Land Law

18th edition

Edited by Cedric D Bell
LLB, LLM, PhD, Barrister
Principal Lecturer in Law, University of Central Lancashire
Director of Training and Research, Rawsthorn Edelstons, Preston
Visiting Professor of Legal Practice, University of Hertfordshire

HLT Publications

HLT PUBLICATIONS
200 Greyhound Road, London W14 9RY

First published 1979
18th edition 1996

ISBN 0 7510 0688 2

British Library Cataloguing-in-Publication.
A CIP Catalogue record for this book is available from the British Library.

Acknowledgement
The publishers and author would like to thank the Incorporated Council of Law Reporting for England and Wales for kind permission to reproduce extracts from the Weekly Law Reports, and Butterworths for their kind permission to reproduce extracts from the All England Law Reports.

Printed and bound in Great Britain

Contents

Preface

HLT textbooks are written specifically for students. Whatever their course, they will find our books clear and concise, providing comprehensive and up-to-date coverage. Written by specialists in their field, our textbooks are reviewed and updated on an annual basis.

As last year we have included a chapter called 'Recent Cases'. This chapter includes the most significant cases that have occured in the last year. In order to assist the student extracts from the judgments and commentary, where appropriate, have been included. In many instances these cases highlight new interpretations of particular facets of existing law.

Knowledge of recent cases is extremely important for those studying for their examinations. It demonstrates not only an active interest in the law as it develops, but also the dynamic nature of the law which is constantly adapting to changing social and economic trends.

This *Land Law* textbook is designed for use by any undergraduates who have land law within their syllabus. It will be equally useful for all CPE students who must study land law as one of the 'core' subjects.

In addition students of certain professional examinations, including those of the Royal Institution of Chartered Surveyors, the Institute of Legal Executives and the Council for Licensed Conveyancers, will find this textbook gives them sufficient information for their appropriate examinations in land law.

This edition includes a summary of the key provisions of the Landlord and Tenant (Covenants) Act 1995, which introduces some of the biggest reforms in real property law for 50 years and which came into force on 1 January 1996. It reforms the doctrines of privity of contract and privity of estate so far as they relate to the relationship of landlord and tenant. Further, this edition features a number of new cases including *Cheltenham & Gloucester Building Society* v *Norgan* [1996] 1 All ER 449, the landmark Court of Appeal ruling on mortgage arrears; *Re Dennis (A Bankrupt)* [1995] 3 All ER 171 on the severance of an equitable joint tenancy by bankruptcy; and *Wheeler and Another* v *J J Saunders Ltd* [1995] 2 All ER 697, an interesting new authority on the acquisition of easements under the doctrine of *Wheeldon* v *Burrows* (1879).

This edition endeavours to state the law as at 1 February 1996.

Table of Cases

Table of Statutes

Glossary

Some terms used in land law

Absolute:	not conditional or determinable (used in relation to estates)
Alienation:	the act of disposing of or transferring to another
Ante-nuptial:	before marriage
Appendant:	attached to land by operation of law
Appurtenant:	attached to land by act of parties
Base fee:	a fee simple produced by partially barring an entail, not absolute: see s1 Fines and Recoveries Act 1833
Beneficial owner:	a person entitled for his own benefit
Caution:	a form of entry protecting an interest in registered land
Cestui que trust:	a beneficiary under a trust
Cestui que use:	a person to whose use property was conveyed
Cestui que vie:	a person for whose life an estate pur autre vie (during the life of another) lasts
Charge:	an encumbrance securing the payment of money – compare legal charge with equitable charge
Commorientes:	persons dying at the same time
Constructive:	inferred or implied
Contingent:	operative only upon an uncertain event
Conversion:	a change in the nature of the property, from real to personal or vice versa
Corporeal:	able to be physically possessed
Coverture:	the continuance of a marriage
Cy-près:	as nearly as possible
Deed:	a document signed, sealed and delivered
Deed poll:	a deed with only one party
Defeasance:	the determination of an interest on a specified event

Demise:	a transfer, usually the grant of a lease
Determine:	come to an end
Devise:	a gift of real property by will
Distrain, distress:	the lawful seizure of chattels without a court action by a landlord to enforce a right against his tenant; usually for non-payment of rent
Dominant tenement:	land to which the benefit of a right is attached
Easement:	a right over land, eg a right of way
Emblements:	growing crops which an outgoing tenant of agricultural land may take
En ventre sa mère:	conceived but not born
Entail:	an estate or interest descending only to the issue of the grantee (fee tail)
Equity of redemption:	the sum of a mortgagor's rights in mortgaged property
Escrow:	a deed which will be completed by delivery
Estoppel:	prohibition of a party from denying facts which he had led another to believe to be true
Execute:	1. to perform or complete, eg a deed 2. to convert, eg transform the equitable interest under a use into a legal estate
Executory:	not yet completed
Feme covert:	married woman
Feme sole:	single woman
Feoffment:	conveyance by livery of seisin, ie formal ceremony of handing over title to the land
Foreclosure:	proceedings by a mortgagee which free mortgaged property from the equity of redemption
Heirlooms:	1. inheritable chattels 2. settled chattels
Hereditaments:	inheritable rights in property
Heritable issue:	descendants capable of inheriting
In esse:	in existence
In gross:	existing independently of a dominant tenement
Incorporeal:	not able to be physically possessed
Incumbrance:	a liability burdening property
Indenture:	a deed between two or more parties, cf deed poll
Instrument:	a legal document
Interesse termini:	the rights of a lessee before entry
Issue:	descendants of any generation
Jus accrescendi:	right of survivorship in joint tenancy
Jus tertii:	a third party's title
Land:	see s205(1)(ix) Law of Property Act 1925
Licence:	a permission, eg to occupy land

Lien:	a form of security for unpaid money
Limitation of actions:	statutory barring of rights of action after a specified period: see Limitation Act 1980
Limitation, words of:	words delimiting the estate granted: see s60 Law of Property Act 1925
Limited owner:	an owner with an estate less than a fee simple
Merger:	the fusion of two or more estates or interests, cf surrender
Mesne:	intermediate
Minority:	the state of being an infant
Mortmain:	holding of land by a corporation
Notice:	actual constructive or imputed knowledge, cf Land Charges Act 1972
Occupancy:	occupation of land
Overreach:	to transfer rights from land to its purchase money
Override:	to render rights void
Partibility:	divisibility of inheritance among children
Per capita:	one share for each person
Per stirpes:	one share for each line of descendants
Portions:	provisions for children, especially lump sums for younger children under a settlement
Possession:	defined to include the receipt of rent and profits: s205(1)(xix) LPA 1925
Prescription:	the acquisition of easements by long user: see Prescription Act 1832
Privity of contract:	the relation of the original landlord and tenant
Privity of estate:	the relationship between the present landlord and tenant
Puisne mortgage:	a legal mortgage not protected by deposit of title deeds, see land charge Class C(i)
Pur autre vie:	for the life of another
Purchase, words of:	words conferring an interest
Purchaser:	one who takes by act of parties, not by operation of law
Release:	waiver of some right or interest
Quicquid plantatur solo, solo cedit:	whatever is affixed to the soil, belongs to the soil
Remainder:	the interest of a grantee subject to a prior grant to another
Restrictive covenant:	a covenant restricting the use of land
Resulting:	returning to the grantor by implication of law or equity
Reversion:	the interest remaining in a grantor
Riparian owner:	the owner of land adjoining a watercourse or road
Seisin:	possession of land by a freeholder
Servient tenement:	land burdened by a right, eg an easement

Settlement:	provision for persons in succession (or the instrument creating it: see Settled Land Act 1925)
Severance:	the conversion of a joint tenancy into a tenancy in common in equity only: see s1(6) Law of Property Act 1925
Severance, words of:	words showing a tenancy in common – must be in the deed itself
Specialty:	contract by deed
Spes successionis:	a possibility of succeeding to property
Squatter:	a person wrongfully occupying land
Statutory trusts:	trusts imposed by statute
Subinfeudation:	alienation by creating a new tenure
Sui juris:	not subject to any legal disability
Surrender:	the transfer of an interest to the person next entitled, cf merger
Tacking:	extension of a mortgagee's security to cover a later loan
Tenement:	property held by a tenant
Term of years absolute:	a defined period for which a tenant holds the land: see s205(1) (xxvii) Law of Property Act 1925
Time immemorial:	from 1189, the first year of the reign of Richard I
Title:	the evidence of a person's right to property
Undivided share:	the interest of a tenant in common which only arises in equity after 1925
User:	use enjoyment (*Note*: not the person who uses)
Vested:	unconditionally owned
Voluntary conveyance:	a conveyance not for valuable consideration
Waiver:	abandonment of a legal right
Waste:	an act altering the nature of the land

Use of the glossary

Other words and phrases will appear in the study of land law and the reader should make his or her own supplement to this glossary when such words appear in his or her reading material. Always do this immediately the word is discovered. In this way the context of the word will be appreciated and recalled for future reference.

1

The Study of Land Law

1.1 The problem of land law

Most students have difficulty when they start to study English land law. This is partly because of the strange technical terms used, and a list of some of the most common of them can be found in the glossary. The main reason, however, is that land law is a logical system, but one that is strange to most people because they rarely encounter it in their daily life. Almost everyone has made at least one contract, and most people can understand torts such as negligence and know about crime at least from television and newspapers, but they only encounter land law when they buy a house.

English land law is firmly based in English history, and can only be understood in the light of its feudal origins. That is why this textbook starts with a historical introduction, which is intended to give those students who have never studied English history the basic information they need. Others may find it a useful revision of a period of history they probably studied several years ago.

1.2 The 1925 property legislation

Arguably the most important year for land law was 1925, when a scheme of legislation was passed, coming into force on 1 January 1926, which reformed and largely codified land law and related subjects, trusteeship and administration of estates. The 1925 legislation was a reform of the old system, not a totally new one, and some knowledge of the pre-1925 law may still be required for examination purposes.

1.3 Methods of study of land law

Because land law is a complete system, it is not possible to study it in small, self-contained sections, and it is necessary in the early parts of the textbook to refer briefly to topics which will not be studied until later, and which may not be understood when first encountered. Do not despair! Many students find that during the first few months of land law study they are in a 'fog', but that suddenly all the pieces of the puzzle fall into place, and the subject becomes much easier.

Finally, this textbook is not intended as, and cannot be, a substitute for a detailed textbook which will give examples and discuss the case law, or statutory provisions and problems, in depth.

In the case of certain topics in the land law syllabus, there are techniques which can help the student to answer the type of questions often set on that topic. These techniques are embodied in worked examples at the end of the chapter dealing with a topic for which such a question-answering technique is helpful.

There are a number of references in the text to 'Cheshire' and 'Megarry and Wade'. The works referred to are *Cheshire and Burn's Modern Law of Real Property* by E H Burn (15th edn, 1994), Butterworths, and *The Law of Real Property* by Megarry and Wade (5th edn, 1984), Sweet and Maxwell.

2

Historical Introduction

2.1 Origins of the feudal system

Round about the fourth century AD the Roman Empire, which had ruled the greater part of Europe for about four to five hundred years, began to collapse. The Roman armies, which had provided law and order, were gradually withdrawn to Rome, and when they left there was no strong local government to replace them. The border areas were attacked by 'barbarians', peoples who had not been under Roman rule who came from the north of Europe. The attacks on England came first from the Picts and Scots, who lived north of the Roman (Hadrian's) Wall, which ran from Carlisle to Newcastle, and then from the Saxons, a Germanic people. The Saxons settled in many parts of the country, being known as the Anglo-Saxons. Later, the eastern part of the country was raided by the Vikings, who came from Scandinavia, and they settled in many parts of eastern England.

The same pattern of withdrawal of troops, attacks by barbarian tribes and breakdown of law and order was repeated in most of Europe. The result was not only murder and pillage; people were unable to farm their land, which resulted in famine. The only way of getting any protection to enable him to farm his land was for the farmer to give his land to the strongest person in the area who had the biggest army, who would then allow the farmer to work it and pay him in kind. In return, the lord was bound to protect his tenant. This became known as the feudal system, where land was held from a lord in return for services, the lord being bound to protect his tenant from those who might seek to dispossess him. Feudalism was the original 'protection racket'.

2.2 The feudal system in England

Not a great deal is known about English land-holding before the Norman Conquest, but there is evidence that there was a form of feudalism in places. However, as in Europe, there was no universal feudal system covering the whole country, because the system had grown from the bottom upwards. The importance of the Norman Conquest of 1066, and the reason why it is the start of English land law, is that a feudal system was imposed from the top, which produced an unusually complete and logical system. This is because the king, William the Conqueror, declared that all the land belonged to him by reason of his victory, and this is why it is still said that ultimately all land in the country belongs to the Crown, and that all 'owners' are merely tenants of one sort or another. This will be examined in more detail in Chapter 4.

William then rewarded his chief followers by making them tenants of large areas of land, and they in turn granted smaller areas to their followers, who might in turn grant land. This meant that a pyramid of land-holding was created, with the king at the top, under him a few chief lords, known as barons, and so on, with a large number of tenants, who each farmed a small area, at the bottom (see diagram).

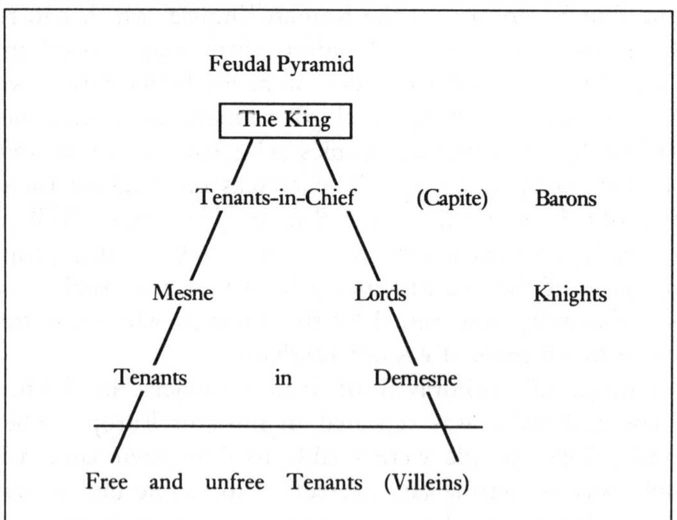

The basis of the feudal system

The basis of the feudal system is that land was given to pay for services. At the time of the Norman Conquest, and for some time thereafter, the economy was purely agricultural and everyone produced their own food. There was very little money, which was not much used, and bartering was the method of obtaining things the people could not produce themselves. This meant that land was the only real source of wealth, and the 'richest' man was the one with the most land. Today we have a money economy, and if we want a pair of shoes, or we want our car mended, we pay for the goods or services with money. In feudal times, goods and services were bought with land. If a 'wealthy' man, a man with ample land, wanted a cook, he would grant enough land to support a man and his family to someone in return for that man's services as a cook. When that man died, the lord would grant the land to someone else, often the man's son, in return for the same services.

The type of service for which the land was granted was known as the 'tenure', various forms of which are examined in more detail in Chapter 3. Most of the king's tenants, who were known as tenants-in-chief, held land in return for providing the king with a specified number of soldiers. They would seek to fulfil this obligation by in turn granting part of the lands granted to them to tenants ('tenants in desmesne' or 'mesne lords') who had to supply some of these soldiers. This would continue down the pyramid until at the bottom there was the soldier who was granted enough land to keep himself and his family in return for doing the required military service.

The manor

The basic unit of the feudal system was the manor. Each manor had a lord (the lord of the manor) and usually consisted of the lord's own land (known as the lord's desmesne), consisting of the manor house and the lord's agricultural land, land held by tenants and waste land on which the tenants grazed their cattle. The lord's land was cultivated by the tenants in return for the land he had granted them. Some of the tenants would be freemen, others would be serfs or villeins. Villeinage was a personal status which was akin to slavery, but was not exactly slavery. The villein had no rights, except physical protection, against his lord and might belong either to the lord or to the manor, but against third parties he had all the rights of a freeman. See Lord Denning MR in *Corpus Christi College* v *Gloucestershire County Council* [1982] 3 All ER 995:

> 'In medieval times the manor was the nucleus of English rural life. It was an administrative unit of an extensive area of land. The whole of it was owned originally by the lord of the manor.'

2.3 The decline of the feudal system

The feudal system in its original form was probably in operation for less than 200 years, and thereafter began to decline for several reasons. Some of the most important of these are:

The impracticability of maintaining an army by feudal means

As we have seen, many of the tenants-in-chief held their land in return for the supply of troops. Such troops, however, were only obliged to serve in the king's army for a fixed number of days per year. It was very difficult to wage an effective military campaign when an army was entitled in the middle of a battle to pack up and go home, and so the king very soon preferred to hire full-time soldiers, especially as money was becoming more important in the economy. He would therefore commute the requirement of actual soldiers to a requirement of a fixed sum of money, which facilitated the raising of a mercenary army.

The rise of a monetary economy and ensuing inflation

As money became more important, many mesne lords preferred to receive from their tenants an easily enforced payment of money rather than actual services, which were harder to enforce. Such payments were fixed, and as the value of money declined, so many lords did not find it worth the bother of enforcing the payments.

2.4 The intervention of statute

The Statute Quia Emptores 1290

We have seen that originally a tenant would usually provide the services he was bound to render by himself granting land in return for services. This creation of 'subtenants' is known as subinfeudation. Lords were entitled to various valuable incidents to their grant as well as the services (see Chapter 3 for details of incidents), but subinfeudation could effectively deprive a lord of these. For example, if A granted to B in knight's service and B then grants to C for a rose each midsummer's day, then if B dies leaving an infant heir, A is entitled to wardship of the heir, but instead of being entitled to the land by reason of the wardship all he gets is an annual rose. In order to protect their incomes arising from incidents, the barons ensured the passing of the Quia Emptores Statute which included the following provisions:

1. Alienation by subinfeudation was forbidden.
2. All free tenants were authorised to alienate all or part of their land by substitution, without the lord's consent, the new tenant standing in the old tenant's place and holding directly from the lord by the same services.
3. On alienation of part the services were to be apportioned.
4. The statute only applied in grants in fee simple.

The effect of this statute was to make land-holding a piece of property which could be freely alienated (the modern concept) rather than a personal relationship between a lord and his tenant (the feudal concept) It also prevented the creation of new tenures, and so thereafter the feudal pyramid could no longer grow – it could only contract. It is useful to see the extent of the statute from the opening words of Chapter 1:

> 'Forasmuch as purchasers of lands and tenements of the fees of great men and other lords have many times heretofore entered into their fees, to the prejudice of the lords, to whom the freeholders of such great men have sold their lands and tenements to be holden in fee of their feoffers, and not of the chief lord of the fees, whereby the same chief lords have many times lost their escheats, marriages, and wardships of land and tenements belonging to their fees which thing seemed very hard and extream unto those lords and other great men and moreover in this case manifest disheritance: Our lord the King (Edward I) in his Parliament at Westminster after Easter, the eighteenth year of his reign ... at the instance of the great men of the realm, granted, provided and ordained, that from henceforth it shall be lawful to every freeman to sell at his own pleasure his lands and tenements, or part of them; so that the feoffee shall hold the same lands or tenements of the chief lord of the same fee by such service and customs as his feoffor held before.'

It should be noted that the Statute Quia Emptores is still in force today. Its effect is demonstrated by any conveyance of land whereby the purchaser takes over completely the role of the vendor. This is further recognised by s60(1) Law of Property Act 1925 (LPA 1925):

> 'A conveyance of freehold land to any person without words of limitation ... shall pass to the grantee the fee simple or other the whole interest which the grantor had power to convey in such land unless a contrary intention appears in the conveyance.'

The use and the Statute of Uses 1535

Quia Emptores 1290 preserved the lord's rights to feudal incidents and thus prevented 'tax avoidance' by means of subinfeudation. This did not, however, prevent tenants from trying to avoid the incidents, which could sometimes amount to a crippling financial burden. There were other defects of the feudal system from the tenant's point of view which he might wish to avoid, the most important of these being:

1. Freehold land could not be devised by will but passed automatically to the heir.
2. Land could only be conveyed by a public ceremony called 'feoffment with livery of seisin' at which both parties had to be present. This made conveyancing difficult or inconvenient.
3. Seisin had to pass immediately, and so it was not in general possible to create future interests in land.
4 If the tenant was convicted of a felony his land was escheat (ie forfeit) to the lord. This was particularly serious in times of political uncertainty, such as the Wars of the Roses, when being on the losing side would usually be followed by escheat.

These disadvantages could all be avoided by the use, whereby land was conveyed to a trusted person, known as the feoffee to uses, who held the land on behalf of the person whom the tenant really intended to benefit, the cestui que use. The common law looked on the feoffee to uses as the absolute owner and refused to enforce what it regarded as only a moral obligation, but once the Court of Chancery became established the Chancellor would enforce the use, and thus protect the cestui que use. The use became very popular in the fifteenth century. In 1535 Henry VIII, realising that his feudal income from incidents had been seriously eroded, forced Parliament to pass the Statute of Uses. The effect of the statute was that when land was conveyed to A to the use of B, and the legal estate passed directly to B, this was called 'executing the use'. Within a century the use had been restored because the courts allowed the Statute of Uses to be evaded by means of the use upon the use; land was conveyed to A to the use of B to the use of C, the first use was executed and B was left holding the legal estate on trust (to use the modern term) for C. Thereafter the modern law of trusts developed, with important effects on land law as will be seen in Chapter 5.

The Tenures Abolition Act 1660 (also known as the Statute for the Abolition of Military Tenures)

The payment of services had ceased to be of any importance by the fifteenth century, but feudal incidents remained important. In particular the Crown, which was always lord and never tenant, derived a great deal of revenue from these incidents. After the triumph of Parliament over the king in the Civil War, Parliament sought to ensure its supremacy by abolishing any independent source of income of the Crown. The Long Parliament in 1646 abolished all forms of tenure, except freehold and copyhold, and most of the feudal incidents, and this was confirmed by Charles II in 1660 by the Tenures Abolition Act. The Crown was instead granted a tax on beer!

3

Tenures

3.1 Introduction

Tenure is the method of holding land, the services to be rendered by the tenant in return for the grant of the land. While these could be of any kind, depending on the lord's needs, in practice they became in general standardised and could be classified. The main division was between free and unfree, and there were various types of free tenure. These are demonstrated in the diagram overleaf.

3.2 Free tenures

Tenures in chivalry

These were also called military tenures and were of two sorts: grand serjeanty and knight services.

Grand serjeanty

These were tenures granted by the king in return for personal services of an honourable nature, such as carrying his banner or being his marshal. There were many such services connected with court ceremonial and with coronations. This type of tenure eventually became confined to tenants-in-chief and was abolished by the Tenures Abolition Act 1660 which, however, preserved some of the honorary services.

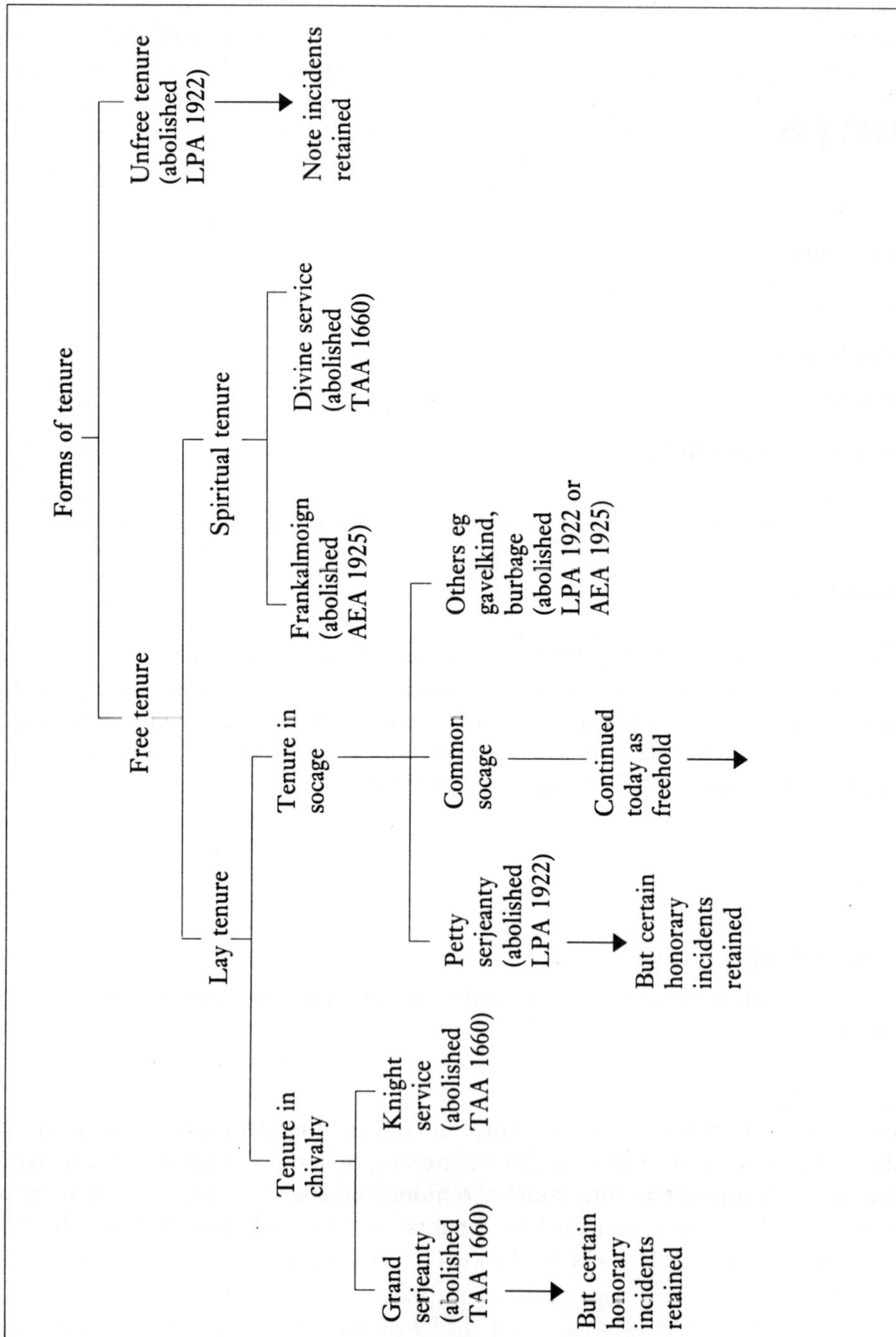

Forms of tenure
Unfree tenure (abolished LPA 1922)
Note incidents retained
Free tenure
Spiritual tenure
Divine service (abolished TAA 1660)
Frankalmoign (abolished AEA 1925)
Lay tenure
Tenure in socage
Others eg gavelkind, burbage (abolished LPA 1922 or AEA 1925)
Common socage
Continued today as freehold
Petty serjeanty (abolished LPA 1922)
But certain honorary incidents retained
Tenure in chivalry
Knight service (abolished TAA 1660)
Grand serjeanty (abolished TAA 1660)
But certain honorary incidents retained

Knight service
This originally obliged the tenant to provide a fixed number of fully armed horsemen (knights) for a fixed number of days a year, but within a century this inconvenient method of raising an army had been replaced by commuting this obligation into a money payment known as scutage. As the value of money fell, scutage ceased in practice to be levied, and payment had generally lapsed by the fourteenth century.

Incidents of tenures in chivalry

Tenures in chivalry were subject to incidents, which were of many types and which provided the main value of the tenure to the lord once the value of the services had become nominal. The most important of these incidents were as described below.

Homage, fealty and suit of court
Homage was the spiritual bond created between man and lord by the taking of the feudal oath, fealty was the tenant's obligation to perform his obligations and suit of court was the tenant's obligation to attend his lord's court and assist in its decisions.

Relief and primer seisin
When an heir of full age succeeded a tenant he had to pay the lord relief, usually one year's value of the land, in order to be admitted in succession to his father. Primer seisin was the right of the king, when he was the lord concerned, to take possession until homage and relief were rendered, which in practice entitled the Crown to a further year's value in addition to the relief.

Wardship and marriage
Where a tenant died leaving an infant heir, the lord had the right to take the profits of the land while the heir remained an infant, but in return he was obliged to maintain and educate the infant.

When the heir reached full age the lord was entitled to a further half year's profits, although by the Magna Carta 1215 this was confined to the king. Marriage was the right to select the heir's spouse and to receive any payments made in respect of the marriage. The heir could reject the proposed spouse, but if the match was 'suitable' (ie the proposed spouse was of an equivalent rank and wealth) he would be fined the amount the lord would have received, and if he married without consent twice that sum. These were particularly valuable incidents.

Aids
On certain occasions the lord could demand a payment from all his tenants, limited by the Magna Carta to the ransom of the lord (when captured in battle), the knighting of his eldest son and the marriage of his eldest daughter.

Escheat and forfeiture

Escheat was the right of the lord to the land when the tenancy came to an end for any reason. The most common causes were the failure of heirs, escheat propter defectum sanguinis, and when the tenant was convicted of a felony and sentenced to death, escheat propter delictum tenentis. Before the land returned to the lord, the Crown had the right to hold it for a year and a day and commit acts of waste.

Forfeiture was the right of the Crown to keep the lands of any person attainted of high treason.

Note: almost all of these incidents were abolished by the Tenures Abolition Act 1660, the only ones of importance which were retained being escheat and forfeiture. Grand serjeanty and knight service were converted into tenures of free and common socage.

Tenures in socage

These were less exalted than military tenures and were found in the bottom part of the feudal pyramid, see Chapter 2, section 2.2. They were of two types:

Petty serjeanty

The tenant was obliged to perform some services for the king of a non-honourable, non-personal nature, such as supplying arrows or firewood. It quickly ceased to be of importance as money became more important, and the king found it easier to pay for such services. After the fifteenth century it could only exist as a tenure-in-chief.

Socage

This was by far the commonest form of tenure, and after 1660 became the only kind of free tenure. While any kind of services could be reserved, the most usual services were of an agricultural nature. This would be fixed both as to nature and extent, and by the end of the fifteenth century had generally been commuted to money payments.

The socage tenures were only subject to aids, relief and escheat, and the relief was fixed at one year's rent, rather than the one year's profit to which military tenures were subject.

Inheritance of free tenures

Primogeniture

In general the system of primogeniture applied, ie the land went automatically to the eldest son. However, socage tenure could vary depending on local customs. When the tenure was 'common socage' the rule of primogeniture applied, but there were some important variations as follows:

Exceptions to the rule of primogeniture

Gavelkind. This applied automatically to all land in Kent and could apply elsewhere. The main feature of such land was partibility, ie on intestacy it descended to all males of the same degree equally and not to the eldest son alone. Other peculiar features of gavelkind were:

DEVISABILITY. This land, unlike all other types, could be freely disposed of by will. Free devisability did not apply to other land until the Statute of Wills 1540, and even then restrictions remained, some as late as 1925.

NO ESCHEAT. No escheat on felony, although forfeiture for high treason applied.

DOWER. A widow was entitled to dower until remarriage in one-half of her deceased husband's estate (in common socage it was only in one-third).

CURTESY. A husband was entitled to a life estate ('curtesy') in all his deceased wife's realty, whether or not issue capable of inheriting the land had been born. In common socage he only received curtesy if there was such an issue.

Borough English. This custom applied in various parts of the country, and was not confined to towns as the name might suggest. When this custom applied, socage land descended to the youngest rather than the eldest son.

Spiritual tenures

These were of two types, frankalmoign by which land was granted to an ecclesiastical corporation in return for no specific services, but under an obligation to pray for the tenant's soul, and divine service in which the tenure was subject to defined services such as saying Mass weekly or giving a specified sum to the poor. This service could be enforced by the normal methods of distraint and forfeiture, unlike the obligations of frankalmoign which could only be enforced by the ecclesiastical courts.

The conveyance of land to ecclesiastical corporations, known as mortmain, was very unpopular with lords because, as a corporation never dies and leaves heirs, there would be a loss of feudal dues from incidents. The Magna Carta and the Statutes of Mortmain 1279 and 1290 forbade the conveyance of land to religious bodies, but pious tenants who were concerned for their spiritual health found a way to avoid this prohibition by the use.

3.3 Unfree tenures

Villeinage

Unfree tenure was called villeinage, and later became known as copyhold – see section 3.4. The main differences between free and unfree tenures were as described below.

No seisin

The tenant of a free tenure had seisin, which meant that the king's courts would protect him if his lord unlawfully sought to eject him from the land. In unfree tenure, the tenant was deemed to hold on behalf of the lord who had the seisin, so the king's courts would not at first protect the tenant whose only remedy was in the lord's court.

Services not fixed

The services attached to free tenure were always fixed in quantity and quality, while those of unfree tenure were not fixed and were usually more onerous. The villein had to work for his lord for a fixed number of days a week, doing whatever was required in the manner in which the lord required him to do it.

Status

Only a free man could hold land in free tenure. The converse was not true, because although a man of villein status could only hold in unfree tenure, some land of villein tenure was held by free men. It was the quality of the services, not the status of the tenant, that distinguished the two forms of tenure.

At first the villein's position was precarious, but it became established that the lord should not forfeit his land unless the tenant had done some act which by the custom of the manor merited forfeiture. The principal incidents were:

1. Agricultural services. They later became commuted to money payments.
2. Fealty and suit of court.
3. Escheat and forfeiture.
4. Heriots. This was a custom that the lord was entitled to take the tenant's best beast or other chattel on the tenant's death.
5. Fines payable on alienation of the land.

Later history of villeinage

During the fourteenth and fifteenth centuries most villein services were commuted to money payments, so the villein became a rent-paying tenant and the lord hired the necessary labour, and at the same time villein status was dying out. By 1550 the king's courts were prepared to protect any tenant whether he held by free or villein tenure.

3.4 Copyhold

Origin of title

The change in status of the villein tenant from an agricultural labourer, often of servile status, to a rent-paying farmer was marked by a change of name, and villein tenure became known as copyhold. The particulars of each holding were entered in the manorial rolls, and copyhold land was conveyed by surrender to the lord who then admitted the new tenant, the transaction being recorded in the court rolls. The transferee was given a copy of the entry, hence 'copyhold'. The transfer was governed by the custom of the manor. Certain incidents, notably fines, heriots and reliefs, continued to apply.

Enfranchisement

Various Acts of Parliament throughout the nineteenth century made possible the enfranchisement (ie conversion to freehold) of copyhold, but much remained until the Law of Property Act 1922 which by s128 and Schedule 12 compulsorily enfranchised all remaining copyhold. The Act divided manorial incidents attached to copyhold into three categories:

1. Those which were obsolete (eg forfeiture for alienation without the lord's consent): these were abolished immediately.
2. Those which had some existing monetary value (eg quit rents): these continued until 1935 to give the parties an opportunity to arrange voluntarily for the incident to be extinguished on the payment of compensation. Failing agreement, application was to be made to the then Minister of Agriculture and Fisheries. These incidents were subsequently extended to 1 November 1950 before they were finally extinguished.
3. Those which were not extinguished and which still attach to the land unless extinguished by mutual agreement and compensation. These are:

    a) tenant's right of common;
    b) rights to minerals;
    c) rights of the lord in respect to markets and fairs and sporting rights;
    d) liability for dykes, ditches, sea or river walls and bridges.

Copyhold today

It should be noted that the third category remains in existence today. For a consideration of these rights in relation to the 'manor' see: *Corpus Christi College* v *Gloucestershire County Council* [1982] 3 All ER 995.

3.5 Conclusion: tenures today

The Tenures Abolition Act 1660 (also known as the Statute for the Abolition of Military Tenures) effectively marked the end of the tenurial system by converting all tenures into socage. A number of forms and incidents were preserved – see diagram at section 3.1 – but these, in turn, were brought to an end by the 1925 property legislation. This means that the only form of tenure which remains today is the former socage tenure now known as freehold. In addition a number of honorary incidents relating to grand and petty serjeanty remain together with the four incidents preserved by the LPA 1922 from the enfranchisement of copyholds.

Although tenure continues as a legal fact it is no longer restrictive in its effect. This is summarised by Cheshire in these words at page 25:

> 'We can, in fact, now describe the theory of tenure, despite the great part that it has played in the history of English law, as a conception of merely academic interest. It no longer restricts the tenant in his free enjoyment of the land.'

4

Estates

4.1 Introduction

Tenure involves the quality of land-holding, that is, the types of services for which land is granted. Estate is the quantity of land-holding, the period for which the land was granted. The importance of estates, and the reason why the law relating to land is much more complicated than the law relating to ownership of other property, is that several people can have different estates in the same piece of land. A might have a life interest, B a life interest in remainder and C the fee simple reversion, while D had a 99-year lease and had granted a seven-year sublease to E. At the same time A may have mortgaged the land to F, while G had a right of way over the land.

The system of estates was amended by the 1925 legislation, but it is necessary to know the old classification to understand the new law.

4.2 Classification of estates

The two main classes are freehold and leasehold. Each class may then be subdivided – but note how some of these subdivisions did not continue, in that form, after 1925. The position in 1925 may be seen in the diagram below.

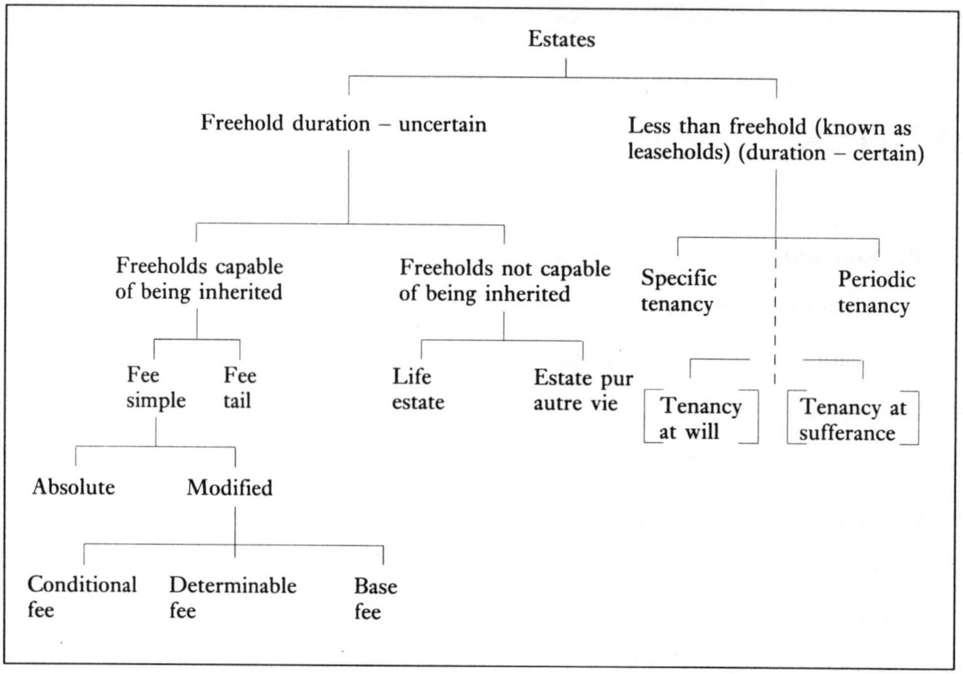

Freehold estates

There were prior to 1925 three freehold estates: fee simple, fee tail, and life estate. These will be dealt with in detail later in this chapter at sections 4.4 to 4.6.

Leasehold estates (sometimes referred to as estates less than freehold)

At first the common law refused to recognise the lease as an interest in land, treating it as a mere personal contract. The leaseholder only became fully protected by the law at the end of the fifteenth century following the introduction of the Action of Ejectment, and in theory a leasehold is still inferior to a freehold. Another result of this historical situation is that leaseholds are treated as personal property, while freeholds and other legal rights in land are real property.

The main categories of leasehold are:

1. Fixed term of certain duration – specific tenancy.
2. Fixed term with duration capable of being rendered certain – renewable periodic tenancies.
3. Tenancies at will and at sufferance may also be classified under leaseholds, although they do not fit easily into the above two major divisions of specific and periodic tenancies – hence the parentheses.

The various types of lease are dealt with in detail in Chapter 10.

4.3 Possession, remainder, reversion and seisin

An estate in land can be held in either possession, remainder, reversion, or seisin.

Possession

Means that the owner of the estate is immediately entitled to possession and enjoyment of the land – this is not necessarily the same as occupation of the land. See the definition of 'possession' in s205(1)(xix) LPA 1925.

Remainder

Means that the owner of an estate in remainder will be entitled to possession after some other person (or persons) has been entitled to possession, not having had any previous interest in the land.

Reversion

Means the residue of the interest possessed by a person who has granted away a lesser estate in possession than he owns.

Seisin

The concept of seisin was extremely important in early land law, and denoted quiet possession of the land. It was a status, not a right, and so a lawful owner put out of possession was 'disseised' and the interloper gained seisin until himself dispossessed by force or law. The important fact was that only freeholders could have seisin, and so if a leaseholder or a copyholder was in possession the seisin remained in the freeholder or lord. For a person to be seised he must hold the freehold estate; the land must be of freehold tenure; and either he must have physical possession of the land or a tenant/leaseholder holds the land for him.

4.4 The fee simple

Definition

While in theory the fee simple owner holds his land in tenure, in practice he is the absolute owner, save that the land will revert to the lord (usually the Crown) if the fee simple owner dies intestate leaving no heirs.

Note the distinction between the fee simple which is absolute and the modified fee simple.

Fee simple absolute

This type of fee is an estate which continues indefinitely, and is the most common.

Modified fee simple

There are three types of modified fee simple:

1. Determinable fee: this is a fee simple which automatically comes to an end on the happening of some specified event which is not certain to occur. If the specified event does occur the land reverts to the grantor.
2. Fee simple upon condition (conditional fee): this is the grant of a full fee simple to which is attached a condition that may operate upon the happening of some specified uncertain event, a condition subsequent.
3. Base fee: this is a special type of fee which arises after the barring of an entail (below) and is determinable upon the failure of heirs of the body of the original grantor. See s1 Fines and Recoveries Act 1833.

Distinction between the determinable fee and the conditional fee
It is often difficult to determine whether a particular grant creates a determinable fee or a conditional fee. A determinable fee has an in-built limitation, often indicated by 'while', 'until', 'so long as', while a conditional fee is a full fee simple with an extra condition tacked on, often shown by words such as 'provided that', 'but if', 'on condition that'. The main differences between the types are:

Determination
The grantor of a determinable fee simple retains a 'possibility of reverter' which means that a determinable fee terminates automatically on the happening of the specified event. The effect is that the legal estate reverts automatically and this, in itself, may create problems as in *Re Rowhook Mission Hall, Horsham* [1984] 3 All ER 179.

A conditional fee gives the grantor a right of entry on the happening of the specified event, and until that right is exercised the fee continues: *Re Clayton's Deed Poll* [1980] Ch 99. But this must be read in the light of the later decision in *Re Rowhook Mission Hall.*

Validity of the condition
If the condition attached to a determinable fee is void for any reason other than perpetuity the whole grant fails. If the condition attached to a conditional fee is void the grantee takes a fee simple absolute.

Effect of a void condition
The courts are therefore readier to find that the condition of a conditional fee is void than to make the same finding in respect of a determinable fee. If the condition in a conditional fee simple is held to be void it is the condition alone that is void, and the grantee takes an absolute interest in the property free from the condition. If the determining event in a determinable fee simple is void then the whole grant is also void. The grounds on which a condition may be held to be void are:

1. Uncertainty: the condition will be void unless it can be precisely determined what will cause its operation; for example, a clause requiring 'residence' may be too vague and imprecise.
2. Alienation: the condition must not take away the power of alienation, because this is totally against the idea of ownership. A partial restraint, not to sell to a particular person, may be valid.
3. Course of law: the condition must not attempt to alter a course of devolution prescribed by law, for example on intestacy, or making it a condition that the grantee does not become bankrupt.
4. Restraint of marriage: the condition must not impose a total or wide restraint on marriage, although a partial restraint may be valid.
5. Public policy: the condition must not be illegal, immoral or otherwise against public policy. Any condition which encouraged separation and divorce would come within this category.

Remoteness and effect of rule against perpetuities

The rule against perpetuities does apply to any such right of re-entry, and the condition must not offend against the rule against perpetuities (see Chapter 16). The perpetuity rules do not apply to determinable fees granted before 1964, but the Perpetuities and Accumulations Act 1964 provides that the possibility of reverter arising on a grant of a determinable fee simple is subject to the rule against perpetuities: see s12.

Existence at law

A determinable fee cannot exist as a legal estate after 1925, but is a settlement under the Settled Land Act 1925 (see Chapter 8). While originally legislation also made a conditional fee a settlement under that Act, it is arguable that the effect of the Schedule to the Law of Property (Amendment) Act 1926 is that a conditional fee can now exist as a legal estate, because the Schedule adds the following words to s7(1) LPA 1925:

> '... a fee simple subject to a legal or equitable right of entry or re-entry is for the purposes of this Act [the Law of Property Act 1925] a fee simple absolute.'

On the same principle, the effect of divesting under the School Sites Act 1841 to create a fee simple absolute is seen in operation in *Re Rowhook Mission Hall, Horsham* (above). To prevent the problem of trustees acquiring a title by adverse possession in order to defeat the revertee as seen in that case, the Reverter of Sites Act 1987 s1 now provides that when the land ceases to be used for a particular purpose, and thus brings the possibility of reverter into effect, the land will be held on trust for sale for the revertee. There will be no automatic reverting of the land, which will thus prevent the trustees using adverse possession to gain a title, and the revertee will become a beneficiary under the statutory trust for sale created by the 1987 Act. Overreaching provisions will apply to enable the trustees to sell free from the interest of the revertee which will become interests in the proceeds of sale. The 1987 Act is retrospective to make the trust for sale apply, even if the purpose failed before the Act came into force on 17 August 1987.

The contents of the Reverter of Sites Act 1987 are set out in Chapter 5, section 5.9.

Rights of the fee simple owner

The right of alienation

The fee simple owner may dispose of his land as he wishes, either by will or inter vivos.

The right to everything in, on or over the land

This was expressed by the medieval lawyers as 'cujus est solum, ejus est usque ad coelum et ad inferos' – all is his, up to the sky and down to the centre of the earth – but this is much wider than reality today. These rights have several limitations:

Rights of others over the land. The owner is subject to rights such as easements, tenancies and mortgages.

Airspace. While the owner of the land can sue in trespass or nuisance for intrusion of his airspace *(Kelsen* v *Imperial Tobacco Co* [1957] 2 QB 334), his rights are restricted to such height as is necessary for the ordinary use of the land and the structures on it *(Bernstein* v *Skyviews Ltd* [1977] 3 WLR 136). In *Bernstein*'s case Griffiths J expressed the modern rule as to rights in airspace in these words:

> 'The problem is to balance the rights of an owner to enjoy the use of his land against the rights of the general public to take advantage of all that science now offers in the use of airspace. This balance is in my judgment best struck in our present society by restricting the rights of an owner in the airspace above his land to such a height as is necessary for the ordinary use and enjoyment of his land and the structures upon it: and declaring that above that height he has no greater rights in the airspace than any other member of the public.'

See also *Woollerton and Wilson* v *Richard Costain* [1970] 1 WLR 411.

Section 76(1) of the Civil Aviation Act 1982 provides that no action shall lie in respect of trespass or nuisance by a flight of an aircraft over property at a reasonable height.

Minerals. The right of the fee simple owner to all minerals under his land has been considerably eroded by statute. At common law the Crown is entitled to all gold and silver, by the Coal Act 1938 all coal was vested in the Coal Commission and is now vested in the National Coal Board, and oil and natural gas are vested in the Crown by the Petroleum (Production) Act 1934.

Treasure trove. By common law the Crown is entitled to treasure trove, that is gold or silver which was deliberately hidden, the true owner being unknown. See *Attorney-General of the Duchy of Lancaster* v *G E Overton (Farms) Ltd* [1982] 1 All ER 524.

Other chattels found on land. The general question of other chattels found on land has been considered by the Court of Appeal in *Parker* v *British Airways Board* [1982] 1 All ER 834. The owner of the land upon which the chattels are found must clearly show he is in control of the land before he can claim title to the chattels.

Wild animals. Wild animals belong to no one, although the land owner has the right to hunt them. As soon as the animal is killed it belongs to the owner of the land on which it was killed.

Water. A landowner has no property in water which flows or percolates through his land, and his rights to draw it off for his own purposes are now severely limited by statute. However he has the sole right to fish in the water, provided that it is not tidal. See *Swindon Waterworks Co Ltd* v *Wilts and Berks Canal Navigation Co* (1875) LR 7 HL 697; *Rugby Joint Water Board* v *Walters* [1967] Ch 397.

The landowner does have the right to abstract subterranean water flowing in undefined channels beneath his land without regard to the consequences to his neighbours. This was established by the House of Lords in *Bradford Corporation* v *Pickles* [1895] AC 587.

Liability in tort. A landowner may be liable in tort for acts done on his land. In particular note the duties of a landowner to his neighbours not to commit acts of trespass, nuisance or negligence.

Statute. Besides the statutes mentioned above there are many other statutes which limit an owner's right to do what he likes with his land. Examples are the Town and Country Planning Acts, the Rent Act and the Housing Acts – see Chapters 10 and 17.

Accretions to land. The owner is entitled to land added by gradual accretion from the sea. See *Southern Centre of Theosophy* v *State of South Australia* [1982] 1 All ER 283.

Creation of a fee simple

The words needed to create a particular estate are known as the words of limitation. The rules relating to the words required to create a fee simple are as follows:

	Inter vivos	*By will*
At common law	'to A and his heirs'	No formal words needed but intent must be shown
By the Wills Act 1837	–	The fee simple passes unless the contrary is shown
By Conveyancing Act 1881	'to A in fee simple'	–
By LPA 1925 s60(1)	the fee simple passes unless the contrary is shown	–

Note: by ss19 and 20 Land Registration Act 1925 the legal estate in registered land does not pass to the transferee until the transfer is completed by registration.

4.5 The fee tail

(*see the Statute De Donis Conditionalibus 1285*)

Definitions

Students interested in the history of the entail should consult Megarry and Wade p76, or a book on legal history. There are three types of entail:

1. Tail general, in which the fee is limited to a person and heirs of his body, ie lineal descendants, of either sex.
2. Tail male, in which the fee is limited to a person and the male heirs of his body.
3. Tail female, limited to a person and the female heirs of his body (very rare).
4. Each of these can be either general, ie not limited to children by a particular spouse, or special, ie limited to children by a particular spouse.

Creation of an entail – words of limitation

The necessary words of limitation were as follows:

	Inter vivos	*By will*
At common law	'heirs' + words of procreation	Informal words showing intent
By Conveyancing Act 1881	'in tail'	–
By LPA 1925 s60(4)	'in tail'	'in tail'

See also s130 LPA 1925.

Ending the entail

This is known as barring the entail. A tenant in tail after possibility, that is, when he cannot possibly have heirs of the requisite type, cannot bar the entail. Otherwise the right to bar cannot be excluded or restricted. The methods available are:

By a disentailing assurance

This can be executed by a tenant in tail in possession of full age, and the effect is to enlarge the fee tail into a fee simple. This defeats the interests of his issue and all subsequent interests but not prior interests.

By a disentailing deed

A tenant in tail in remainder, ie who has not yet succeeded to the entail, can bar the entail by deed with the concurrence of the protector of the settlement who is the owner of the prior life interest under the settlement; and, if there is more than one prior life interest, the first in time or any person who would have a prior interest if he had not disposed of it.

A tenant in tail in remainder can execute a disentailing deed without this consent, but he will only create a base fee (see sl Fines and Recoveries Act 1833). However, a base fee may be enlarged into a fee simple by the following:

1. Execution of a fresh disentailing deed with the consent of the protector or after the former tenant in tail in remainder becomes entitled to possession.
2. By union of the base fee with the reversion or remainder in fee simple.
3. By will, if the testator is in possession.
4. By expiry of 12 years after the date on which the tenant in tail in remainder became entitled to possession.

By will

Section 176 LPA 1925 made it possible for entails to be barred by wills executed after 1925. This only applies to entails in possession and the tenant in tail must be of full age. The will must refer specifically to the entailed property, or the instrument creating the entail, or entailed property generally. Entails cannot be barred by infants, lunatics and bankrupts.

4.6 The life estate

Definition

There are two types of life estate, which since 1925 can only exist as equitable interests:

1. For the life of the tenant – this can arise expressly or by operation of law, eg a tenant in tail after possibility.
2. Estate for life of another – estate pur autre vie – this may be granted expressly or may arise when a tenant for life assigns his interest.

Rights of a tenant for life

The rights of a tenant for life over the land are considerably restricted by the common law rules relating to waste and to fixtures.

4.7 Waste

Waste is any act which alters the nature of the land. This change in the land is not necessarily detrimental to the land. The idea behind the rules is that a tenant for life is only entitled to the income from the land, and must not act so as to affect its capital value.

Types of waste

There are four types of waste: ameliorating, voluntary, permissive and equitable.

Ameliorating waste
This is an act which improves the land. A court would not in general look favourably upon an action to restrain such acts unless the whole character of the property is changed. See *Doherty* v *Allman* (1878) 3 App Cas 709.

Voluntary waste
This is a positive act which damages the land, such as opening a mine or cutting timber. A tenant for life is liable for voluntary waste unless the grant expressly exempts him from such liability, when he is said to be 'unimpeachable of waste'. See *Honywood* v *Honywood* (1874) LR 18 Eq 306; *Dashwood* v *Magniac* [1891] 3 Ch 306.

Permissive waste
This is a failure to do something which ought to be done. A tenant for life is not liable for permissive waste unless the grant imposes upon him an obligation to repair. See *Powys* v *Blagrave* (1854) 4 De GM & G 448.

Equitable waste
This was defined by Lord Campbell in *Turner* v *Wright* (1860) 2 De GF & J 234 as '... that which a prudent man would not do in the management of his own property'.

Even when a tenant for life is unimpeachable for waste, equity will not allow him to ruin the property by acts of destruction (*Vane* v *Lord Barnard* (1716) 2 Vern 738), unless he can show that the document giving his life interest also shows a clear intention to allow him to commit such acts of equitable waste. See s135 LPA 1925:

> 'An equitable interest for life without impeachment of waste does not confer upon the tenant for life any right to commit waste of the description known as equitable waste, unless an intention to confer such right expressly appears by the instrument creating such equitable interest.'

4.8 Fixtures

The law of fixtures is also important in relation to leaseholds, to which some special rules apply in addition to these general principles.

Definition

A fixture is a chattel which has become part of the land by being attached to it, often stated as the Latin maxim 'quicquid plantatur solo, solo cedit' (whatever is affixed to the soil, belongs to the soil). Fixtures are real property, and belong to the owner of the land unless a contrary intention can be shown.

The distinction between fixtures and chattels

In order to decide whether a particular object is a fixture or a chattel, the courts apply two tests known as the degree and the purpose of annexation:

The degree of annexation
This is the first test to be applied and means that, prima facie, an object is a fixture if it is firmly attached to the land, but not a fixture if it is only resting on the ground by its own weight. See *Dean* v *Andrews* (1985) The Times 25 May: a large prefabricated greenhouse bolted to a concrete plinth which was not affixed to the ground but merely rested on the ground under its own weight (and that of the greenhouse) was held NOT to be a fixture. See also *Holland* v *Hodgson* (1872) LR 7 CP 328. When considering fixtures in relation to leases the test is often said to be whether the object can be removed without doing serious damage to the premises. Originally the degree of annexation was the only test applied by law, but it operated harshly, and so the courts began to use a second test.

The purpose of annexation
If the object was attached to the land with the intention that it should be part of the land, it is a fixture; if it was attached to the land merely for its better enjoyment as a chattel, it remains a chattel. The test was at first applied only to limited owners, eg life tenants. In *Leigh* v *Taylor* [1902] AC 157 a tenant for life had securely fastened

valuable tapestries to the walls, but the House of Lords held that she had done this merely for their better enjoyment and they passed to her estate.

The same test was applied in *D'Eyncourt* v *Gregory* (1866) LR 3 Eq 382 to objects (garden statues) not attached to the land but merely resting on it. They were held to be an integral part of the landscaping and therefore fixtures.

In *Berkley* v *Poulett* (1976) The Times 3 November the same test was applied as between vendor and purchaser by the majority of the Court of Appeal. It is not possible to reconcile the many cases on fixtures, and even the above two tests may not always be conclusive. See *Hamp* v *Bygrave* (1982) 266 EG 722.

The right to remove fixtures

Prima facie a fixture cannot be removed from the land and belongs to the fee simple owner. There are however certain limited exceptions to this rule.

Landlord and tenant

Certain fixtures, known as 'tenant's fixtures', may be removed by the tenant during his tenancy or a reasonable time thereafter. There are three classes of tenant's fixtures.

1. Trade fixtures, those attached by the tenant for the purpose of his trade or profession. See *New Zealand Government Property Corporation* v *H M & S Ltd* [1982] 1 All ER 624.
2. Ornamental and domestic fixtures which can be removed without substantial damage to the building.
3. Agricultural fixtures. By s13 of the Agricultural Holdings Act 1948 an agricultural tenant may remove fixtures which he installed for agricultural purposes before the end of the term or within two months thereafter if he gives one month's written notice; and all rent is paid and obligations performed, no avoidable damage is done in the removal and any damage done made good; and the landlord has not served a written counter-notice and paid a fair value for the fixtures.

Tenant for life and remainderman

The position is the same as between landlord and the tenant, except that the 1948 Act provisions do not apply.

Mortgagor and mortgagee

All fixtures on mortgaged land are included in the mortgage, and the mortgagor may not remove them during the currency of the mortgage, even those affixed after the mortgage commenced. This becomes important where the mortgagee contemplates the remedy of taking possession of the mortgaged property. See *Hobson* v *Gorringe* [1897] 1 Ch 182; *Reynolds* v *Ashby & Son* [1904] AC 466.

Vendor and purchaser

All fixtures pass to the purchaser on conveyance unless otherwise agreed: see *Hamp* v *Bygrave* (above). Where certain garden ornaments could have been either fixtures or chattels in their own right, it was held that the ornaments were part of the property on which they were situated because they had been expressly referred to as such in both the particulars of sale and the inquiries before contract. In addition they had been regarded as part of the freehold by the vendors during their negotiations with the purchasers and, as such, were held to pass with the land on the conveyance to the purchasers. (See also *Dean* v *Andrews* (1985) The Times 25 May.)

4.9 Reverter of Sites Act 1987

'1(1) Where any relevant enactment provides for land to revert to the ownership of any person at any time, being a time when the land ceases, or has ceased for a specified period, to be used for particular purposes, that enactment shall have effect, and (subject to subs(4) below) shall be deemed always to have had effect, as if it provided (instead of for the reverter) for the land to be vested after that time, on the trust arising under this section, in the persons in whom it was vested immediately before that time.

(2) Subject to the following provisions of this Act, the trust arising under this section in relation to any land is a trust to sell the land and to stand possessed of the net proceeds of sale (after payment of costs and expenses) and of the net rents and profits until sale (after payment of rates, taxes, costs of insurance, repairs and other outgoings) upon trust for the persons who but for this Act would from time to time be entitled to the ownership of the land by virtue of its reverter.

(3) Where:

a) a trust in relation to any land has arisen or is treated as having arisen under this section at such a time as is mentioned in subs(1) above; and

b) immediately before that time the land was vested in any persons in their capacity as the minister and churchwardens of any parish,

those persons shall be treated as having become trustees for sale under this section in that capacity and, accordingly, their interest in the land shall pass and, if the case so requires, be treated as having passed to their successors from time to time.

(4) This section shall not confer any right on any person as a beneficiary:

a) in relation to any property in respect of which that person's claim was statute-barred before the commencement of this Act, or in relation to any property derived from any such property; or

b) in relation to any rents or profits received, or breach of trust committed, before the commencement of this Act; and anything validly done before the commencement of this Act in relation to any land which by virtue of this section is deemed to have been held at the time on trust for sale shall, if done by the beneficiaries, be deemed, so far as necessary for preserving its validity, to have been done by the trustees.

(5) Where any property is held by any persons as trustees of a trust which has arisen under this section and, in consequence of subs(4) above, there are no beneficiaries of that trust, the trustees shall have no power to act in relation to that property except:

a) for the purposes for which they could have acted in relation to that property if this Act had not been passed; or

b) for the purpose of securing the establishment of a scheme under s2 below or the making of an order under s2 of the Education Act 1973 (special powers as to trusts for religious education).

(6) In this section:

"churchwardens" includes chapel wardens;

"minister" includes a rector, vicar or perpetual curate; and

"parish" includes a parish of the Church in Wales;

and the reference to a person's claim being statute-barred is a reference to the Limitation Act 1980 providing that no proceedings shall be brought by that person to recover the property in respect of which the claim subsists.

Charity Commissioners' schemes

2(1) Subject to the following provisions of this section and to ss3 and 4 below, where any persons hold any property as trustees of a trust which has arisen under s1 above, the Charity Commissioners may, on the application of the trustees, by order establish a scheme which:

a) extinguishes the rights of beneficiaries under the trust; and

b) requires the trustees to hold the property on trust for such charitable purposes as may be specified in the order.

(2) Subject to subsections (3) and (4) below, an order made under this section:

a) may contain any such provision as may be contained in an order made by the High Court for establishing a scheme for the administration of a charity; and

b) shall have the same effect as an order so made.

(3) The charitable purposes specified in an order made under this section on an application with respect to any trust shall be as similar in character as the Charity Commissioners think is practicable in all the circumstances to the purposes (whether charitable or not) for which the trustees held the relevant land before the cesser of use in consequence of which the trust arose; but in determining the character of the last-mentioned purposes the Commissioners, if they think it appropriate to do so, may give greater weight to the persons or locality benefited by the purposes than to the nature of the benefit.

(4) An order made under this section on an application with respect to any trust shall be so framed as to secure that if a person who:

a) but for the making of the order would have been a beneficiary under the trust; and

b) has not consented to the establishment of a scheme under this section,

notifies a claim to the trustees within the period of five years after the date of the making of the order, that person shall be paid an amount equal to the value of his rights at the time of their extinguishment.

(5) The Charity Commissioners shall not make any order under this section establishing a scheme unless:

a) the requirements of s3 below with respect to the making of the application for the order are satisfied or, by virtue of subs(4) of that section, do not apply;

b) one of the conditions specified in subs(6) below is fulfilled;

c) public notice of the Commissioners' proposals has been given inviting representations to be made to them within a period specified in the notice, being a period ending not less than one month after the date of the giving of the notice; and

d) that period has ended and the Commissioners have taken into consideration any representations which have been made within that period and not withdrawn.

(6) The conditions mentioned in subs(5)(b) above are:

a) that there is no claim by any person to be a beneficiary in respect of rights proposed to be extinguished:

i) which is outstanding; or

ii) which has at any time been accepted as valid by the trustees or by persons whose acceptance binds the trustees; or

iii) which has been upheld in proceedings that have been concluded;

b) that consent to the establishment of a scheme under this section has been given by every person whose claim to be a beneficiary in respect of those rights is outstanding or has been so accepted or upheld.

(7) The Charity Commissioners shall refuse to consider an application under this section unless it is accompanied by a statutory declaration by the applicants:

a) that the requirements of s3 below are satisfied with respect to the making of the application or, if the declaration so declares, do not apply; and

b) that a condition specified in subs(6) above and identified in the declaration is fulfilled;

and the declaration shall be conclusive for the purposes of this section of the matters declared therein.

(8) A notice given for the purposes of subs(5)(c) above shall contain such particulars of the Commissioners' proposals, or such directions for obtaining information about them, and shall be given in such manner, as they think sufficient and appropriate; and a further such notice shall not be required where the Commissioners decide, before proceeding with any proposals of which notice has been so given, to modify them.

Applications for schemes

3(1) Where an application is made under s2 above by the trustees of any trust that has arisen under s1 above, the requirements of this section are satisfied with respect to the making of that application if, before the application is made:

a) notices under subs(2) below have been published in two national newspapers and in a local newspaper circulating in the locality where the relevant land is situated;

b) each of those notices specified a period for the notification to the trustees of claims by beneficiaries, being a period ending not less than three months after the date of publication of the last of those notices to be published;

c) that period has ended;

d) for a period of not less than twenty-one days during the first month of that period, a copy of one of those notices was affixed to some object on the relevant land in such a position and manner as, so far as practicable, to make the notice easy for members of the public to see and read without going on to the land; and

e) the trustees have considered what other steps could be taken to trace the persons who are or may be beneficiaries and to inform those persons of the application to be made under s2 above and have taken such of the steps considered by them as it was reasonably practicable for them to take.

(2) A notice under this subsection shall:

a) set out the circumstances that have resulted in a trust having arisen under s1 above;

b) state that an application is to be made for the establishment of a scheme with respect to the property subject to the trust; and

c) contain a warning to every beneficiary that, if he wishes to oppose the extinguishment of his rights, he should notify his claim to the trustees in the manner, and within the period, specified in the notice.

(3) Where at the time when the trustees publish a notice for the purposes of subs(2) above:

a) the relevant land is not under their control; and

b) it is not reasonably practicable for them to arrange for a copy of the notice to be affixed as required by paragraph (d) of subs(1) above to some object on the land,

that paragraph shall be disregarded for the purposes of this section.
(4) The requirements of this section shall not apply in the case of an application made in respect of any trust if:
a) the time when that trust is treated as having arisen was before the commencement of this Act; and
b) more than twelve years have elapsed since that time.'

Commentary

The Act excludes from s7(1) LPA 1925 certain statutes which allowed for sites to be made available for schools, churches, libraries or museums, including the School Sites Act.

The effect is to replace the right of reverter, in such cases, with a statutory trust for sale. Upon the particular use coming to an end the land will be held on trust for sale for the revertee, who becomes the beneficiary under this statutory trust for sale.

This ends the automatic revesting of the land and will, in the cases where the 1987 Act applies, prevent the trustees from obtaining a title by adverse possession as occurred in *Re Rowhook Mission Hall* [1985] Ch 62.

5

Law and Equity

5.1 Two legal systems

The common law rules concerning land were almost fully developed when the Chancellor started to exercise a separate jurisdiction in the fifteenth century, because matters concerning land were the first to come to the king's courts.

The Chancery jurisdiction over land developed because the Chancery would enforce the use, or trust as it was later called. Land was put into uses for several purposes, often to evade the effects of the common law. From this jurisdiction developed a whole range of equitable estates, ie enforceable only in the Court of Chancery, brought into being by the use or the use upon a use, which exactly mirrored the range of legal estates, and so in one piece of land one person could have a fee simple protected by the common law courts (the legal fee) and a different person a fee simple protected by the Court of Chancery (the equitable fee). Until the Judicature Acts of 1873 and 1875 these were two separate court systems, with their own rules and procedure. Now, although law and equity are 'fused' in that they are administered by the same courts by the same process, they are still to some extent different systems of law. Land law, more than any other subject, uses and exploits these parallel legal and equitable interests in land to produce often elegant, sometimes bewildering, solutions to complex problems of land ownership.

Definition

Equity may be defined as a system of doctrines and procedures which developed side by side with the common law and statute law.

5.2 Contributions by equity to land law

1. The trust.
2. Remedies such as specific performance of contracts for the sale or leasing of land. This also gave rise to the rules relating to the agreement for a lease. See Chapter 10.
3. Mortgagor's equity of redemption. This will be explained in Chapter 14.
4. Restrictive covenants. These are dealt with in Chapter 11.

5.3 The difference between legal and equitable rights

The difference arose because of the fact that the common law only recognised legal ownership and gave no effect to trusts, which were enforceable only in equity. Legal interests in land are therefore rights in rem, enforceable against anyone; equitable interests were at first rights only in personam, enforceable against the trustee personally. This was clearly a very limited protection, and so the Court of Chancery gradually extended it, enforcing equitable interests against persons who took under the trustee on various grounds. Equity, however, would not enforce a trust against an innocent purchaser of the land who knew nothing about the trust, as that enforcement would itself be inequitable, and so an equitable right was still not as strong as a legal right.

5.4 The doctrine of notice

These equitable rules became embodied in what is known as the doctrine of notice. This can be expressed as the following maxim:

> 'Legal rights are good against the whole world; equitable rights are good against all persons except a bona fide purchaser of the legal estate for value without notice of the equitable interests in that land, and those claiming under him.'

This bona fide purchaser is often known as 'equity's darling'. The essential features of this privileged person are that he is:

1. *Bona fide* – any dishonesty, sharp practice or other inequitable practice will forfeit equity's protection.
2. *Purchaser for value* – 'purchaser ' excludes those who inherit the land or acquire it by operation of law. 'For value', while it does not necessarily mean 'full value', means money or money's worth or marriage. The decision of the House of Lords in *Midland Bank Trust Co Ltd* v *Green* [1981] AC 513 shows that the consideration need not be adequate. See also s17(1) Land Charges Act 1972 for the definition of 'purchaser'.
3. *Of a legal estate* – this is essential; the purchaser of an equitable interest is in general bound by prior equitable interests whether he had notice of them or not.

4. *Without notice* – the purchaser must have no knowledge of the equitable interest at the time he purchased his interest. There are three types of notice:
   a) *Actual notice* – this must be within his own knowledge and must not be merely a vague reference, except that such vague knowledge might lead to constructive notice (below).
   b) *Constructive notice* – a purchaser cannot attempt to avoid equitable interests by shutting his eyes and ears and thus not having actual notice. He is deemed to have notice of all matters about which a reasonably diligent purchaser would have inquired and which would have come to his notice on such an inquiry. This would be derived either from not following up some information or by deliberately abstaining from making any inquiries. As to the need to inspect the land, see *Hunt* v *Luck* [1902] 1 Ch 428.

      If a person in occupation deliberately withholds information about his interest he may be estopped from relying on the defence that the inquirer had constructive notice arising from the occupation. See *Midland Bank Ltd* v *Farmpride Hatcheries Ltd* (1981) 260 EG 493.
   c) *Imputed notice* – if a purchaser employs an agent, eg a solicitor, in the purchase, any actual or constructive notice which that agent receives in the course of the same transaction is imputed to the purchaser.

      The application of s199(1)(ii)(b) LPA 1925 in the context of a surveyor acting on behalf of a mortgagee was seen in *Kingsnorth Finance Co Ltd* v *Tizard* [1986] 2 All ER 54. The surveyor was held to have imputed notice, on behalf of the mortgagee, of a wife's occupation where the potential mortgagor had described himself as being 'single'. This gave the court the opportunity to consider the meaning of 'occupation' in the context of unregistered land. The wife had made contributions to the purchase price and her occupation was such as to give the mortgagee imputed notice of her equitable rights in the property.
5. *Successors in title* – the protection, once acquired, extends to all persons claiming through the original purchaser, even though they are not purchasers for value.
6. While the doctrine of notice has become less important since the passing of the 1925 legislation, for reasons we shall see in the next chapter, it still has a part to play in several aspects of land law. See the Land Charges Act 1972, and note ss198 and 199 Law of Property Act 1925. It is essential to know the above rules and when they may still apply today, eg restrictive covenants created before 1926, and where the rules of equitable estoppel may apply in the case of licences (see Chapter 14).

5.5 Powers

A power enables a person who is not the owner of property to dispose of it or exercise certain administrative powers over it. Since 1925 most powers are equitable.

The most important types of power are powers of trustees and powers of appointment. Powers of appointment can be classified as:

1. *General powers* – the appointor may appoint to any person including himself. He will not be required to obtain the consent of another person. He is treated as the virtual owner until an appointment is made.
2. *Special powers* – the appointor must appoint one of a specified class of persons known as the objects of the power.
3. *Hybrid powers* – the appointor may appoint to any person except himself, or may only appoint with the consent of another. A general testamentary power is a hybrid power.

Exercise of powers of appointment

When the donor specifies that the power is to be exercised in a certain way or subject to certain formalities, the direction must be followed or the exercise is void. An appointor of a special power must observe the limits imposed on the exercise. If he makes an appointment which partly comes within the scope of the power but is otherwise too wide, the part within the scope is valid and the rest void. If he makes an appointment which does not come within the scope at all, the whole appointment is void.

Fraud on a power

A fraud on a power is where the power has been used for a purpose beyond that intended by the instrument creating the power, and the effect is that the appointment is void in so far as it is fraudulent. By s157 LPA 1925 a purchaser in good faith of property fraudulently appointed is protected provided that he bought for money or money's worth without notice of the fraud from an appointee aged more than 25 who was entitled in default of appointment.

Release and disclaimer of powers

A power is discharged by exercise. A donee of a power may release it or contract not to exercise it by s155 LPA 1925 unless it is a trust power when he is under a duty to exercise it. He may disclaim it by deed: s156 LPA 1925. He may also impliedly extinguish it by any dealing inconsistent with the further exercise of the power.

6

The 1925 Legislation – Including Registration of Incumbrances

6.1 Introduction

There had been considerable statutory reform of land law during the nineteenth century, but a need for a comprehensive code of property legislation was felt, which resulted in the magnificent achievements of the draftsmen and legislature known as the 1925 legislation. This was a series of Acts, most of which were passed in 1925 and came into effect on 1 January 1926, which are:

The Law of Property Act 1922	(LPA 1922)
The Settled Land Act 1925	(SLA 1925)
The Law of Property Act 1925	(LPA 1925)
The Land Charges Act 1925	(LCA 1925)
The Land Registration Act 1925	(LRA 1925)
The Trustee Act 1925	(TA 1925)
The Administration of Estates Act 1925	(AEA 1925)

Since 1925 there has been further, piecemeal, legislation. The most important Acts are:

The Law of Property (Amendment) Act 1926	(LP(A)A 1926)
The Perpetuities and Accumulations Act 1964	(PAA 1964)
The Law of Property (Joint Tenants) Act 1964	(LP(JT)A 1964)
The Law of Property Act 1969	(LPA 1969)
The Land Charges Act 1972	(LCA 1972)
The Local Land Charges Act 1975	(LLCA 1975)

(The LCA 1972 and LLCA 1975 consolidate the law of land charges, replacing the LCA 1925)

The Rentcharges Act 1977	
The Land Registration Act 1986	(LRA 1986)
The Land Registration Act 1988	(LRA 1988)

6.2 The purpose of the 1925 legislation

There are two main purposes of the legislation:

To assimilate so far as is possible the rules relating to real property and to personal property

This is of lesser importance in the study of land law. The main reforms were:

1. By s130 LPA 1925 an entailed interest could be created in personalty as well as realty.
2. On intestacy by ss45 and 46 AEA 1925 (as amended) both real and personal property pass in the same way (apart from entails).
3. Realty and personalty are now both available to pay the deceased's debts, which formerly had to be satisfied from personalty alone, s34(3) and Schedule 1 AEA 1925.
4. The rule in *Dearle* v *Hall* (1828) 3 Russ 1 governing the priority of assignment of equitable interests applies equally to interests in realty and personalty by s137 LPA 1925.
5. By s60(1) LPA 1925 a conveyance of freehold land passes the whole interest of the vendor without the need for words of limitation.
6. Substantial changes were made in the method of creating legal mortgages. See ss85–87 LPA 1925 (Chapter 14).

The simplification of conveyancing

When a purchaser buys land he wants to know, first, whether the vendor in fact owns the title he is purporting to sell and, second, whether the land is incumbered by any interests belonging to third parties. We have already seen that a purchaser is in a much better position in respect of equitable interests owned by others than legal interests, and so the fewer legal interests there are the easier the purchaser's task is. On the other hand, owners of equitable interests also need protection. The 1925 legislation sought to satisfy as far as possible these conflicting claims of the purchaser and the owner of the equitable interest by:

1. Reducing the number of legal estates and interests that can exist in land (see s1 LPA 1925 below).
2. Protecting certain equitable interests by registration or transferring them to money in the hands of trustees (overreaching).
3. Expanding the system of title registration.

6.3 The reduction of the legal estates and interests

Section 1 LPA 1925

Legal estates

Section 1(1) LPA 1925 states that:

> 'The only estates in land which are capable of subsisting or of being conveyed or created at law are –
> 1. an estate in fee simple absolute in possession;
> 2. a term of years absolute.'

This means that all other interests, eg entails, life estates, which could previously be legal estates can now only exist as equitable interests behind a trust.

Legal interests

Section 1(2) deals with legal interests, that is rights over another's land, as follows:

> 'The only interests or charges in or over land which are capable of subsisting or of being conveyed or created at law are:
> 1. an easement, right or privilege in or over land for an interest equivalent to an estate in fee simple absolute in possession or a term of years absolute;
> 2. a rentcharge in possession issuing out of or charged on land being either perpetual or for a term of years absolute;
> 3. a charge by way of a legal mortgage;
> 4. a charge on land not created by an instrument;
> 5. rights of entry exercisable over or in respect of a legal term of years absolute, or annexed, for any purpose, to a legal rentcharge.'

Equitable interests

Section 1(3) concludes the reorganisation by stating that:

> 'All other estates interests and charges in or over land take effect as equitable interests.'

Estates and interests under 1 LPA 1925

Fee simple absolute in possession

'Fee simple' – the meaning of fee simple has been dealt with in Chapter 4 (section 4.4). 'Absolute' is used as opposed to a limited fee simple such as a determinable fee simple or a conditional fee. The effect of the Law of Property (Amendment) Act 1926 has already been noted, and the full effect of s7(1) in relation to fee simple which may be divested together with the 1926 amendment should be considered when any right of re-entry has been reserved (see Chapter 4, section 4.4):

> ' "In possession" means that the estate is immediate, not in remainder or reversion, and is defined to include the receipt of rents and profits as well as physical possession. (See s205(1)(xix) LPA 1925.) Thus a landlord who owns the fee simple absolute in possession has a legal estate even though he has parted with possession to the tenant (who may also have a legal estate). In addition s1(5) provides that: "A legal estate may subsist concurrently with or subject to any other legal estate in the same land." '

This may be demonstrated by the following diagram:

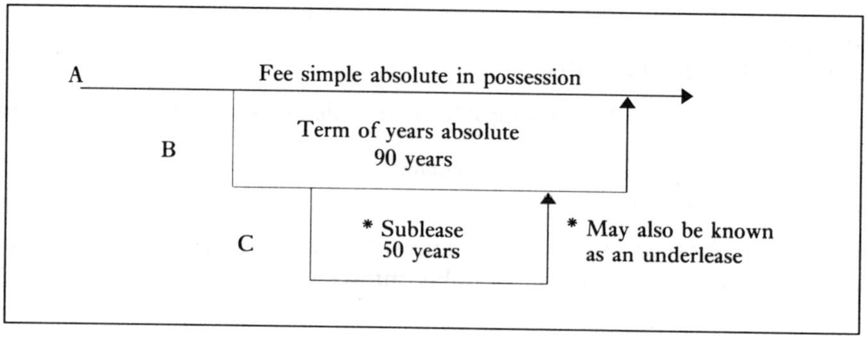

In this case A owns the fee simple absolute in possession. He grants a lease to B for 90 years. A continues to be in 'possession' because of s205(1)(xix) LPA 1925 which defines possession to include the receipt of rents and profits. B has a term of years absolute which will remain 'absolute' even if A has reserved a right of re-entry in the event that B breaks any covenants in the lease.

In turn B has granted a sublease to C. This is also a legal estate, being a term of years absolute. There is no requirement that B must be 'in possession'.

The whole example illustrates the fact that any number of legal estates may subsist concurrently within the terms of s1(5) LPA 1925.

Term of years absolute

A 'term of years absolute' is defined by s205(1)(xxvii) LPA 1925 as including a term of less than one year, or for a year or years, or from year to year, which appears to include all periodic tenancies. 'Absolute' does not appear to have any meaning, because a term of years is absolute even though it is subject to determination by notice, re-entry or operation of law. Megarry and Wade refer to an interesting example of a term of years absolute that is neither a term of years nor absolute. This would arise in the case of a monthly tenancy, 'less than a year', subject to a right of re-entry for failure to pay rent or breach of any other covenant in the lease.

Legal easements: s1(2)(a) LPA 1925

This covers both easements and profits à prendre (Chapter 12), but note that they can only be legal if held for equivalents of the two legal estates. An example of a non-legal easement could be an easement for life which only exists as an equitable easement today. See s2(3) LPA 1925.

Rentcharges: s1(2)(b) LPA 1925

A rentcharge is a right to be paid a periodical sum of money charged on land. This section has been considerably modified by the effect of the Rentcharges Act 1977, which forbids the creation after 22 August 1977 of any new rentcharges except those which come under the Settled Land Act 1925 (which could not be legal anyway), 'estate rentcharges' imposed to ensure the performance of covenants, and rentcharges imposed by statute or by a court.

Section 2 Rentcharges Act 1977 prohibits the creation of any new rentcharge except those mentioned above, of which the 'estate rentcharge' should be noted. The 'estate rentcharge' is defined to include a rentcharge created to meet the cost of the performance of covenants for the provision of services or the carrying out of maintenance or repairs by the owner of the rentcharge. The importance of the estate rentcharge lies in providing a way round the problem that the burden of a positive covenant, eg to repair, does not run (see Chapter 11).

The effect is to preserve certain rentcharges paid by the individual owners of some freehold properties on estates which have been deliberately laid out for landscape or amenity purposes, the upkeep of which is financed by such payments. All other existing rentcharges are to be phased out within 60 years.

Legal charge: s1(2)(c) LPA 1925

See Chapter 14. One of the two methods of creating a legal mortgage after 1925. This was introduced in the LPA 1925 – see s87 of that Act.

A charge on land not created by an instrument: s1(2)(d) LPA 1925

Unimportant today due to the repeal of the significant parts of the subsection.

Rights of entry: s1(2)(e) LPA 1925

These are rights of entry reserved in a lease enabling the landlord to recover the land if the tenant does not pay the rent or breaks his covenants, or those which allow a rentcharge owner to secure payment by taking possession of the land.

Any other former estate or interest which does not come within the above list must be equitable: s1(3) LPA 1925.

6.4 Protection of the equitable interests

The 1925 legislation makes a broad distinction between what can be called 'commercial' and 'family' interests in land. Those estates and interests which are legal estates and interests under s1 LPA 1925 are those which are commonly bought and sold; those which are equitable only, such as life interests, generally arise as a result of a will or a family settlement. The same broad distinction is made between those equitable interests which arise from, or may be the subject of, a commercial transaction, which are generally protected by registration, and those arising from settlements which are protected by the mechanism of overreaching. The former equitable rules of notice have been affected by the 1925 legislation – but those earlier rules do continue to be important.

The land charges register

The word 'registration' relates to two distinct concepts. The first is the registration of incumbrances (in unregistered land) as a replacement for the equitable doctrine of notice. This must not be confused with the registration of title at the Land Registry which is dealt with later (Chapter 7). The land charges register was intended to provide a means of protecting owners of equitable interests coming within the registrable classes, while at the same time making it easy for a purchaser to discover what equitable incumbrances he will be bound by. The problems which arise are due to the exceptions which make the land charges register an incomplete record of incumbrances which may affect unregistered land.

Prior to 1 July 1995, a land charge could only be registered against an estate owner and nobody could be an estate owner after he had died. Since that date it has been easier to register a land charge where an owner has died because s15 of the Law of Property (Miscellaneous Provisions) Act 1994 enables the charge to be registered against the owner's name after his death.

Principles of registration

The registration of a registrable interest replaces the doctrine of notice, so far as that interest is concerned. The principles relating to a registered land charge represent the combined effect of:

Section 4 Land Charges Act 1972: failure to register makes the interest void against a 'purchaser' – as defined in s17 LCA 1972. See *Midland Bank Trust Co Ltd v Green* [1981] AC 513 (below).

Section 198 Law of Property Act 1925: registration is deemed to constitute actual notice to all persons for all purposes connected with the land. This means that a registered charge is binding on a purchaser whether he knew about it or not, and an unregistered charge is not binding on a purchaser even if he had notice of it.

The meaning of the word 'purchaser' was considered in *Midland Bank Trust Co Ltd* v *Green*, where a wife purchased a farm from her husband for a considerable undervalue, the purpose of the sale being to defeat the exercise of an option by the son. The option was not registered. The House of Lords held that the unregistered option, under s13(2) Land Charges Act 1925 (now s4(6) Land Charges Act 1972), was void against 'a purchaser of a legal estate for money or money's worth'. These words contained no requirement that the purchaser must take in good faith or that the 'money or money's worth' must be more than nominal. See also s17 LCA 1972.

Registrable interests

The 1925 Act – now replaced by the LCA 1972 – imposed a duty to keep five separate registers; these are set out in s1(1) LCA 1972 as:

1. A register of land charges.
2. A register of pending actions.
3. A register of writs and orders affecting land.
4. A register of deeds of arrangement affecting land.
5. A register of annuities.

The register of land charges is undoubtedly the most important for land law purposes and this will be dealt with later. The following points should be noted in relation to the other registers:

The register of pending actions. This relates to 'any action information or proceeding pending in court relating to land or any interest in or charge on land' (s17(1) LCA 1972). The meaning of 'pending land action' is further considered in *Selim Ltd* v *Bickenhall Engineering Ltd* [1981] 1 WLR 1318 and *Haslemere Estates Ltd* v *Baker* [1982] 1 WLR 1109.

An action for breach of a landlord's repairing covenant is not a pending land action because it does not amount to a claim to an interest in the particular land. See *Regan & Blackburn Ltd* v *Rogers* [1985] 1 WLR 870.

The register of writs and orders affecting land. These include writs and orders enforcing judgments and orders of the court and would include any receiving order in bankruptcy made after 1925.

The register of deeds of arrangement affecting land. A deed of arrangement is defined in the Deeds of Arrangement Act 1914 as any document whereby control over a debtor's property is given for the benefit of his creditors.

The register of annuities. This register was closed in 1925 and dealt with annuities created after 25 April 1855 and before 1 January 1926.

The register of land charges. As indicated above this is the most important of the registers for land law purposes, and is dealt with in more detail below.

The register of land charges

Registrable land charges are divided into five classes by s2 LCA 1972.

Class A – charges imposed by statute which only arise on application by some interested person (unimportant): s2(2) LCA 1972.

Class B – charges imposed automatically by statute (unimportant): s2(3)LCA 1972.

Class C – this class is divided into four categories: s2(4) LCA 1972.

C(i) – a puisne mortgage, ie a legal mortgage of the legal estate not protected by deposit of title deeds. *Note*: this is a legal interest and is an example of a non-equitable matter covered by the LCA 1972.

C(ii) – a limited owner's charge. This charge is given to a tenant for life who himself pays any inheritance tax and entitles him to the same rights as a mortgagee against the settled land.

C(iii) – a general equitable charge. This is a residuary class, and covers things such as equitable mortgages of a legal estate unprotected by deposit of title deeds and an unpaid vendor's lien.

C(iv) – an estate contract, in other words a contract by the owner of a legal estate to convey or create a legal estate which is binding and enforceable. This covers contracts for the sale, lease or mortgage of land, and equitable leases arising from a purported lease lacking in the necessary formalities. See *Hollington Brothers Ltd* v *Rhodes* [1951] 2 All ER 578. The class also includes options to purchase and a right of pre-emption: see *Pritchard* v *Briggs* [1980] Ch 338, in which a conflict arose between persons holding a right of pre-emption and an option to purchase respectively on the same property where both were correctly registered as estate contracts under s2(4)(iv) LCA 1972. Although the right of pre-emption was registered first, it was held by the Court of Appeal that the option to purchase had priority because a right of pre-emption is not an interest in land, even though it is registrable under the LCA 1972. A person who has a right to have land offered to him first if the owner of the land decides to sell can take no initiative. He cannot call for a conveyance to himself, he has only the hope that the owner will decide to sell the land. The grant of a right of pre-emption confers no present or contingent interest in land. See also *Taylor Fashions Ltd* v *Liverpool Victoria Trustees Co Ltd* [1981] 1 All ER 897.

Estate contract does include a lessee's option to renew an estate contract even though the option runs with the reversion.

Class D – this class is divided into three categories: s2(5) LCA 1972.

D(i) – a charge for unpaid inheritance tax in favour of the Inland Revenue (unimportant).

D(ii) – restrictive covenants made after 1925, not being covenants in a lease (covenants created before 1926 continued to depend on the rules of notice).

D(iii) – equitable easements arising or created after 1925. This section is very vaguely worded but has been interpreted by the House of Lords in *Shiloh Spinners Ltd* v *Harding* [1973] AC 691 as having a narrow meaning, confined to rights equivalent to easements and profits. Lord Wilberforce considered whether an equitable right of entry was included and said: '... Class D(iii) should be given its plain prima facie meaning and that so read it does not comprise equitable rights of entry'.

Class E – annuities created before 1926 but registered after 1925 (unimportant): s2(6) LCA 1972.

Class F – charge arising from the Matrimonial Homes Act 1983: s2(7) LCA 1972. This is the right of a spouse who does not own a legal estate in the matrimonial home to occupy the home: s1 Matrimonial Homes Act 1983; see *Wroth* v *Tyler* [1974] Ch 30 in which Megarry J described the effect of the original Act of 1967 in these words:

> '... the essentials of the right given by the Act [1967] to an occupying spouse [are] as follows. The right is in essence a personal and non-assignable statutory right not to be evicted from the matrimonial home in question during marriage or until the court otherwise orders: and this right constitutes a charge on the estate or interest of the owning spouse which requires protection against third parties by registration.'

The use of Class F land charges was considered in *Barnett* v *Hassett* [1981] 1 WLR 1385, in which it was held that a spouse who has no intention to occupy the matrimonial home is not permitted to register a Class F charge merely in an attempt to freeze the proceeds of an intended sale.

Unregistrable interests

There are certain interests which do not come within the provision of the Land Charges Act 1972, but do not arise under a trust or settlement, and so are not overreachable. Some of these are clearly unregistrable because of the wording of s2 LCA 1972, eg restrictive covenants and equitable easements created before 1926. Others have been declared by the courts to be unregistrable, for example:

1. Beneficial interests under bare trusts.
2. Equitable rights of entry: *Shiloh Spinners* v *Harding* (see Lord Wilberforce, above).
3. Beneficial interests under resulting trusts: see *Caunce* v *Caunce* [1969] 1 WLR 286, and cf *Williams & Glyn's Bank* v *Boland* [1981] AC 487.
4. Contractual licences: see *Binions* v *Evans* [1972] Ch 359.
5. Equitable rights based on estoppel: see *E R Ives Investments Ltd* v *High* [1967] 2 QB 379 (see also Chapter 13). This is probably the most significant application of the doctrine of notice today as the rules relating to proprietary estoppel continue to be developed by the courts.
6. A charging order on an undivided share of land is now possible under the Charging Orders Act 1979, but the Act did not make such order registrable under the Land Charges Act 1972.

The doctrine of notice applies to unregistrable interests. The effect of constructive notice today was discussed in *Midland Bank Ltd* v *Farmpride Hatcheries Ltd* (1981) 260 Estates Gazette 493, and the application of the rule in *Hunt* v *Luck* [1902] 1 Ch 428 continues to be relevant in the case of the tenant who has a legal lease not capable of protection by registration as a land charge Class C(iv) or in the case of a person having the benefit of a licence by estoppel. As to the effect of imputed notice, see *Kingsnorth Finance Co Ltd* v *Tizard* [1986] 2 All ER 54.

Overreaching

A settlement of land, in the broadest meaning of the word, is an arrangement creating a succession of interests in property. The 1925 legislation allows two methods of doing this, a settlement under the Settled Land Act 1925, and a trust for sale. These are explained in detail in Chapter 8. Because limited interests in land are now necessarily equitable, in both types of settlement there are one or more persons holding the legal estate on trust for the beneficiaries.

In order to enable easy dealing with land subject to a settlement or trust for sale, a method of selling it free from the equitable interests of the beneficiaries, while protecting them, is necessary. This is done by providing that if the purchase money for the land is paid to at least two trustees of the settlement (unless a trust corporation is a trustee, when the money may be paid to it) the purchaser takes free of equitable interests under the settlement, which are said to be 'overreached'. The beneficiaries' interests are transferred to the purchase money.

Further details of the overreaching provisions are given in Chapter 8.

Effects of a sale of unregistered land on legal and equitable rights

Unregistered land means land of which the title is not registered as explained in Chapter 7.

1. The purchaser takes subject to all legal rights except:
   a) those legal rights which are registrable and are unregistered, eg puisne mortgage (land charge Class C(i));
   b) those few legal rights which are overreachable.
2. The purchaser takes subject to all equitable rights except:
   a) registrable equitable rights which are unregistered: s4 LCA 1972;
   b) overreachable equitable rights, provided that the overreaching mechanism is gone through;
   c) unregistrable and non-overreachable rights in respect of which he is a bona fide purchaser of a legal estate for value without notice.

The general effect of the registration of land charges

Section 198 LPA 1925 provides that registration under the Land Charges Act is to be deemed to constitute notice of the matter registered 'to all persons and for all purposes'. There are, however, a few exceptions to s198 LPA 1925 where actual knowledge is required. These are:

Tacking: s94(2) LPA 1925
Where a prior mortgage expressly states that it is to be a security for any further advances, then registration of such a later mortgage is not deemed to be actual notice and will not prevent tacking (see Chapter 14).

Discharge of a mortgage: s96(2) LPA 1925
When a mortgagor has discharged his first mortgage, the first mortgagee is not deemed to have notice of any subsequent mortgages simply because the later mortgages were registered. Thus subsequent mortgagees, who will not have the title deeds, must both register their mortgage as land charges Class C(i) or Class C(iii) and give actual notice to the prior incumbrancers.

Actual knowledge at the date of the contract: s24 LPA 1969
Whether a purchaser knew of a registered land charge when he entered into the contract is to be decided by reference to his actual knowledge. Section 24 LPA 1969 provides:

> 'Where under a contract for the sale or other disposition of any estate or interest in land the title to which is not registered under the Land Registration Act 1925 ... any question arises whether the purchaser had knowledge at the time of entering into the contract, of a registered land charge, that question shall be determined by reference to his actual knowledge and without regard to the provisions of s198 of the Law of Property Act 1925.'

The effect of s24 LPA 1969 is to make a land charge search before the exchange of contracts unnecessary because the only knowledge which counts at the time of exchange of contracts is the actual knowledge of the prospective purchaser. It should be noted that the Act refers to 'actual knowledge', which appears to exclude the rules of constructive notice in this particular area.

The two major exceptions to the application of s24 are that the section does not relate to contracts for the sale of registered land, and nor does it dispense with the need for a search in the local land charges register (see section 6.5 below).

6.5 Local Land Charges Act 1975

Definition of a local land charge

A local land charge is broadly defined in s1 Local Land Charges Act 1975 Act to include charges under the Public Health and Highways Acts, restrictions and positive obligations imposed by a local authority or Minister of the Crown if they bind successive owners of the land, and matters expressly declared to be local land charges. Entries in the land charges register are made against the relevant land.

Effect of failure to register a local land charge

Section 10 LLCA 1975 should be noted; it provides that from 1 August 1977 failure to register a charge in the local land charges register shall not affect the enforcement of the charge, but that a purchaser shall be entitled to compensation for any loss suffered by reason that the charge was not registered or was not shown as registered by an official search certificate. Previously a local land charge had been void against a purchaser for money or money's worth of a legal estate in the land affected unless registered before completion of the purchase. The result is that while a local land charge certificate will no longer be conclusive, a certificate from the central land charges register still remains conclusive under s10(4) Land Charges Act 1972.

Examples of local land charges

Local land charges include various public matters relating to financial charges, some planning charges and lists of buildings of special architectural or historical interest.

The one private matter which will be found in the local land charges register is a light obstruction notice registered under the provisions of the Rights of Light Act 1959 (see Chapter 12).

6.6 Entries on the land charges register

The land charges register is a 'names' register and a person wishing to protect a registrable interest must register it against the name of the landowner for the time being: s3(1) LCA 1972. This gives rise to several problems which are:

Registration against the wrong name

This does not invalidate the registration if it is made in a name which could reasonably be regarded as a usual variation of the correct name (*Oak Co-operative Building Society* v *Blackburn* [1968] Ch 730), although it will not bind a purchaser who searches against the correct name because a clear search is conclusive by virtue of s10(4) LCA 1972 (*Diligent Finance Co Ltd* v *Alleyne* (1972) 23 P & CR 346).

Search against the wrong name

A purchaser who searches against the wrong name will be bound by the interests registered against the correct name, or even against a usual variant of the correct name (*Oak Co-operative* v *Blackburn* (above)).

Names behind the root of title

Before a purchaser buys land the vendor must prove that he has title, ie he owns the interest he is selling. This is done by producing the documents that trace the title to the land in question. It would be an impossible task for a vendor to produce every document, and instead he need not produce a document older than a specified date before the transaction which shows the ownership of the land unless the contract provides otherwise. This is known as the 'root of title'. Until 1969 the specified period was 30 years; it is now 15 years (s23 LPA 1969). As registration of incumbrances goes back to 1925, it is often the case that there are previous owners whose names are not revealed by examination of the title documents against whom incumbrances may have been registered. A scheme of compensation for purchasers affected by undiscoverable land charges was introduced by s25 LPA 1969. See also section 6.4 as to the effect of s24 LPA 1969.

6.7 Searching in the land charges register

A prospective purchaser can only discover registered incumbrances by searching the register against the correct names of all the persons he knows to have owned the land in question. In view of the decision in the *Oak Co-operative* case (above) he would also be well advised to search against all the usual variants of the correct names.

The search may be made in person, but it is much safer to have an official search made by the Land Registry and obtain an official certificate. Nowadays an official search is done by computer. The advantages of an official search certificate are:

1. It is conclusive in favour of the person requesting the search, provided that his application correctly specifies the persons and the land concerned. This means that he takes free of any rights it fails to disclose, even if properly registered.
2. It protects any solicitor or trustee making a search from liability for any error in the certificate.
3. It provides protection from incumbrances registered in a period of 15 working days from the date of the certificate, so that if the purchase is completed within that period the purchaser takes free from such incumbrances.

If the official search certificate fails to reveal a properly registered charge the purchaser takes free of the charge and so the owner of the interest loses it. No provision was made by Parliament to compensate the owner of the interest in such a case, but an action for damages for negligence lies against the public authority responsible. This should be compared with local land charges position since 1 August 1977: see *Ministry of Housing and Local Government* v *Sharp* [1970] 2 QB 223.

Compare s10 Local Land Charges Act 1975 (section 6.5 above).

6.8 Priority notices

Very often on the sale of land a series of operations all take place at the time of completion; for example, the conveyance which inter alia creates a restrictive covenant will be completed a few moments before a mortgage on the property. If the normal rules of registration applied, the restrictive covenant would be void as against the mortgagee. The vendor can, however, protect his restrictive covenant by giving a priority notice to the registrar at least 15 days before the transaction. Then, if he registers his covenant within 30 days of the entry of the priority notice the registration dates back to the moment of the creation of the restrictive covenant and hence is binding on the mortgagee. This priority notice provision applies to all registrable charges.

6.9 Vacation of the registration of a land charge

The court has a wide jurisdiction, both inherent, *Calgary and Edmonton Land Co Ltd* v *Dobinson* [1974] Ch 102, and statutory under s1(6) LCA 1972, to order the removal of any registration from the register when the registration was improper or has ceased to apply. See *Barnett* v *Hassett* [1981] 1 WLR 1385.

The problem of what matters are registrable has been further considered in *Selim Ltd* v *Bickenhall Engineering Ltd* [1981] 3 All ER 210, where an application to the court for leave to sue a tenant who was protected by the Leasehold Property (Repairs) Act 1938 was held to be registrable as a 'pending land action' under s17(1) Land Charges Act 1972. See also *Haslemere Estates Ltd* v *Baker* [1982] 3 All ER 525 where a claim based on proprietary estoppel in respect of time spent and expenditure incurred in respect of obtaining a planning permission and agreeing a form of lease was a claim to money and not a pending land action.

6.10 Worked example

The following is an example of a typical LLB examination question set on the contents of this chapter.

The answer is only intended to set out the points which should be covered by the student when answering, and it is for each student to develop his or her own style of writing.

Q In 1970 Peter bought the fee simple absolute of Windmill Farm. The farm is subject to a covenant prohibiting any further building, entered into by Peter's predecessor in title in 1920, and in 1975 Peter covenanted with his neighbour not to use the Long Meadow for other than agricultural purposes. In 1980 Peter mortgaged the farm to the Temple Building Society by way of legal charge.

The Society took the title deeds, but later allowed Peter to borrow them and never asked for their return. In 1985 Peter let Tithe Cottage, one of the farm buildings, to Mrs Stanley for 15 years at £500 pa in writing but not under seal. In 1990 Peter executed a deed declaring himself to be trustee of the farm for his wife. Peter recently sold and conveyed the legal fee simple in the whole farm to William without disclosing any of the above matters. Advise William as to whether he is bound by them.

A Assuming this to be *unregistered land*, the effect of the various transactions is as follows:

The 1920 restrictive covenant

Covenants made before 1926 are not registrable as land charges and the doctrine of notice applies. William does not have actual notice, and provided that he does not have constructive or implied notice he will not be bound by this covenant. This is one of the occasions when the examiner will require a knowledge of pre-1926 land law.

The 1975 restrictive covenant

This is registrable as a Class D(ii) land charge. If it is registered, registration constitutes actual notice (s198 LPA 1925), and so William is bound; if it is not registered it is void against a subsequent purchaser for money or money's worth of a legal estate (s4 LCA 1972), and so William will not be bound. As to the meaning of 'purchaser', see *Midland Bank Trust Co Ltd* v *Green* [1981] 2 WLR 28 and s17 LCA 1972.

The 1980 mortgage

This was originally protected by deposit of title deeds and so was a legal interest not requiring registration. William would be bound irrespective of notice. It is possible, however, that the return of the title deeds to Peter made the mortgage registrable as a puisne mortgage, Class C(i), and, if so, it would be binding if registered and void if unregistered. Even if it does not become registrable it is possible that the Society has lost its priority against William if its failure to regain the title deeds was gross negligence (see Chapter 14). See *Oliver* v *Hinton* [1899] 2 Ch 264.

The 1985 lease

This is an equitable lease as it is for more than three years but not made by deed (see Chapter 10) and is registrable as an estate contract, Class C(iv). If registered it is binding on William, if unregistered it is void. See *Hollington Brothers Ltd* v *Rhodes* [1951] 2 All ER 578.

The 1990 trust

This appears to be a bare trust rather than a settlement. Bare trusts are not overreachable, nor are they registrable, and so the doctrine of notice applies. This was assumed to be the position by the Court of Appeal in *Binions* v *Evans* [1972] Ch 359.

In recent years LLB examiners have gone on to ask if the answer would differ if the title to the land was registered. After Chapter 7 has been studied the reader is advised to return to this example to check if his answer would differ if the title to Windmill Farm was registered.

7

Registration of Title

7.1 Introduction

Registration of title was introduced in the nineteenth century and extended by the Land Registration Act 1925. The idea lying behind registration is that there should be a register containing all the relevant details about all land in England and Wales. Compulsory registration of title has been extended to the whole of England and Wales since 1 December 1990.

There were two reasons for the establishment of such a system:

1. To provide a simpler and faster method of proving title when the land is conveyed.
2. To provide better protection for purchasers and for the owners of equitable interests in the land conveyed.

Proof of title

A vendor must be able to prove that he is entitled to the land before he can pass good title to a purchaser. Under the pre-1926 system such proof was provided by the production of the title documents to the land, ie the conveyances or leases. The vendor had to be able to show the chain of ownership for the last 30 (now 15) years. And each time the land was sold, all these documents had to be examined. Under the LRA 1925 a single register entry is substituted for the series of title deeds as proof of title, and a prospective purchaser need only examine this register entry.

Protection of interests in the land

A purchaser learnt of the existence of some of the interests, both legal and equitable, affecting the land from the title deeds, but many were not disclosed. All purchasers were bound by any legal interests and all purchasers, except a bona fide purchaser for value of the legal estate without notice, were bound by any equitable interests. On the other hand the owner of an equitable interest in the land would lose that interest to a purchaser of the legal estate without notice. In order to protect both purchasers and the owners of equitable interests, the register entry under the LRA 1925 is intended to provide an accurate record of all interests in or over all land.

The Land Registration Act 1986 received the Royal Assent on 30 June 1986 and came into force on 1 January 1987. The Act implements the Law Commission's Report on Land Registration – Law Commission No 125. The main effect of the changes is that every conveyance on the sale of freehold land and every lease for more than 21 years or the assignment of a lease with more than 21 years to run must be submitted for registration within two months of the date of the deed.

Minor interests index

Section 5 Land Registration Act 1986 *repeals* s102(2) LRA 1925. With consequent changes to the Land Registration Rules 1925 the effect is to abolish the Minor Interests Index and provide that priority between dealings with equitable interests in registered land is to be determined by the rule in *Dearle* v *Hall* (1828) 3 Russ 1. This will be the order in which notice is received by the trustees.

Land Registration Act 1988

This Act came into force on 3 December 1990 and opens the Land Registry to inspection by anyone, removing the restrictions on access to the register without the authorisation of the registered proprietor. This new right of access extends to inspecting and making copies of entries on the register and any consequent documents held by the Land Registry, but does not include leases and charges on the land.

The consequences of having an 'open register' are many and varied. For example, a developer trying to assemble a site for development can now discover who owns the plot he needs to acquire and can then approach the owner directly with an offer to buy it. Further, the tenant of a long lease can now discover the identity of his landlord without having to correspond with, for example, a managing agent. Finally, it greatly facilitates the enforcement of judgments and could be of use to private investigators and investigative journalists.

Registration of Title Order 1989

The Registration of Title Order 1989 (SI 1989/1347) completed the extension of registration of title to the whole of England and Wales. From 1 December 1990 the whole of England and Wales is now subject to compulsory registration of title at the next appropriate transaction.

Land Registration Act 1988 (Commencement) Order 1990 (SI 1990/1759)

This Order brought the Land Registration Act 1988 into force from 3 December 1990. In addition, new rules – known as the Land Registration (Open Register) Rules 1990 – govern the administration of the open register procedure. For example, it currently costs £5 to obtain a copy of the register and £5 for a copy of a file plan.

7.2 Registration of title and the doctrine of notice

The equitable doctrine of notice so far as it relates to land with registered title is abolished by the LRA 1925. Its place is taken by registration. Failure to register renders an equitable interest void against a purchaser, whether or not he had notice. This simple principle is however modified by s70(1) LRA 1925, in particular s70(1)(g) (see section 7.8 below), so that unregistered equitable interests may still bind a purchaser of registered land who has constructive or imputed notice of their existence. The effect of the saving provision in s70(1)(g) LRA 1925 should be understood.

Minor interests and the doctrine of notice

The general rule is that only minor interests protected on the register will bind a purchaser: s20(1) LRA 1925 (for minor interests see sections 7.9 and 7.10).

Actual knowledge or notice of an unprotected minor interest will not affect a purchaser who takes free from that interest. This is the effect of s59(6) LRA 1925, which provides that notice will not make an unprotected minor interest bind a purchaser.

This is part of the general policy of the LRA 1925: that the state of the register is the paramount feature. This rule should create the distinction between estates and interests on the register which are binding against everyone and those not on the register which are not binding unless they come within s70(1) as overriding interests. This was the intention of the LRA 1925 and should be the only distinction which can be made. Attempts have been made, however, to reintroduce the concept of 'notice' into registered land, in spite of s20(1) LRA 1925.

Section 20(1) LRA 1925 provides that a transferee for value under a registered disposition of an absolute freehold title takes free of 'all estates and interests whatsoever' unless they are protected on the register OR take effect as overriding interests.

The problem cases

The two cases which have sought to introduce the concept of 'notice' are discussed below. The first case is *Peffer* v *Rigg* [1978] 3 All ER 745. The facts are set out in full in the casebook. The difficulties arose out of a matrimonial problem where the interest in the former matrimonial home was transferred by the husband, Rigg, to his former wife for a nominal sum of £1. Peffer was a co-owner with Rigg in equity even though the title was in Rigg alone. The question before the court was whether Mrs Rigg took free from Peffer's equitable interest. It was held that she knew the property was held on trust for sale (due to the equitable tenancy in common) and when it was transferred to her she knew of Peffer's interest in the house. Since the consideration was nominal then under s20(4) LRA 1925 she took the property subject to Peffer's unregistered interest. Even if the consideration was valuable consideration, as part of the general divorce settlement, Mrs Rigg did not take free of Peffer's interest because only a purchaser in good faith can take advantage of s20(1) LRA 1925. Thus only a transferee who has both given valuable consideration and acted in good faith can be protected. Mrs Rigg could not be in good faith where she had notice of something which affected her title. In addition she knew the property was held on trust for sale (equitable tenancy in common) and so she took it on a constructive trust. Graham J summarised his decision with these words:

> 'If ... sections 20 and 59 are read together ... they can be reconciled by holding that if the "transferee" spoken of in s20 is in fact a "purchaser" he will only be protected if he has given valuable consideration and is in good faith. He cannot in my judgment be in good faith if he has in fact notice of something which affects his title as in the present case ...'

He then concluded in these terms:

> '... this view of the matter seems to me to enable the two sections to be construed consistently together without producing the unreasonable result of permitting a transferee

> purchaser to take advantage of the Act, and divest himself of knowledge of defects in his own title and secure to himself a flawless title which he ought not in justice to be allowed to obtain.'

The second case is *Lyus* v *Prowsa Developments Ltd* [1982] 1 WLR 1044. Here the proprietor company of a building estate with registered title created a registered mortgage in favour of a bank. The proprietor then contracted to sell a plot on the estate to Lyus who paid a deposit and registered a caution. The plot would be transferred to Lyus, when a house had been built on it. The registered proprietor became the subject of a compulsory winding-up order before the house was completed. The bank, as mortgagee, agreed to sell the plot to the defendants subject to the contract with Lyus, and the defendants, in turn, agreed to sell the plot to a third party. This final agreement was completed by a transfer which contained no reference to the contract with Lyus. Dillon J held that the third party was bound on the basis that a constructive trust was imposed on the defendants with a similar trust imposed on the third party. He summarised his decision in these words:

> '... the court may yet intervene to raise a constructive trust on appropriate terms if to leave the defendant retaining the property free from all interest would be tantamount to sanctioning a fraud on the part of the defendant.'

The effect of the two cases

If a purchaser has express knowledge of an unprotected minor interest he may still be bound by it if circumstances arise where a constructive trust should be imposed. This appears to be the introduction of the doctrine of notice into registered land without regard to s59(6) LRA 1925.

Alternatives to counter this view

1. Try s74 LRA 1925 which provides that no person dealing with a registered estate is to be affected by notice of a constructive trust, or
2. Rely upon the words of Lord Wilberforce in *Williams & Glyn's Bank* v *Boland* [1980] 2 All ER 408.

In considering the effect of the doctrine of notice in relation to s70(i)(g) LRA 1925 Lord Wilberforce stated:

> '... to have regard to ... the doctrine of notice ... would run counter to the whole purpose of the Act. The purpose, in each system, is the same, namely, to safeguard the rights of persons in occupation, but the method used differs. In the case of unregistered land, the purchaser's obligation depends on what he has notice of, notice actual or constructive. In the case of registered land, it is the fact of occupation that matters. If there is actual occupation, and the occupier has rights, the purchaser takes subject to them. If not he does not. No further element is material.'

Conclusion

It is a danger if the clear principles of the LRA 1925 are allowed to became clouded by the introduction of the rules of notice, and it may be that the words of Lord Wilberforce will become the basis for future decisions on this matter. This, at least, would uphold the main ethos of the 1925 property legislation to simplify conveyancing.

To some extent the legislature has clouded the issue by s5 Land Registration Act 1986. In abolishing the Minor Interests Index it is provided that priority between dealings with equitable interests in registered land is to be determined by the rule in *Dearle* v *Hall* (1828) 3 Russ 1. This means priority is established by the order in which notice is received by the trustees. This must undermine the clear distinction Lord Wilberforce was seeking to establish in the above quotation (see 'Alternatives to counter this view', above).

7.3 Relationship between the Land Charges Act 1972 and the Land Registration Act 1925

Land Registration Act 1925

The system of registration under the LRA 1925 now extends to cover the whole of England and Wales. However, this system was introduced gradually, starting in the larger towns. Regions are declared to be areas of compulsory registration under the LRA 1925. Land within a compulsory area must be registered. However, registration under the LRA 1925 occurs only when the land is sold. Once land is registered under the LRA 1925, it is called 'registered land'. Until the land is so registered, it remains 'unregistered land'. This will continue for some considerable time in the future.

Land Charges Act 1925 (now 1972)

The LCA 1925 (now the LCA 1972) was introduced as a stop-gap measure, to provide protection for equitable interests in land not yet registered under the LRA 1925. The LCA 1972 applies to all land until that land is registered under the LRA 1925.

The relationship

The two systems of registration are independent and should not be confused. If land is registered the LRA 1925 applies. If land is unregistered the LCA 1972 applies. It is impossible for both systems of registration to apply to the same land at the same time. Either one or the other applies, not both. In relation to cxamination questions the candidate must be able to distinguish the respective effects of the two systems within any one problem area. The invitation is often to consider whether the answer would differ if the title to the land were not registered, or vice versa. However, the system of registration under the LRA 1925 is defined partly in terms of the LCA 1972, and so there is some link between the two systems.

7.4 Classes of rights in registered land

Under the LRA 1925 all estates and interests in land are divided into three categories.

Registered interests/dispositions (see section 7.7)

These correspond to the legal estates and interests set out in ss1(1) and 1(2) LPA 1925. Note that not all leases are registrable dispositions (see section 7.12).

Overriding interests (see section 7.8)

These are rights that bind a purchaser even though they cannot be registered. They consist of:

1. Legal interests which are not registered dispositions.
2. Equitable or legal interests which are registrable as minor interests but protected as overriding interests under s70(1)(g) LRA 1925, if not so registered.

Minor interests (see section 7.9)

All interests which are neither registered dispositions nor overriding interests are minor interests and should be registered. Failure to register renders a minor interest void against a purchaser unless it is protected under s70(1)(g).

7.5 Contents of the title register

Where land is registered under the LRA 1925, all legal estates in land, both freehold and leasehold (except where the lease is for 21 years or less), have a title register. This takes the place of title deeds and is kept in the Land Registry. The estate owner is given a copy of the entry in the land register, called a land certificate – this is merely a copy of the entries in the register and is not a document of title such as the conveyance in unregistered land. The title register to the land should contain all the information which a potential purchaser would want to know.

Each register is divided into three sections:

The property register

This describes the land, giving the address and a map reference, and shows where it is on a map. It also includes details of rights over other land of which the registered land has the benefit, ie where the registered land is the dominant tenement in respect of an easement.

The proprietorship register

This contains the name and address of the estate owner (freeholder or leaseholder), and the nature of his title (see section 7.11). It also contains details of any cautions, inhibitions and restrictions (see section 7.10) affecting the registered proprietor's right of dealing with the land. These would arise where the land is held under a trust for sale or a strict settlement.

The charges register

This contains details of rights owned by others over the registered land. These include:

1. Minor interests.
2. Registered dispositions other than freehold estates.

Not included are local land charges, which are registered separately in the registers kept in the local land charges registries. See also s70(1)(i) LRA 1925.

7.6 Getting on the register

Areas of compulsory registration of title – registration at the next major transaction

The whole of England and Wales is now designated as a compulsory area for registration of title. As a result land must be registered when the fee simple is sold or when a lease for 21 years or more is created or assigned. In the absence of a sale of the freehold or the creation or assignment of such a lease, the land need not be registered, even though in a compulsory area.

The LRA 1986 reduced the required period of the lease from 40 to 21 years. In a compulsory area, land must be registered when the fee simple is sold or when a lease for more than 21 years is created or when a lease with more than 21 years to run is assigned.

Once land has been registered, the register is kept at the Land Registry. The registered owner (known as the proprietor) is given a copy of the register, called a land certificate. This, so far as the registered proprietor is concerned, takes the place of the title deeds as evidence of his title although this land certificate is not, in itself, a document of title.

Effect of failure to register: s123 LRA 1925

The land must be registered in order for the freehold to be sold or a long lease to be created. Failure to register the land renders a purchaser's title void, unless application is made to register the title within two months of purchase. If the vendor has received the purchase money, he will hold the legal estate on trust for the purchaser. Note that under the LRA 1925 the land is registered under the name of the land, not under the name of the estate owner as is the case with charges under the LCA 1972.

Potential problems

A person seeking to register a minor interest may still have difficulty as a notice can only be entered on the register on production of the land certificate, which requires the co-operation of the registered proprietor. See section 7.10 below for the alternatives available.

7.7 Registered interests/dispositions

These are set out in LRA 1925 ss18 and 19 (freehold land) and ss21 and 22 (leasehold land), and consist of:

1. Fee simple absolute in possession.
2. Legal leases exceeding 21 years.
3. Legal rentcharges.
4. Legal easements.
5. Legal mortgages.

The conveyance or creation of these estates or interests can only be accomplished by registration. Until and unless the grant is registered in the appropriate way it is ineffective (s19 LRA 1925). The legal estate or interest remains vested in the grantor and the deed of grant is void (s39 LRA 1925).

The proper method of registration depends on the estate or interest:

Fee simple

The grantee's (transferee's) name is entered in the proprietorship register and that of the grantor is crossed out. The transferee thereupon becomes the registered proprietor of the freehold estate.

Legal lease

A lease cannot be a registered disposition if the term is for 21 years or less, or if it has a mortgage term subject to a right of redemption.

All other leases are registered dispositions. On their creation or assignment, the lessee's name is entered in the proprietorship register of the leasehold estate. A notice is also entered in the charges register of the freehold estate affected. (For further details of the registration of leases see section 7.12.)

Legal easement

A notice is entered in the charges register of the servient tenement; the details may also be entered in the property register of the dominant tenement.

Note: only legal easements created by express grant or reservation are registered dispositions. Legal easements created by implied grant are overriding interests. See s70(1)(a) LRA 1925.

Legal rentcharge

A notice is entered in the charges register of the land subject to the rentcharge.

Legal mortgage

A notice is entered in the charges register of the mortgaged land. During the mortgage the land certificate will be retained by the Land Registry and the mortgagee will receive a charge certificate.

Note: when land in an area which has become a compulsory area is unregistered, a purchaser of the legal estate or a long lease can only acquire a good legal title to the freehold or leasehold estate if the land is registered and the disposition is registered.

7.8 Overriding interests

Definition

These are defined in s3(xvi) LRA 1925 as:

> 'all the incumbrances, interests, rights and powers not entered on the register, but subject to which registered dispositions are to take effect'.

Effect

These are, therefore, rights which bind a purchaser without appearing on the register, even though he has no knowledge of them. They provide the most common pitfall for a purchaser of registered land and:

> 'provide a cavernous crack in the fundamental mirror principle under which the register is supposed to reflect accurately and irrefutably the current facts material to a particular title' (Hayton, *Registered Land*).

For land law purposes many examination questions involve a knowledge of overriding interests.

Types of overriding interest

There are two classes of overriding interest:

1. Those specifically listed in s70(1) LRA 1925, although often in broad and uncertain terms.
2. Minor interests which are not protected by registration but are protected under s70(1)(g) and converted into overriding interests.

Section 70(1) LRA 1925

The interests listed under s70(1) LRA 1925 are:

> 'a) Rights of common, drainage rights, customary rights (until extinguished), public rights, profits à prendre, rights of sheepwalk, rights of way, watercourses, rights of water and other easements not being equitable easements required to be protected by notice on the register.
> b) Liability to repair highways by reason of tenure and other tenurial obligations.
> c) Liability to repair the chancel of a church.
> d) Liability in respect of embankments and sea and river walls.
> e) Tithe redemption annuities.
> f) Rights acquired or being acquired under the Limitation Act 1980.
> g) The rights of every person in actual occupation of the land or in receipt of the rents and profits thereof save where inquiry is made of such person and the rights are not disclosed.
> h) In the case of a possessory, qualified, or good leasehold title, all estates, rights, interests and powers excepted from the effects of registration.
> i) Rights under local land charges unless and until registered on the register at the Land Registry on the particular title concerned. [Such registration at the Land Registry is rare and the normal practice is to rely upon registration in the local land charges register.]
> j) Fishing, sporting, seignorial and manorial rights and franchises.
> k) Leases granted for a term not exceeding 21 years (s70(1)(k) LRA 1925 as amended by s4(1) LRA 1986).
> l) Mineral rights in respect of land registered before 1926.'

The most important of these are s70(1)(a), (f), (g) and (k), which will now be considered in more detail.

Section 70(1)(a). Most problems with this section arise from the strange jumble of interests listed, this jumble being due to the legislative history of this provision. The section is obviously intended to protect legal easements and profits, which is the position in unregistered land, but the meaning of the words 'equitable easements required to be protected by notice' is unclear, because there is no such requirement elsewhere in the Act. Equitable interests may be protected by notice, but they may also be protected by a caution. It has been held in a county court case, *Payne* v *Adnams* [1971] CLY 6486, that this means no equitable easements are excluded from s70(1)(a), but the general opinion of textbook writers and the Land Registry is that equitable easements cannot be overriding interests. This opinion must now be read in the light of the decision of Scott J in *Celsteel Ltd* v *Alton House Holdings Ltd* [1985] 1 WLR 204. The judge decided that under r258 of the Land Registration Rules 1925 an equitable easement was 'a right enjoyed with the land' for the purpose of that rule. As it affected the registered title it was an 'overriding interest' which did not need to be protected by notice on the register. For examination purposes this decision should be considered within the potential question of the treatment of equitable easements in registered and unregistered land (see also Chapter 6). Equitable profits à prendre can, on the other hand, be overriding interests.

In addition the interests covered by s70(1)(a) include:

1. Legal easements or profits à prendre created before the servient tenement was registered.
2. Legal easements or profits à prendre created other than by express grant or reservation, ie by implied grant, under s62 LPA 1925 or the rule in *Wheeldon* v *Burrows* (1879) 48 LJ Ch 853 CA, or by prescription.

Section 70(1)(f). This provides for the rights arising by adverse possession. Once the owner's title has been extinguished the squatter may apply to be registered in the owner's place, and until this is done the owner holds the property on trust for the squatter. See s75 LRA 1925. If he sells before this is done the squatter's title is binding on the purchaser. This is considered further in Chapter 15. See *Bridges* v *Mees* [1957] Ch 475; *Chowood* v *Lyall* [1930] 2 Ch 156.

Section 70(1)(k). Section 70(1)(k) is intended to protect those leases which cannot be registered dispositions because they are for 21 years or less.

Section 4 LRA 1986 amends s70(1)(k) LRA 1925. Any lease granted for a term of 21 years or less is now an overriding interest. This removes the previous exemptions relating to leases without a rent or granted with a premium. Thus the provisos for such a lease are now that the term does not exceed 21 years, and that the lease was granted.

It appears that the distinction between a lease within s70(1)(k) and an agreement for a lease not within s70(1)(k) is retained. In addition, leases for three years or more not granted by deed which take effect in equity are outside s70(1)(k) because such leases are not by deed and so cannot be said to have been 'granted'. See *City Permanent Building Society* v *Miller* [1952] Ch 840.

Leases for 21 years or less which do not qualify under s70(1)(k) are registrable as minor interests, or may come within s70(1)(g) as 'rights' protected by 'actual occupation'.

Legal leases for a term not exceeding 21 years taking effect in possession or within one year from the date thereof granted at a rent without taking a fine take effect as though they were registered dispositions immediately upon being granted, ss18(1), 19(2) and 22(2), subject to minor interests on the register and overriding interests.

Section 70(1)(g). All the interests specifically listed in s70(1) are legal interests. The intention of the Act was to preserve legal interests as good against all the world, while making equitable interests registrable as minor interests. However, the wording of s70(1)(g) has allowed the courts to interpret this subsection as including equitable interests, which are thereby made overriding interests. This distorts the basic structure of the Act and can result in bona fide purchasers of the legal estate of registered land being bound by unregistered equitable interests of which they have no notice, actual or constructive.

Section 70(1)(g) provides:

> 'The rights of every person in actual occupation of the land or in receipt of the rents or profits therefrom save where inquiry is made of such person and the rights are not disclosed.'

Before s70(1)(g) can apply three conditions must be satisfied:

1. There must be a right 'subsisting in relation to the land' which is capable of being protected by s70(1)(g). In *Webb* v *Pollmount Ltd* [1966] Ch 584 such a right was defined as being:

   > 'an interest in the land capable of enduring through different ownerships of the land according to normal conceptions of title to real property'.

   Neither occupation nor notice of occupation can by itself create the overriding interest. There must be an existing 'right', protected by occupation, before s70(1)(g) can apply.

   Interests in land which have been held to qualify as such 'rights' include:

   a) The equitable interests of co-owners holding under a statutory trust for sale: *Williams & Glyn's Bank* v *Boland* [1981] AC 487. The implications of this decision have been considered by the Law Commission which concludes that as the law stands at present little can be done to alleviate the problems caused to purchasers or mortgagees by the protection afforded to the rights of persons in actual occupation. (Law Commission Report on the Implications of *Williams & Glyn's Bank* v *Boland*: Law Com No 115).

      In early 1985 the government introduced, in the House of Lords, a Land Registration and Law of Property Bill to take account of some of the problems posed by the decision in *Williams & Glyn's Bank* v *Boland*. There was failure to agree on the limits of any necessary amendments to s70(1)(g) LRA 1925 and the Bill was withdrawn. The law now remains as expressed by the House of Lords in the *Boland* decision. It is anticipated that the Law Commission will look further at the situation with a view to further amending legislation being published, and may also give some consideration to the protection available for married couples compared with non-married couples in relation to the family home.

b) The right to specific performance of an estate contract: *Bridges* v *Mees* [1957] Ch 475.
c) The right to specific performance of an option: *Webb* v *Pollmount* (above).
d) An unpaid vendor's lien over the land sold: *London and Cheshire Insurance Co Ltd* v *Laplagrene Property Co Ltd* [1971] Ch 499.
e) An unsuccessful purchaser's lien (over the land he failed to buy) for his deposit: *Lee-Parker* v *Izzet* [1971] 1 WLR 1688.
f) The right of a tenant to make deductions from his rent in respect of the cost of repairs when the landlord is in breach of a repairing covenant: *Lee-Parker* v *Izzet* (above).
g) The rights of the deserted wife in occupation of the matrimonial home were considered by the Court of Appeal in *National Provincial Bank Ltd* v *Hastings Car Mart* [1964] Ch 665 but reversed by the House of Lords on appeal in *National Provincial Bank Ltd* v *Ainsworth* [1965] AC 1175, which led to the passing of the Matrimonial Homes Act 1967 – now the Matrimonial Homes Act 1983. Section 2(8)(b) of the 1983 Act provides that:

> '... a spouse's right of occupation shall not be an overriding interest within the meaning of that Act [LRA 1925] affecting the dwelling house notwithstanding that the spouse is in actual occupation of the dwelling house.'

See (c) below.

h) The rights of a beneficiary under a resulting bare trust: *Hodgson* v *Marks* [1971] Ch 892.
i) The right to rectify when accompanied by actual occupation: *Blacklocks* v *J B Developments (Godalming) Ltd* [1981] 3 All ER 392.

Rights which can only be minor interests, and hence cannot be protected by s70(1)(g), are:

a) The rights of a beneficiary under a Settled Land Act settlement: s86(2) LRA 1925.
b) The rights of a tenant arising from a notice under the Leasehold Reform Act 1967 of his desire to have the freehold or an extended lease: s5(5) Leasehold Reform Act 1967.
c) The rights of occupation of a spouse under Matrimonial Homes Act 1983, see (g) above.

This confirmed the rejection by the House of Lords in *National Provincial Bank* v *Ainsworth* [1965] AC 1175 of the Court of Appeal view that a deserted spouse's right of occupation was a 'right' within s70(1)(g).

Such a right was created by the Matrimonial Homes Act 1967, but it can be protected against third parties only by registration of a Class F land charge in the charges register of registered land: s2(8)(a) Matrimonial Homes Act 1983.

d) An access order under the Access to Neighbouring Land Act 1992. This order is not an overriding interest and must be protected by a notice or caution. See s5 of the Access to Neighbouring Land Act 1992 which adds a new s49(1) to the LRA 1925. The effect of the access order is to enable a landowner to go onto adjoining land to carry out work which is reasonably necessary to preserve his land.

A question arises whether contractual licences or licences protected in equity or by estoppel (see Chapter 13) are capable of being rights falling within s70(1)(g). On strict land law principles perhaps they should not be, but then neither should equitable tenancies in common. The decision in *Re Sharpe (A Bankrupt)* [1980] 1 All ER 198 does suggest that the equitable proprietary rights of a licensee which arise from expenditure on the land (the estoppel factor) are capable of falling within s70(1)(g) LRA 1925 when accompanied by actual occupation.

2. The owner of the right must be in actual occupation of the land or in receipt of the rents or profits therefrom affected by the right.

'Actual occupation' is not defined by the Act. It has been held to mean physical presence on the land, not some entitlement in law to occupy the land: *Williams & Glyn's Bank* v *Boland* (above).

A tenant under an unregistered registrable lease who does not occupy the premises himself and allows someone else to live there rent-free, under a licence or a tenancy at will, does not qualify under either head (*Strand Securities* v *Caswell* [1965] Ch 958) even though he has a right to possession. The physical presence must be reasonably continuous: *Epps* v *Esso Petroleum Co* [1973] 1 WLR 1071.

A person may be in actual occupation even though this is not readily ascertainable from inspection of the property: *Hodgson* v *Marks* (above).

The date when the owner must be in occupation was said to be the date of the mortgage in *Paddington Building Society* v *Mendelsohn* (1985) 50 P & CR 244. This will exclude from the protection of s70(1)(g) many purchasers who do not occupy until after the mortgage is completed which is usual in the case of many purchases of residential premises.

This point was confirmed by the House of Lords in *Abbey National Building Society* v *Cann* [1990] 2 WLR 832. Lord Oliver confirmed that the relevant date for determining the existence of an overriding interest under s70(1)(g) LRA 1925 is the date of registration *but* the relevant date for determining whether the claimant was in actual occupation for the purposes of s70(1)(g) is the date of completion.

The brief facts of *Cann* were that in May 1984 George Cann (the son) applied for a loan of £25,000 on a flat. Contracts were exchanged in July 1984, a legal charge was executed on 6 August 1984 and the money was advanced. Completion took place on 13 August 1984 and on 13 September 1984 George was registered as proprietor and the building society was registered as proprietor of the charge.

Mrs Cann was the mother of George and she claimed the benefit of an overriding interest under s70(1)(g). She said that on 13 August 1984 there was a period of 35 minutes between actual occupation by her son and certain carpet layers and the completion of the transaction. The House of Lords rejected her claim. Mrs Cann knew that George would need a mortgage for the balance of the purchase money, and as she impliedly authorised raising the mortgage, Lord Oliver said that:

> '... she must necessarily have authorised him to that extent to create a charge ... having priority to her interest'.

The society was an equitable chargee for money actually advanced with priority over Mrs Cann's expectation of an interest if and when the property was acquired. Mrs Cann raised the question of the gap between occupation and completion which she said fed the estoppel against the society on the basis of *Church of England Building Society* v *Piskor* [1954] Ch 553. The House of Lords also rejected this claim. There was no scintilla temporis on 13 August between the acquisition of the property and the creation of the charge which could feed any estoppel in Mrs Cann. In the words of Lord Oliver they were '... precisely simultaneous ... [and] ... indissolubly bound up together'. Any purchaser who relies on such a mortgage acquires an equity of redemption and Lord Oliver described the effect of this:

> '... from the very inception [land] charged with the ... loan without which it could never have been transferred at all'.

The House of Lords concluded that *Church of England Building Society* v *Piskor* was wrongly decided.

In future the appropriate date for ascertaining the existence of an overriding interest under the LRA 1925 will be the date of registration, but the date for determining whether the claimant was in actual occupation will be the date of completion.

This rule was applied by the House of Lords in *Lloyds Bank plc* v *Rosset* [1990] 2 WLR 867 where the majority decision of the Court of Appeal was reversed. Mrs Rosset and her builders had commenced renovation work on the property in early November 1982. Contracts were exchanged for the purchase on 23 November 1982. Mr Rosset took out a loan by way of overdraft on 14 December 1982 and completion in the name of Mr Rosset alone took place on 17 December with the bank taking a charge to secure the loan. The charge was registered on 7 February 1983.

Mrs Rosset claimed she had a beneficial interest in the property by way of a constructive trust which qualified as an overriding interest and which was binding on the bank under s70(1)(g) because she was in actual occupation both at the charge and registration. She claimed a significant contribution in kind to the acquisition because of the work done towards renovation and this gave rise to the constructive trust in her favour. No evidence was produced to show that Mrs Rosset would eventually have an interest in the property. The purchase was from Mr Rosset's resources and made in his name alone. The House of Lords said there was no constructive trust in favour of Mrs Rosset. Lord Bridge expressed the decision in a very forthright manner. The amount of renovation work

> '... expressed as a contribution to a property ... exceeding £70,000 ... [was] ... so trifling as to be almost de minimis'.

Lord Bridge went on say:

> 'If Courts must rely on conduct of parties to infer a common intention to share property beneficially and to give rise to a constructive trust direct contributions to ... purchase price by ... partner ... not the legal owner whether initially or by payment of mortgage instalments, would readily justify ... the creation of a constructive trust ... extremely doubtful whether anything less would do.'

The work done by Mrs Rosset in the renovation of the future matrimonial home which was then bought by Mr Rosset in his own name with his own finance was not sufficient to justify any inference of a common intention that she should have a beneficial interest in the property. As a consequence she had no 'right' within the terms of s70(1)(g) LRA 1925.

3. The saving clause to s70(1)(g) requires that the purchaser must have made inquiry of the owner of the right, and not been told of the right – 'save where inquiry is made of such person and the rights are not disclosed'.

   Inquiry of the vendor alone will not suffice, it must be the person in 'actual occupation' (*Hodgson* v *Marks* (above)), nor will an inquiry made for another purpose, eg under s40 Landlord and Tenant Act 1954: see *London and Cheshire Insurance* v *Laplagrene* (above).

   The examination candidate must be able to consider whether this saving clause introduces some further element of 'notice' into registered land. This point is considered in *Real Property and Real People* by K J Gray and P D Symes at Chapters 9 and 10.

Effect of s70(1)(g)

If the three requirements are satisfied, the right claimed is converted by actual occupation from a minor interest into an overriding interest – which, of course, need not be protected by registration. See *Williams & Glyn's Bank* v *Boland* [1981] AC 487.

The date at which there must be actual occupation is the date of the conveyance to a purchaser. If the owner of the right subsequently ceases occupation, the right remains an overriding interest. It is not converted back into a minor interest. See *London and Cheshire Insurance* v *Laplagrene* (above).

Where land is registered, the conveyance is effected by the registration of the registered disposition. Any disposition of registered land is subject to all overriding interests existing at the date of registration, which is of necessity later than the date of the disposition. It has been held that a purchaser is subject to an overriding interest which did not exist at the date of the conveyance but which arose before registration. See *Grace Rymer Investments Ltd* v *Waite* [1958] Ch 831.

This decision must now be read in the light of the subsequent decision in *Paddington Building Society* v *Mendelsohn* (1985) 50 P & CR 244.

The effect of the decision in *Williams & Glyn's Bank* v *Boland* must now be read in the light of the decision of the House of Lords in *City of London Building Society v Flegg* [1987] 2 WLR 1266.

If a legal charge is granted by trustees for sale of registered land holding for tenants in common who remain in occupation, but with no knowledge of the creation of the charge, the interest of the tenants in common is transferred to the equity of redemption held by the trustees and the capital monies raised by the charge. The tenants in common could not claim an overriding interest under s70(1)(g) LRA 1925 to enable them to remain in occupation because their beneficial interest in the land was overreached by the legal charge, leaving nothing to which a right of occupation could attach. The payment to two trustees distinguishes this case from the *Boland* decision. The distinction was expressed by Lord Templeman. He referred to *Boland* and continued:

> 'There the husband was sole proprietor who was trustee for himself and his wife as tenants in common. The wife's beneficial interest coupled with actual occupation constituted an overriding interest to which the husband's mortgagee took subject. But in that case the interest of the wife was not overreached or overridden because the mortgagee advanced capital moneys to a sole trustee. If the mortgagee's interest had been overreached by advancing capital moneys to two trustees there would have been nothing to justify the wife in remaining in occupation as against the mortgagee.
>
> There had to be a combination of an interest which justified continuing occupation plus actual occupation to constitute an overriding interest. Actual occupation was not an interest in itself.'

In considering s70(1)(g) the actual occupation is only the initial basis for the claim. This occupation should be regarded as the 'key to the door'. Use the key to open the door to discover what 'rights' the occupier has claim to. It is only these rights which can satisfy the overriding interest provisions of s70(1)(g) LRA 1925.

The Law Commission Working Paper No 106, *Trusts of Land: Overreaching* (1988), considers the problems arising from the decision of the House of Lords in *City of London Building Society* v *Flegg.*

7.9 Minor interests

Definition

All interests which are neither registered dispositions nor overriding interests are minor interests and must be protected by registration. A full definition of 'minor interest' is contained in s3(xv) LRA 1925 as:

> '... the interests not capable of being disposed of by registered dispositions and capable of being overridden (whether or not a purchaser has notice thereof) by the proprietors unless protected as provided by this Act and all rights and interests which are not registered or protected on the register and are not overriding interests, and include:
> (a) In the case of land held in trust for sale, all interests and powers which are under the Law of Property Act 1925 capable of being overridden by the trustees for sale, whether or not such interests and powers are so protected: and
> (b) In the case of settled land, and interests and powers which are under the Settled Land Act 1925, and the Law of Property Act 1925, or either of them, capable of being overridden by the tenant for life or statutory owner, whether or not such interests and powers are so protected as aforesaid.'

Thus minor interests form a residuary group.

There are two classes of minor interest:

1. Interests capable of being overreached on a proper sale. These are the interests of the beneficiaries under a trust for sale or a strict settlement.
2. Interests which will not bind a purchaser unless registered. These include equitable interests registrable under the LCA 1972 for unregistered land and the miscellaneous equitable interests which are not registrable under that Act, eg interests under bare trusts, beneficial interests under resulting trusts. Legal interests arising under a lease for 21 years or less, granted rent-free or at a fine, must also be registrable as minor interests.

7.10 Protection of minor interests

There are four methods of protecting minor interests. Protection is effective from the date of registration.

Notice – s52(1) LRA 1925

This is entered in the charges register, and ensures that any future dealings with the land take place subject to the interest protected by the notice. It can only be entered if the land certificate is produced, and so in general it can only be entered if the registered proprietor agrees.

The protection afforded to a charge protected by notice is, in may situations minimal. This was demonstrated by the Court of Appeal in *Mortgage Corporation Ltd* v *Nationwide Credit Corporation Ltd* [1993] 4 All ER 623. The case concerned the priority of two mortgages, neither of which was a registered charge. Rather, both were equitable minor interests. The plaintiffs' legal charge was executed on 10 July 1989 but they took no steps to protect it. The defendants' legal charge was executed on 31 July 1989 and they entered a notice under s49 LRA 1925 in August 1989 in the charges register of title. The plaintiffs subsequently obtained a possession order against the registered proprietors and sold the property. Since the sale proceeds were insufficient to repay both parties in full the defendants withdrew their s49 notice to facilitate completion of the sale, with the question of priority between the plaintiffs' and defendants' charges being determined post completion by the court. The issue was whether the plaintiffs had priority as first in time or whether the defendants had priority by virtue of the entry of the s49 notice.

The court considered s52(1) LRA 1925. That subsection did not deal with priorities as between competing minor interests. Rather it was directed to preserving the priority of a minor interest protected by a notice against a subsequent registered disposition. It did not have the effect of creating priority over an earlier unprotected minor interest (ie it did not apply on these facts). The court also considered s106 LRA 1925 by virtue of which a charge protected by a s49 notice but not registered was no longer capable of being overridden as a minor interest. However, it only took effect in equity unless and until it became a registered charge (here neither mortgage was a registered charge). In the absence of any provision in the Act, the priorities were governed by the equitable rule that where the equities are equal, the first in time prevails. The fact that the plaintiffs had done nothing whereas the defendants had entered a s49 notice did not mean the equities were not equal. Accordingly, the plaintiffs' charge had priority over the defendants' charge (the former's priority in terms of creation gave the better equity).

Caution – ss53–56 LRA 1925

A caution merely gives the person entering it a right to be warned of any impending transaction with the land and gives him time to object. When the land is unregistered a caution against first registration may be entered, but the more usual caution is one against dealings. A caution is used when a notice cannot be entered because the land certificate cannot be obtained. It is weaker protection than a registered land charge in unregistered land because:

1. It puts the onus on the cautioner to take steps to protect his interests.
2. It can be 'warned off' at any time by the registered proprietor requiring notice to be given to the cautioner that he must defend his claim within a given time.

The entry of a caution to protect an interest in land does not confer priority on that interest over a subsequently registered charge. This was established by the Court of Appeal in *Clark and Another* v *Chief Land Registrar and Another* (1994) The Times 10 May. There the plaintiffs, who were judgment creditors, obtained a charging order against a house jointly owned by their debtors. They protected that order by entering cautions on the register in August and November 1990. Subsequently, the second defendant advanced a sum of money to the debtors secured by way of legal charge on the property. The second defendant sought registration of the legal charge in December 1990. At that point the Land Registry ought to have informed the plaintiffs (cautioners) of the proposed registration of this charge so that they could object but it failed to do so. Subsequently when the debtors' property was sold the sale proceeds were insufficient to meet the claims of the cautioners and the legal chargee. The question arose whether the registration of a caution protected the plaintiffs' interest in land or simply gave them the opportunity to gain protection by the entry of a notice when a subsequent dealing with the land was proposed.

After examining ss54–56 LRA 1925 the court concluded that the registration of the caution simply gave the plaintiffs a right to be given notice of any proposed dealing. It did not entitle them to assert the priority of their interest over the second defendant's subsequently registered land charge (in other words, the lodging of a caution against dealings did not automatically achieve priority for the interest in respect of which it was lodged). However, the plaintiffs were entitled to an indemnity from the Chief Land Registrar under s83 LRA 1925 for failing to give them notice of a charge over the land subsequently registered by the second defendant.

Finally, it is important to re-emphasise that if the land certificate cannot be obtained (ie it is not available to the applicant) a caution must be used.

Inhibitions – s57 LRA 1925

An inhibition is an order of the court or the registrar forbidding all dealings with the land either for a specified time period or until a specified event or until further notice. This is usually a last resort, although it is used routinely when the registered proprietor becomes bankrupt.

Restrictions – s58(1) LRA 1925

A restriction prevents dealing with the land until some condition is complied with, but unlike an inhibition it is not hostile to the registered proprietor. It is used, for example, when land is held on trust for sale or is settled land, to ensure that the overreaching mechanism is gone through.

In the case of a strict settlement the restriction will take the following form:

> 'No disposition by the proprietor of the land under which capital money arises is to be registered unless the money is paid to A B of ... and C D of ... (the trustees of a settlement of whom there must be not less than two nor more than four unless a trust corporation is the sole trustee) or into court. Except under an order of the registrar no disposition by the proprietor of the land is to be registered unless authorised by the Settled Land Act 1925.'

Official search certificate

A bona fide purchaser for value can protect himself against interests which are registered after he has purchased the land but before he has been registered as proprietor by obtaining an official search certificate. This gives the purchaser a temporary 30 working days 'priority period' so that, provided that he registers within that time, he is not bound by any minor interests which may be registered during the 30 working days. If the purchaser's application to register is correct and is delivered to the appropriate office of the Land Registry within the 30 working days, any entries on the register made during that 'priority period' will be postponed to this application of the purchaser: Administration of Justice Act 1982.

Summary

From the previous paragraphs it is now possible to demonstrate in diagrammatical form the relationship between the various types of interest identified in the LRA 1925 and to indicate whether or not they will appear on the register itself.

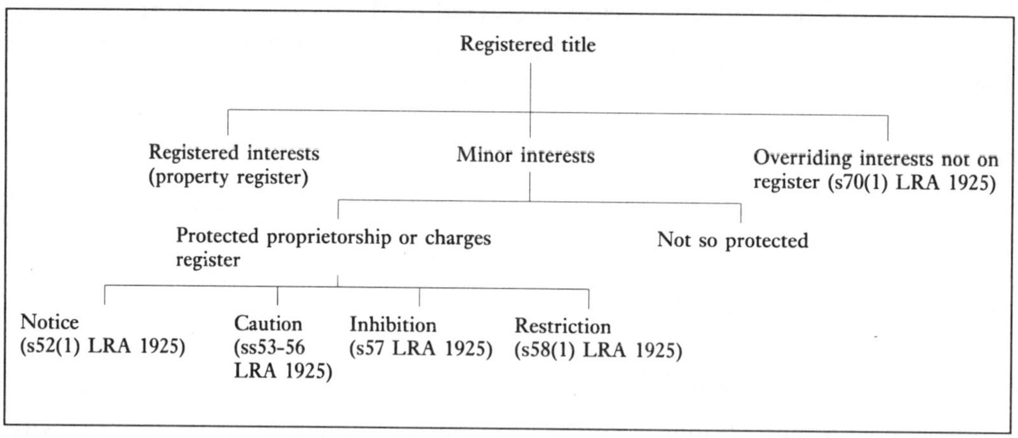

7.11 Registration of title: classes of title

Where land is registered for the first time the nature of the title described in the proprietorship register will depend upon the proof of title which the estate owner can produce. There are seven classes of title, three for freeholds and four for leaseholds.

Freehold titles

Absolute titles

Where the registrar is satisfied that an applicant has shown a good title to the land, he will be registered as having an absolute title, and described as such in the proprietorship register. An absolute title vests the fee simple in possession in the first registered proprietor subject only to entries on the register, overriding interests, and minor interests of which he has notice where the interests are held by beneficiaries under a trust of which he is a trustee.

Qualified title

This has the same effect as an absolute title except that the proprietor holds subject to an interest specified on the register, or to interests arising prior to a specified date. This type of title is registered where the estate owner cannot produce all the documents necessary to provide a good root of title.

Possessory title

This means that the title is subject to all estates rights and interests adverse to the first registered proprietor and subsisting at the date of first registration, even if not shown on the register. Thus the pre-registration title must be investigated in the traditional way.

This type of title is registered where the applicant claims title through adverse possession or where he cannot produce any documents of title apart from the conveyance to himself. See also Chapter 15 for further treatment of adverse possession under the Limitation Act 1980.

Leasehold titles

In general terms any leasehold interest in land may be registered if it is for a term of years absolute where more than 21 years remain unexpired. See section 7.12.

Absolute leasehold title

This has the same effect as an absolute freehold title, and also guarantees that the lessor has power to grant the lease and that the lease was properly granted. The lessee takes subject to the interests binding an absolute freehold owner and also subject to all the covenants and obligations of the lease.

Qualified leasehold title

This has the same effect as a qualified freehold title.

Possessory leasehold title

May be granted to a lessee in possession.

Good leasehold title

Where a lessee is unable to produce documentary evidence of his landlord's title to the land, and the freehold is not registered, he can only acquire a good leasehold title. This does not guarantee that the lease was properly granted.

Conversion of titles

Section 1 Land Registration Act 1986 substitutes a new s77 to the Land Registration Act 1925 relating to the conversion of titles. The effect is that titles may be converted to better titles in the following circumstances:

1. Good leasehold – may be upgraded to absolute at any time. It *must* be upgraded on the application of the proprietor if the registrar is satisfied as to the freehold title.
2. Possessory – may be upgraded to absolute (freehold) or good leasehold. It *must* be upgraded on the application of the proprietor provided that either the registrar is satisfied as to the title or the land has been registered with possessory title for at least 12 years and the registrar is satisfied that the proprietor is in possession.
3. Qualified – may be converted to absolute (freehold) or good leasehold at any time and *must* be on the application of the proprietor if the registrar is satisfied as to the title.

7.12 Registration of leaseholds

The provisions relating to the registration of leaseholds as registered dispositions are complicated and illogical, but their effect is as follows:

Registration of a lease is forbidden, even if the land is in a compulsory area, if the lease was for 21 years or less, or contains an absolute prohibition against assignment, or is a mortgage term subject to a right of redemption.

Registration of a lease is compulsory if the following apply:

1. The land is in a compulsory registration area and the new lease is for 21 years or more, or a lease with at least 21 years to run is assigned.
2. The title to the freehold or leasehold out of which the lease is granted is already registered and the lease is for more than 21 years.

When considering the registration of leaseholds, the provisions of both s70(1)(k) and s70(1)(g) LRA 1925 may still have to be considered. Under s70(1)(k) LRA 1925 (as amended by s4 LRA 1986) leases granted for a term not exceeding 21 years are overriding interests. Until the words were deleted by the LRA 1986, s70(1)(k) did require such leases to be 'granted at a rent'. On the basis of this it was held in *City Permanent Building Society* v *Miller* [1952] Ch 840 that a lease which had not been 'granted' was not within this provision because it was not granted by deed and any agreement for a lease must be protected as a 'right' under s70(1)(g) LRA 1925. The change to s70(1)(k) will not affect this interpretation because the word 'granted' is retained in the amended s70(1)(k) LRA 1925.

It is suggested that by using s3(x) LRA 1925, under which 'lease' is defined to include '... an underlease and any tenancy or agreement for a lease, underlease or tenancy', an opportunity may have been lost to give some clarification to this point.

If the definition of 'lease' in s70(1)(k) could have been extended to the amended s70(1)(k) the new provision would then have covered both leases and agreements for leases and there would no longer be any need to use s70(1)(g) LRA 1925 to establish that an agreement for a lease is an overriding interest. It is interesting to note that Fox LJ did not take the opportunity to discuss this point in *Ashburn Anstalt* v *Arnold* [1988] 2 All ER 147 where the leasehold interest was held to be an overriding interest under s70(1)(g) LRA 1925. This will not be affected by the decision of the House of Lords in *Prudential Assurance Co Ltd* v *London Residuary Body* [1992] 3 WLR 279 which overruled *Ashburn Anstalt* v *Arnold.* This decision confirms that s70(1)(g) LRA 1925 is to be regarded as a safety net when there is controversy over whether the interest is a lease or not. If there is 'actual occupation' then the arrangement may well be protected as a 'right' within s70(1)(g) LRA 1925.

In the meantime it appears that the decision in *City Permanent Building Society* v *Miller* remains as valid law and the distinction between a lease which is granted by deed and other leases and agreements for a lease remains significant.

7.13 Rectification of the register

Need for rectification

Because mistakes can be made on registration, particularly on first registration, and because the registered title may become incorrect over a period, for instance if a person acquires squatter's title, provision is made for correcting entries on the register; this is known as rectification. The court has confirmed that there is no general discretion to order rectification of the register in any case in which it might be thought just to do so. See *Norwich and Peterborough Building Society* v *Steed* (1992) The Times 18 March. Corresponding provision is made for compensating those who suffer loss through rectification. See s83 LRA 1925 and section 7.14.

Power to rectify – s82 LRA 1925

Section 82(1) LRA 1925 gives a wide discretion to rectify to both the court and the registrar. This is, however, qualified by the restrictions contained in s82(3), as amended by s24 Administration of Justice Act 1977, which provide that the register can only be rectified against a registered proprietor in possession if:

The rectification gives effect to an overriding interest or an order of the court

This follows from the fact that the registered proprietor took subject to such interests existing at the date of registration. See *Chowood* v *Lyall* [1930] 2 Ch 156.

The registered proprietor has caused or substantially contributed to the error or omission by fraud or lack of proper care

This ground for rectification was substantially amended by s24 AJA 1977. The previous provision read:

> 'where the registered proprietor against whom rectification is sought is a party or has caused or substantially contributed by his act, neglect or default to the fraud, mistake or omission in consequence of which such rectification is sought'

and this was interpreted in *Re 139 High Street, Deptford* [1951] Ch 884 and *Re Sea View Gardens, Claridge* v *Tingey* [1967] 1 WLR 134 as covering cases where the registered proprietor innocently lodges documents for registration which do not in fact convey the land in respect of which registration was obtained. It remains to be seen how the courts will interpret this provision.

This ground will only apply when the mistake was made by the first registered proprietor and rectification is claimed against him.

Where for any other reason it would be unjust not to rectify the register against the proprietor

This gives a wide residuary discretion. The provisions were considered in *Re 139 High Street, Deptford* (above) and in *Epps* v *Esso Petroleum Co* [1973] 1 WLR 1071.

In every case the remedy of rectification is discretionary. See *Re Sea View Gardens* (above); *Epps* v *Esso Petroleum Co* (above).

Effect of rectification

When the person successfully claiming rectification is replaced as the registered proprietor, he will normally take free of incumbrances created by the wrongfully registered proprietor unless he is by his conduct estopped from taking priority. See *Argyle Building Society* v *Hammond* (1984) The Times 19 October; see also *Re Dances Way, West Town, Hayling Island* [1962] Ch 490.

The effective date is the date of the application for registration. Where the rectification results in the entry of a notice on the register, earlier dispositions will not be affected by the interest the subject of the notice.

This ability to seek rectification is one of the dangers in registered land. It can have a serious effect on the claims of certainty of title which are made on behalf of registered land as a supposed advantage over land with unregistered title. Megarry and Wade raise the problem at page 227 and conclude:

> 'The liberal provision for rectification is a distinctive feature of the English system ... It greatly eases the task of the registrar in accepting titles for registration without excessive precautions and formality. Even more, perhaps, than in the case of unregistered land, it emphasises the principle that titles are relative, not absolute, and that no title is completely free from the danger that some better right to the land may be established.'

The reader is directed to page 235 of Megarry and Wade for a final conclusion based on rectification as pointing yet again to 'the central dilemma of the law of property'.

7.14 Compensation

Need for indemnity

By s83 LRA 1925 a person who suffers loss by reason of rectification or non-rectification of the register, or by reason of the destruction or loss of documents by the registry or inaccurate searches, may claim compensation.

Limitations of s83 LRA 1925

This is much less than a complete indemnity because:

1. No compensation is payable when the rectification is to give effect to an overriding interest because no loss has been suffered by the rectification. The proprietor's title has been subject to the overriding interest all the time and the rectification merely formalises the position. See *Re Chowood's Registered Land* [1933] Ch 574.
2. When the claimant successfully claims rectification there is no compensation even if he suffers loss.
3. No compensation is payable if the person claiming it caused or substantially contributed to the loss by fraud or lack of care (s83(5) LRA 1925).
4. The claim for compensation must be made within the limitation period. See *Epps* v *Esso Petroleum Co* (above).

Amount of compensation

Compensation is calculated in accordance with the following principles:

1. Where the register is rectified, the value of the lost interest at the date of rectification.
2. Where the register is not rectified, the value of the lost interest at the date the mistake was made. See *Epps* v *Esso Petroleum Co* (above).

7.15 Worked example

Problem questions frequently deal with the topics of overriding interests and of rectification and compensation. In addition problem questions may look to a comparison between the solution offered where the title to the land is not registered and where the title to the land is registered.

Q In 1975 Adrian bought Whiteacre from Bruce. The title had not previously been registered but the land was in an area of compulsory registration so A obtained registration as proprietor with absolute title. The title deeds submitted to the registry showed Whiteacre as including a small strip of wasteland along the eastern border which had since 1960 been used by Charles who parked his caravan on it and kept hens on one end of it, and a cottage which had been sold to Denis in 1973. The registered title included both of these.

Advise Charles, Denis and Adrian. Would your answer be different if Adrian had sold Whiteacre to Edward last year and he was now registered as proprietor?

A Assuming Charles to be in adverse possession of the waste strip, and the facts here are similar to those of *Bridges* v *Mees* (1957) where adverse possession was found, Charles had acquired squatter's rights in the strip by 1975. Such rights are an overriding interest under s70(1)(f) and Adrian took subject to them. Charles can apply for rectification of the register to have himself registered as the proprietor: *Chowood* v *Lyall* (1930). Adrian will not be able to claim compensation as none is payable when the rectification is to give effect to an overriding interest: *Re Chowood's Registered Land* (1933). He will, however, be able to sue Bruce for breach of covenant as to title.

Denis may also apply for rectification of the register. This is a case where rectification may be ordered if the mistake was caused or substantially contributed to by fraud or lack of proper care on the part of the registered proprietor (s82(3)(a) LRA 1925). In *Re 139 High Street, Deptford* (1951), a case decided on the previous provisions, land belonging to another was included in the registered title because of a mistake in a document innocently lodged in the application for first registration, but this section was held to apply and rectification ordered. It is not yet known how the courts will interpret the words 'lack of proper care', but this would seem to be a case where there has been some carelessness, although it is not clear who has been careless. Denis is therefore likely to obtain rectification. Adrian may apply for compensation under s83 LRA 1925, but this can be refused where the applicant caused or substantially contributed to the loss by fraud or negligence (s83(5)(a)), although there are no decisions on the standard of care required. If the land has been bought by Edward, he will have taken subject to Charles' overriding interest and therefore rectification can be ordered and no compensation is payable, as above. In respect of Denis' claim, however, the provisions of s82(3)(a) do not apply in this case as the section only applies when the registered proprietor against whom rectification is sought himself caused the mistake. In this case, the mistake was made by Adrian, but rectification is sought against Edward. The registrar and the court have a discretion to rectify under s82(3)(c) in any case, where it would be unjust not to do so, and this would seem to be such a case. Edward would be entitled to compensation.

8

Settlements of Land

8.1 Introduction

As has already been noted, under the 1925 legislation there are two methods of creating a succession of interests in land, settlements under the Settled Land Act 1925 and trusts for sale which are generally controlled by the Law of Property Act 1925: *Re Ogle's Settled Estates* [1927] 1 Ch 229 in which Romer J stated:

> 'In some parts of the Act no doubt settlement means merely the document or documents creating the settlement: see, for example, ss1(4), 47 and 64. But, in general, a settlement for the purposes of the Act is a state of affairs in relation to certain land, brought about by one or more documents, the particular state of affairs being one or more of those specified in sub-ss (i) to (v) of s1(1) of the Settled Land Act 1925.'

The main difference between the two methods of settlement is that in the case of the strict settlement the legal ownership and the powers of dealing with the land are vested in the tenant for life, who will normally be the beneficiary who is at present entitled to possession of the land. He has a dual role and is in the position of a trustee as well as being a beneficiary. The onus is upon him to exercise his powers (see section 8.7) in the best interests of all the beneficiaries including himself. The trustees of the settlement will oversee the exercise of these powers and will either be told of the tenant for life's intention to use them or give their consent to his doing so. Any money received as a result of exercising of these powers will be paid to the trustees of the settlement.

In the case of the trust for sale, the legal ownership and the powers of dealing with the property are vested in separate trustees for sale. It is the trustees for sale who will receive any money derived from the exercise of their powers.

For examination purposes this distinction between the strict settlement and the trust for sale is vital in case the examiner requires to know who will exercise the various powers in given circumstances.

8.2 Settlements under the Settled Land Act 1925

What constitutes settled land? By s1(1) of the Settled Land Act 1925 a settlement is created by any document or documents which deal with land in one of the ways set out in the subsection. The most important of these are:

1. Where the land stands for the time being limited in trust for any persons by way of succession. The most common example of such a limitation is 'to A for life and then to B in fee simple'. There are certain special sorts of succession which are included in separate heads in s1(1). They include:
2. Entails, eg 'to A for an entailed interest'.
3. An estate subject to a gift over on the failure of issue or other event (but see Chapter 4, section 4.4, for conditional fees, for example 'to A in fee simple but if A dies without issue then over to B').

4. A determinable fee (see, again, Chapter 4, section 4.4), for example 'to A in fee simple until A commits some act of bankruptcy'.
5. Where land is given to an infant.
6. Where the land is subject to a family rentcharge (such charges are not affected by the Rentcharges Act 1977), for example 'to A in fee simple but charged with the payment of £1,000 per annum to A's widow during her lifetime'.

8.3 How is a settlement created?

By s4(1) SLA 1925 every settlement must be effected by two documents, a trust instrument and a vesting deed. The latter contains all that a purchaser of the settled land needs to know, while the details of the trust are contained in the trust instrument which the purchaser is not entitled to see. These details are said to be 'behind the veil' or to be subject to the 'curtain principle'. The object is to enable the land to be sold easily in spite of the beneficial interests of the settlement.

Contents of the vesting deed – the public document

The vesting deed must (s5(1)):

1. Describe the settled land.
2. Declare that the settled land is vested in the person named as tenant for life on the trusts contained in the trust instrument.
3. Contain the names of the trustees of the settlement.
4. Contain any additional powers of the tenant for life.
5. Name the persons with power to appoint new trustees.

The purpose of the vesting deed is to vest the legal fee simple in the person who for the time being is to have the enjoyment of the land itself. The tenant for life obtains the legal estate which is held on the trusts of the settlement.

Contents of the trust instrument – the private document

The trust instrument must (s4(3)):

1. Declare the trusts affecting the settled land.
2. Appoint or constitute trustees of the settlement.
3. Contain the power, if any, to appoint new trustees of the settlement.
4. Set out any additional powers.
5. Bear any stamp duty payable.

This trust instrument declares the beneficial interests of the tenant for life and successors and is said to be 'behind the curtain'.

Where the settlement is made by will, the will itself is the trust instrument. The testator's personal representatives must vest the legal estate in the tenant for life by means of a vesting assent, which acts as the vesting deed.

If after the execution of the principal vesting deed more land is acquired within the settlement, it will be conveyed to the tenant for life by a subsidiary vesting deed.

Pre-1926 settlements

Before the SLA 1925 settlements could be created by a single document. To bring pre-1926 settlements into line with the new legislation it was provided that the single document should be treated as the trust instrument, and that as soon as was practicable the trustees of the settlement should, and, if so requested by the tenant for life, must, execute a vesting deed. However, it was also provided that in such cases a purchaser is entitled to look at the trust instrument as well as the vesting deed.

Incompletely constituted settlements

If an inter vivos settlement is not made by means of these two documents, a vesting deed and a trust instrument, then by s4(1) the legal estate is not transferred and therefore remains in the settlor. The only way this can be put right is by the trustees executing a vesting deed (s9(2)) (a rare example of a legal estate being conveyed by a person who does not have it himself).

Furthermore, until there are two documents, s13, the so-called 'paralysing' section, operates. This provides that a tenant for life can make no disposition of the legal estate in the land until a vesting deed has been executed in accordance with the Act. Any purported disposition before this has been done operates as a contract to carry out the transaction after the vesting deed has been executed. This, of course, would be a registrable estate contract. There are exceptions to the paralysing effect of s13:

1. Where the disposition is made by a personal representative.
2. Where the disposition is made to a purchaser of a legal estate without notice of the settlement – although after 1925 this must be registered as a land charge Class C(iv).
3. Where the settlement has come to an end. A settlement will end where one person becomes solely and absolutely entitled and the trusts set out in the trust instrument are concluded. *Re Alefounders' WT* [1927] 1 Ch 360.
4. Where s1 Law of Property (Amendment) Act 1926 applies. This provides that where a person of full age is entitled to land subject to family charges (which make the land settled land by s1(1)(v)), the person entitled may sell the land subject to those charges without going through the SLA 1925 formalities.

This only applies where the only reason that the land is settled is because of the charges, and gives the estate owner the choice of going through the SLA procedure and selling free of the charges which are overreached, or conveying subject to the charges without the SLA formalities. The latter is not attractive to a purchaser because he only has the protection of a personal indemnity from the vendor.

When there has been an incompletely constituted settlement a purchaser may look at the trust instrument.

8.4 Who is the tenant for life?

The tenant for life is very important as the focus of the strict settlement because by s16(1) the legal estate is vested in him, and by s108 all the powers of management of the settled land are exercisable by him. The person who is tenant for life is defined by ss19 and 20 SLA 1925.

Section 19 contains the general definition which applies to most settlements:

> 'The person of full age who is for the time being beneficially entitled under a settlement to possession of the settled land for his life is for the purposes of this Act the tenant for life of that land ...'

However, because of the wide definition of settled land in s1(1) SLA 1925, it is necessary to define 'tenant for life' in special cases with more particularity. This is done by s20 which provides that each of the following persons being of full age shall, when his estate or interest is in possession, have the powers of a tenant for life under the Act:

1. A tenant in tail.
2. A person with a conditional fee.
3. A person entitled to a base or determinable fee.
4. A tenant for years determinable on life, not holding merely under a lease at a rent. This definition excludes a person paying even a nominal rent.
5. A person entitled to the income of land under a trust during his own or any other life.
6. A person entitled in fee simple subject to family charges (this class of tenant for life can sell the land subject to the charge, see above).

If the land is subject to an immediate binding trust for sale, the person so entitled is not a tenant for life and the land is not settled land.

8.5 When there is no tenant for life

There are certain circumstances in which, although the land is settled land, there is no tenant for life. The most common of these are:

1. Where the person entitled is an infant.

2. Where no person is entitled to the whole income, for example, where only a definite fraction of the income is to be paid to the person entitled, the remainder to be accumulated (*Re Frewen* [1926] Ch 580), or where a fixed annual amount (an annuity) is to be paid.
3. Where no person is entitled to the income, that is, where there is a discretionary trust.

When there is no tenant for life, then by s23 the powers of the tenant for life are vested in the statutory owner, defined in s117(1)(xxvi) as either:

1. The person of full age on whom the settlement expressly conveys the powers of a tenant for life ; *or*
2. (more commonly) the trustees of the settlement.

8.6 Who are the trustees of the settlement?

Section 30 SLA 1925 sets out five definitions, each of which must be applied in turn; in other words, if there is no person within head (1) then head (2) must be examined, but if there are persons within head (1) then they will be trustees of the settlement and there is no need to look at head (2). The sequence should be noted carefully with particular reference to the first two heads.

The various heads are:

1. The persons who under the settlement are trustees with power to sell or to consent to or to approve sale. In any event such power of sale will only be exercised by the tenant for life, but the attempt is enough to make such persons the trustees of the settlement.
2. The persons expressly declared by the settlement to be 'trustees for the purposes of the Settled Land Act'. The appointment must be declared to be 'for the purposes' of the SLA 1925.
3. Persons who under the settlement are trustees with power to sell other land comprised in the settlement.
4. Persons who under the settlement are trustees with future powers to sell or under a future trust for sale.
5. Persons appointed by deed by those able to dispose of the whole equitable interest in the settled land.

When a settlement arises under a will or intestacy, and there are no trustees under any other provisions, the personal representatives are trustees of the settlement until others are appointed (s30(3)).

Where none of the above provisions apply, or where it is in any other case expedient, an application can be made to the court under s34 by the tenant for life, statutory owner or other person interested for appointment of trustees of the settlement. In such a case the court will not appoint the tenant for life as trustee of the settlement. See *Re Harrop* (1883) 24 Ch D 617. Otherwise there is no general restriction on the tenant for life becoming a trustee of the settlement, although such an appointment may not always be practicable. See s68(3) SLA 1925.

8.7 Powers of the tenant for life

Today some examiners limit this topic to certain powers. However, for the benefit of readers who do need to know the full scale of the powers of the tenant for life, the remaining powers are included to give the complete picture.

In *Re Mundy and Roper's Contract* [1899] 1 Ch 275 Chitty LJ described the powers of the tenant for life in these words:

> 'The object is to render land a marketable article, notwithstanding the settlement. Its main purpose is the welfare of the land itself and of all interested therein, including the tenants and not merely the persons taking under the settlement ... The scheme adopted is to facilitate the striking off from the land of the fetters imposed by the settlement; and this is accomplished by conferring on tenants for life in possession and others considered to stand in a like relation to the land, large powers of dealing with the land by way of sale, exchange, lease and otherwise and by jealously guarding those powers from attempts to defeat them or to hamper this exercise.'

This jealous 'guarding' is now supported by s106 SLA 1925 which provides that these powers given by the SLA to the tenant for life cannot be excluded, restricted or modified by the settlement or by any contract made by the tenant for life.

The various powers of the tenant for life may be demonstrated by the following diagram relating to the authorisations necessary before the respective powers are exercised.

Powers exercisable on giving notice to the trustees	*Powers exercisable* (A) *With the consent of the trustees*	*Powers exercisable without either notice to or consent of the trustees or the court*
1. Sale, ss38-39 2. Lease, ss41-48 3. Exchange, ss38-40 4. Grant Options, s51 (all the above require *general notice* which states the intention to exercise a power but without being specific) 5. Mortgage, s71 (following the giving of *specific notice*)	1. Compromise or settle disputes, s58(1) 2. Release rights imposed on other land for benefit of settled land, s58(2) (B) *With the consent of the trustees or the court* 1. To cut and sell timber, s66 2. To dispose of the principal mansion house, s65(1) (C) *With the consent of the court* 1. To sell heirlooms, s67 2. To effect any transaction not otherwise authorised by the Act or settlement if it is for the benefit of the land or beneficiaries, s64 3. To grant building/mining leases for terms longer than in the Act, s46	1. Make improvements, ss83-89 2. Accept surrenders of leases, s52 3. To take leases of other lands, s53 4. To make leases of less than 21 years, s42(5)

There is no statutory system of controlling the exercise by the tenant for life of his powers in respect of the legal estate nor can the settlor impose controls (see below), but there are certain safeguards against his abusing them. These are:

1. His position as trustee for all the beneficiaries under the settlement (s107). He is therefore liable to an action for breach of trust if he abuses those powers which he holds both for his own benefit and as trustee for all the beneficiaries under the settlement.
2. In the case of the most important of the powers he has to give notice to the trustees of the settlement. The notice must be in writing and must be given at least one month before the transaction in question to no fewer than two trustees. However this requirement does not give much protection because:

   a) The trustees are under no duty to interfere with an improper transaction.

b) In most cases a general notice is sufficient – except in the case of mortgages where specific notice is required – s101 SLA 1925.
c) Any trustee may in writing accept less than one month's notice or waive it altogether.
d) A person dealing in good faith with a tenant for life is not concerned to inquire whether notice has been given.

3. In some cases he must obtain the consent of the trustees or an order of the court before he exercises his powers. The tenant for life is free to deal with his own beneficial interest as he pleases and his right to do so is inherent and not given by statute.

Powers exercisable on notice

Power of sale: ss38–39
The tenant for life may sell all or any part of the settled land or any easement, right or privilege of any kind over the land. However, as well as giving notice he must obtain the best consideration in money that can reasonably be obtained and the purchase money must be paid to at least two trustees (unless a trust corporation is trustee when the money can be paid to the trust corporation). See *Wheelwright* v *Walker* (1883) 23 Ch D 752. (For provisions protecting a purchaser from a tenant for life see section 8.13.)

Power to exchange: ss38–40
Settled land, or any part of it, or any easement right or privilege over it may be exchanged for other land etc. Any adjustment in money for difference in value, 'equality of exchange' capital money, may be paid and received.

Power to lease: ss41–48
The settled land, or any part of it, or any easement right or privilege over it, may be leased for periods not exceeding:

1. 999 years for building or forestry.
2. 100 years for mining.
3. 50 years for any other purpose eg a residential lease.

Every lease must comply with the following conditions:

1. It must be made by deed.
2. It must take effect in possession not more than one year after its date, or in reversion after an existing lease with not more than seven years to run at the date of the new lease.
3. It must reserve the best rent obtainable in the circumstances, regard being had to any fine taken and to any money to be spent by the tenant in improving the land.

Any fine is capital money.

4. It must contain a covenant by the lessee for payment of rent and a condition of re-entry on rent not being paid within a specified time not exceeding 30 days.
5. A copy (known as a counterpart) of the lease must be executed by the lessee and given to the tenant for life. There is an exception to these rules where the lease is for not more than 21 years and is for the best rent without taking a fine and does not exempt the lessee from liability for waste. Then the lease:
6. May be made without giving notice to the trustees.
7. If the lease is for not more than three years it may be made by writing provided that there is an agreement to pay the rent.

A lease which does not comply with these requirements is void, except so far as it binds the equitable interest of the tenant for life. However, by s152 LPA 1925, if the lease was made in good faith and the lessee has taken possession, the lease will be effective in equity as a contract for a lease.

Power to mortgage: s71

If the tenant for life wishes to raise money for his own benefit, in the absence of a special provision in the settlement, he can only do so by mortgaging his beneficial interest. This will necessarily be an equitable mortgage as the security, the tenant for life's own life interest, can only be equitable. The legal estate can only be mortgaged for the following purposes:

1. To provide money required to be raised under the provisions of the settlement.
2. To provide money where reasonably required for specified purposes. These are all concerned with the settled land and the most important are:
3. To discharge an incumbrance.
4. To pay for authorised improvements to the land (the most common purpose).
5. Equality of exchange.
6. Payment of the costs of the above and certain other transactions.

In creating such a mortgage, specific notice must be given to the trustees of the settlement.

Power to grant options: ss90(1)(i) and 51

A tenant for life may grant an option in writing to purchase or take a lease of all or any part of the settled land or of any easement, right or privilege over it, provided that:

1. The price or rent must be the best reasonably available and must be fixed at the time of granting the option.
2. The option must be exercisable within an agreed number of years not exceeding ten.
3. The option may be granted with or without any consideration being paid, but if it is paid it is capital money.

Powers exercisable only with consent

Consent of the trustees

Power to dispose of the principal mansion house: s65. If either the settlement was made before 1926 and does not expressly dispense with consent, or the settlement was made after 1925 and expressly requires consent, then consent is required before the tenant for life can sell or lease the principal mansion house. If the house is usually occupied as a farmhouse, or if the site of the house together with its grounds is less than 25 acres, then it is not a principal mansion house within the section. In all other cases, it is a question of fact.

Power to cut and sell timber: s66. Consent is only required where the tenant for life is impeachable for waste. If consent is required, three-quarters of the proceeds are capital money and the remaining one-quarter will go to the tenant for life as income.

Power to compromise claims: s58(1)

Consent of the court

Power to sell settled chattels (known as 'heirlooms'): s67. Such a sale of heirlooms requires the order of the court – consent of the trustees will not suffice.

Power to effect any proper transactions: s64. This section gives the court a residual power to permit any other transaction with the settled land or capital money which would be for the benefit of the land or the beneficiaries.

In *Hambro* v *Duke of Marlborough* [1994] 3 All ER 332, the court gave the widest possible meaning to its power under s64 by concluding that under this provision it could approve a scheme which would have the effect of removing the land from the Settled Land Act 1925 by creating a trust for sale. The case concerned Blenheim Palace and estate which was given to the first Duke of Marlborough and his issue by the nation as a reward for his services. The conveyance established a strict settlement. The eleventh Duke was tenant for life and the Marquess of Blandford, his eldest son, would become tenant for life in due course. However, owing to the irresponsible behaviour of the Marquess, the plaintiffs (settlement trustees) sought an order under s64 which in effect would have limited the right of the Marquess to manage the Blenheim estate. Under the scheme put forward by the trustees the trust fund was to be held to pay the income to the eleventh Duke for life and subject thereto on protective trusts for the Marquess for his life and capital on the trusts of the existing settlement. Furthermore, the Duke was to execute a conveyance of substantially all the land comprised in the settlement to the trustees of the new trust to be held by them on trust for sale. This scheme would have taken the land out of the Settled Land Act by creating a trust for sale and it would have varied the beneficial interest of the Marquess without his consent. The Marquess opposed the application of the trustees. The court held that it had jurisdiction under s64 to approve the scheme. By virtue of s64 it could approve any transaction which was for the benefit of the settled land even if thereafter the land ceased to be settled land within the Settled Land Act 1925. Furthermore, the court held that it could approve a transaction which varied the beneficial interest of an ascertained beneficiary of full age and capacity who did not consent, provided that the variation was for the benefit of the settled land, or all the beneficiaries under the settlement. Accordingly, the person whose beneficial interest was affected would obtain some countervailing advantage either as one of the beneficiaries or as someone interested in the settled land which was being benefited.

Powers exercisable without either giving notice or obtaining consent

Powers to effect improvements: ss83–89 and Schedule 3

Improvements are special operations of a capital nature, as opposed to current repairs which must be paid out of income. If the improvements are to be paid out of the capital money or money raised by a mortgage of the settled land, the tenant for life must comply with the provisions of ss83–89 and Schedule 3. Improvements are classified as follows according to their place in Schedule 3 SLA 1925:

Part I. There are 25 heads, including drainage, building bridges and farm buildings. The tenant for life cannot be required to pay for such improvements and the estate itself pays for them.

Part II. There are six heads, including building houses and repair of dry rot damage. The tenant for life may be required by the trustees to repay the capital by up to 50 half-yearly instalments. Any such repayment will be by way of a rentcharge paid by the tenant for life.

Part III. There are three heads, including the provision of heating or lighting or vehicles used on the estate for farming purposes. The trustees must require repayment by the tenant for life by not more than 50 half-yearly instalments.

8.8 Personal nature of the statutory powers: s108

No powers over settled land can be given to anyone other than the tenant for life. A settlement may confer powers in addition to the statutory powers on the tenant for life, but any attempt by the settlor to give these additional powers to any other person or to provide that the statutory powers should be exercised by some person other than the tenant for life is invalidated by s108 SLA 1925, and the additional powers contained in the settlement are by that section conferred on the tenant for life.

8.9 Protection of the statutory powers: s106

The statutory powers cannot be ousted, curtailed or hampered, and s106 makes void any provision in the settlement which has the effect of preventing or discouraging the tenant for life from exercising the statutory powers. Thus:

1. A provision requiring him to obtain the consent of some person to the sale or lease of land is void.
2. A provision which provides that he should forfeit his beneficial interest if he should exercise any of his powers is void.

However, such conditions must be carefully construed as they are only invalid so far as they attempt to fetter exercise of the statutory powers. For example, a provision that the tenant for life will forfeit his interest if he ceases to reside on the settled land will be void if he ceases to reside because he has exercised a statutory power, eg sold or leased the land, but valid if he ceases to reside for some other reason; for instance, if he voluntarily decides to emigrate, and so leaves the property, the forfeiture clause will be valid. See *Re Haynes, Kemp* v *Haynes* (1887) 37 Ch D 306, *Re Trenchard* [1902] 1 Ch 378 and *Re Acklom* [1929] 1 Ch 195.

Where a fund is provided by the settlor for the upkeep of the property during the tenant for life's residence, it has been held that he can still claim for payments after letting the land but not after selling. See *Re Patten* [1929] 2 Ch 276, *Re Burden, Mitchell* v *St Luke's Hostel Trustees* [1948] Ch 160, *Re Aberconway's Settlement Trusts* [1953] Ch 647.

Romer J expressed the general principle in these words in *Re Burden*:

> '... there is nothing whatever in the section (s106) to convert the trust from a direction to pay outgoings into a direction to pay money out to the tenant for life.'

8.10 Powers remain with the tenant for life: s104

A tenant for life cannot assign, release or contract not to exercise his powers in respect of the legal estate even though he has disposed of his entire beneficial interest. There are, however, three cases in which the powers may become exercisable by someone other than the tenant for life:

1. If he assigns his beneficial interest to the person next entitled under the settlement with intent to extinguish it, then the statutory powers become exercisable by the assignee (provided that he is of full age). The tenant for life is treated as if he were dead (s105). The assignment must be to the person next entitled for the section to apply. See *Re Maryon-Wilson's Instruments* [1971] Ch 789.
2. If he ceases to have a substantial interest in the land and either consents to an order being made or has unreasonably refused to exercise his powers, the court may make an order authorising the trustees of the settlement to exercise the

statutory powers in his name (s24). For s24 to apply there must be more than neglect and a clear refusal by the tenant for life to exercise his powers.

3. Where the tenant for life is a mental patient, his statutory powers may be exercised under an order of the Court of Protection.

The consent of an assignee of the tenant for life's beneficial interest is not required for the exercise of any of the statutory powers, but he must be given notice of any intended transaction.

8.11 Death of the tenant for life

If the land remains settled, the deceased tenant for life's special personal representatives, the SLA trustees, must take out a grant of probate or letters of administration limited to the settled land, and then convey the land by vesting assent to the person entitled. If, on the other hand, the land ceases to be settled land, then the land will vest in the deceased tenant for life's ordinary personal representatives who will then convey it by simple assent to the person next entitled.

8.12 Acquisition by the tenant for life of the settled land: s68

The tenant for life may acquire all or any part of the settled land for himself, but in such a case the trustees of the settlement exercise the powers of the tenant for life in carrying out the transaction.

8.13 Dispositions by the tenant for life and protection of purchasers

There are several provisions regulating dispositions and protecting purchasers.

Section 13 SLA 1925 both regulates dispositions and protects purchasers (see section 8.3). Recall that s13 does contain an exception in favour of a purchaser of a legal estate without notice.

Section 18 states that any disposition other than one authorised by the SLA 1925 is void except in so far as it binds the tenant for life's equitable interest. A purchaser would therefore take subject to the beneficial interests whether he had notice or not. Further, even if the disposition is authorised, any capital money must be paid to at least two trustees of the settlement (or a trust corporation) or the beneficial interests will not be overreached.

Protection under s95

If the money arising under a transaction is paid to the trustees the payer is not concerned to see that the money is properly applied. This is particularly important when settled land is mortgaged, as if the money is used improperly the mortgage is unauthorised and, without the effect of this section, would be void by s18.

Protection under s110

Section 110(1) provides that a purchaser dealing in good faith with a tenant for life shall be deemed to have given the best price etc, and to have complied with the provisions of the SLA. Section 110(2) also provides that a purchaser shall not be entitled to inspect the trust instrument, but is entitled to assume that the particulars given in the vesting deed are correct. Section 110(3) protects the purchaser from personal representatives.

Conflict between s18 and s110

Problems have arisen when a purchaser has dealt in good faith with a person he thought was an absolute owner, but who was in fact a tenant for life making an unauthorised transaction. In the first instance case of *Weston* v *Henshaw* [1950] Ch 510, it was held by Danckwerts J that the protection of s110 only applied to a purchaser dealing with a person whom he knew to be a tenant for life. Cheshire points out at page 817 that this decision is

> 'the only decision in unregistered land which is an exception to the immunity of the bona fide purchaser for value of the legal estate without notice'.

In the later case of *Re Morgan's Lease* [1972] Ch 1 (also at first instance), Ungoed-Thomas J, relying on the Court of Appeal decision on the equivalent provision in the Settled Land Act 1882, in *Mogridge* v *Clapp* [1892] 3 Ch 382, which was not cited in the earlier case, decided that s110 did apply to a purchaser who was in fact dealing with a tenant for life even though he did not know it. Ungoed-Thomas J stated:

> 'Thus my conclusion is that s110 applies whether or not the purchaser knows that the other party to the transaction is a tenant for life.'

Most authors appear to favour this latter decision. Megarry and Wade remind their readers at page 342 that s110 does require the purchaser to be acting in good faith, and this aspect must always be applied in problems relating to the conflict between ss18 and 110 SLA 1925.

When the settlement has come to an end

A problem could arise when a settlement has come to an end because a tenant for life has forfeited his beneficial interest, but the tenant for life has not vested the legal estate in the person entitled and deals with the land as if the settlement were continuing. The purchaser would not appear to be protected by s110(2) as this applies to a 'purchaser of a legal estate in settled land'.

While there is no authority on this point, it would seem probable that the purchaser would acquire the legal estate, as this was still vested in the tenant for life, but take it subject to the equitable interests.

8.14 Capital money

Capital money, which may either have been provided by the settlor or arise from disposition of the settled land, eg sale or three-quarters of the sum received upon the sale of timber, must be invested in one or more of the ways specified in s73 SLA 1925, including trustee securities, paying for authorised improvements, or purchase of land held on fee simple or on a lease with 60 years or more still to run. The tenant for life may select the mode of investment (s75(3)), even though he does not have direct control of the capital money.

8.15 Functions of Settled Land Act trustees

1. To receive and hold capital money – see section 8.14.
2. To receive notice from the tenant for life when required.
3. To give consent when required.
4. To act as special personal representatives on the death of the tenant for life when the settlement continues.
5. To act as statutory owner when there is no tenant for life.
6. To exercise the powers of the tenant for life when he wishes to acquire the settled land for his own benefit.
7. To execute the vesting deed when the settlement is imperfectly constituted.
8. To exercise the powers of the tenant for life where the tenant for life has ceased to have a substantial interest and has either consented or the court has made an order. See s24.
9. To execute a deed of discharge when necessary on the determination of the settlement. See s17 SLA 1925. Such a deed is not necessary:
   a) If the settlement has come to an end by the death of the tenant for life, because the ordinary PRs' simple assent is sufficient to show the land has ceased to be settled. See *Re Bridgett and Hayes' Contract* [1928] Ch 163.
   b) If the settlement has come to an end before a vesting instrument has been executed. See *Re Alefounders' WT* [1927] 1 Ch 360.
10. To exercise a general supervision. The function is neatly summarised by Cheshire at page 199:

> 'The role of the trustees is to manage and protect the money that is paid to them.'

8.16 Trusts for sale

Distinction between settlements under the Settled Land Act 1925 and trusts for sale

Trusts for sale, which are expressly excluded from the SLA 1925 (see s1(7) SLA 1925: 'this section does not apply to land held upon trust for sale') are defined by s205(1)(xxix) LPA 1925 and s117(1)(xxx) SLA 1925 as 'an immediate binding trust for sale', and the most important distinction is that when land is held on trust for sale the legal estate and powers of dealing with the land are vested in the trustees, as opposed to a settlement when they are vested in the tenant for life. The main question today is to decide which method is most suitable to satisfy the requirements of the would-be settlor.

Definition – 'immediate binding trust for sale'

Trust for sale. This means that there must be a duty to sell and thus a true trust for sale, and not just a mere power to sell. If the settlor does not impose a duty to sell the settlement will then come under the SLA 1925. See ***Re Newbould*** (1913) 110 LT 6.

Immediate. This means that if the trust for sale arises in the future there will be a settlement rather than a trust for sale. But s25(1) LPA 1925 does provide a power to postpone sale. Thus the trust for sale must be effective immediately even though the duty to sell can then be postponed.

Binding. This word has been used by the courts to determine when a settlement under the SLA 1925 gives way to a trust for sale under the LPA 1925 in cases where there is first a settlement and a trust for sale arises before all the limitations are exhausted. In *Re Leigh's Settled Estates (No 1)* [1926] Ch 852 it was held that any prior equitable interest which the trustees for sale could not overreach prevented the trust for sale from being 'binding' so the settlement continued. This was later rejected, but the new rule laid down in *Re Parker's Settled Estates* [1928] Ch 247 that a binding trust for sale was one which would embrace 'the whole legal estate which is the subject matter of the settlement' has the same effect. In the case in question, there was an outstanding legal term which meant that the whole legal estate was not vested in the trustees for sale and, as a consequence, the land was not held on trust for sale.

Types of trust for sale

A trust for sale may arise:

1. *Expressly* by the wording of the settlement. There is no requirement of two documents as there is for settlements under the SLA. As a matter of practice it is

often found that two documents have been used for precisely the same reason as in the SLA, in order to keep the trusts off the title.

2. *By statute.* The most common examples of trusts for sale imposed by statute are:
   a) When two or more persons are jointly entitled to land (see Chapter 9).
   b) When a person dies intestate, then a trust for sale is imposed on his estate by s33 of the Administration of Estates Act 1925. From 1 July 1995, where a person dies intestate his property passes to the Public Trustee until the grant of administration (s14 of the Law of Property (Miscellaneous Provisions) Act 1994), whereas before that date it vested in the President of the Family Division.
   c) If trustees lend money on mortgage and the property becomes vested in them, eg by foreclosure.

8.17 Position of trustees for sale

Power to postpone sale

Unless a contrary intention appears, a power to postpone sale is implied in every trust for sale by s25 LPA 1925. However, because there is a trust for sale, there is a duty to sell, and the rule is that any trustee can compel his co-trustees to do their duty but they must be unanimous if they wish to exercise a power. Therefore the land must be sold unless all trustees agree to postpone. See *Re Mayo* [1943] Ch 302. However, the court will not enforce a sale if that would defeat the object of the trust or if it would be in breach of a contractual obligation on the trustees. See *Re Buchanan-Wollaston's Conveyance* [1939] Ch 738.

This rule has particular application in respect of the family home. See *Jones* v *Challenger* [1961] 1 QB 176; *Bedson* v *Bedson* [1965] 2 QB 666; *Re Evers' Trust, Papps* v *Evers* [1980] 1 WLR 1327; *Re Holliday (A Bankrupt)* [1980] 3 All ER 385; *Cousins* v *Dzosens* (1981) The Times 12 December; *Bernard* v *Josephs* [1982] 3 All ER 162; *Dennis* v *McDonald* [1982] Fam 63; *Burns* v *Burns* [1984] 1 All ER 244; *Grant* v *Edwards* [1986] 3 WLR 114.

The above cases on family home matters also illustrate the conflict which may arise between the statutory power to postpone sale under s25 LPA 1925 and the wide discretion given to the court under s30 LPA 1925 to 'make such order as it thinks fit' on an application by 'any person interested' (in the property). The court has to decide not only on the duty or power dichotomy, but also whether the purpose of the trust can still be achieved.

Upon an application for a s30 order for sale, the court looks for any 'secondary' or 'collateral' purposes to the trust – that is, any reason for the purchase of the land other than sale. A common example of a secondary purpose is the purchase of the property as a family home.

Where the court finds the existence of a secondary purpose and where that purpose is still subsisting the court will not usually grant the order. In *Jones* v *Challenger* (above) above the secondary purpose had come to an end. There a house had been purchased jointly by a married couple for a matrimonial and family home and at the relevant time the children had grown up and left and the marriage had ended in divorce. Accordingly, a s30 order was made compelling the reluctant ex-spouse to join in a sale of the property.

The court takes into account the need for a roof over a family, particularly where there are young children involved. In *Re Evers' Trust* (above) the court refused on these grounds to order a sale in spite of the fact that the land was subject to a duty to sell.

In *Re Citro, Domenico (A Bankrupt)* [1991] Ch 142 the Court of Appeal held that a collateral purpose would not be treated as subsisting when that purpose was to provide a matrimonial home and one of the parties ceased through bankruptcy to own his share. There a husband was adjudicated bankrupt, his only asset being a half share of the beneficial interest in the matrimonial home. His wife had a beneficial interest in the matrimonial home and lived in it with their children. The trustee in bankruptcy applied under s30 LPA 1925 for possession in order to sell the house. In granting the orders sought, the Court of Appeal concluded that the interest of the creditors prevailed over those of the wife and children, although they did postpone sale for six months.

These issues were recently considered by the Court of Appeal in *Abbey National Building Society* v *Moss* (1993) The Times 30 November. There a mother owned the property in question outright. She was persuaded by her daughter to transfer the property into their joint names in order to simplify the passing of the property on the mother's death. However, the transfer was on condition that the house would never be sold during the mother's lifetime without her consent. Subsequently the daughter borrowed £30,000 from the plaintiff on the security of the house. The mother and daughter then fell out, the daughter left the country having defaulted on the mortgage, and the plaintiff sought possession of the house under s30 LPA 1925.

The Court of Appeal concluded that the trust for sale could not be implemented without the mother's consent (that is, she had to consent before a sale of the property took place). Until she consented, a secondary or collateral purpose was in existence (that the mother should remain in the property during her lifetime). The court emphasised that it would not usually allow a trust for sale to defeat a secondary or collateral purpose just because one of the original parties to the trust assigned her interest. Here it could not have been within the contemplation of either the mother or the daughter that the assignment (whether voluntary or involuntary) by the daughter of her interest could lead to the house being sold against her mother's wishes. Further, in the court's view it was impossible to conclude that the secondary purpose had come to an end just because the daughter had lost her beneficial interest through the mortgage, because the secondary purpose was completely unaffected by that event (it would have been different if the secondary purpose had been that both mother and daughter were to have lived together in the house). Finally, the court said that in *Re Citro* (above) it was limited to situations where one of the parties ceased to have an interest by reason of bankruptcy or insolvency. Accordingly, it was inapplicable here and the mother's appeal against a sale order was allowed.

Other powers

By s28(1) LPA 1925 the trustees for sale have all the powers of a tenant for life of settled land and of Settled Land Act trustees. If, however, the consent of any person is required for sale, these powers can only be exercised subject to the same consent.

Curtailment of the powers

Trusts for sale may be made subject to a condition that the land shall not be sold without the consent of the named person or persons (s28(1)). If the trustees fail to obtain such consent they will be in breach of trust, but by s26(1) LPA 1925 a purchaser for value need only ensure that the consent of two such persons is obtained and he is then protected. The consent of an infant may be given by his parent or guardian, and of a mental patient by the Court of Protection. The court has power to dispense with consents that cannot be obtained by s30 LPA 1925.

The effect of allowing such consent (compare the position under the Settled Land Act) is that the powers of the trustees may be effectively curtailed. In *Re Inns* [1947] Ch 576 the person whose consent was required was a contingent remainderman who would only benefit if the land remained unsold, but the court said, obiter, that this was a valid requirement. This answers a popular question as to the most effective method of keeping land unsold today. It appears from *Re Inns* that the combined effect of the power to postpone sale in s25(1) LPA 1925 and the need for consents under s28(1) LPA 1925 may be to keep the land unsold. This leads to the conclusion that to achieve the original intention of a strict settlement today, to retain land in the family, it may well be better to create a trust for sale rather than a strict settlement under the SLA 1925. The problem with the latter, of course, is that the SLA gives the tenant for life a power of sale and this cannot be taken away from him because of the provisions of s106 SLA 1925.

8.18 Position of the beneficiaries

A person with an immediate life interest in the whole property may be permitted to occupy it himself.

Delegation

By s29 the trustees may in writing revocably delegate to such a person certain powers, including those of leasing and management. If they refuse to delegate these powers the court may direct them to do so under s30.

Consultation

By s26(3) the trustees must, so far as is practicable, consult the persons of full age for the time being beneficially interested in possession and must, so far as is consistent with the general interests of the trust, give effect to their wishes or to the wishes of the majority in terms of value. A purchaser is not concerned to see that such wishes are complied with. However, this provision only applies to statutory trusts for sale (see section 8.16) and to express trusts which expressly indicate that the section should apply.

Powers of the court

If the trustees refuse to sell or exercise any of their powers or if any requisite consent cannot be obtained, 'any person interested' may apply to the court under s30 for an order giving effect to the proposed transaction and the court may make such an order as it thinks fit. The operation of s30 LPA 1925 has been the subject of much recent litigation (see section 8.17).

Doctrine of conversion

Theoretically there is no overreaching in a trust for sale because of the effect of the doctrine of conversion, ie that from the very creation of the trust the beneficiary's rights are rights in money not in land. However, the same provisions apply to trusts for sale: the purchase money must be paid to at least two trustees or a trust corporation in order for the purchaser to take free of the rights of the beneficiaries.

Although the decision in *Irani Finance Ltd* v *Singh* [1971] Ch 59 remains generally correct as to the effect of conversion, the detailed decision would now be different in the light of s2 of the Charging Orders Act 1979.

After *National Westminster Bank Ltd* v *Stockman* [1981] 1 All ER 800, a charging order may now be imposed on land held on trust for sale.

In a dispute as to priority between a mortgage and a charging order it has been held that the mortgage had priority to an unregistered charging order nisi which was earlier in time.

It was further held that even though the Charging Orders Act 1979 allowed a charging order to be made on an undivided share in land, the earlier interpretation in *Irani Finance Ltd* v *Singh* of 'land' as not including an undivided share in the proceeds of the sale of land held on trust for sale still stood for the purposes of the definition of 'land' in s17 Land Charges Act 1972. Browne-Wilkinson V-C concluded:

> 'Nor was it necessarily Parliament's intention to make charging orders on undivided shares registrable: to do so would cut across the whole system of separating the legal estate. To have introduced such a conveyancing revolution would have required clear words.'

In *Cedar Holdings Ltd* v *Green* [1981] Ch 129 a husband and wife were the joint legal and equitable owners of a house registered in their joint names. Following their divorce the husband borrowed money from Cedar Holdings Ltd, offering them as security a charge on the house. The charge was executed by the husband and a woman impersonating his wife. The property expressed to be charged was 'land' and it was held by the Court of Appeal that a beneficial interest in the proceeds of sale of land held on statutory trusts for sale was not an interest in land within s63(1) Law of Property Act 1925.

This decision of the Court of Appeal was said by Lord Wilberforce in *Williams & Glyn's Bank* v *Boland* [1981] AC 487 to be wrongly decided.

Following this the Court of Appeal has now confirmed that a valid equitable charge could be created over a husband's equitable interest. The Court of Appeal decided in *First National Securities Ltd* v *Hegarty* [1984] 3 All ER 641 that a charging order should be made absolute to leave an 'innocent' wife whose signature had been forged to an application under s30 LPA 1925. In that situation she must then rely upon the discretion of the court to make 'such order as it thinks fit'.

Another decision of the Court of Appeal is in *Thames Guaranty Ltd* v *Campbell* [1984] 2 All ER 585. In this case the husband deposited the land certificate as security for the charge on the family home without the knowledge of his wife. The court declined to recognise this as an equitable charge on the husband's interest, but ordered that the land certificate should be returned to the wife. She was co-owner and was, accordingly, entitled to the return of the land certificate to the joint custody of herself and her husband. Slade LJ stated:

> '... Mr Campbell had not obtained the consent of his co-proprietor to the creation of any charge, nor had he given a notice of severance of joint tenancy. There ... was ... no equitable charge on the freehold title, even after the deposit of the land certificate had been made.'

This case highlights a problem to which we will return in Chapter 14.

It is a risk to rely upon a mortgage by deposit as a security. In the *Hegarty* case (above) the mortgagee did have a charge against the husband's beneficial interest but not in the *Campbell* case (above).

8.19 Ad hoc settlements and trusts for sale

A complicated and little-used machinery was set up in order to overreach certain prior equitable interests which were not overreached by the usual methods in both settlements and trusts for sale. An ad hoc settlement or trust for sale can be used, with special trustees approved by the court or a trust corporation.

8.20 Settlements and registered land

Where the settlement is placed in the context of registered land many examination candidates appear to imagine many unseen problems. The following additional points should be noted:

Strict settlements under the SLA 1925

1. The title will be registered in the name of the tenant for life.
2. The existence of the settlement would be revealed by a restriction entered as a minor interest in the proprietorship register. It would take the following form:

   'Restriction registered on the ... day of ... 1986.

   No disposition by the proprietor of the land under which capital money arises is to be registered unless the money is paid to A of ... and B of ... (the trustees of the settlement of whom there must be not less than two nor more than four unless a trust corporation is the sole trustee) or into court. Except under an order of the registrar no disposition by the proprietor is to be registered unless authorised by the Settled Land Act 1925.'

3. If the tenant for life of a strict settlement of registered land mortgages his life interest, how can the mortgagee preserve his priority? This was formerly achieved by the entry of a priority caution in the Minor Interests Index under s102(2) LRA 1925.

   This procedure was ended by the Land Registration Act 1986 by the repeal of s102(2) LRA 1925. The result is to abolish the Minor Interests Index and provide that priority between dealings with equitable interests in registered land is to be determined by the rule in *Dearle* v *Hall* (1828) 3 Russ 1. This will mean that the order of priority will be the order in which notices are received by the trustees of the settlement.

   As a consequence the rules of priority for equitable mortgages are now the same in both registered and unregistered land by the application of this rule.

Trusts for sale under the LRA 1925

Where registered land is subject to a trust for sale, whether the trust for sale is made expressly or by statute, the legal title is registered in the names of the trustees for sale (s94(1) LRA 1925). If more than four trustees exist the usual rule as to the first four named who are adults will apply.

The interests of the beneficiaries are minor interests which must be protected by the entry of a restriction in the proprietorship register. The restriction will be similar to that used in the case of a strict settlement. It must show that any disposition can only be made by order of the registrar or the court unless the proprietors are entitled for their own benefit (as in the case of a matrimonial home) or can give valid receipts for capital money.

If the purchaser from the registered proprietor complies with the restriction, that will override the beneficial interests with an effect similar to overreaching in the case of a strict settlement in unregistered land.

8.21 Comparison of the strict settlement and the trust for sale

Feature	*Strict settlement*	*Trust for sale*
1. Controlling Act	Settled Land Act 1925	Law of Property Act 1925
2. Legal Estate	Vested in tenant for life or statutory owners, s19(1)	Vested in trustees for sale, s28(1)
3. Documents	Two documents must be used - the vesting deed and the trust instrument, s4(1)	Only one document required but two are often used to keep the trusts off the title
4. Sale	Tenant for life has a power to sell, s38	Trustees for sale under a duty to sell, s205(1)(xxix)
5. Conversion	No application to a strict settlement	Converts land held on trust for sale into personalty
6. Restrictions on powers	Settlor cannot restrict the powers of the tenant for life, s106	Settlor can place restrictions by way of consents and there is a power to postpone sale, s25, s26(1), and *Re Inns* (1947)
7. Application of capital money	Decided by the tenant for life on the basis of the settlement, s73 and s75(2)	Decided by the trustees for sale, s28(1)
8. Conclusion	See Megarry and Wade at Page 410 '... Settlements and Trusts for sale have changed places since the middle of the last century'.	

8.22 Worked examples

Q Dan died in 1990, leaving by his will his large Victorian house, which had been the matrimonial home, to his trustees on trust to permit his widow Doris to reside there for as long as she wished, and on her death or ceasing to reside on trust for their children in equal shares. Doris finds the house is too large for her and wishes to move to somewhere smaller, but she has no money of her own.

Advise her as to whether she can carry out the following plans and, if so, what steps must be taken to carry them out:

1. Mortgage the house in order to purchase somewhere smaller.
2. Sell the house and from the proceeds buy somewhere smaller.
3. Let the house and use the income to rent somewhere smaller.

A Although the house was devised to Dan's trustees there is no indication that this is an immediate binding trust for sale. This is therefore a settlement under the Settled Land Act 1925, and Doris is the tenant for life.

The settlement provides that she is to forfeit her interest if she ceases to reside in the house. This provision will be void by s106 SLA 1925 in so far as it prevents or hampers her from exercising her statutory powers as tenant for life. It is clear from cases such as *Re Orlebar* (1936) and *Re Trenchard* (1902) that the tenant for life will not forfeit his interest if he ceases to reside because he has exercised his statutory power of sale or leasing, but he will forfeit his interest if he ceases to reside for some other reason.

Examining the three proposals in turn:

1. The tenant for life can only mortgage the legal estate in the settled land for the statutory purposes set out in s71, and the provision of alternative accommodation for the tenant for life is not one of these. Doris is free to mortgage her beneficial interest, but this is unlikely to raise very much money. Further, it is not necessary for a mortgagor to give up possession of the mortgaged premises, and so if she ceases to reside it will not be as a result of exercising her interest. This plan is therefore not of any use.
2. Doris is entitled to sell the settled land, provided that she obtains the best consideration that can reasonably be obtained, and she will not forfeit her interest if she ceases to reside for this reason. The money must, however, be paid to the trustees who must invest it according to the provisions of s73 SLA 1925, although the tenant for life has the right to direct how the money should be invested (s75(2)). While the purchase of freehold or long leasehold land is an approved investment, this only allows the purchase of land as an income-producing asset and not for the beneficiary to live in.

   Doris or the trustees may, however, apply to the court under s75(3) to sanction the use of capital money to buy a smaller home for Doris, and the court will consider the interests of all the beneficiaries in deciding whether to make such an order. If this course of action is adopted it will be necessary for the trustees to vest the legal estate in Doris by a vesting assent (assuming the trustees also to be Dan's executors).
3. Doris can let the settled land, provided that the conditions of ss41–42 are fulfilled. This would be a residential lease, and so it must be for 50 years or less, be by deed for the best rent reasonably available, if any fine is taken it is capital money, and contain a covenant by the lessee for payment of rent and a right of forfeiture, and a counterpart lease must be executed by the tenant and given to the tenant for life. If the term exceeds 21 years, notice must be given to the trustees. A lease for three years or less can be in writing. The lease will only be effective if the legal estate has been vested in Doris (s13 SLA). Doris as tenant for life is entitled to the income from the settled land, and so she can use the money to rent a home for herself. This is the simplest method of achieving the desired end.

Q T, by his will, left his large house 'to my wife W for life or until remarriage and then to be sold and the proceeds shared between my children'. Two years later

W remarried secretly and then, as tenant for life, sold the house to P who paid the purchase money to the Settled Land Act trustees. The children have just discovered that their mother has remarried. Advise them as to what steps they can take to recover their shares.

A The children have a clear action for breach of trust against W, but this will only be of assistance if she has money.

The children are entitled to the capital money held by the SLA trustees.

There is no clear statutory provision or authority as to P's position. As the legal estate was still vested in W she could convey the legal estate to him. He was not able to inspect the trust instrument (s110(2)), and so he could not know that in fact the settlement had come to an end and that W was no longer tenant for life. It is arguable, however, that he is not protected by s110(1) because the settlement has come to an end, and so he is not a 'purchaser of a legal estate in settled land', and therefore took subject to the children's interest.

9

Co-ownership

9.1 Introduction

Creation

Co-ownership arises when two or more persons hold an interest in land at the same time. Their interests in land must be concurrent rather than consecutive. If land is conveyed to A and B in fee simple in possession, then A and B are co-owners. If land is conveyed to A for life, the remainder to B, then A and B both have an interest in the same land, but their interests are consecutive, not concurrent, and they are not co-owners.

Where land is held by co-owners, then during their lifetimes each is entitled to live on or share in the proceeds of the land. See *Bull* v *Bull* [1955] 1 QB 234. But on the death of a co-owner (say A), there are two possible ways in which his interest in the land could devolve. It could pass to the remaining co-owner (B), so that B becomes the sole owner of the land. Or the interest could pass under A's will or intestacy to a third party, eg two children C and D, so that B and C and D then become co-owners of the land. The problems arise as to their respective shares.

This may be illustrated by the following diagram, assuming A and B make an equal contribution to the purchase price.

Joint tenancy	*Tenancy in common*
A–B	A–B
A dies leaving two children C and D. The result is: B takes all as survivor.	A dies leaving two children C and D. The result is: C – D – B
	1/4 1/4 1/2

Where the first arrangement exists, A and B hold the land as 'joint tenants', and B's entitlement to A's share on A's death is known as the 'right of survivorship'. Under the second arrangement, A and B hold the land as 'tenants in common' and B, C and D continue to hold as tenants in common.

Co-owners must hold their land either as joint tenants or as tenants in common. The main distinction between the two means of holding the land is that the right of survivorship applies only to joint tenancies and that only the joint tenancy can exist at law after 1925.

Note:

1. The word 'tenant' in the context of co-ownership has nothing to do with a tenant under a lease. It is derived from tenure and describes how the land is held.
2. The right of survivorship is also known by its Latin form, as the jus accrescendi.
3. By the Bodies Corporate (Joint Tenancy) Act 1899 a corporation may acquire and hold any property in joint tenancy in the same manner as if it were an individual.

Joint tenancy

Under a joint tenancy the joint tenants are considered to be a single composite person who is the land owner. All the joint tenants own all the land and no single joint tenant can point to any part of the land as his alone. However, each joint tenant has a potential share in the land equal to that of all the other joint tenants. If there are four joint tenants, each has a potential quarter share. This word 'potential' should always be used to describe the prospective interest of the surviving joint tenants at any time.

The right of survivorship follows logically from the concept of a single composite owner. The loss (through the death of a joint tenant) of part of the composite owner does not prevent the continued existence of the composite owner so long as there are at least two surviving co-owners. If A, B, C and D hold land as joint tenants, the joint tenancy will continue until there is only one survivor who will be solely entitled to the land. This may generally be referred to as the 'lottery effect' with the prize going to the person who lives the longest.

A joint tenant cannot dispose of his interest by will. The right of survivorship will take precedence over any attempted disposition by will and over the usual rules on intestacy. This rule is expressed in Latin as jus accrescendi praefertur ultimae voluntati. But a joint tenant can dispose of his interest during his lifetime. His interest will consist of his potential share, and the person to whom it is granted will hold that interest as a tenant in common, not as a joint tenant, and so will not be affected by the jus accrescendi. But such disposition can only take place in equity because s1(6) LPA 1925 provides that:

> 'A legal estate is not capable of subsisting or of being created in an undivided share in land.'

Alternatively, a joint tenant can avoid the jus accrescendi by transforming his joint tenancy into a tenancy in common during his lifetime. This is called 'severance' and is dealt with in detail at section 9.9.

Tenancy in common

A tenancy in common arises where land is limited to two or more persons with words of severance, which indicate an intention that the parties are to take separate shares.

Under a tenancy in common each co-owner remains an individual land owner with a distinct share in the land. These shares need not be equal. If A and B are tenants in common, their shares could be half each or three-quarters and one quarter. While the size of each co-owner's share is known, the share does not represent any particular piece of land. Each tenant has a share in all the land. Hence these shares are known as 'undivided shares' in land, the phrase used in the LPA 1925 to describe tenancies in common.

When the land is sold, the proceeds of sale are divided according to the tenants' respective shares. The right of survivorship does not apply, and so a tenant in common can dispose of his interest both inter vivos and by will.

Severance

A joint tenant who wishes his interest to pass to a person other than the remaining joint tenants cannot give effect to his wishes by will. Any attempt to dispose of his interest by will is ineffective, as the right of survivorship comes into operation on his death. However, he can avoid the right of survivorship by converting his joint tenancy into a tenancy in common during his lifetime. This process is called severance (see section 9.9).

If A, B and C are joint tenants and A severs his interest, B and C remain as joint tenants, with mutual rights of survivorship, while A's interest becomes a tenancy in common of one-third of the equitable interest. A no longer has any rights of survivorship, but he can dispose of his interest by will. At the same time A will remain a joint tenant at law, and A, B and C will hold the legal estate as joint tenants for A as a tenant in common in equity and B and C as joint tenants in equity.

Where there are only two joint tenants, severance by one converts the interest of the other into a tenancy in common, as there cannot be a sole joint tenant. Again such effect only applies in equity; while the two will continue as joint tenants at law, they will both become tenants in common in equity: *Williams* v *Hensman* (1861) 1 John & H 546.

Severance can be effected by:

1. Alienation inter vivos by a joint tenant.
2. Mutual agreement among joint tenants.
3. The provisions of s36(2) LPA 1925.

These methods are dealt with in detail in section 9.9.

Legal and equitable interests under co-ownership

There is no requirement that the legal and equitable interests in land held under co-ownership should be identical, and frequently they differ. A key to the proper understanding of co-ownership is always to consider the legal estate separately from the equitable interest. This is an area where the drawing of diagrams to illustrate the respective interests is an invaluable aid to understanding the principles.

Prior to the 1925 legislation joint tenancies and tenancies in common could exist both at law and in equity. Now only a joint tenancy can exist at law and a tenancy in common must be held behind a trust. Hence the legal title of land held under co-ownership must always be held as a joint tenancy. The equitable interest can be held as a joint tenancy or as a tenancy in common or as a mixture of both.

The separation of the legal and equitable interests

The following examples show the importance of considering the legal and equitable interests separately.

If A, B and C are co-owners as joint tenants, then they hold the legal estate on trust for themselves as joint tenants in equity.

Legal estate	*Equitable interest*
A, B, C as joint tenants	A, B, C as joint tenants

If C dies, the jus accrescendi operates both at law and in equity, so that A and B are left as legal and equitable joint tenants.

A, B as joint tenants	A, B as joint tenants

The combined effect of the above two examples may be illustrated as:

A B C	–	joint tenants at law
A B C	–	joint tenants in equity

Death of C and the effect of the right of survivorship:

A B	–	joint tenants at law
A B	–	joint tenants in equity

Alternatively, where A, B and C are joint tenants both at law and in equity, C can sever his equitable joint tenancy. The effect of this is that A, B and C remain joint tenants at law, holding the equitable interest on trust for A and B as joint tenants and C as a tenant in common.

Legal estate	*Equitable interest*
A, B, C as joint tenants	A, B as joint tenants of two-thirds C as tenant in common of one-third

The effect of this may be shown as:

A	B	C	–	joint tenants at law
A/B		C	–	equity
joint tenants two-thirds		tenant in common one-third		

If A, B and C are co-owners as tenants in common, they hold the legal estate as joint tenants on trust for themselves as equitable tenants in common.

Legal estate	*Equitable interest*
A, B, C as joint tenants	A, B, C as tenants in common

If C dies, the jus accrescendi operates on the legal estate so that A and B acquire C's legal estate and remain joint tenants, but they hold C's equitable interest under his tenancy in common on trust for his personal representatives.

Legal estate	*Equitable interest*
A, B	A, B, C's personal representatives as tenants in common

The combined effect of the last two examples may be illustrated as:

A	B	C	–	joint tenants at law
	|			
A	B	C	–	tenants in common in equity

Death of C and assuming each contributed an equal share to the purchase price.

A	B		–	joint tenants at law
	|			
A	B	PRs of C	–	tenants in common in equity
one-third	one-third	one-third		

It should be noted that the legal owner(s) need not be the same person(s) as the equitable co-owners. A and B can jointly hold the legal estate on trust for C and D as equitable joint tenants or equitable tenants in common.

Determination of the type of co-ownership

As the legal estate must always be held under a joint tenancy, it is the equitable interest that reflects whether land is held under a joint tenancy or a tenancy in common.

How the equitable interest is held will depend upon the means by which the co-ownership came into existence, and whether there has been severance of any or all of the equitable interests after the creation of a joint tenancy.

9.2 Creation of a joint tenancy

The essence of the joint tenancy is that the joint tenants do not have separate interests in the property. Together they are entitled to the same interest. A joint tenancy can be created expressly or impliedly. In either case the 'four unities' must be present before there can be a joint tenancy.

The four unities (PITT)

These are:

1. *Unity of possession.* This means that each co-owner is equally entitled to possession of the whole land and can sue if excluded from any part of the land. The essential feature is described by Megarry and Wade at page 419:

   > '... each co-owner is as much entitled to possession of any part of the land as the others.'

2. *Unity of interest.* The interest of each co-owner must be identical with regard to the extent, duration and nature of the interest held in the land. None of the individual co-owners can dispose of the interest by himself because he does not have the whole estate, as seen in *Thames Guaranty Ltd* v *Campbell* [1984] 2 All ER 585.
3. *Unity of title.* Each co-owner must claim title under the same document or act; for instance, all the co-owners acquired their interest from the same conveyance.
4. *Unity of time.* The interest of each co-owner must vest at the same time.

If there is no unity of possession there is no co-ownership; if one of the other three (interest, title or time) is missing there may be a tenancy in common but not a joint tenancy.

Express creation

This occurs when a grant to co-owners expressly states that the land is to be held jointly and the four unities are present.

Implied or presumed creation

Where a grant of land to co-owners is silent as to how the land is to be held, there is a presumption at law that the land will be held as a joint tenancy provided that:

1. the four unities are present; and
2. the presumption of a joint tenancy is not rebutted by:

   a) words of severance; or
   b) factors showing that a tenancy in common was intended; or
   c) factors giving rise to an equitable presumption of a tenancy in common. See section 9.3.

9.3 Creation of a tenancy in common

As with a joint tenancy, a tenancy in common can be created expressly or impliedly. In either case there must be unity of possession, without which there cannot be any form of co-ownership. But there is no requirement for the other unities to be present.

Express creation

A grant to co-owners stating that they are to hold as tenants in common creates an equitable tenancy in common, provided that there is unity of possession.

Implied or presumed creation

A grant of land to more than one person where the grant is silent as to how the land is to be held will take effect in equity as a tenancy in common if:

1. Any of the four unities (apart from unity of possession) is missing; or
2. Words of severance were used in the grant. These are words showing an intention on the part of the grantor that the co-owners were each to have distinct, but undivided, shares in the land, rather than to hold the land as a notional composite person. Words that have been held to give co-owners undivided shares in land and so create a tenancy in common are:

   To A and B equally
   To A and B in equal shares
   To be divided among A and B
   Among A and B

   The words must be clear. A conveyance which contained the following addendum:

   > 'To hold in fee simple as beneficial joint tenants in common equal shares'

   was held to create a joint tenancy in *Joyce* v *Barker Bros Builders Ltd* (1980) 40 P & CR 512. This decision has been challenged in *Martin* v *Martin* (1987) 54 P & CR 238 where identical words were said to be words of severance which override the joint tenancy and create a tenancy in common. In the opinion of Millett J these words must be considered as being in two separate deeds with the first, notional, deed creating a joint tenancy in equity which the second, notional, deed severed to create a tenancy in common in equity.

   This decision should not be seen to affect the general rules of interpretation that in the case of a conveyance inter vivos the interpretation is achieved by taking the first words which create a sensible grant. In the case of a will, however, the last words which create a sensible meaning will prevail; or
3. The grant as a whole showed that a tenancy in common was intended.

Equitable presumptions in favour of a tenancy in common

A rebuttable equitable presumption which overrides the presumption at law of a joint tenancy arises in certain circumstances. In general, these are circumstances where it would be inequitable for there to be a joint tenancy with the consequent right of survivorship and equal division of the proceeds of sale.

First, where the purchase money for land conveyed into the names of more than one person was provided by those persons in unequal shares, the legal estate will be held by the owners as joint tenants on trust for themselves as equitable tenants in common holding undivided shares proportionate to their respective contributions. See *Bull* v *Bull* [1955] 1 QB 234. But no such presumption arises in the case of equal shares where they will be presumed to be joint tenants.

Secondly, where two or more persons advance money on mortgage, whether in equal or unequal shares.

Thirdly, where the land is partnership property. See *Lake* v *Craddock* (1732) 3 P Wms 158 where it was held that the right of survivorship is incompatible with a commercial undertaking – jus accrescendi inter mercatores pro beneficio commerci locum. It is clear that this is only a presumption which may be subject to any express declaration to the contrary in favour of a joint tenancy. See also *Barton* v *Morris* [1985] 2 All ER 1032, in which a farm was conveyed to two people expressly as joint tenants with the bulk of the purchase money being provided by one of them. The property was run as a guest house and small farm, and the person who provided the bulk of the purchase money kept partnership accounts showing the farm as a partnership asset. Nicholls J held that in view of the express declaration in the conveyance that the property was to be held on joint tenancy, he could not accept that there had been any course of dealing with the property from which a severance of the joint tenancy could be inferred. Thus the presumption of a tenancy in common derived from the fact of the partnership accounts could not prevail over the express words of the conveyance.

The Privy Council has indicated that the list is not exhaustive and, in particular, has added a fourth category of presumption in favour of a tenancy in common in equity: where the grantees hold the premises for their several individual business purposes. The case in which this arose was *Malayan Credit Ltd* v *Jack Chia MPH Ltd* [1986] 1 All ER 711, which concerned a five-year lease of one floor of an office block in Singapore. The floor area and responsibility for outgoings was apportioned between tenants as to 62 per cent and 38 per cent respectively, and each tenant used the accommodation for their separate commercial activities. Sale of the property was ordered with a division of the proceeds of sale in the above proportions.

Lord Brightman said:

> 'Where premises are held by two persons as joint tenants at law for their several business purposes, it is improbable that they would intend to hold as joint tenants in equity.'

He was of the opinion that the equitable presumptions in favour of a tenancy in common should not be restricted to the usual three (above). He concluded:

> 'There are other circumstances in which equity may infer that the beneficial interest is intended to be held as – tenants in common – one such case is where the grantees hold the premises for their several individual business purposes.'

This new presumption fits neatly between the first and third existing presumptions discussed above: where the purchase money is provided in unequal shares, and in the case of partnership property.

9.4 Resulting trusts and co-ownership

A presumed equitable joint tenancy or tenancy in common can arise where land is conveyed into the name of one person. Where two or more persons contribute to the purchase money of land which is conveyed into the name of only one of them (or into the names of fewer than contributed), there is a rebuttable equitable presumption that they were all intended to share ownership of the land. To give effect to this presumption, equity imposes a resulting trust on the person(s) in whom the legal estate is vested, to hold the equitable interest on trust for all the contributors as equitable co-owners. If the purchase money was contributed in equal shares, the equitable interest will be held as a joint tenancy. Otherwise the equitable presumption of a tenancy in common will prevail. See *Williams & Glyn's Bank* v *Boland* [1980] 3 WLR 138.

The burden of proof in such a case may be high. If there is no express agreement or express trust the right to a beneficial interest under a trust could only be established by moving an express or imputed intention that a party other than the legal owner should have a beneficial interest in the property. The effect of this intention must make it inequitable for the legal owner to claim the sole beneficial interest. This was the effective decision of the Court of Appeal in *Bristol & West Building Society* v *Henning* [1985] 1 WLR 778.

The decision in *Bristol* must be compared with the subsequent decision of the Court of Appeal in *Grant* v *Edwards* [1986] 3 WLR 114. The court had to consider again the evidence necessary to establish a common intention that a co-habitee was to have a beneficial interest. Nourse LJ set out the test in these words:

> '... where there is no written declaration or agreement, nor any direct provision by the plaintiff of part of the purchase price so as to give rise to a resulting trust in her favour, she had to establish a common intention between her and the defendant, acted upon by her, that she should have a beneficial interest in the property. If she could do that equity would not allow the defendant to deny that interest and would construct a trust to give effect to it.'

The House of Lords has expressed similar views in respect of the alleged constructive trust of Mrs Rosset in *Lloyds Bank plc* v *Rosset* [1990] 2 WLR 867. The words of Lord Bridge are worth repeating:

> 'Direct contributions to ... purchase price by [a] partner ... not the legal owner whether initially or by payment of mortgage instalments, would readily justify ... the creation of a constructive trust ... extremely doubtful whether anything less would do.'

The same principle applies where one person spends money on permanent improvements to another's land with the intention of acquiring an interest in that land, although only a tenancy in common can be acquired as the unities of time, title and interest are absent.

In *Hussey* v *Palmer* [1972] 1 WLR 1286, A paid for an extension to B's house so that A could live in the house. A was held to be an equitable tenant in common of a share proportionate to her expenditure. In the Court of Appeal, Lord Denning considered the case to be within those where one person contributed towards the purchase price of a house so that the owner held on constructive trust for the contributor. The fact that the court will look at the circumstances of each case to decide in what way the equity could be satisfied is seen by the above decision in *Bristol & West Building Society* v *Henning*.

The equitable presumption of a resulting trust can be rebutted by evidence showing that the contribution was intended as a loan or gift. *Hussey* v *Palmer* (above) should be compared with the decision in *Re Sharpe (A Bankrupt)* [1980] 1 All ER 198 (see Chapter 13) in which Browne-Wilkinson J made the following comment on *Hussey* v *Palmer*:

> 'Counsel ... relied on *Hussey* v *Palmer* where the Court of Appeal by a majority held that, even though the plaintiff in that case described moneys used to improve a property as having been paid by way of loan to the owner of the property, she was entitled to an equitable interest in the property. However, her equitable interest was not, apparently, a share of the proceeds of sale, but something akin to a lien for the moneys advanced.
>
> 'The facts in that case were very special and I think the clue to the decision may be that the court reached the view that, although described in evidence as a loan, the parties did not in fact intend a loan since there was never any discussion of repayment.'

The judge then went on to apply that decision to the facts of *Re Sharpe* by saying:

> 'In my judgment, if, as in this case, moneys are advanced by way of loan there can be no question of the lender being entitled to an interest in the property under a resulting trust. If he were to take such an interest, he would get his money twice; once on repayment of the loan and once on taking his share of the proceeds of sale of the property.'

9.5 Co-ownership under the 1925 legislation

Before 1926 both joint tenancies and tenancies in common could exist as legal estates. Considerable conveyancing problems could arise with legal tenancies in common as the conveyance had to be signed by all the legal tenants in common, who could be numerous and whose names would not necessarily be on the original deed.

As part of the general ruling of the 1925 legislation and specifically in order to remedy the above problem (for land other than settled land), the following principles were laid down by ss34–36 LPA 1925:

1. Tenancies in common cannot exist as legal estates, but only as equitable interests.
2. A joint tenant cannot convert his joint tenancy to a tenancy in common (ie sever his joint tenancy) at law, but only in equity.
3. The legal estate of land held in equity by co-owners is always held as a joint tenancy.
4. The legal joint tenancy is held by trustees on trust for sale for the equitable co-owners, who may be tenants in common or joint tenants.

Abolition of a legal tenancy in common (for land other than settled land)

This is recognised by s1(6) LPA 1925:

> 'A legal estate is not capable of subsisting or of being created in an undivided share in land.'

This was achieved by two provisions:

1. A legal tenancy in common cannot exist or be created after 1925 (s34 LPA 1925). Section 34(1) provides:

   > 'An undivided share in land shall not be capable of being created except ... as hereinafter mentioned.'

   The detailed provisions are to be found in s34(2) LPA 1925. The effect is that any attempt to create a legal tenancy in common takes effect as a joint tenancy at law and a tenancy in common in equity. Note that the 1925 legislation refers to tenancies in common as 'undivided shares in land'.

   As a consequence, if land is conveyed to A and B to hold as legal tenants in common, A and B will hold the legal estate as joint tenants on trust for themselves as tenants in common in equity.
2. A legal joint tenancy cannot be severed after 1925 (s36(2) LPA 1925). Section 36(2) provides:

   > 'No severance of a joint tenancy of a legal estate, so as to create a tenancy in common in land, shall be permissible.'

   Where land is held under a joint tenancy both at law and in equity only the equitable interest can be converted to a tenancy in common.

   If A, B and C are joint tenants at law and in equity, C's severance of his joint tenancy can only take effect in equity. He will remain a joint tenant at law, and because he holds the legal estate as a trustee, he will continue to hold the legal estate until he dies or resigns as trustee, even though he may have severed his equitable interest by selling it to D. This is a particular point of many co-ownership questions and emphasises the need for separation of the legal estate from the equitable interest when answering co-ownership problems.

Imposition of a trust for sale

Whenever there is beneficial co-ownership in possession of land (other than settled land) the legal estate must be held on trust for sale (ss34 and 36 LPA 1925).

If the conveyance does not expressly provide for a trust, a statutory trust is imposed. The terms are set out in s35 LPA 1925. All the usual rules applying to trusts for sale (see Chapter 8, section 8.16) apply to the statutory trusts. The use of s36(4) SLA 1925 in *Bull* v *Bull* [1955] 1 QB 234 to rectify the lack of any expression of trust is considered below.

Identity of trustees for sale

The identity of the trustees for sale depends on how the co-ownership came into existence. There are three possibilities:

1. Express grant to trustees on trust for two or more beneficiaries. The named trustees are the trustees for sale, holding, in the absence of express trusts, on the statutory trusts set out in s35 LPA 1925,

   eg grant to X and Y to hold on trust for A and B

X, Y	trustees for sale, holding legal estate as joint tenants on trust for
A, B	beneficiaries (beneficial co-owners).

2. The named trustees including or consisting entirely of the beneficial co-owners,

eg X, Y, A	A, B
on trust for	on trust for
A, B	A, B, C.

3. Conveyance of estate in possession to two or more persons. In the absence of named trustees, the trustees for sale are the beneficial co-owners. If there are more than four beneficial co-owners, then the trustees are the first four named in the conveyance provided that they are all of full age. See s34 Trustee Act 1925 which provides in s34(2):

   > 'In the case of settlements and dispositions on trust for sale of land made or coming into operation after the commencement of this Act
   > a) The number of trustees thereof shall not in any case exceed four, and where more than four persons are named as such trustees, the four first named (who are able and willing to act) shall alone be the trustees, and the other persons named shall not be trustees unless appointed on the occurrence of a vacancy;
   > b) The number of the trustees shall not be increased beyond four.'

   eg conveyance to A and B, who are both of full age

A, B	trustees for sale, holding legal estate as joint tenants on trust for
A, B	beneficial co-owners;

   eg conveyance to A, B, C, D, E and F, who are all of full age

A, B, C, D	trustees for sale, holding legal estate as joint tenants on trust for
A, B, C, D, E, F	beneficial co-owners.

Joint tenancies

In the case of equitable joint tenancies, the trust for sale is imposed by s36 LPA 1925:

> 'Where a legal estate (not being settled land) is beneficially limited to or held in trust for any persons as joint tenants, the same shall be held on trust for sale, in like manner as if the persons beneficially entitled were tenants in common, but not so as to sever their joint tenancy in equity.'

Tenancies in common

In the case of tenancies in common, the trust for sale is imposed by s34 LPA 1925 and the trustees for sale hold the legal estate as joint tenants for the co-owners as beneficial (equitable) tenants in common. While the scheme of the Act appears to be the imposition of a trust for sale in all cases of co-ownership, s34 does not on the face of it cover all cases of tenancies in common. It deals with the case where:

> 'land is expressed to be conveyed to any person in undivided shares, and those persons are of full age'.

In many cases it will be found that there is no such expression in the conveyance. In particular s34 does not cover the following cases:

1. A conveyance to A and B as joint tenants in circumstances where equity presumes a tenancy in common, for example where the purchase money was contributed in unequal shares.
2. A conveyance to X, purchasing as trustee for A and B who have contributed the purchase money in unequal shares (see *Bull* v *Bull* (above)).
3. A declaration by A, as sole owner, that he holds on trust for himself and B as tenants in common.
4. A conveyance to A (an infant) and B (an adult) as tenants in common.
5. A conveyance to A as sole owner, when the purchase price was contributed in unequal shares by A and B: A holds the legal estate for himself and B as beneficial tenants in common.

Two solutions have been used by courts, where a conveyance was made in circumstances where equity presumes a tenancy in common.

In *Re Buchanan-Wollaston's Conveyance* [1939] Ch 738 the court held that the case fell within s36, but this solution involves ignoring the word 'beneficially' in that section. But in *Bull* v *Bull* (above) the Court of Appeal relied on s36(4) SLA 1925 (see section 9.6) which provides that an undivided share in land cannot be created

> 'except under a trust instrument or under the Law of Property Act 1925, and shall then only take effect behind a trust for sale'.

More recently, the courts have not concerned themselves with the specific wording of s34 LPA 1925 and have acted on the basis that the overall scheme was the imposition of a trust for sale on all beneficial tenancies in common.

The words of Lord Denning in *Bull* v *Bull* (above) should be noted with care. He described the effect of the transaction thus:

> 'The son is, of course, the legal owner of the house: but the mother and son are, I think, equitable tenants in common. Each is entitled in equity to an undivided share in the house, the share of each being in proportion to his or her respective contribution ... Each of them is entitled to the possession of the land and to the use and enjoyment of it in a proper manner.'

Lord Denning then went on to discover the trust for sale:

> 'I realise that since 1925 there has been no such thing as a legal tenancy in common. All tenancies in common now are equitable only and they take effect behind a trust for sale.'

The problem of conveyances of this nature was then analysed:

> 'The son is the legal owner and he holds it on the statutory trusts for sale. He cannot at the present moment sell the house because he cannot give a valid receipt for the proceeds. It needs two trustees to give a receipt. The son could get over this difficulty by appointing another trustee who would agree with him to sell the house, the two trustees would no doubt have to consider the mother's wishes, but as the son appears to have made the greater contribution he could in theory override her wishes about a sale. The difficulty of the two trustees would be a practical difficulty because so long as the mother is there, they could not sell with vacant possession.'

In *Williams & Glyn's Bank* v *Boland* [1981] AC 487 this approach by Lord Denning was accepted by the House of Lords without question. Lord Wilberforce stated:

> 'Each wife contributed a substantial sum of her own money towards the purchase of the matrimonial home or to paying off a mortgage on it. This, indisputably, made her an equitable tenant in common to the extent of her contribution.'

Lord Scarman also used *Bull* v *Bull* in saying:

> 'Each wife enjoys, by reason of her interest, a present right of occupation as well as a right to a share in the proceeds of sale, if and when the house is sold'.

This approach is not without critics and the reader is recommended to consider the full discussion of the problem which can be found in *Real Property and Real People* (1981) by K J Gray and P D Symes at pages 256–60. The authors conclude at page 259:

> 'It is disappointing that the House of Lords did not address itself to a more fundamental reconsideration of an appropriate regime for co-ownership of land. This is especially so at a time when the orthodox trust for sale analysis, introduced in such cavalier fashion in *Bull* v *Bull*, now emerges not simply as an overworked device, but as an approach in the family home context which has created more problems than it has solved. Nevertheless, even though it may be regretted that the House of Lords did not inquire more searchingly into the precise source of the trust for sale in *Bull* v *Bull*, ... *Boland* at last provides clear House of Lords authority for the proposition that a trust for sale arises (by implication) whenever a legal estate in land is vested in one owner following a joint purchase using the moneys of more than one contributor.'

9.6 Co-ownership and settlements

Strict settlement

Where two or more persons become beneficially entitled in possession to land which is held under a strict settlement, the consequence depends upon whether their interest is as joint tenants or tenants in common.

Joint tenants

Where the beneficiaries are entitled as joint tenants, the land remains settled land and a trust for sale is not imposed. The joint tenants (provided that they are all of full age) together constitute the tenant for life and can call for the legal estate to be vested in them as joint tenants (s19(2) SLA 1925).

Where land is limited to A and B for life, C for life, etc, A and B hold the legal estate as joint tenants and as tenant for life on trust for themselves and the remaining beneficiaries.

Tenants in common

Where the beneficiaries are entitled in possession as tenants in common, the land cannot become or remain settled land. By s36 SLA 1925 the strict settlement is converted to a trust for sale which will continue until the death of the last tenant in common. The trustees for sale are the trustees of the settlement. They hold the legal estate on the statutory trusts set out in s36(6), which are identical to those in s35 LPA 1925.

Trust for sale

Again reference should be made to s36(4) SLA 1925 which provides that a tenancy in common shall not be capable of creation except under a trust instrument or under s34(2) LPA 1925, and shall then take effect under a trust for sale.

End of the settlement

Land ceases to be settled land when the only subsisting limitation is an absolute interest vested in a person or persons of full age, even if that interest must be held behind a trust, for example:

To A for life, then to B and C jointly.
To A for life, then to B and C in equal shares.

In either case, the settlement comes to an end on A's death, and the land vests in A's ordinary personal representatives. In the case of a joint tenancy, the equitable joint tenants are empowered by s7(5) SLA 1925 to require A's ordinary PRs to convey the legal estate to them. B and C will then hold the legal estate as joint trustees for sale. In the case of a tenancy in common, it was held (somewhat paradoxically) in *Re Cugny's Will Trusts* [1931] 1 Ch 305 that s36 SLA 1925 still applied, so the trustees of the settlement (which came to an end on A's death) can require A's ordinary PRs to convey the legal estate to them as trustees for sale on trust for B and C as equitable tenants in common.

9.7 Minors and co-ownership

Section 19 LPA 1925 and the SLA 1925 set out the following principles governing co-ownership by minors:

1. A conveyance to two or more persons as joint tenants, all of whom are minors, takes effect as a settlement under the SLA 1925, the legal estate being held by a statutory owner (s19(1) LPA 1925).
2. A conveyance to two or more persons as tenants in common, all of whom are infants, takes effect as a trust for sale (s1(1)(ii)(d) and s36 SLA 1925).
3. A conveyance to two or more persons, some of whom are infants, takes effect as a trust for sale. The trustee(s) for sale is(are) the co-owner(s) of full age. All the co-owners irrespective of their age hold the equitable estate as tenants in common or joint tenants according to the terms of the conveyance.

9.8 House deposit and co-ownership

The effect of a parent paying the deposit on a first matrimonial home as a wedding present has been considered by the courts. In *McHardy & Sons* v *Warren* (1994) The Times 8 April the husband held the legal title to the matrimonial home (which was unregistered) in his sole name. The wife's claim to a beneficial interest arose because her father-in-law had paid the deposit (£650) on the first matrimonial home as a wedding present to his son and daughter-in-law (the defendants). The court held that where a parent so acts then the bride and groom are to have equal interests in the home and not an interest by reference to the percentage which the deposit bore to the full price. Further, it was irrelevant that the property was in the husband's name alone. Accordingly, the home was held by the husband on an implied trust for sale for himself and his wife in equal shares.

This is a somewhat doubtful decision. In particular, why should half of a deposit give the spouse legal title to half the beneficial interest without consideration as to who paid the rest of the purchase price subsequently?

9.9 Ending of co-ownership

Joint tenancy and tenancy in common both come to an end

First, if the land is divided physically between the co-owners or the land sold and the proceeds divided: this is known as partition. See also s28(3) LPA 1925.

Secondly, if the entirety of the land becomes vested in one person: this is known as union. By the Law of Property (Joint Tenants) Act 1964 a purchaser from a sole surviving joint tenant is bound to assume that the survivor is solely and beneficially entitled if he conveys 'as beneficial owner' unless a memorandum of severance is endorsed on the conveyance which created the joint tenancy.

Thirdly, the problem of making title by the surviving joint tenant has created difficulties since 1925. By the Law of Property (Amendment) Act 1926 it was provided that the surviving joint tenant who is solely and beneficially entitled to the land could deal with the legal estate as if it were not held on trust for sale. This did not satisfy conveyancers because the deceased tenant – without the knowledge of the survivor – could have severed his interest. To overcome this rule many purchasers insisted that a second trustee be appointed in order to make title.

This is no longer necessary because s1(1) Law of Property (Joint Tenants) Act 1964 provides that the survivor of joint tenants shall, in favour of the purchaser, be deemed to be solely and beneficially interested if he conveys as beneficial owner.

This provision is subject to two major exceptions:

1. where a memorandum of severance has been endorsed on the conveyance by which the legal estate was vested in the joint tenants;
2. where the title to the land is registered (s3 1964 Act). This recognises the paramount position of the land register and the fact that the purchaser can rely upon the entries in the register. The purchaser will then only be affected by any severance of the joint equitable interest which has been entered on the register.

A joint tenancy may be severed and converted into a tenancy in common

It is possible to sever the equitable joint tenancy without disturbing the joint tenancy of the legal estate. Severance, to be effective, must be done during the joint tenant's lifetime. There are a variety of ways in which an equitable joint tenancy can be severed. In the ensuing paragraphs the following are considered:

1. alienation;
2. acquisition of another estate in land;
3. homicide;
4. notice in writing;
5. bankruptcy;
6. course of dealing.

It is important to emphasise that severance can only effect the equitable interest, not the legal estate. First, severance can be effected by a joint tenant alienating his interest *inter vivos.* The assignee becomes a tenant in common, although the other co-owners remain joint tenants as between themselves. A partial alienation, such as a mortgage, is sufficient to sever a joint tenancy, but a mere incumbrance is not.

Secondly, severance can be effected by a joint tenant acquiring another estate in the land. This destroys the unity of interest.

Thirdly, severance can be effected by homicide. The rule that no-one may benefit from his crime means that one joint tenant who kills another cannot benefit from that other's death by the operation of the principle of survivorship.

Fourthly, by virtue of s36(2) LPA 1925 an equitable joint tenancy can be severed by a joint tenant giving written notice to the other joint tenants. Any form of written notice will suffice provided it is given to all the other joint tenants and it shows a sufficient wish to effect an immediate severance. In *Re 88 Berkley Road London NW9* [1971] Ch 648 it was held that a notice had been properly served if it was sent by recorded delivery even if it was not received by the addressee. An unequivocal intention is sufficient. This was satisfied in *Re Draper's Conveyance* [1969] 1 Ch 486 where a wife who was a joint tenant of the matrimonial home asked the court (by way of issuing a summons) for an order granting her share in the property as soon as possible. However, in *Harris* v *Goddard* [1983] 1 WLR 1203 a mere prayer in a divorce petition under s24 Matrimonial Causes Act 1973 relating to the former matrimonial home was held not to be a notice of a desire to sever the joint tenancy under s36(2) LPA 1925. This was because in contrast to *Re Draper's Conveyance* (above) there was held to be no sufficient immediate intention to receive a specific share. Rather it was simply a request for the future.

Fifthly, an equitable joint tenancy can be severed by an act of bankruptcy by one joint tenant. Such severance occurs on the date of the act of bankruptcy and not on the later date of adjudication of bankruptcy. This was established in *Re Dennis (A Bankrupt)* [1995] 3 All ER 171. There D and his wife owned two properties as beneficial joint tenants. In September 1982, D committed an act of bankruptcy (he failed to comply with a bankruptcy notice) and so a bankruptcy petition was presented against him. D's wife died in February 1983, leaving her estate to her two children in her will. In May 1983 a receiving order was made against D, and in November 1983 he was adjudicated bankrupt. The question arose whether the vesting of D's property in the trustee, which severed the joint tenancies, occurred at the date of the act of bankruptcy by retrospective effect of the adjudication, or at the date of adjudication of bankruptcy. If the former, the joint tenancies were severed before the wife's death and her share as a tenant-in-common would devolve under her will. If the latter, the joint tenancies were not severed before the wife's death and the wife's share would pass on her death to D as survivor, with the result that on adjudication the whole interest in the properties vested in the trustee and was available to D's creditors. The Court of Appeal held that where a joint tenant of property was adjudged bankrupt under the Bankruptcy Act 1914, the title of the trustee in bankruptcy to that property related back to the first act of bankruptcy even though the debtor was not adjudged bankrupt until some later date. Consequently, in this case the joint tenancies had been severed on D's act of bankruptcy in September 1982 (ie before the wife's death) and therefore the wife's share devolved under her will. Accordingly, the court declared that a one-half share in the properties formed part of the wife's estate. (See also *Re Palmer (Deceased) (A Debtor)* [1994] 3 All ER 835.) For further details of these cases see Chapter 18, section 18.1.

Finally, severance can be effected by a course of dealing. In *Burgess* v *Rawnsley* [1975] Ch 429 a widow, R, met a widower, H. They became good friends and bought a house together in which to live. Each paid half of the purchase price and held both the legal title and equitable interest as joint tenants. Subsequently, the relationship broke down and the elderly couple reached a verbal agreement whereby H was to buy R out. However, before this was reduced to writing H died. The Court of Appeal unanimously held that severance had occurred. Although the contract to sell was unenforceable because of the lack of written evidence required by s40 LPA 1925, there was a course of dealing which was sufficient to effect a severance. Lord Denning MR considered how far a course of dealing might provide the necessary evidence of severance and stated:

> 'The thing to remember today is that equity leans against joint tenants and favours tenancies in common ... it is sufficient if there is a course of dealing in which one party makes clear to the other that he desires that their shares should no longer be held jointly but in common. Similarly it is sufficient if both parties enter on a course of dealing which evinces an intention by both of them that their shares shall henceforth be held in common and not jointly.'

The mutual agreement need not be specifically enforceable. The significance of the agreement is not that it binds the parties, but that it serves as an indication of a common intention to sever. Since *Burgess* v *Rawnsley* (above) was decided, s40 LPA 1925 has been repealed by s2 Law of Property (Miscellaneous Provisions) Act 1989 (contracts for the sale or disposition of an interest in land have to be 'made in writing': see section 10.4.) It is not clear what impact this will have on *Burgess* v *Rawnsley* (1975) and it is possible that the decision will be unaffected by the legislative change. In *Gore and Snell* v *Carpenter* (1990) 61 P & CR 456 it was held that mere negotiations were not sufficient for severance where there was no express agreement to sever and the negotiations did not amount to a sufficient course of dealing for severance.

The burden of proof is on the person seeking to establish a severance. A memorandum of severance should, for the protection of the severed interest, be endorsed upon the conveyance which created the joint tenancy.

9.10 Rights between co-owners

Where a trust for sale arises by statute or by implication, the beneficiaries are entitled to possession of the land pending sale: see *Bull* v *Bull* [1955] 1 QB 234.

In *Jones* v *Jones* [1977] 1 WLR 438 it was held that one tenant in common who was not in occupation was not entitled to rent from another tenant in common, even though that other occupies the whole. But see *Dennis* v *McDonald* [1982] Fam 63 which shows that payments between the parties may be ordered. Here an occupation rent was ordered to be paid.

In a landlord and tenant context, notice to determine a joint periodic tenancy served on the landlord by one of two joint periodic tenants will determine the tenancy even if the other joint tenant does not concur: *Hammersmith and Fulham London Borough Council* v *Monk* [1991] 3 WLR 1144 HL.

9.11 Other forms of co-ownership

Coparcenary

When a person died intestate before 1926 his realty descended to his heir, who could in certain circumstances be more than one person; for example, where the deceased had no sons but two or more daughters, the daughters were the heir. These persons held the realty as coparceners. Coparcenary resembled tenancy in common in that there was no right of survivorship, but for some purposes it was treated as a joint tenancy. Since s45 AEA 1925 coparcenary can now arise only in the case of entailed interests and must necessarily be equitable.

Tenancy by entireties

Before the Married Women's Property Act 1882, if land was granted to a husband and wife in such circumstances that they would ordinarily take as joint tenants they took as tenants by entireties and there was no right of severance. The tenants were one person (the husband!). The MWPA 1882 prevented the creation of such tenancies after 1882 and made it possible for a woman to own her own property. However, under the rule in *Re Jupp* (1888) 39 Ch D 148, if land was granted to H and W and X, H and W were still regarded as only one person in relation to X, who therefore took half, and H and W took the other half. This rule was abolished by s37 LPA 1925, which provides that:

> 'A husband and wife shall for all purposes of acquisition of any interest in property ... be treated as two persons.'

9.12 Party walls

Boundary walls may be in sole ownership of one owner or in some form of co-ownership between the respective neighbours. In *Watson* v *Gray* (1880) 14 Ch D 192, Fry J considered four possible alternatives:

1. The adjoining owners own the wall as tenants in common.

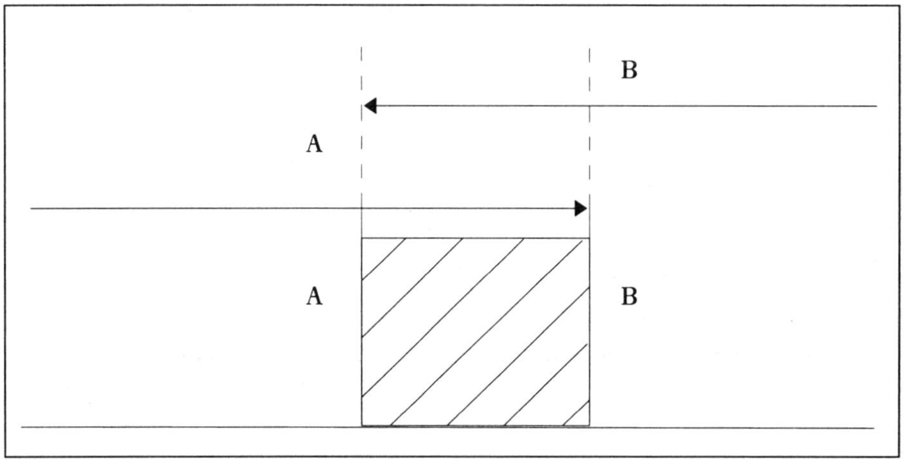

Before 1926 such adjoining owners were deemed to be tenants in common of the party wall itself.

2. Each adjoining owner might own to the mid-point of the wall. The wall would thus be divided vertically into two with half the thickness belonging to each adjoining owner.

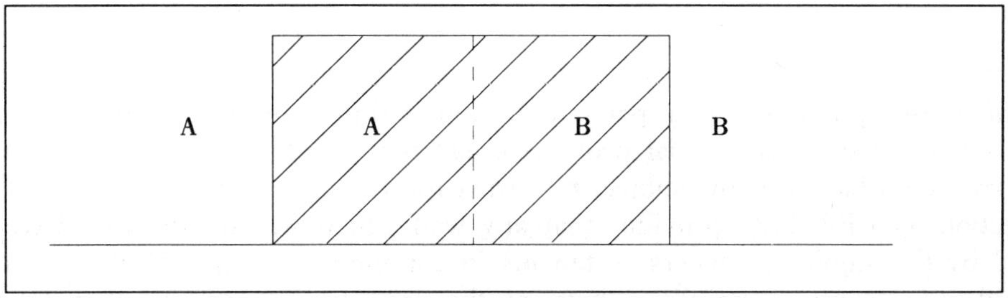

3. Each neighbour might own half as in (2) above but each half-width enjoys a cross-easement of support against the other.

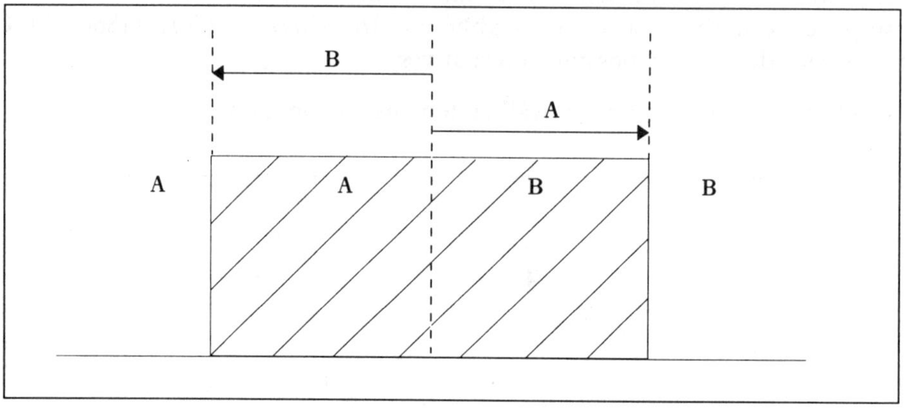

See below for the effect of s38 LPA 1925.

4. The wall is owned entirely by the owner of one property, subject to an easement of support in favour of the adjoining owner to have it maintained as a dividing wall.

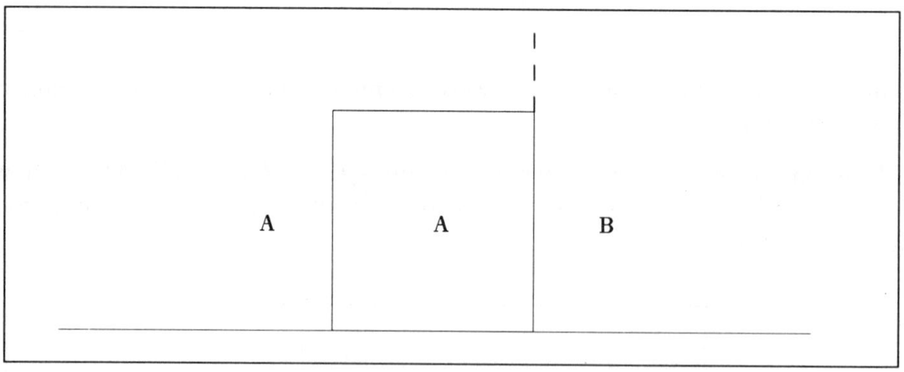

The presumption was that party walls fell within category (1) above, but this could be rebutted. If no special provisions had been made, then party walls in this category would have become subject to a trust for sale after 1925.

Section 38 LPA 1925 provides that any wall which would otherwise have been owned by the adjoining owners as tenants in common (category (1) above) shall be deemed to be severed vertically as between the respective owners and that the owner of each part shall have such rights of support and uses over the other part as he would have enjoyed as a tenant in common (category (3) above). See also Schedule 1 Part V paragraph 1 LPA 1925. Thus the effect of s38 is that all party walls formerly in category (1) are converted into category (3).

9.13 Worked examples

Q Albert, Boris, Charles and David are all married men with families, and in 1992 they buy a seaside cottage for holidays, each putting up a quarter of the price. It is conveyed to all four of them jointly. In 1994 Charles is killed in a car crash, and in 1995 Albert sells his share to Edward. David has become unemployed and wants the cottage sold in order to get some money; he is unable to sell his share. Can David force a sale, and if so who can sell and what share in the proceeds will David get?

A In answering this kind of question the student is advised to use the following type of diagram to help him sort out the legal and equitable situation.

Legal		*Equitable*	
1992	A, B, C, D as trustees for sale	A, B, C, D joint tenants – price in equal shares	
1994	A, B, D	A, B, D	
1995	A, B, D	E tenant in common of one-third	B, D joint tenants of two-thirds

Or this form of diagram may be used in the alternative:

1992	A B C D	– Joint tenants	– Law
	A B C D	– Joint tenants	– Equity
1994	A B D	– Joint tenants	– Law
	A B D	– Joint tenants	– Equity
1995	A B D	– Joint tenants	– Law

BD joint tenants of two-thirds	E tenant in common of one-third

This shows that the effect of the conveyance was to vest the legal estate in the four purchasers (assuming them all to be of full age) as trustees for sale for themselves as beneficial joint tenants. It is arguable that this property is a form of 'partnership' property, so they would take as tenants in common, but probably the presumption only applies when there is a legal partnership.

On Charles' death in 1994 the jus accrescendi operates on both sides of the line, leaving Albert, Boris and David holding on trust for sale for themselves as beneficial joint tenants.

The effect of the sale by Albert of his share is to sever his equitable interest. Edward therefore takes a one-third share as tenant in common, Boris and David remaining joint tenants of the remaining two-thirds. Albert's act has no effect on the legal estate unless he formally retires as trustee.

The trustees have a duty to sell with a statutory power to postpone sale, and unless they all agree on postponement the property should be sold: *Re Mayo* (1943). Therefore, prima facie, David can compel his co-trustees to sell the legal estate. However, if they will not do so willingly he will have to apply to the court for an order for sale under s30 LPA 1925, and the court may refuse to grant such an order if to do so would be a breach of contract or would defeat a continuing purpose of the trust. See *Jones* v *Challenger* (1961); *Re Buchanan-Wollaston's Conveyance* (1939). The purpose for which the cottage was purchased was to provide a holiday home, which purpose is continuing, and so David may not get an order for sale.

If the land is sold it must be conveyed by the trustees. The act of sale puts an end to Boris and David's joint tenancy, and so the proceeds will be split equally, one-third to each of David, Boris and Edward.

Q Jack and Jill, who were living together but did not intend to get married, decided to buy a house. Jill contributed half the deposit, but because the building society would not grant a mortgage to an unmarried couple, the conveyance and the mortgage were in Jack's name only. They lived together in the house, Jill paying half of all the outgoings. They have now ceased to be lovers; Jack is seeing another woman and has told Jill she must leave the house by the end of the month, as he has found a purchaser for the house and is emigrating to Australia. Advise Jill.

A If Jill made the payments with the intention, known to Jack, that she should have an interest in the property, then equity imposes a constructive trust upon Jack. It would appear that Jill should have little difficulty in persuading a court that this was her intention. Jack therefore holds the legal estate on trust for sale for himself and Jill. Prima facie as they contributed equally they will be joint tenants unless there is evidence that they intended to have separate shares. Even if they took as joint tenants it is arguable that Jack's course of conduct is sufficient to sever the joint tenancy. See *Burgess* v *Rawnsley* (1975). As co-owners, whether joint tenants or tenants in common, they have an equal right to possession (*Bull* v *Bull* (1955)), and Jill cannot be made to leave by Jack.

Jill must also seek to protect her position with regard to the proposed sale of the property. She may not be able to prevent the sale, as the purpose for which the house was bought, to provide a home for them both, appears to have come to an end, and so the principle in *Re Buchanan-Wollaston's Conveyance* (1939) would not apply. She must, however, ensure that her beneficial interest comes to the notice of the purchaser so that he can insist on another trustee being appointed to receive the purchase money, which will ensure that she gets her half share. If the land is unregistered, then it seems from the decision in *Caunce* v *Caunce* (1969) that her interest is not registrable as a land charge, the purchaser will not be bound by it unless he has notice. It is possible that her presence on the premises might be constructive notice, but it is much safer to ensure that he has actual notice. She cannot register a Class F charge as this is confined to spouses.

If the land is registered she can protect her interest as a minor interest by the entry of a caution on the register. If she has not done so, then, after the decision of the House of Lords in *Williams & Glyn's Bank* v *Boland* (1981), her interest as an equitable tenant in common arising under a resulting trust is capable of being an overriding interest. Provided that Jill is in actual occupation when Jack sells the house, the purchaser will take the land subject to Jill's equitable half share. Alternatively, the purchaser, if he inspects the property, will discover Jill's occupation and should make inquiries as to whether she has any interest. When her interest was discovered, the sale can still go ahead if Jack consents to the appointment of another trustee for sale so that the overreaching provisions of s2 LPA can come into operation.

10

Leases and Tenancies – Including Covenants Relating to the Leasehold

10.1 Introduction

Land held under a lease or tenancy is held for a legal estate, 'a term of years absolute' as defined in ss1(1)(b) and 205(1)(xxvii) LPA 1925. The complete definition in s205(1)(xxvii) LPA 1925 should be read and understood:

' "Term of years absolute" means a term of years (taking effect either in possession or in reversion whether or not at a rent) with or without impeachment for waste, subject or not to another legal estate, and either certain or liable to determination by notice, re-entry, operation of law or by a provision for cesser on redemption, or in any other event (other than the dropping of a life, or the determination of a determinable life interest), but does not include any term of years determinable with life or lives or with the cesser of a determinable life interest, nor, if created after the commencement of this Act, a term of years which is not expressed to take effect in possession within twenty-one years after the creation thereof where required by this Act to take effect within that period; [see s149(3) LPA 1925] and in this definition the expression "term of years" includes a term for less than a year, or for a year or years and a fraction of a year or from year to year.'

Section 1(5) LPA 1925 provides:

'A legal estate may subsist concurrently with or subject to any other legal estate in the same land.'

Hence the same land may be held both as a legal freehold estate and as a legal leasehold estate at the same time, and there may be two or more leasehold estates subsisting in the land at the same time.

Both landlords and tenants have legal estates in possession, because 'possession' is defined by s205(1)(xix) LPA 1925 as including 'receipt of rents and profits or the right to receive the same, if any'.

The effect of the grant of a leasehold estate is that the fee simple owner grants to the leaseholder, for a fixed or ascertainable length of time, the right to deal with the land as though he owned it (subject to certain limitations). Until and unless the lease ends, the fee simple owner is no longer entitled to physical possession of the land, but only to the 'reversion' on the lease, which amounts to legal possession of the land.

L's fee simple absolute in possession is illustrated below:

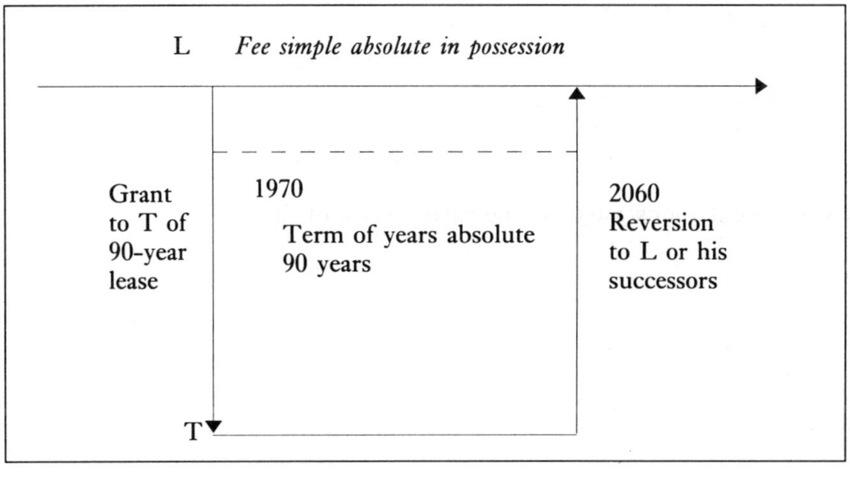

10.2 Definitions

Lease: a contract either in writing or by deed granting a leasehold estate in land.
Tenancy: the interest held under a lease. A tenancy can be granted orally, by a tenancy agreement.
Demise: the grant of a tenancy.
Covenant: a promise expressly made in a lease, or implied into a lease or tenancy agreement by statute or at common law.
Rent: the consideration given by a tenant to his landlord in return for the grant of a tenancy. Rent is paid throughout the term. It usually takes the form of money, but need not.
Fine or premium: a lump sum paid by a tenant at the beginning of the term. If a fine is paid, usually it is only very low, or no rent is payable for the remainder of the term.
Determination: the coming to an end of a tenancy.
Reversion: the interest in the land held by a landlord during the subsistence of a lease.

A number of words are used interchangeably for 'landlord' and 'tenant'.

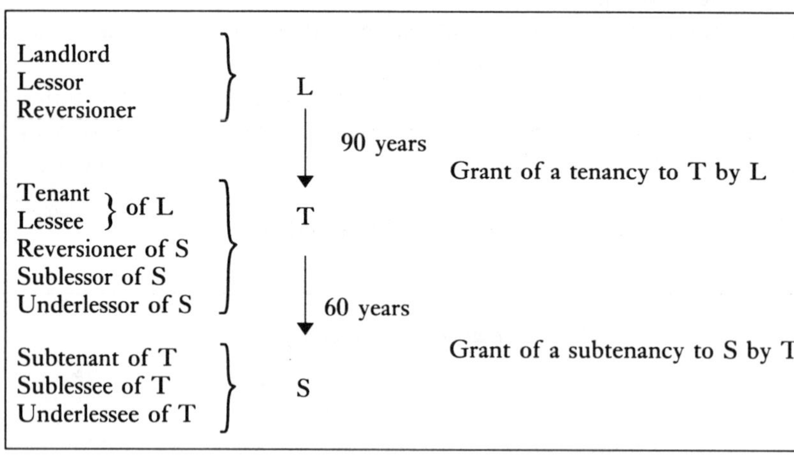

This may also be demonstrated by the earlier style of diagram:

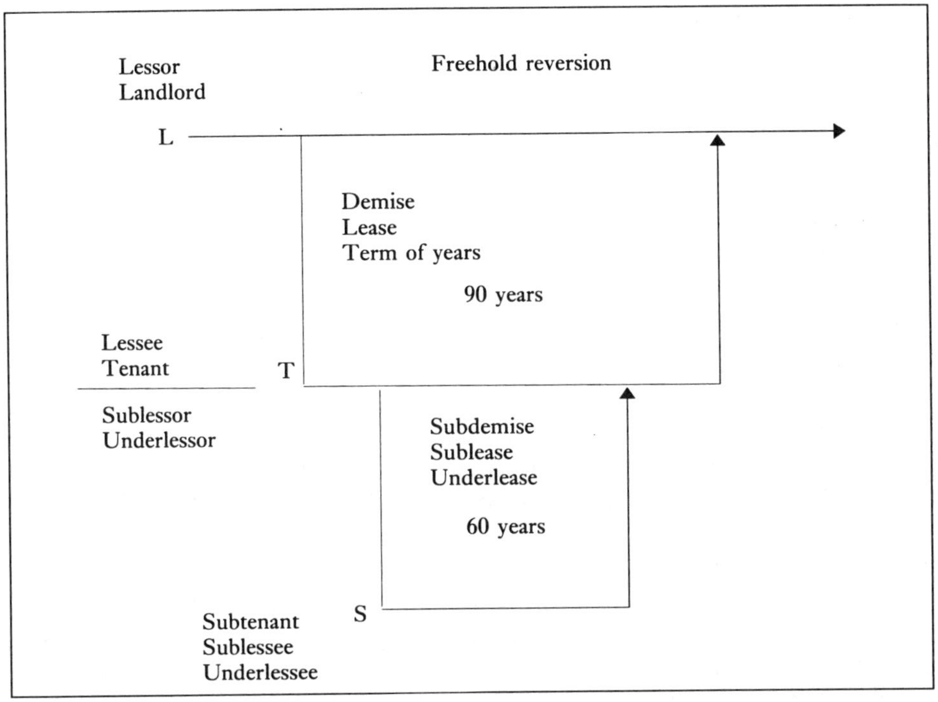

10.3 Assignments and subtenancies

Assignment

While the lease continues, both a landlord and a tenant can assign their interest in the land. The landlord can assign his reversion and the tenant his lease.

Assignment of the reversion

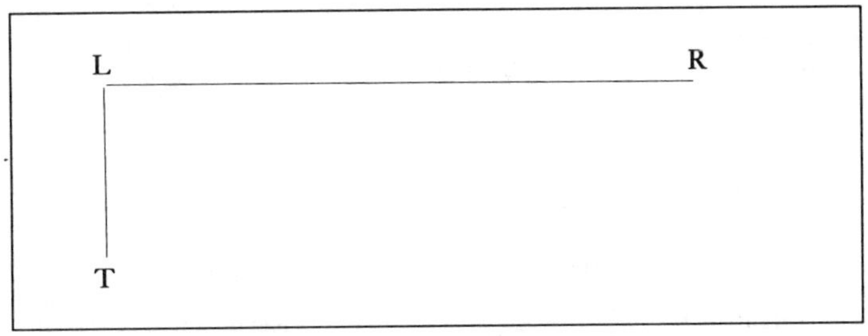

The landlord assigns his reversion by selling his fee simple estate to R during the term of the lease. R steps into L's shoes and becomes T's landlord. L no longer has any rights in the land, or any rights under the lease.

Assignment of the lease

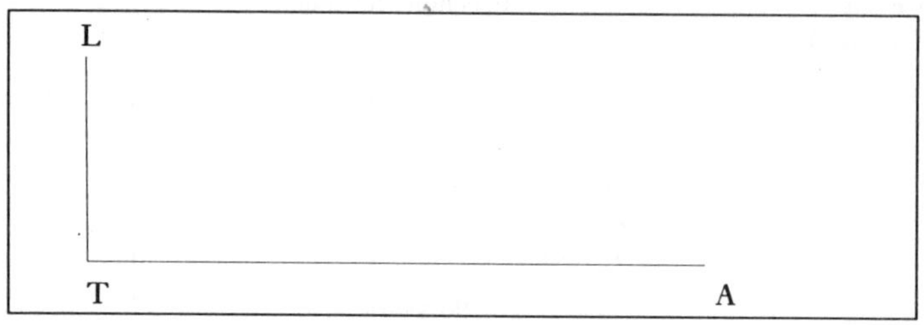

An assignment of a lease is the grant by the tenant to the assignee of the whole interest under the lease. The assignee (A) steps into T's shoes, and the original tenant no longer has any rights to possession of the land comprised in the lease.

If the original tenant, T, has granted any subtenancies prior to the assignment, then so far as the subtenants are concerned T's assignment is an assignment of his reversion on their subtenancies, and the assignee, A, becomes their landlord.

Subtenancy

Care must be taken to distinguish the effect of an assignment of the residue of the lease from the creation of a subtenancy. A subtenancy is the grant by the tenant of less than his whole interest under the lease. This can be achieved by either a grant to the subtenant of only part of the land comprised in the tenancy, or a grant of all the land to the subtenant for a term shorter than that held by the tenant.

The subtenant holds his land of the tenant. So far as the subtenant is concerned, the tenant is his landlord, and the tenant holds the reversion on the subtenant's interest; see diagram below:

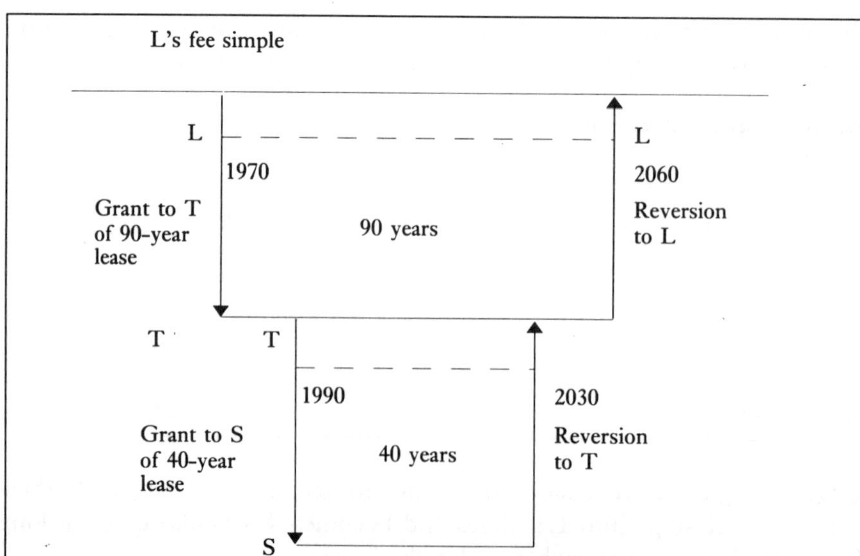

Note that in all cases where leases or subleases are created there must always be a reversion to the landlord.

If the tenant's lease comes to an end prematurely, then all subtenancies also come to an end at the same time. Hence if T's lease is determined by forfeiture (see section 10.10 below) in 2000, S's tenancy also determines and L holds an unincumbered fee simple.

Once the tenant's lease ends, he becomes a trespasser, as do any subtenants.

The grant to a subtenant of a term of equal length to or greater length than that held by a tenant takes effect as a legal assignment, even in the absence of a deed. The supposed subtenant steps into the tenant's shoes and holds the land for the same term and on the same conditions as the tenant.

10.4 The essentials of a lease

In order to grant a valid legal estate, a lease must comply with three requirements: it must be in the correct form; it must be certain in duration; and the tenant must have exclusive possession. These will be dealt with in turn.

The formal requirements must be met

Section 52(1) LPA 1925 provides:

> 'All conveyances of land or any interest therein are void for the purposes of conveying or creating a legal estate unless made by deed.'

Hence legal leases must be made by deed. This is the general rule to which one exception exists. Section 54(2) LPA 1925 provides the exception:

> 'Nothing in the foregoing provisions ... shall affect the creation by parol of leases taking effect in possession for a term not exceeding three years ... at the best rent which can be reasonably obtained without taking a fine.'

Thus a valid legal lease may be made orally or in writing provided that:

1. It is for a term not exceeding three years, whether or not the lessee has power to extend the term; and
2. It takes effect in possession; and
3. It is at the best rent reasonably obtainable without taking a fine.

All periodic tenancies (see section 10.6 below) and terms certain of three years or less fall within this exception. It should be noted that s54(2) does include leases for precisely three years.

A lease for more than three years not made by deed is void at law, but can take effect at equity as a specifically enforceable contract for a lease provided that:

1. It was granted for value; and
2. It was made in writing to satisfy s2(1) Law of Property (Miscellaneous Provisions) Act 1989.

This contract must incorporate all the agreed terms and, instead of being signed by the potential defendant alone, must now be signed by or on behalf of each party to the contract: s2(3).

The effect is to repeal s40 LPA 1925 in total. No longer can a contract merely be evidenced in writing, it must be *made in writing*. Section 40(2) LPA 1925 is also repealed, and this sees the end of the doctrine of part performance so far as it relates to land law. It has been suggested that this void created by the end of the application of part performance may well be filled by the rules of estoppel. The Law Commission had suggested that estoppel could 'achieve very similar results where appropriate to those of part performance'.

The exceptions to s2 LP(MP)A 1989 are set out in s2(5) as:

1. a contract to grant a lease not exceeding three years under s54(2) LPA 1925;
2. a contract made at public auction;
3. a contract regulated under the Financial Services Act 1986;
4. contracts creating resulting, implied or constructive trusts.

Section 2 LP(MP)A 1989 came into force on 27 September 1989 and does not relate to contracts made before that date. It provides:

> '2(1) A contract for the sale or other disposition of an interest in land can only be made in writing and only by incorporating all the terms which the parties have expressly agreed in one document or, where contracts are exchanged, in each.
> (2) The terms may be incorporated in a document either by being set out in it or by reference to some other document.
> (3) The document incorporating the terms or, where contracts are exchanged, one of the documents incorporating them (but not necessarily the same one) must be signed by or on behalf of each party to the contract.
> (4) Where a contract for the sale or other disposition of an interest in land satisfies the conditions of this section by reason only of the rectification of one or more documents in pursuance of an order of a court, the contract shall come into being, or be deemed to have come into being, at such time as may be specified in the order.
> (5) This section does not apply in relation to:
> a) a contract to grant such a lease as is mentioned in s54(2) of the Law of Property Act 1925 (short leases);
> b) a contract made in the course of a public auction; or
> c) a contract regulated under the Financial Services Act 1986;
> and nothing in this section affects the creation or operation of resulting, implied or constructive trusts.
> (6) In this section:
> "disposition" has the same meaning as in the Law of Property Act 1925;
> "interest in land" means any estate, interest or charge in or over land or in or over the proceeds of sale of land.
> (7) Nothing in this section shall apply in relation to contracts made before this section comes into force.
> (8) Section 40 of the Law of Property Act 1925 (which is superseded by this section) shall cease to have effect.'

One of the points of controversy surrounding s2 LP(MP)A 1989 is whether an exchange of correspondence regarding an oral agreement concerning land can meet the requirements of s2. In *Hooper* v *Sherman* [1994] NPC 153 the Court of Appeal, in a case not concerning leases, held (by a majority) that an exchange of letters could create an enforceable contract within s2. In *Commission for the New Towns* v *Cooper (GB) Ltd* [1995] 2 All ER 929 a different Court of Appeal reached a contrary decision. There the court held that the closing stages of correspondence by which an agreement was reached, ie the final offer or counter-offer and an unqualified acceptance of it, could not also constitute the 'exchange of contracts' which was required by s2 before a contract could be made. An additional exchange of documents setting out or incorporating all 'the terms which the parties have agreed' must take place or the parties must sign a simple document which sets them out. An obvious consequence of these conflicting decisions is uncertainty for conveyancing practitioners. A definitive decision on the point from the House of Lords would be welcome. See Chapter 18, section 18.2, for further details of these cases.

All legal leases must be assigned by deed, even if created orally: *Julian* v *Crago* (1991) The Times 4 December.

The lease may contain an option to purchase the reversion or an option to renew the lease: *Taylor Fashions Ltd* v *Liverpool Victoria Trustees Co Ltd* [1981] 1 All ER 897.

An incidental change effected by s1 LP(MP)A 1989 is that deeds will no longer be 'signed, sealed and delivered'. Section 1(3) removes the need for sealing the deed, which will now be valid if it is merely signed and delivered.

Differences between legal and equitable leases

A specifically enforceable lease is regarded as a valid equitable lease under the rule in *Walsh* v *Lonsdale* (1882) 21 Ch D 9 on the principle that 'equity regards as done, that which ought to be done'. As a consequence examiners frequently ask the candidates to consider whether an equitable lease is as good as a lease. It is true that an equitable lease is as good as a legal lease for many purposes except that an equitable lease:

1. depends for its validity on the discretionary remedy of specific performance, which may not be available – for example, if the tenant is in breach of a covenant. See *Sudbrook Trading Estate Ltd* v *Eggleton* [1982] 3 WLR 315;
2. does not carry with it easements and other rights under s62 LPA 1925 (see Chapter 12) because it is not a conveyance;
3. is void against a subsequent purchaser of the land if:
   a) the land is unregistered and the agreement is not registered as an estate contract (Class C(iv) land charge). See *Hollington Bros Ltd* v *Rhodes* [1951] 2 All ER 578;
   b) the land is registered and the lessee is not in actual occupation or has not protected his interest by an entry on the register.

In addition, there is no privity of estate (see section 10.11) between the landlord and an assignee of the tenant under an equitable lease.

The commencement date and duration of the term must be certain

In order to comply with the definition of term of years absolute in s205(1)(xxvii) LPA 1925 both the commencement date and the duration of the term must be certain or capable of being ascertained at the outset of the term. A lease which does not comply with this requirement is void, and leases which are therefore void under this rule are:

1. leases for life: see s149(6) LPA 1925, section 10.6 (below) and *Binions* v *Evans* [1972] Ch 359;
2. leases for perpetuity: see section 10.6;
3. leases for an uncertain period (eg 'a lease for the duration of the war'): see *Lace* v *Chantler* [1944] KB 368.

The decision in *Lace* v *Chantler* was reviewed and applied by the House of Lords in *Prudential Assurance Co Ltd* v *London Residuary Body* [1992] 3 WLR 279. A brief review of the facts will help to see how this question of uncertainty can arise.

In 1930 land fronting a highway was sold to the then London County Council for future road widening. It was leased back to the plaintiffs' predecessors in title at a yearly rent of £30.00. The agreement stated that

> 'the tenancy shall continue until ... the land is required by the Council for the purposes of ... [road widening]'.

Sixty years later the highway had still not been widened, and the reversion was now in the London Residuary Body (LRB) which was not a highway authority. The LRB served a six months' notice to quit purporting to end the tenancy. The current rental value of the land was estimated to be over £10,000 per annum. The plaintiffs sought a declaration that the notice to quit was null and void because the tenancy could only be determined if the land was required for road widening purposes.

The House of Lords reversed the decision of the Court of Appeal in *Lace* v *Chantler* and held that all leases and tenancy agreements must be certain in duration. Here the lease was for an uncertain period and was void. The land was held on a yearly tenancy created by the tenants' possession plus the payment of a yearly rent, and only those terms in the agreement which were consistent with a yearly tenancy would apply. The term relating to road widening was inconsistent with the ability of either party to determine a yearly tenancy on six months' notice, and as a result the tenancy had been lawfully determined.

Lord Templeman (at p283) gave a most useful description of how such a yearly tenancy can come into existence:

> 'When the agreement in the present case was made, it failed to grant an estate in land. The tenant however entered into possession and paid the yearly rent of £30 reserved by the agreement. The tenant entering under a void lease became by virtue of possession and the payment of a yearly rent, a yearly tenant holding on the terms of the agreement so far as those terms were consistent with the yearly tenancy.
>
> A yearly tenancy is determinable by the landlord or the tenant at the end of the first or any subsequent year of the tenancy by six months' notice ...'

He went on to consider how a periodic tenancy of this nature can be said to be certain, and continued (at p285):

> 'A tenancy from year to year is saved from being uncertain because each party has power by notice to determine at the end of any year. The term continues until determined as if both parties made a new agreement at the end of each year for a new term for the ensuing year.'

This confirms that the existing rule that the lease must be certain or capable of being made certain at the outset of the term does apply to periodic tenancies.

Lord Templeman then said:

> 'A power for nobody to determine or for one party only to be able to determine is inconsistent with the concept of a term from year to year.'

This was a reference to the decision in *Re Midland Railway Co's Agreement* [1971] Ch 725 which had been applied by the Court of Appeal in *Ashburn Anstalt* v *Arnold* [1989] Ch 1. These cases had decided that the landlord could bar himself from determining the lease. As Lord Templeman observed:

> 'That case, if it was correct, would make it unnecessary for a lease to be of a certain duration.'

In the circumstances it was held that both of these cases were wrongly decided, and they were overruled. Lord Templeman concluded:

> 'A grant for an uncertain term does not create a lease. A grant for an uncertain term which takes the form of a yearly tenancy which cannot be determined by the landlord does not create a lease.'

The rule is now much clearer. If the lease is void but a periodic tenancy then arises from the payment and acceptance of rent, such periodic tenancy will not incorporate any provisions for determination set out in the void lease which are inconsistent with the periodic tenancy.

Exclusive possession

The tenant must be given exclusive possession, that is the right to exclude other persons including the landlord from the premises.

If exclusive possession is not given then the grantee is only a licensee; for example, a lodger or hotel guest has only a licence to use his room. The significance of exclusive possession as an essential feature in identifying a lease has been emphasised by the House of Lords in *Street* v *Mountford* [1985] 2 WLR 877. See section 10.5.

10.5 Distinction between a lease and a licence

If exclusive possession is not granted, the agreement can only be a licence. The grant of exclusive possession is a factor indicating that a lease has been granted, but it is not a decisive factor as it is possible for the grantee to be given exclusive possession and still not have a lease. Whether an agreement constitutes a lease or a licence depends on the true intention of the parties.

This intention must now be considered in the light of the decision by the House of Lords in *Street* v *Mountford* (above). Tests used by the courts in determining the intention to create a licence include:

1. The words used: the way the parties describe their agreement is evidence of their intention but not conclusive: see *Addiscombe Garden Estates* v *Crabbe* [1958] 1 QB 513.
2. Concurrent rights of possession: where the landlord reserves concurrent rights of possession there is only a licence: see *Shell-Mex and BP* v *Manchester Garages* [1971] 1 WLR 612. But the reservation of a right of access for specific purposes does not prevent the grant of a lease: see *Heath* v *Drown* [1973] AC 498.
3. Family arrangements: family and similar arrangements are usually regarded as licences, there being no intention to create a formal landlord-tenant relationship: see *Errington* v *Errington and Woods* [1952] 1 KB 290.
4. Employees: employees who are required to reside in premises as a necessary part of their duties (eg caretakers, house surgeons) are licensees.
5. Mistresses: where a mistress occupies premises provided by her lover, the courts have recently tended to regard her as a licensee: see *Tanner* v *Tanner* [1975] 1 WLR 1346; *Horrocks* v *Forray* [1976] 1 WLR 230; *Helby* v *Rafferty* [1978] 3 All ER 1016; *Carega Properties SA* v *Sharratt* [1979] 2 All ER 1084; *Dyson Holdings Ltd* v *Fox* [1976] QB 503.
6. Circumstances: the court will in all cases look at the circumstances in which the agreement was reached, and this is the ultimate test: see *Abbeyfield (Harpenden) Society Ltd* v *Woods* [1968] 1 WLR 374; *Marchant* v *Charters* [1977] 1 WLR 1181.

The Rent Act 1977 does not apply to licences, and so landlords attempt to avoid the protection of the Act by granting licences, just as the occupier seeks to create a lease in order to obtain security of tenure.

In *Somma* v *Hazelhurst* [1978] 1 WLR 1014 a landlord did succeed in establishing that he had granted a licence of a bed-sitting room. The important factors were that the written agreement reserved to the licensor the right to designate who should share the room with the licensee, and also made each licensee occupying the room separately responsible for paying a proportion of the rent. See also *Buchmann* v *May* [1978] 2 All ER 993.

The decision in *Somma* v *Hazelhurst* was expressly disapproved by the House of Lords in *Street* v *Mountford* (above). Lord Templeman concluded with these words:

> 'My Lords the only intention which is relevant is the intention demonstrated by the agreement to grant exclusive possession for a term at a rent. Sometimes it may be difficult to discover whether on the true construction of an agreement, exclusive possession is conferred. Sometimes it may appear from the surrounding circumstances that there was no

> intention to create legal relationships. Sometimes it may appear from the surrounding circumstances that the right to exclusive possession is referable to a legal relationship other than a tenancy. Legal relationships to which a grant of exclusive possession might be referable and which would or might negative the grant of an estate or interest in the land include occupancy under a contract for the sale of the land, occupancy pursuant to a contract of employment or occupancy referable to the holding of an office. But whereas in the present case the only circumstances are that residential accommodation is offered and accepted with exclusive possession for a term at a rent, the result is a tenancy ... Henceforth, the courts which deal with these problems will, save in exceptional circumstances, only be concerned to inquire whether as a result of an agreement relating to residential accommodation the occupier is a lodger or a tenant. In the present case I am satisfied that Mrs Mountford is a tenant.'

The House of Lords also disapproved the decisions in *Aldrington Garages Ltd* v *Fielder* (1978) 32 P & CR 461 and *Sturolson & Co* v *Weniz* (1984) 272 EG 326.

From this decision it is clear that if exclusive possession has been granted there is no longer any need to analyse further the detailed rights and obligations of the arrangement. Exclusive possession is now crucial in establishing the evidence of a tenancy and the absence of a licence. The only relevant general test in relation to residential accommodation is to establish whether the occupier is a lodger or a tenant. See also *Royal Philanthropic Society* v *County* (1985) 276 EG 1068; *Bretherton* v *Paton* (1986) 278 EG 615.

This question of exclusive possession may continue to create problems when applied in the strict tenant or lodger dichotomy. If an occupier does not have exclusive possession but the landlord provides no services, the courts may well have difficulty in applying Lord Templeman's test. This was seen in *Brooker Settled Estates Ltd* v *Ayers* (1987) The Times 13 February where the Court of Appeal held that the fact that the occupier was not a lodger, because the landlord did not provide attendance or services, did not necessarily mean there was exclusive possession giving rise to a tenancy. A tenant must satisfy the tests of exclusive possession for a term at a rent.

In the opening sentence of the above quotation from Lord Templeman in *Street* v *Mountford*, reference was made to 'a term at a rent'. The need for rent was challenged by Fox LJ in *Ashburn Anstalt* v *Arnold* [1988] 2 All ER 147 on the basis that the need for rent was negatived by the definition of 'term of years absolute' in s205(1)(xxvii) LPA 1925 as

> ' ... a term of years (taking effect either in possession or in reversion whether or nor at a rent)'.

Fox LJ went on to say:

> 'In the circumstances I conclude that the reservation of a rent is not necessary for the creation of a tenancy. That conclusion involves no departure from Lord Templeman's proposition ... We are saying only that we do not think that Lord Templeman was stating the quite different proposition that you cannot have a tenancy without a rent.'

It is submitted that this argument will not be affected by the overruling of *Ashburn*

Anstalt v *Arnold* by the House of Lords in *Prudential Assurance Co Ltd* v *London Residuary Body* [1992] 3 WLR 279.

The Court of Appeal has given further guidance on this question of rent and leases in *Skipton Building Society* v *Clayton* (1993) The Times 25 March. In this case the rent-free nature of the lease was brought within s149(6) LPA 1925 in order to 'take effect as a lease ... for a term of 90 years ...'.

The non-exclusive possession agreement

The problem whether exclusive possession has been granted was further considered in *Hadjiloucas* v *Crean* [1987] 3 All ER 1008, where the Court of Appeal concluded that the words of Lord Templeman may be too wide to cover some non-exclusive possession agreements, and do not necessarily cover certain examples of multiple occupation. Purchas LJ suggested that the circumstances must be considered against the factual background, the factual matrix, and as a result: each occupier is a licensee if he cannot exclude others; or there may be parallel leases where each tenant has a right to exclude all others; or the agreement may produce a joint tenancy with a collective form of exclusive possession in all the co-owners.

The joint tenancy approach

This solution was adopted by the Court of Appeal in *AG Securities* v *Vaughan* [1988] 2 All ER 173 where a majority of the Court held that, even though the separate agreements of each of four occupiers expressly excluded a right for that occupant to have exclusive possession of a four-bedroom flat, nevertheless the four occupants had between them a collective form of exclusive possession of the whole flat. This meant that together they had a lease as co-owners even though there was no joint liability to pay a single rent. The majority in the Court of Appeal was satisfied that the four unities of possession, interest, title and time existed as pre-conditions of such a joint tenancy. The existence of the four unities, and in particular the unities of title and time, was challenged in a dissenting judgment by Sir George Waller in which he concluded

> '... there cannot be a joint tenancy where there are serious doubts about each of the four unities.'

The decisions in *AG Securities* v *Vaughan* and *Antoniades* v *Villiers* were heard by the House of Lords as a joint appeal and reported together at [1988] 3 WLR 1205. In *AG Securities* v *Vaughan* the appellants owned a block of flats, one of which contained six rooms in addition to a kitchen and bathroom. They furnished four rooms as bedrooms, a fifth as a lounge and the sixth as a sitting room and entered into short-term agreements with four individuals, each referred to in the relevant agreement as 'Licensee'. The agreements were made at different times and on different terms and were normally for six months' duration. Each agreement provided that the licensee had

> 'the right to use [the flat] in common with others who have or may from time to time be granted the like right ... but without the right to exclusive possession of any part of the ... flat'.

When a licensee left, a new occupant was mutually agreed by the appellants and the remaining licensees. The court held that the occupants were indeed licensees.

Lord Bridge of Harwich:

> 'These rights and obligations having initially been several, I do not understand by what legal alchemy they could ever become joint. Each occupant had a contractual right, enforceable against the appellants, to prevent the number of persons permitted to occupy the flat at any one time exceeding four. But this did not give them exclusive possession of the kind which is distinctive of a leasehold interest. Having no estate in land, they could not sue in trespass. Their remedy against intruders would have been to persuade the appellants to sue as plaintiffs or to join the appellants as defendants by way of enforcement of their contractual rights.
>
> The arrangement seems to have been a sensible and realistic one to provide accommodation for a shifting population of individuals who were genuinely prepared to share the flat with others introduced from time to time who would, at least initially, be strangers to them. There was no artificiality in the contracts concluded to give effect to this arrangement. On the contrary, it seems to me to require the highest degree of artificiality to force these contracts into the mould of a joint tenancy.'

Lord Oliver of Aylmerton:

> 'The respondents are compelled to support their claims by a strange and unnatural theory that, as each occupant terminates his agreement, there is an implied surrender by the other three and an implied grant of a new joint tenancy to them together with the new incumbent when he enters under his individual agreement ... this appears to me to be entirely unreal. For my part, I (find) no unity of interest, no unity of title, certainly no unity of time and, as I think, no unity of possession. I find it impossible to say that the agreements entered into with the respondents created either individually or collectively a single tenancy either of the entire flat or of any part of it.'

In *Antoniades* v *Villiers* the attic of the respondent's house was converted into furnished residential accommodation. Wishing to live together there, the appellants signed identical agreements called 'licences' which were executed at the same time and stressed that they were not to have exclusive possession. In particular, the agreements provided that

> 'The licensor shall be entitled at any time to use the rooms together with the licensee and permit other persons to use all of the rooms together with the licensee.'

No attempt was made by the respondent to use the rooms or to have them used by others. Stressing, too, that the real intention of the parties was to create a licence not coming under the Rent Acts, the agreements provided for a monthly payment of £87 and stated that they were determinable by one month's notice by either party. The court held that the agreements created a joint tenancy.

Lord Bridge of Harwich:

'Here the artificiality was in the pretence that two contemporaneous and identical agreements entered into by a man and a woman who were going to live together in a one-bedroom flat and share a double bed created rights and obligations which were several rather than joint. As to the nature of those rights and obligations, the provisions of the joint agreement purporting to retain the right in the respondent to share the occupation of the flat with the young couple himself or to introduce an indefinite number of third parties to do so could be seen, in all the relevant circumstances, to be repugnant to the true purpose of the agreement. No one could have supposed that those provisions were ever intended to be acted on. They were introduced into the agreement for no other purpose than as an attempt to disguise the true character of the agreement which it was hoped would deceive the court and prevent the appellants enjoying the protection of the Rent Acts. As your Lordships all agree, the attempt fails.'

Lord Templeman:

'My Lords, in *Street* v *Mountford* this House stipulated with reiterated emphasis that an express statement of intention is not decisive and that the court must pay attention to the facts and surrounding circumstances and to what people do as well as to what people say ...

... My Lords, in the second appeal now under consideration, there was, in my opinion, the grant of a joint tenancy for the following reasons. (1) The applicants for the flat applied to rent the flat jointly and to enjoy exclusive occupation. (2) The landlord allowed the applicants jointly to enjoy exclusive occupation and accepted rent. A tenancy was created. (3) The power reserved to the landlord to deprive the applicants of exclusive occupation was inconsistent with the provisions of the Rent Acts. (4) Moreover, in all the circumstances the power which the landlord insisted on to deprive the applicants of exclusive occupation was a pretence only intended to deprive the applicants of the protection of the Rent Acts.'

The lease-licence debate continues, and the courts can now take advantage of the two decisions of the House of Lords in *AG Securities* v *Vaughan* and *Street* v *Mountford* [1985] 2 WLR 877. These decisions were applied by the Court of Appeal in *Aslan* v *Murphy* [1989] 3 All ER 130 and *Mikeover* v *Brady* [1989] 3 All ER 618. See also *Norris* v *Shecksfield* [1991] 1 WLR 1241.

The debate also arises in the context of the provision of accommodation for the homeless. In *Family Housing Association* v *Jones* [1990] 1 WLR 779, a tenancy was confirmed even though the Association retained a key, but this was overruled by the House of Lords in *Westminster City Council* v *Clarke* [1992] 2 WLR 229. It was held that an agreement known as a 'licence to occupy' did not grant exclusive possession of any particular room and did not create a landlord and tenant relationship. The council could change the hotel accommodation, and the occupier could be required to share a room with other persons. This degree of control was necessary to ensure the smooth running of the hotel.

In *Stribling* v *Wickham* (1989) 27 EG 81 the Court of Appeal had a further opportunity to consider whether a number of agreements, each purporting to grant an individual licence, also create a joint tenancy. The court held that the separate agreements genuinely represented the reality of the transaction, and, as none of the sharers could be regarded as a tenant of any individual part, they must be licensees. The following points were suggested by way of guidance:

1. All the circumstances surrounding the creation of the agreements must be considered, including the relationship between the prospective occupiers and the intended and actual mode of occupation.
2. The actual mode of accommodation may not be used to construe documents, but may be used to determine whether any parts of the documents should be ignored as being parts which the parties never intended to act upon.
3. The court must determine the true nature of the transaction. This agreement was said to be 'a genuine and sensible arrangement for the benefit of both sides'.
4. The fact that the agreements were all entered into at one time as replacements of earlier agreements was not significant if the earlier agreements were entered into separately.

Street v *Mountford* (above) was decided in the context of residential occupation, and the courts must decide whether to apply the decision by analogy in the case of commercial leases.

10.6 Types of tenancy

Terms certain

These are leases for a fixed period of time. The length of time can vary from a few weeks to thousands of years, but it cannot be unending because every lease must have a reversion.

A term certain comes to an end at the end of the fixed term. No noticc to quit is required to determine this type of tenancy; it is said to end by effluxion of time.

A term certain can be brought to an end before the expiry of the term by:

1. forfeiture: where the tenant is in breach of an obligation in the lease (see section 10.7).
2. notice to quit: provided that provision for determination by notice to quit is made in the lease. In the absence of express provision, notice to quit cannot be used to determine terms certain.

Yearly tenancies

These may be created expressly or by implication of law. A tenancy by implication arises when there is no express agreement as to the nature of the tenancy, but rent is paid and accepted with reference to an annual sum. See Lord Templeman's speech in *Prudential Assurance Co Ltd* v *London Residuary Body* [1992] 3 WLR 279 at p283, discussed in section 10.4 above. At common law, in the absence of agreement to the contrary, at least half a year's notice is required to determine a yearly tenancy, such notice expiring at the end of a completed year of the tenancy. If the tenancy began on one of the 'usual quarter days' (25 December, 25 March, 24 June, 29 September) two quarters' notice is required. In all other cases six calendar months' notice must be given. The rent may be paid at more frequent intervals than one year; it is common in yearly tenancies to provide for the rent to be paid quarterly.

Other periodic tenancies

These can be created in the same way as a yearly tenancy, in other words expressly or by implication. The notice period, however, is a full period expiring at the end of one of the periods of the tenancy. This is subject to any contrary agreement. When the tenancy is that of premises used as a dwelling, at least four weeks' notice is required by statute, and this notice must be given in the form required by statute (s5 Protection from Eviction Act 1977). The Court of Appeal had held in *Re Midland Railway Co's Agreement* [1971] Ch 725 that the landlord could limit his ability to serve notice to determine the lease. This decision was overruled by the House of Lords in *Prudential Assurance Co Ltd* v *London Residuary Body* (above). As a consequence, any provision which either grants a power to determine an uncertain lease, *or* prevents the termination of an uncertain lease during a period of uncertainty, will itself be void.

In *Centaploy Ltd* v *Matlodge Ltd* [1974] Ch 1, Whitford J expressed the principle in these words:

> '... it must be basic to a tenancy that at some stage the person granting the tenancy shall have the right to determine and a tenancy in which the landlord is never going to have the right to determine at all is, as I see it, a complete contradiction in terms.'

Tenancy at will

A tenancy at will arises whenever a tenant, with the landlord's consent, occupies land on terms that either party may determine the tenancy at any time. Unless the parties agree that the tenancy should be rent free, the tenant must pay an agreed rent or a reasonable sum for his use and occupation of the land. If there was no agreement as to rent, and subsequently the tenant commences to tender rent on a regular basis and the rent is accepted, the tenancy is converted into a periodical tenancy, the period being related to the period of payment of rent. Where a person went into possession during negotiations for a lease this was held to create a tenancy at will in *British Railways Board* v *Bodywright Ltd* (1971) 220 EG 651 which was applied in *Javad* v *Aqil* (1990) The Times 29 May.

Tenancy at sufferance

This can only arise when a tenant holds over after the expiry of a valid tenancy without the landlord either consenting or objecting. The tenant is liable to pay a reasonable sum for use and occupation, and the tenancy may be determined at any time or may be converted into a periodical tenancy in similar circumstances to the tenancy at will above.

Leases for lives

A lease, whether made before 1926 or after 1925, for a life or lives, or for a term of years determinable with life or lives or on the marriage of the lessee, is by s149(6) LPA 1925 converted into a lease for 90 years determinable after the end of the life or lives or on the marriage of the lessee, as the case may be, by the giving by either party of not less than one month's notice expiring on one of the quarter days, applicable to the tenancy. This provision applies only to a lease at a rent or fine. A term determinable with life at no rent or fine may fall within s20(1)(iv) SLA 1925, creating a strict settlement. See *Binions* v *Evans* [1972] Ch 359, as considered and applied in *Ungurian* v *Lesnoff* [1989] 3 WLR 840 by Vinelott J.

In *Bass Holdings Ltd* v *Lewis* (1986) 280 EG 771 Lewis was the tenant of a public house. His three-year lease included a provision for termination after the three years 'on six months' notice or on the death of the tenant by notice of not less than 14 days'. The Court of Appeal was not impressed by the tenant's argument that this provision brought the lease within s149(6) LPA 1925. This was not a lease for life or lives within s149(6). For the Act to apply the lease must be granted either for a term limited by reference to a life or lives, or for a term of years conditionally upon the survival of a life or lives. Nourse LJ concluded:

> 'I add by way of illustration that the simplest example of a term of years limited conditionally upon the survival of a life or lives is a lease to A for a term of 20 years if he shall so long live.'

Perpetually renewable leases

These are leases which give the lessee the right to renew the lease for another period as often as it expires. They are converted by s145 and Schedule 15 LPA 1922 into terms of 2,000 years determinable only by the lessee by not less than ten days' notice expiring on any of the old renewal dates. If the lease provides for the payment of a fine on renewal then:

1. If the lease was granted before 1926 the fine was converted into additional rent spread over the period between the renewal dates.
2. If the lease was granted after 1925 the provision for payment of a fine is void.

The lessee is bound to notify the lessor of any assignment of the term, and if the lessee does assign he ceases to be liable on the covenants in the lease (an exception to the general rule). A perpetually renewable lease may be inadvertently created by unrestricted renewal clauses, eg 'on the same terms and conditions, including this clause'. See *Re Hopkin's Lease, Caerphilly Concrete Products Ltd* v *Owen* [1972] 1 WLR 372 and compare with *Marjorie Burnett Ltd* v *Barclay* (1980) 258 EG 642.

The essence of the perpetually renewable lease is that the renewal clause itself is included. In *Parkus* v *Greenwood* [1950] Ch 644 a lease for three years included a clause that:

> '... the lessor will on the request of the tenant grant him a tenancy at the same rent containing the like provisions as are herein contained including the present covenant for renewal.'

The courts lean against perpetual renewability, as was expressed by Nourse J in *Marjorie Burnett Ltd* v *Barclay* (above):

> 'It seems clear, therefore, that the court must bear in mind the leaning against perpetually renewable leases and must find expressed in the lease an express covenant or obligation for perpetual renewal. The court must look ahead to see what the second lease would contain when the requirements of the first lease had been duly complied with.'

Reversionary leases

The grant of a lease at a rent or a fine is void if it is to commence more than 21 years after the date of the grant (s149(3) LPA 1925), as is a contract to grant a lease if the lease is to commence more than 21 years after the grant. However, a contract to grant a lease more than 21 years after the date of the contract is valid – the LPA 1925 relates the period of 21 years to the date of the lease and not the date of the contract. See *Re Strand and Savoy Properties Ltd* [1960] Ch 582; *Weg Motors Ltd* v *Hales* [1962] Ch 49.

Such a contract may, however, be subject to the perpetuity rule (see Chapter 16).

10.7 Terms implied into leases

Obligations are implied into leases both at common law and by statute. These obligations can be expressly excluded from leases, but in the absence of express provision, both landlords and tenants are subject to implied covenants. There are two situations to consider:

1. the position in the absence of express provision; and
2. usual covenants.

Position in the absence of express provision

Where a lease has *actually been granted* and it does not contain covenants concerning certain matters these matters will be regulated by implied covenants (see below). However, as Lord Cozens Hardy MR stated in *Malzy* v *Eichholz* [1916] 2 KB 308 if the lease does contain an express covenant 'there is no room for an implied covenant covering the same ground or any part of it' (at pages 313, 314).

The landlord's obligations

Covenant for quiet enjoyment. This means that the landlord undertakes that the tenant shall be free from disturbance by adverse claims or physical interference with the tenant's enjoyment of the demised premises by the landlord himself or by persons claiming under him. Harassment and intimidation of the tenant is a breach of this covenant (as well as being a criminal offence under s1 Protection from Eviction Act 1977): see *Kenny* v *Preen* [1963] 1 QB 499, but interference with privacy by erecting a staircase giving a view into the demised premises is not: see *Browne* v *Flower* [1911] 1 Ch 219.

The covenant does not extend to the acts of persons having title paramount, *Jones* v *Lavington* [1903] 1 KB 253, nor to the wrongful acts of persons claiming under them.

For the remedies available for breach, see later and *Sampson* v *Hodson-Pressinger* [1981] 3 All ER 710.

The landlord is not in breach of his covenant for quiet enjoyment where the acts which constitute the interruption of the tenant's rights are due to the exercise of rights created by a title which is superior to that of landlord. See *Celsteel Ltd* v *Alton House Holdings Ltd (No 2)* [1987] 1 WLR 291.

Not to derogate from the grant. This prevents the landlord from doing anything or permitting anything to be done which would render the premises unsuitable for the purpose for which they were let. See *Aldin* v *Latimer Clark, Muirhead & Co* [1894] 2 Ch 437; *Harmer* v *Jumbil Tin Areas Ltd* [1921] 1 Ch 200. But this does not extend to acts merely making the lease less profitable (*Port* v *Griffith* [1938] 1 All ER 295), or to a mere invasion of privacy. See *Browne* v *Flower* (above).

Obligations as to repairs and fitness for occupation. At common law there is no general obligation imposed on a landlord to repair premises, nor is there any term implied into the lease that the premises should be suitable, either physically or legally, for the purposes for which they are let. See *Hill* v *Harris* [1965] 2 QB 601.

There are five exceptions to this general rule:

FURNISHED DWELLING HOUSES. Under the rule in *Smith* v *Marrable* (1843) 11 M & W 5 there is an implied condition in the letting of a furnished dwelling house that it should be reasonably fit for human habitation at the beginning of the tenancy. The obligation does not continue thereafter to require the landlord to maintain the dwelling in a habitable condition.

Failure to comply with this condition is a repudiatory breach of contract, which allows the tenant to treat the contract of tenancy as at an end.

BLOCKS OF FLATS. There is an implied condition in every lease of a flat in a block of flats that the landlord will take reasonable steps to keep the common parts (lifts, staircases, etc) retained by him in repair. See *Liverpool City Council* v *Irwin* [1977] AC 239.

DWELLING HOUSES LET FOR LESS THAN SEVEN YEARS. Section 32 Housing Act 1961, which has now been consolidated in ss11–16 Landlord and Tenant Act 1985, implies into the leases of dwelling houses let for less than seven years, granted after 24 October 1961, a covenant by the landlord:

1. to keep in repair the structure and exterior of the dwelling house, including drains, pipes and gutters;
2. to keep in repair and proper working order the installations in the house:
   a) for the supply of water, gas and electricity and for sanitation (including basins, sinks, baths and sanitary conveniences, but not other fixtures, fittings and appliances for making use of water, gas and electricity);
   b) for space heating or heating water.

This covenant overrides any express covenant to repair by the tenant, and the landlord cannot make the tenant pay for repairs he is obliged to do under this covenant. See *Brikom Investments Ltd* v *Seaford* [1981] 2 All ER 783.

The duty on the landlord under s11 Landlord and Tenant Act 1985 is to carry out the repairs within a reasonable time of receiving notice of the need for repair. In *Morris* v *Liverpool City Council* (1988) 14 EG 59 it was held that failure to carry out permanent repairs within a week of notification where temporary repairs had been made was not unreasonable.

For the purposes of s11 Landlord and Tenant Act 1985, knowledge of the need of repairs may be obtained in various ways. In *Hall* v *Howard* (1989) 57 P & CR 226 a valuation report had been sent to the landlord during unsuccessful negotiations for the purchase of the reversion. This report identified certain structural defects within s11. The Court of Appeal held that the valuation report, in spite of the different content, would put a reasonable landlord on notice of a possible breach of the repairing covenant implied by s11.

The construction of the former s32 Housing Act 1961 was further considered in *Re the Estate of Valboug Cecile Godman Irvine* v *Morgan* (1992) 24 HLR 1.

HOUSES LET AT LOW RENT. By s6 Housing Act 1957, when a house is let at a rent not exceeding £80 pa in Greater London and £52 pa elsewhere, there is an implied condition that the house is fit for human habitation at the commencement of the tenancy, and an implied obligation on the landlord to keep it in such a condition throughout the tenancy. The obligation only extends to defects of which the landlord has notice. In determining whether the house is unfit for human habitation regard must be had to the matters set out in s4(2) HA 1957, including repair, natural lighting, and ventilation. The provisions of ss4–6 Housing Act 1957 are now consolidated in ss8–10 Landlord and Tenant Act 1985.

DEFECTIVE PREMISES ACT 1972. The landlord may also be under an obligation under s4 of this Act to all persons who might be affected by defects in the premises to take reasonable care to see that they and their property are reasonably safe from injury or damage.

The tenant's obligations

To pay the rent. At common law a landowner has a right to recover from any person occupying his land as a tenant a reasonable sum for use and occupation unless the circumstances indicate otherwise.

To pay rates and taxes. This means usual local authority rates, council tax and other rates assessed in respect of the premises except such as are imposed expressly upon the landlord. The obligation will normally arise due to the occupation of the premises by the tenant.

Not to commit waste. The tenant commits waste if he causes any alteration or damage to the premises which injures the reversion. If the lease is for a fixed term, the tenant is liable for both permissive and voluntary waste and he must therefore keep the premises in repair. See *Yellowly* v *Gower* (1855) 11 Exch 274.

In the case of a periodic tenancy the tenant is liable for voluntary waste only, and he must use the premises in a 'tenant-like manner'. See *Warren* v *Keen* [1954] 1 QB 15.

To permit the landlord to enter and view the premises. To do this when the landlord is obliged to repair them.

Usual covenants

The parties may have agreed to be bound by the 'usual covenants'. They are a species of implied term. The phrase 'usual covenants' is generally taken to refer to the following covenants:

By the tenant –	to pay tenant's rates and taxes;
	to pay rent;
	to keep the premises in repair and deliver them up in repair;
	if the landlord has undertaken to repair, to permit the landlord to enter and view the state of repair;
	a condition for re-entry on non-payment of rent.
By the landlord –	for quiet enjoyment.

But in *Chester* v *Buckingham Travel Ltd* [1981] 1 All ER 386 it was decided that this list was not exhaustive and the decision as to whether any covenant is 'usual' must depend upon the circumstances of each case. The research will include the practice in any particular area and the character of the property.

10.8 Express covenants in leases

A carefully drafted lease may contain a large number of express covenants, some by the landlord, but most of them by the tenant, which regulate in detail the parties' conduct under the lease. Some of the most common are discussed below.

In all cases it is necessary to decide whether any alleged breach falls within the precise wording of the covenant. The most usual covenants are:

Covenant to pay rent

This should stipulate the rent and the dates on which it is payable. If it is not expressly made payable in advance it is payable in arrear. It remains payable even though the premises are destroyed or rendered uninhabitable, unless the lease expressly stipulates otherwise. See *Cricklewood Property and Investment Trust Ltd* v *Leightons Investment Trust Ltd* [1945] AC 211.

The application of the doctrine of frustration to leases was further considered in *National Carriers Ltd* v *Panalpina Northern Ltd* [1981] AC 675. In general the amount payable cannot be altered while the tenancy subsists unless the lease so provides or the parties agree. Modern commercial leases do contain rent review clauses.

The landlord can enforce payment of rent:

1. By suing in contract for the money.
2. By distress. This is an ancient remedy which is governed by archaic and technical rules, and is little used today. For details see the standard textbooks.
3. By forfeiture (see section 10.10).

In *P & A Swift Investments* v *Combined English Stores Group plc* [1988] 2 All ER 885 the House of Lords had to consider whether a covenant by a surety guaranteeing the payment of rent and the observance of covenants was a covenant which touched and concerned the land. The test for establishing whether a covenant does touch and concern was confirmed under three propositions:

1. Does it only benefit the reversioner for the time being?
2. Does it affect the nature, quality mode or user or value of the land?
3. It is not expressed to be personal.

If all these three propositions are satisfied, a covenant to pay a sum of money can be a covenant touching and concerning the land if it is connected with something to be done on, to or in relation to that land. When these propositions are applied, a covenant by a surety which guarantees performance of the tenant's covenants touching and concerning the land itself touches and concerns the land and is enforceable by an assignee of the reversion against the surety without express assignment.

Covenant to insure

Such a covenant, which may be given by either party, is breached if the premises are at any time uninsured, even if no fire occurs. The covenant may be to insure with a named company, or one approved by the landlord. If the tenant has covenanted to repair and the premises are destroyed or damaged by fire he is bound to restore in any case, but if there is no such covenant he is only obliged to restore if the fire was caused by his negligence. See *Beacon Carpets Ltd* v *Kirby* [1984] 2 All ER 726.

Covenants as to user

It is common for the landlord to restrict the use to which the tenant may put the demised premises.

Covenants not to assign, underlet or part with possession of the demised premises

A breach of this covenant is not capable of remedy, and the notice served under s146(1) need not require the breach to be remedied. See *Scala House and District Property Co Ltd* v *Forbes* [1974] QB 575.

1. An absolute covenant: in such a case the tenant may not assign etc the demised premises. The landlord may, of course, waive the covenant.
2. A qualified covenant not to assign etc without the landlord's consent: by s19(1) Landlord and Tenant Act 1927 such consent is not to be unreasonably withheld. If the landlord gives reasons for refusal the burden of proving unreasonableness is on the tenant, otherwise it is on the landlord.

A requirement in a lease that a tenant must offer to surrender his lease before he can seek consent to an assignment is valid, despite s19 LTA 1927. See *Adler* v *Upper Grosvenor Street Investments Ltd* [1957] 1 WLR 227; *Bocardo SA* v *S & M Hotels Ltd* [1980] 1 WLR 17.

In many of the cases on this topic it is a question of construction on the terms of the lease.

Reasonableness

This is a question of fact, but a refusal must relate to the proposed assignee as tenant rather than as an individual, or to the nature of the property. Examples of reasonable refusal are:

1. where the proposed assignee's references are unsatisfactory;
2. where the proposed subletting was at a high premium and a low rent which devalued the landlord's interest in the property;

3. where the proposed assignee was a development company interested only in sharing in development to take place after the end of the lease to the detriment of the landlord: see *Pimms Ltd* v *Tallow Chandlers Co* [1964] 2 QB 547;
4. where the assignee would acquire a statutory protection that the assignor did not have: see *Bookman (Thomas)* v *Nathan* [1955] 1 WLR 815;
5. where the assignee would acquire a right to buy the freehold under the Leasehold Reform Act 1967 which the assignor did not have: see *Bickel* v *Duke of Westminster* [1976] 3 WLR 805; *Norfolk Capital Group* v *Kitway* [1977] QB 506.

Examples of unreasonable refusal are:

1. where the landlord wished to recover the premises for himself: see *Bates* v *Donaldson* [1896] 2 QB 241;
2. where the assignee was a diplomat with diplomatic immunity;
3. if the refusal is aimed to achieve some collateral purpose not connected with the terms of the tenancy: see *Bromley Park Garden Estates Ltd* v *Moss* [1982] 1 WLR 1019.

By statute (s24 Race Relations Act 1976, and Sexual Discrimination Act 1975), consent to assignment is unreasonably withheld if it is on the basis of race, colour, creed or sex. There is an exception for small premises where the person withholding consent will continue to reside on the premises. By s19 LTA 1927 no fine shall be payable in respect of a licence to assign unless the lease expressly provides for it.

If the tenant assigns or sublets without consent he is in breach of the covenant. If consent is unreasonably refused he can:

1. go ahead with the transaction, wait for the landlord to sue and then set up the unreasonable refusal by way of defence; or
2. apply to the county court under s53 LTA 1954 for a declaration that consent has been unreasonably withheld.

In *Old Grovebury Manor Farm Ltd* v *W Seymour Plant Sales and Hire Ltd (No 2)* [1979] 1 WLR 1397 it was held that an assignment in breach of covenant was effective between the parties so that a s146 notice should be served on the assignee by the landlord.

The question of reasonableness for the purposes of s19(1) Landlord and Tenant Act 1927 was reviewed in *International Drilling Fluids Ltd* v *Louisville Investments (Uxbridge) Ltd* [1986] 2 WLR 581, and Balcombe LJ deduced the following propositions from the authorities:

1. The purpose of the covenant was to protect the lessor from having his premises used or occupied in an undesirable way or occupied by an undesirable tenant or assignee.
2. As a corollary a landlord was not entitled to refuse his consent to an assignment on grounds which had nothing whatever to do with the relationship of landlord and tenant.

3. The onus of proving consent had been unreasonably withheld was on the tenant.
4. It is not necessary for the landlord to prove that the conclusions which led him to refuse consent were justified, if they were such as a reasonable man would have so concluded.
5. It might be reasonable to refuse consent on the grounds of the proposed user even though that purpose was not forbidden by the lease.
6. There were conflicting authorities as to whether it was right to have regard to the consequences for the tenant if consent is refused. The two streams of authority could be reconciled by showing that while a landlord usually considers his own relevant interests, there might be cases where there was such a disproportion between the benefit to the landlord and the detriment to the tenant if consent is refused that it became unreasonable for the landlord to refuse consent.
7. Subject to these propositions it was a question of fact, depending on all the circumstances, as to whether the landlord's consent to an assignment was being unreasonably withheld.

These propositions were considered in *Ponderosa International Development Inc* v *Pengap Securities (Bristol) Ltd* (1986) 277 EG 1252.

If the landlord is slow in giving consent the tenant may lose his potential assignee. The Landlord and Tenant Act 1988 introduced new statutory duties from 29 September 1988. The effect is that in the case of a qualified covenant against assignment, subletting, charging or parting with possession, certain additional obligations are imposed on the person who is to give approval. Upon receiving a written application for consent a duty is owed to the tenant to give consent within a reasonable time, unless it is reasonable to refuse consent, and to serve written notice of the decision on the tenant. Any conditions must be included in that written notice. Reasons for refusal must be set out, and the onus of proof lies on the person giving the decision and serving the appropriate written notice. This reverses proposition three propounded by Balcombe LJ in *International Drilling Fluids* above and places the burden on the landlord to proceed quickly to give consent or provide adequate reasons for withholding consent.

Where property is let on an assured periodic tenancy under the Housing Act 1988, and nothing is said about assignment or subletting, then s15 implies a qualified covenant against assignment, subletting or parting with possessions. In this case there is no implied provision that the landlord must not unreasonably withhold consent.

Where a qualified covenant exists not to assign, underlet or part with possession of the demised premises without the consent of the landlord, this is already subject to the qualification that such consent shall not be unreasonably withheld (s19(1) Landlord and Tenant Act 1927).

By virtue of s1 Landlord and Tenant Act 1988 the onus of proof of reasonableness is now placed on the landlord.

If a landlord receives a written application for consent from the tenant a duty is then owned to the tenant within a reasonable time to give that consent (unless the landlord can reasonably refuse) and to serve a notice on the tenant of that decision. Any conditions of that consent must be set out in the notice.

Reasons for any refusal must be specified in the notice, and although the emphasis is still on reasonableness the burden of proof is now shifted from the tenant to the landlord.

Covenants to repair

The fact that one party to a lease does not covenant to repair does not mean that the other party is impliedly obliged to.

Scope of the covenant

Many of the leading cases explaining the meaning of 'repair' were reviewed in *Elite Investments Ltd* v *T I Bainbridge Silencers Ltd* (1986) 280 EG 1001. The courts continue to face the problem of repair in the context of inherent defects to the premises. The following cases should be noted:

Ravenseft Properties Ltd v Davstone (Holdings) Ltd [1979] 1 All ER 929. The insertion of expansion joints into the concrete cladding of a building did not change the character of the building and fell within the express covenant to repair. The joints formed a relatively trivial part of the whole building and the tenant was liable under the covenant to repair.

Elmcroft Developments Ltd v *Tankersley Sawyer* (1984) 270 EG 140. The landlords were required to insert a damp-proof course in the performance of their repairing covenant. This did not require the landlord to provide a new or wholly different thing from that demised, nor did it change the nature or character of the premises.

Quick v *Taff-Ely Borough Council* [1985] 3 All ER 321. If the damage caused to property falls outside the repairing covenant, then remedying an inherent defect is *not* within the covenant to repair. Thus condensation due to faulty design and construction of the windows in a council house did not mean that the building was in need of repair.

Post Office v *Aquarius Properties Ltd* [1987] 1 All ER 1055. The defect was in the structure of the basement of an office. This did not get worse but continued to allow water into the basement. The tenant was not liable, on the covenant to repair, to remedy these defects in the original construction of the building.

Stent v *Monmouth Borough Council* (1987) 282 EG 705. A defective front door to a council house let in water which caused damage to the tenant's carpets. The landlord was held liable to remedy the defective door. There was actual damage which was sufficient to establish a breach of the landlord's repairing obligation.

It is possible to establish the following general principles from the above cases:

1. If the problem is caused by an inherent defect then remedial work is not within the covenant to repair unless the defect has caused some damage to the building or its contents.

2. If the inherent defect causes deterioration to the building, this does not justify carrying out remedial work beyond the terms of the repairing covenant.
3. If it is found that remedial work is necessary within the terms of the covenant to repair, then this may extend to the remedy of the inherent defect itself.
4. There is no 'disrepair' within the covenant to repair if there is no proof of physical deterioration to the building.

If the tenant covenants to do all the inside repairs and permits the landlord access for any reasonable purpose, problems may arise if no express obligation is imposed on either party to keep the outside of the premises in repair. This problem arose in *Barrett* v *Lounova (1982) Ltd* [1989] 1 All ER 351 where the outside of the property was in a bad state of repair and the tenant claimed that the landlord was in breach of an implied covenant to keep the outside of the premises in reasonable repair.

The Court of Appeal confirmed that such a repairing covenant could be implied against the landlord if a tenant's covenant as to inside repairs becomes impossible to perform where there is no equivalent obligation on the landlord to execute outside repairs. The imposition of such an obligation to execute outside repairs would be necessary in order to give business efficacy to the tenancy agreement.

Repairs and estoppel

If occupiers of property carry out repairs and improvements which enhance the value of the property, they do not acquire an interest in the property by way of proprietary estoppel unless they can show that they had acted in the belief that they would acquire an interest in the property. Such a belief must have been encouraged by the landlord. See *Brinnand* v *Ewens* (1987) The Times 4 June (considered further in Chapter 13).

Whether or not a defect is within the scope of a covenant to repair is a question of fact and a question of degree.

A party who covenants to repair is not obliged to renew (ie entirely reconstruct the premises). See *Lurcott* v *Wakeley* [1911] 1 KB 505; *Lister* v *Lane and Nesham* [1893] 2 QB 212; *Brew Bros* v *Snax* [1970] 1 QB 612. Nor is he obliged to make improvements.

Often 'fair wear and tear' is excepted. This exempts the covenantor from liability for the normal action of time and weather, and the normal and reasonable use for which the premises were let. In *Regis Property Co Ltd* v *Dudley* [1959] AC 370 Lord Denning described the extent of this exclusion:

> 'It exempts a tenant from liability for repairs that are decorative and for remedying parts that wear out or come adrift in the course of reasonable use, but it does not exempt him from anything else.'

Standard of repair

The standard of repair required depends on the character of the demised premises and their locality at the time the lease was granted. See *Proudfoot* v *Hart* (1890) 25

QBD 42; *Anstruther-Gough-Calthorpe* v *McOscar* [1924] 1 KB 716. This standard of repair is expressed as such repairs as having regard to the age, character and locality of the premises would make them reasonably fit for occupation by a reasonably minded tenant of the class which would be likely to take it.

Damages for breach

Normally an injunction or decree of specific performance cannot be obtained for a breach of a repairing covenant. If, however, the landlord is in breach and the tenant is unable to repair because the breach concerns property not demised to him, specific performance may be decreed. See *Jeune* v *Queens Cross Properties Ltd* [1974] Ch 97.

By s18(1) Landlord and Tenant Act 1927 damages for breach of a tenant's covenant may not exceed the damage to the reversion. If the premises are to be demolished or structurally altered in such a way as to make the repairs useless, no damages are payable. For the right to serve a counter-notice under the Leasehold Property (Repairs) Act 1938 see section 10.10 below. If the landlord is in breach of his repairing covenant, the tenant may do the repair himself and deduct the cost from the rent. See *Lee-Parker* v *Izzet* [1971] 1 WLR 1688.

The measure of damages suffered by the landlord in the diminution of value of the reversion will usually be equivalent to the cost of repairs.

See *Calabar Properties Ltd* v *Stitcher* [1983] 3 All ER 759.

10.9 Determination of tenancies

There are nine ways in which a lease or tenancy may come to an end: expiry, notice to quit, forfeiture, merger, surrender, frustration, becoming a satisfied term, enlargement and disclaimer.

Expiry

This applies only to terms certain, which come to an end on the expiry of the term granted. There are statutory exceptions to this rule, which allow certain terms to continue after the end of the term until the tenancy is determined according to the methods laid down by statute: for business tenancies, Landlord and Tenant Act 1954 Part II, and for agricultural tenancies, Agricultural Holdings Acts 1948 and 1984 (see sections 10.14 and 10.15 below). Where the statutes do not apply, a tenant holding under a term certain becomes a trespasser when the term ends, and the landlord is entitled to possession.

Notice to quit

This is the method by which all periodic tenancies can be determined. Terms certain can be determined by notice to quit, but only where the right to do so is expressly stated in the lease.

Notice to quit is a notice served on the tenant by the landlord requiring the tenant to quit the premises and give up possession at the end of the next period of the tenancy. There is no need to show any reason for the notice to quit. The landlord under a periodic tenancy has a right to recover possession in this way.

The length of the notice is dependent on the type of periodic tenancy. In all cases the notice must expire on the anniversary of the day on which the tenancy commenced. See *Dodds* v *Walker* [1981] 2 All ER 609.

Weekly tenancy	–	one week's notice (for dwelling houses, by s5 Protection from Eviction Act 1977, there must be four weeks' written notice).
Monthly tenancy	–	one month's notice.
Half-yearly/yearly tenancy	–	six months' notice.

Forfeiture

A landlord can forfeit a tenancy at any time where the tenant is in breach of covenant, so long as the right to forfeit (or re-enter) is reserved in the lease. This is normally known as a 'proviso for re-entry'. Every lease should contain such a right of re-entry as a matter of course.

Forfeiture is normally used to determine terms certain, where the term still has some time to run. Periodic tenancies can be forfeit, but the procedure would be appropriate only for longer periodic tenancies.

Merger

Where a tenant acquires his landlord's interest in the land, the tenancy merges with the reversion and determines. Merger may also take place where both interests become vested in a third party.

Surrender

Where a tenant gives up his interest under a tenancy to his landlord, the tenancy ends. Surrender can occur expressly or by operation of law, where a tenant accepts a new tenancy during the currency of an existing one.

Frustration

It used to be thought that a contract of tenancy could never be frustrated. Hence the liability to pay rent continued, even though the demised premises no longer existed, having been burnt down or bombed.

In *National Carriers Ltd* v *Panalpina (Northern) Ltd* [1981] AC 675 the House of Lords held that leases were capable of frustration, but only in very special circumstances: 'Not never, but hardly ever.'

Becoming a satisfied term

This would apply to a portions term created under the SLA 1925.

Enlargement

The lease will be enlarged into the fee simple under s153 LPA 1925. The lease must originally have been created for over 300 years at no rent and over 200 years must still be outstanding, for example mortgages by demise where the mortgagee has obtained possession of the mortgaged premises.

Disclaimer

Where the tenant denies the landlord's title, for example by tendering rent to a third party.

10.10 Forfeiture

Before a landlord can forfeit a lease he must:

1. Establish that he has the right to forfeit the lease by ensuring the lease contains the necessary forfeiture clause.
2. Ensure that there is no waiver of that right.
3. Comply with s146 LPA 1925 (for all breaches except breach of a covenant to pay rent).
4. Bring possession proceedings in court.

A lease is not forfeited until the proceedings are served on the tenant. Once the lease has been declared forfeited by a court, the tenant and any subtenants may apply for relief from forfeiture.

The right to forfeit

The right to determine a tenancy by re-entry arises where:

1. The lease expressly provides for a right of forfeiture on breach of a covenant by a tenant and the tenant is in breach. A typical forfeiture clause reads:

   > 'Provided always and it is hereby agreed:
   >
   > That if the rent hereby reserved or any part thereof shall at any time be in arrear for twenty-one days after becoming payable (whether formally demanded or not) or there shall be any breach of the foregoing covenants on the part of the Tenant ... then the Landlord may ... re-enter upon the premises and determine the tenancy.'

2. The tenant denies the landlord's title by operation of law.

3. The demise is made conditional upon performance by the tenant of his obligations under it.

At common law a landlord is entitled to re-enter and take possession if he can do it peaceably. Section 6 Criminal Law Act 1977 makes it an offence to use any force, and so it is advisable to enforce forfeiture by legal proceedings. In the case of premises let as a dwelling, s3 Protection from Eviction Act 1977 makes legal proceedings compulsory.

It is important to show that the conduct complained of does constitute a breach of covenant.

Waiver

The landlord may lose his right to forfeit by expressly or impliedly waiving the breach of covenant. Waiver will be implied if the landlord, with knowledge of the tenant's breach, does some act which shows that he regards the tenancy as continuing. The most common form of waiver is the demand and acceptance of rent. See *Central Estates (Belgravia) Ltd* v *Woolgar (No 2)* [1972] 1 WLR 1048.

The effect of waiver depends on the type of breach. Breaches are divided into two categories:

1. Once and for all breaches: breach of a covenant not to sublet or assign; possibly a very serious breach of an immoral use covenant.
2. Continuing breaches: all other breaches, eg repairs.

Waiver of a once and for all breach waives the right to forfeit altogether. Waiver of a continuing breach operates only for the period in relation to which rent was accepted.

Section 146 notice

Section 146(1) LPA 1925 provides a preliminary procedure designed to protect tenants from forfeiture for breach of covenant, without first being given a chance to remedy the breach.

For all breaches other than a failure to pay rent, a landlord cannot forfeit a lease unless he has served a s146 notice on the tenant and the tenant has failed to comply with the notice within a reasonable time.

Section 146(1) provides that a notice must be served on the tenant and that the notice must:

1. specify the breach complained of;
2. require the tenant to remedy the breach (if it is capable of remedy) within a reasonable time;
3. require monetary compensation for the breach.

The landlord must give the tenant a reasonable time to comply with the notice. What is a reasonable time depends on the nature of the breach. Breaches are divided into:

Irremediable breaches
These are of two types:

1. Parting with possession to a subtenant: see *Scala House and District Property Co Ltd* v *Forbes* [1974] QB 575.
2. Serious immoral use: see *Rugby School Governors* v *Tannahill* [1935] 1 KB 87; compare with *Glass* v *Kencakes* [1966] 1 QB 611.

Remediable breaches
These include most other kinds of breach.

Only a short period of time need be given to the tenant before commencing proceedings. For breach of a covenant to repair, three months is reasonable.

Breach of covenant to repair

The Leasehold Property (Repairs) Act 1938, as amended by s51 Landlord and Tenant Act 1954, applies where:

1. The breach is of a repairing covenant.
2. The lease was for at least seven years.
3. There are at least three years of the lease left to run
4. The lease is not an agricultural tenancy.

The 1938 Act, where it applies, requires the landlord's s146 notice to inform the tenant of his rights under that Act. Under it the tenant, by serving a counter-notice within 28 days, can require the landlord to obtain the sanction of the court before commencing possession proceedings. See *Land Securities plc* v *Receiver for the Metropolitan Police District* [1983] 1 WLR 439.

In order for the court to give the landlord leave to proceed he must prove:

1. The immediate remedying of the breach is necessary to prevent substantial diminution in the value of his reversion.
2. The immediate remedying is to give effect to some enactment or by-law.
3. The immediate remedying is in the interests of the occupier.
4. A small expense to remedy compared with greater expense if the necessary work is postponed.
5. Special circumstances render it just and equitable in the opinion of the court that leave should be given. See s1(5) Leasehold Property (Repairs) Act 1938.

In *SEDAC Investments Ltd* v *Tanner* [1982] 3 All ER 646 it was held that if the landlord effects the repairs as an emergency then the court cannot subsequently give him leave to proceed under the 1938 Act because the repairs have by then been carried out. The judge (Mr Michael Wheeler QC) said:

> 'The whole scheme of s1 of the [1938] Act appeared to hinge upon the service of a valid notice by the lessor and if therefore to be effective, the s146 notice had to be served before the breach was remedied, the conclusion could only be that if a lessor remedied a breach and then attempted to serve on the lessee a notice under s146(1) and so deprived the lessee of his right to serve a counter-notice, the court had no jurisdiction to give the lessor leave to commence proceedings for damages.'

The courts have had a further opportunity to consider the solution, which may be that instead of suing for breach of the covenant to repair the landlord should claim for the debt due, as this action is not caught by the 1938 Act. This was the method used successfully in *Hamilton* v *Martell Securities Ltd* [1984] 1 All ER 665. Vinelott J held that where the landlord had carried out repairs, the claim for the cost against the tenant was for a debt due under the lease rather than a claim for damages for breach of the covenant to repair, and so no leave under the 1938 Act was required in order to bring the action against the tenant.

Exceptions to s146(1)

A s146 notice need not be served in the following cases:

1. breach of covenant to pay rent;
2. breach of covenant to allow inspection in mining leases;
3. bankruptcy of the tenant in lease of any of the following:

    a) agricultural land;
    b) mining lease;
    c) public house;
    d) furnished house;
    e) any property where the personal qualifications of the tenant are important. See *Bathurst (Earl)* v *Fine* [1974] 1 WLR 905.

    In such cases the landlord can forfeit immediately when bankruptcy occurs.

In any other lease where there is a proviso for re-entry on bankruptcy, s146(10) LPA 1925 provides that:

1. If the trustee in bankruptcy sells within a year, despite proceedings for forfeiture, he can claim relief even after the year has expired and the court can confirm the title of the purchaser.
2. If the trustee in bankruptcy does not sell within the year, although the landlord cannot forfeit without serving a statutory notice during the year, he may forfeit without serving a notice after the expiration of a year.

Relief from forfeiture

Tenants

Where a tenant is in breach of covenant, the court must allow the landlord to forfeit the lease and order possession. Section 146(2) LPA 1925 gives the court a wide discretion to allow the tenant relief from forfeiture, on terms that the breach ceases. Where the breach is irremediable (see 'Section 146 notice' above) the court will not allow relief from forfeiture. Nor will relief be allowed where the landlord has already re-entered. Section 146(2) only applies while the landlord is 'proceeding' to enforce his rights and not where he has in fact entered before the tenant seeks relief.

Where the breach relates to only one part of the demised premises, that part alone may be forfeited. See *GMS Syndicate Ltd* v *Gary Elliott Ltd* [1982] Ch 1.

Subtenants and mortgagees

If the head lease is forfeited, any sublease or mortgage falls with it. However, s146(4) LPA 1925 gives the sublessee (or mortgagee or chargee) a right to apply to the court for relief against forfeiture of the head lease, whatever the ground of forfeiture and even if the head lessee could not himself have applied for relief. If relief is granted the court may make an order vesting the whole or any part of the demised premises in the subtenant for a term not longer than the sublease and on such conditions as the court thinks fit.

Forfeiture for non-payment of rent

At common law a landlord cannot exercise a right of re-entry unless he has first made a formal demand, that is, he or his agent have demanded the exact sum due in the demised premises on the day it is due at such convenient hour before sunset as will give time to count out the money. This requirement can be dispensed with:

1. if expressly excluded by the lease (which it is in all standard form leases);
2. under the Common Law Procedure Act 1852 if half a year's rent is in arrear, and insufficient goods to satisfy the arrears are available for distress.

If the landlord brings an action for possession the tenant has the right under s212 Common Law Procedure Act 1852 to have the action discontinued if he pays all arrears and costs at any time before the trial. However, it was held in *Standard Pattern Co Ltd* v *Ivey* [1962] Ch 432 that this section is confined to cases where at least half a year's rent is due.

Even after judgment has been given the court can give the tenant relief from forfeiture. The power to do so was originally equitable but is now governed by ss210–212 Common Law Procedure Act 1852. The tenant must apply within six months of the judgment, and relief will be granted if he pays the rent due and the landlord's costs, and if it is equitable in the circumstances to grant it.

The six-month time limit does not apply if the landlord re-entered other than by an action for possession. Relief may be granted on terms, eg that the tenant should do outstanding repairs. Relief will not be granted if the landlord has re-let the premises. See *Stanhope* v *Howarth* (1886) 3 TLR 34.

A subtenant where the head tenancy is forfeit for failure to pay rent can seek relief from forfeiture under s146(4) LPA 1925.

Alternative jurisdiction is in the county court. If the tenant begins proceedings for relief in the county court under s138 County Courts Act 1984, then this excludes any possible relief against forfeiture through the High Court. See *Di Palma* v *Victoria Square Property Co Ltd* [1985] 3 WLR 207.

The Court of Appeal has now confirmed the decision of Scott J at first instance. Lawton LJ concluded:

> 'It followed that on the plain meaning of the words used in the section Parliament intended that a tenant who did not do the acts specified should not later be able to apply to the High Court for relief from forfeiture.'

Section 55 Administration of Justice Act 1985 has amended s138 County Courts Act 1984 following the decision of the Court of Appeal in *Di Palma* v *Victoria Square Property Co Ltd* [1985] 3 WLR 207. The effect of s55 Administration of Justice Act 1985 is to allow a tenant to apply for relief against forfeiture in the County Court at any time during the six months following re-entry of the landlord. This right of relief is also available to a sublessee or a mortgagee. This amendment effectively gives the tenant the same rights to relief as were already available in the High Court and should avoid the anomalies – which were highlighted in this decision and in *Jones* v *Barnett* [1984] Ch 500 – of the choice of court in which to commence proceedings.

10.11 Enforceability of covenants in leases

General principles

Definition of covenant

The strict definition of a covenant is a promise contained in a deed. However, promises contained in written documents or implied into tenancy agreements are also described as covenants, and are enforceable in the same way as covenants in a deed.

Methods of enforcement

Where covenants are enforceable between a landlord and a tenant, either party has a choice of methods of enforcement.

Where a landlord is in breach the tenant can either sue in contract for damages for breach of contract, or seek specific performance of the covenant (usual for a repairing covenant) or an injunction to restrain the landlord's breach (covenants other than repairing covenants) and damages. See *Sampson* v *Hodson-Pressinger* [1981] 3 All ER 710.

For breach of repairing covenants, the tenant is also entitled to do the repairs himself and withhold the cost from his rent.

Where the tenant is in breach the landlord can:

1. Sue in contract for damages for breach of contract.
2. Seek an injunction to restrain the breach and damages.
3. Forfeit the lease for breach of covenant, provided that:

    a) the lease contains a proviso for forfeiture (or re-entry) for breach of covenant by the tenant; and
    b) the landlord has not waived the breach; and
    c) a s146 notice (if required) has been served on the tenant, and the tenant has not remedied the breach within a reasonable time of service of the notice.

Enforceability – two regimes

The law in this area has recently undergone significant reform with the coming into force on 1 January 1996 of the Landlord and Tenant (Covenants) Act 1995. This Act applies a new enforcement regime to all new tenancies *granted* on or after 1 January 1996. Accordingly, the Act is not retrospective and therefore the old regime is still applicable in respect of leases *granted* before that date. In the ensuing paragraphs the law applicable to leases granted before 1 January 1996 and the law applicable to tenancies granted after 31 December 1995 is summarised.

Tenancies granted before 1 January 1996

Covenants in leases are enforceable between parties where there is privity of contract or privity of estate.

Privity of contract and estate. There is privity of contract between the original parties to a lease, and any third parties with whom the lease was said to be made (s56 LPA 1925). There is privity of estate between a tenant and his immediate landlord. Hence there is no privity of estate between a landlord and a subtenant.

Enforceability between original parties to lease. There is privity of contract between the original parties to the lease, so that all covenants are enforceable. Both landlord and tenant remain liable to each other for the whole term of the lease, even though either has assigned his whole interest in the land.

The only exception to this rule is that the tenant under a perpetually renewable lease is not liable after he has assigned his interest. See Schedule 15 paragraph 11(i) LPA 1922.

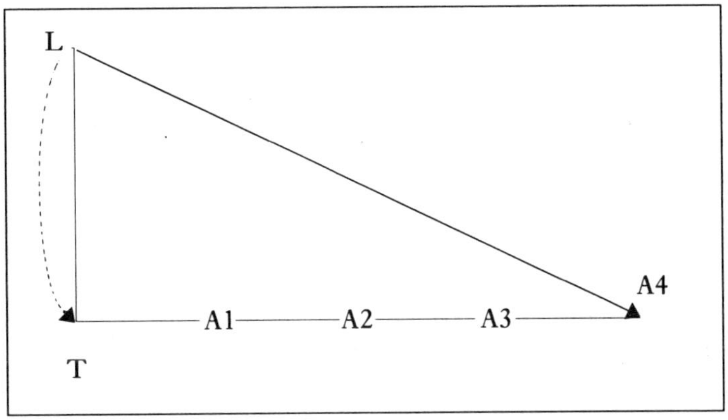

Where an assignee is in breach of covenant, L has a choice. He can sue either A4 (the assignee in possession) or T.

If T is sued for A4's breach, he has two remedies available to him. First, he can sue A1 under the covenant of indemnity implied into every assignment for value by s77 LPA 1925; A1 can then sue A2 and so on along this chain of indemnity covenants. Secondly, he can sue A4 directly in quasi-contract. See *Moule* v *Garrett* (1872) LR 7 Ex 101. This is based on the principles of quasi-contract and will only apply where the covenants touch and concern the land, and the liability of T and A4 is the same liability to L, the landlord. The law implies an obligation between joint debtors to repay money paid by one of them for the exclusive benefit of the other when both are legally liable to a common creditor. Under this rule, if T satisfies A4's debt he has the same right of indemnity as a surety.

Enforceability between assignees. When either the lease or the reversion or both have been assigned there is no privity of contract, but there is privity of estate arising out of the relationship of landlord and tenant. Covenants in the original lease are enforceable between persons standing in the relationship of landlord and tenant, even though one, or both, of them are not the original parties.

Where the tenant has assigned his interest

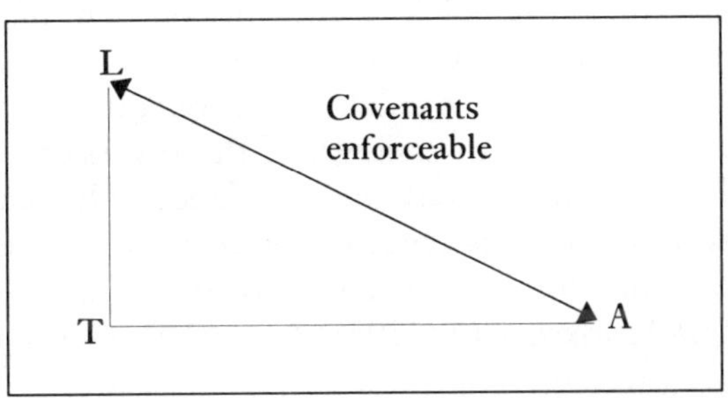

Covenants in the original lease are enforceable by and against the assignee of the tenant if:

1. the covenant touches and concerns the land, that is, it is related to the land itself or concerns the landlord as landlord and the tenant as tenant; and
2. the lease is a legal lease; and
3. the assignment is a legal assignment.

An assignee of the lease remains liable only so long as he remains a tenant, and is not liable for breaches committed after he has assigned the lease. Nor is an assignee liable for breaches committed prior to the assignment to him.

A tenant who suffers loss as a result of a breach of the landlord's covenant which was committed while he was, in fact, the tenant has a right to sue the landlord for loss after the tenant has assigned the residue of the lease. See *City and Metropolitan Properties Ltd* v *Greycroft Ltd* (1987) 283 EG 199.

Where the landlord has assigned the reversion

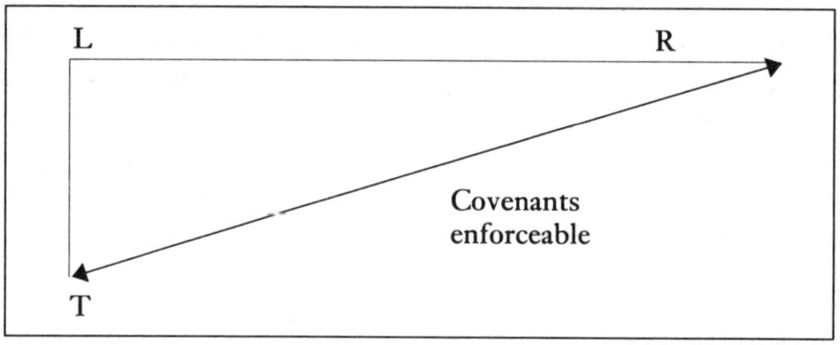

The assignee of the reversion, R, can enforce all covenants contained in the original lease against T provided that the covenants 'have reference to the subject matter of the lease'. This has the same meaning as 'touch and concern the land'.

At common law the assignee of the reversion had no power to enforce covenants in the original lease. This power was conferred by statute. Section 141 LPA 1925: the benefit of covenants that have reference to the subject matter of the lease runs with the reversion. Section 142 LPA 1925: the burden of covenants that have reference to the subject matter of the lease runs with the reversion. The benefit of a covenant is the capacity to sue. The burden of a covenant is the liability to be sued.

As with assignees of the lease, an assignee of the reversion cannot sue or be sued after he has parted with his interest in the land. The courts have, however, interpreted s141 so as to allow an assignee of the reversion to sue a tenant for breach when there is no privity of contract at the time of the breach. In *London and County (A & D) Ltd* v *Wilfred Sportsman Ltd* [1971] Ch 764 Russell LJ said:

'The language of s141 ... is such as in my judgment, to indicate plainly that an assignee of the reversion may sue and re-enter for rent in arrear at the date of the assignment when the right of re-entry has arisen before the assignment.'

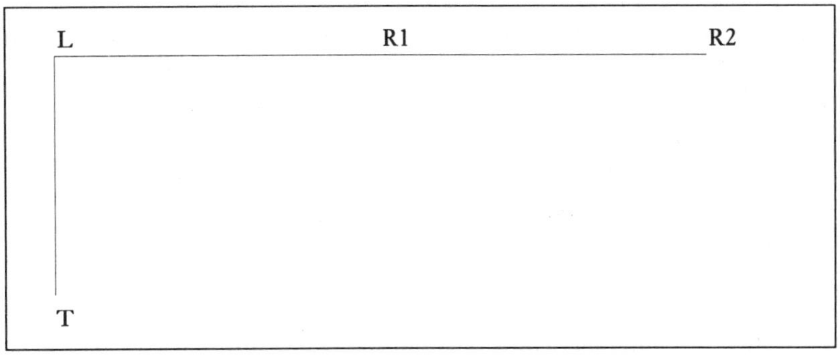

Thus R2 was held to be entitled to sue T for breaches committed by T even though the reversion was vested in R1 at the time of the breach.

The principle was extended in *Arlesford Trading* v *Servansingh* [1971] 3 All ER 113:

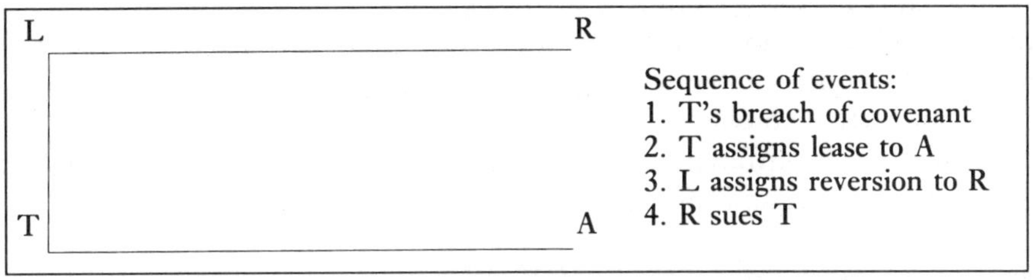

The assignee of the reversion was held entitled to recover arrears of rent (under T's covenant to pay rent) from T, even though those arrears arose before the assignments by T to A, and by L to R. Hence R was able, by virtue of s141 LPA 1925, to sue on a covenant even though there was at no time either privity of contract or privity of estate between R and T. Finally, it is important to note that ss141 and 142 LPA 1925 do not apply to new tenancies under the Landlord and Tenant (Covenants) Act 1995.

Tenancies granted after 31 December 1995

The Landlord and Tenant (Covenants) Act (LT(C)A) 1995 received the Royal Assent on 19 July 1995 and came into force on 1 January 1996. It reforms the doctrines of privity of contract and privity of estate so far as they relate to the relationship of landlord and tenant. The main catalyst of the legislation was the fact that during the recent recession many former tenants were dismayed to discover that they could be required to settle the debts of their insolvent successors long after they had assigned their leases. Such a possibility made prospective tenants wary about taking long leases because of privity of contract (ie that an original tenant would remain liable for future rent and other covenants in the lease throughout the term even after he has parted with all interest in the property).

The need to reform this area of land law was identified by the Law Commission in their 1988 Report 'Landlord and Tenant Law: Privity of Contract and Estate' (Law Com No 174). They concluded that 'it is intrinsically unfair that anyone should bear burdens under a contract in respect of which they derive no benefit and over which they have no control', with the proviso that 'the liability should be preserved where it is necessary but abandoned where it is not'. The Act gives effect to that conclusion. In the ensuing paragraphs an outline of some of the main changes introduced by the LT(C)A is given.

Key points

1. Applies to all new tenancies (both residential and commercial) *granted* on or after 1 January 1996.
2. Tenancies made pursuant to an agreement entered into before 1 January 1996 are exempt from the new provisions.
3. Makes provision for persons bound by covenants of a tenancy to be released from such covenants on the assignment of the tenancy.
4. Applies to all covenants in a tenancy apart from certain covenants arising by operation of statute under the Housing Act 1985 (covenants for repayment of discount on early disposals).
5. The LT(C)A 1995 differentiates between new tenancies (those granted after the Act came into force) and other tenancies.

Transmission of covenants. The LT(C)A 1995 introduces a statutory code for the transmission of the benefit and burden of leasehold covenants in respect of new tenancies. Under the new Act the benefit and burden of all covenants pass upon assignment – whether it is the tenant who is assigning the leasehold interest or the landlord assigning the reversion. Accordingly, there is no longer any need to differentiate between covenants that 'touch and concern' the land and those that do not (s3). For example, on an assignment of a tenancy the assignee tenant becomes bound by the tenant covenants, to the extent that immediately before the assignment they bound the assignor, and becomes entitled to the benefit of the landlord covenants to a corresponding extent.

Release of former tenants. After a tenant assigns, he is released from his covenants and ceases to be entitled to the benefit of the landlord's covenants (s5). However, to this rule there are two categories of exception:

1. Excluded assignments – s11 provides that assignments that are either in breach of a covenant (ie unauthorised assignments) or by operation of law (ie following death or insolvency) cannot release the assigning landlord or tenant from his

obligations under the covenants contained in the assigned tenancy. In these situations an assigning tenant or landlord cannot be released from the relevant covenants of the tenancy until there is a subsequent assignment that is lawful (ie not excluded).

2. Lease terms expressed to be made personal to a named person (s3(6)).

Landlord's right to release. It is not only tenants who can obtain release on assignment. Section 7 provides a new procedure whereby landlords can obtain release from their covenants under a lease when they sell their reversionary interest. However, it is important to note that the release of a landlord is not automatic. To obtain release, a landlord must serve a notice on the tenant as prescribed by s8 either before or within four weeks from completion of the reversionary assignment. If the tenant does not respond to the notice within the prescribed time the covenants in respect of which the notice is served are released. If the tenant responds in writing objecting to the release the landlord can apply to the county court for a declaration that the release sought is reasonable.

Section 24 somewhat restricts the scope of the release provisions. Any release arising under the LT(C)A 1995 does not affect any liability (of either landlord or tenant) arising from a breach of covenant occurring before the release.

Amendment to Landlord and Tenant Act 1927. Since the release of a former tenant can weaken a landlord's financial position, the Landlord and Tenant Act 1927 has been amended to give landlords more control over future assignments. Section 22 amends the 1927 Act by inserting a new s1A into it. This enables a landlord and tenant to detail in the lease what terms or conditions must be satisfied for the landlord to give his consent to an assignment. If thereafter the terms or conditions are not satisfied and the landlord does not consent to the assignment, his consent will not be regarded as having been unreasonably withheld. However, the amendment to s19 of the 1927 Act *cannot* apply to residential premises. It only applies to business premises.

Authorised guarantee agreement. Section 16 provides that a tenant who is released from a covenant on an assignment may enter into or be required by the landlord to enter into an 'authorised guarantee agreement'. Such an agreement requires the assigning tenant to guarantee the performance by the assignee tenant (ie the person to whom he immediately assigns but not subsequent assignees) of the covenants from which he has been released by the assignment.

New protection for former tenants. After 1 January 1996, the only former tenants who can be held liable for debts of a successor are those holding under an 'old lease' (ie one executed before 1 January 1996) or former tenants under a 'new' lease who have entered into a s16 authorised guarantee agreement. In either case, a former tenant will not be liable to pay any amount unless notice has been served on him by the landlord within six months of the debt becoming due (s17).

Finally, to guarantee the performance by the assignee tenant s19 strengthens the position of a former tenant who is obliged to pay the debts of a successor. Once such a former tenant has discharged his obligations under s17 he has the right to call upon the landlord to grant him an overriding lease (overriding the lease of the defaulting assignee). Such a lease is a tenancy of the landlord's reversion and puts the former tenant in the position of intermediate landlord in relation to the defaulting tenant. In the latter capacity the former tenant can exercise all the usual remedies available to a landlord, including the right to forfeit. This development is designed to meet the concerns of many original tenants who, in the recent recession, found themselves powerless to control accruing liabilities due to the default of their successors in title.

Conclusion. The LT(C)A 1995 introduces some of the biggest reforms seen in the last 50 years. The way the property market operates will never be the same again. Any agreement restricting the operation of the LT(C)A 1995 is void: s25. It is important to emphasise that it is the date of the grant of the tenancy which is the determining factor and not the date when the term commences (ie it is the date of the grant which puts a tenancy either side of the cut off). The Act repeals ss141 and 142 LPA 1925 for the vast majority of leases granted on or after 1 January 1996. It is submitted that the Act will have at least three consequences. First, it will create a two-tier leasehold market – old leases subject to privity of contract and new tenancies with automatic tenant release. Accordingly, since it is not retrospective, practitioners dealing with leases will have to distinguish carefully between a new tenancy to which the Act applies and an old lease covered by the privity of contract and estate regime. Second, given the amendment to s19 of the Landlord and Tenant Act 1927, it is submitted that the content of the assignment clause in new tenancies is going to be a key area in leasehold negotiations, since it enables landlords to specify in that clause the security/creditworthiness criteria that a prospective assignee will have to meet. Third, it may result in an increased use of subletting to avoid the consequences of tenant release (the Act has no application to subletting).

Enforcement by and against subtenants

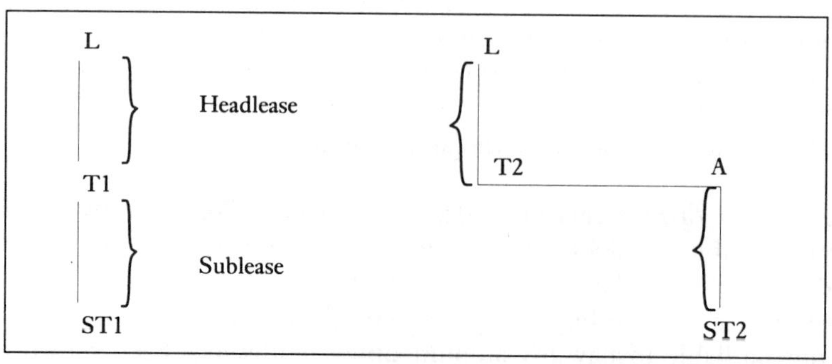

There is neither privity of estate nor privity of contract between a landlord and a subtenant. Privity of estate exists only between a landlord and his immediate tenant.

Liability of subtenants to head landlord

Hence, in neither of the examples given above, can L sue ST directly, under the rules dealing with the enforcement of covenants in leases, for conduct by ST that amounts to a breach of a covenant in the head lease. A subtenant is liable to his immediate landlord for breaches of covenants in the sublease (in the examples, T1 or A), but he is not liable at common law to the head landlord for breach of covenant.

A landlord can enforce a covenant against a subtenant either indirectly or in equity.

Indirect enforcement at common law

By s79 LPA 1925, a covenant relating to any land of a covenantor (the original tenant) is deemed to be made by the covenantor on behalf of himself, his successors in title (assignees) and persons deriving title under him or them (subtenants).

The effect of this provision is that a tenant is liable to his landlord if a subtenant is in breach of covenants contained in the head lease, so long as those covenants relate to the land. The landlord can therefore sue the tenant, or forfeit his lease for breach. Once the tenant's lease is forfeit, the subtenant's lease also comes to an end.

Both the subtenant and the tenant can seek relief from forfeiture, under ss146(4) and 146(2) LPA 1925 respectively.

Note: in order to gain possession from a subtenant, a landlord must forfeit the tenant's lease. Both the tenant and the subtenant then become trespassers.

Enforcement in equity

A landlord can enforce a covenant directly against a subtenant in equity under the rule in *Tulk* v *Moxhay* (1848) 2 Ph 774 so long as:

1. The covenant is negative in substance; and
2. It touches and concerns the land held under the sublease; and
3. There was no intention expressed in the sublease that the subtenant should not be liable (subject to the burden); and
4. The subtenant has actual, constructive or imputed notice of the existence of the covenant. Covenants contained in leases are not registrable, so liability depends on notice.

(See Chapter 11 for further details of restrictive covenants.) If these conditions are satisfied a landlord can sue a subtenant for breach of a covenant in the head lease, and enforce the covenant by means of an injunction, or obtain damages in lieu. Note that a landlord cannot forfeit a subtenant's lease, even though he can establish liability under the rule in *Tulk* v *Moxhay*.

Liability of head landlords to subtenants

A subtenant cannot sue the head landlord directly for his breach of the covenants in the head lease under the rules relating to leasehold covenants, but under the rules relating to freehold land a subtenant may be able to sue the head landlord.

The original landlord. Where the original landlord has not assigned his reversion, a subtenant can enforce both positive and negative covenants directly against the landlord provided that:

1. The covenants relate to the land comprised in the sublease; and
2. The sublease does not state that the subtenant is to be deprived of the benefit of the covenants in the head lease.

The capacity of a subtenant to sue is based on s78(1) LPA 1925, which provides that a covenant relating to any land of the covenantee (the tenant) shall be deemed to be made with his successors in title (assignees) and the persons deriving title under him or them (subtenants).

In *Smith and Snipes Hall Farm* v *River Douglas Catchment Board* [1949] 2 KB 500 it was held that a covenant made with a freeholder could be enforced at common law by a tenant. This argument can be applied to subtenancies.

A successor in title of the original landlord. Where the original landlord has assigned his reversion, a subtenant can enforce only negative covenants against the assignee of the reversion under the rule in *Tulk* v *Moxhay.*

10.12 Statutory protection of tenants

Tenants are protected against their landlords by a complex and interrelated series of statutes. The type of protection depends upon the type of tenancy. Tenancies are divided into three types:

1. residential;
2. agricultural;
3. business.

Tenancies must fall within one of these categories, and cannot fall within more than one. The categories are mutually exclusive.

10.13 Residential tenancies

The legislation affording protection to residential tenants is found in four main statutes: the Rent Act 1977; the Protection from Eviction Act 1977; the Housing Act 1980; and the Rent (Amendment) Act 1985. Some protection is also given by the Landlord and Tenant Act 1954 and the Leasehold Reform Acts 1967–79.

The basic structure of protection is set out in the Rent Act 1977. A tenancy which qualifies under the Act (called a protected tenancy) enjoys the benefit of both control over the amount of rent that may be charged and restrictions on the ability of landlords to regain possession. In order to qualify the tenancy must be one under which:

1. A dwelling house is let as a separate dwelling (s1); and
2. The rateable value of that dwelling house does not exceed £1,500 (in London) or £750 (outside London) (s3); and
3. Rent is paid, and that rent is not less than two-thirds of the rateable value of the dwelling house at the date it was first let (s5).

Once it is established that a tenancy is protected, then the tenant's continued right to possession is safeguarded in two ways:

First, the landlord is not entitled to possession as of right once the contractual tenancy ends, either by effluxion of time where the tenancy is a term certain, or by notice to quit in the case of a periodic tenancy. In either case, provided that the tenant is occupying the dwelling house as his residence immediately before the end of the contractual tenancy, the tenancy is converted into a statutory tenancy. The statutory tenancy continues so long as the tenant remains in occupation and only ends when possession is ordered by the court (s2). In *Hampstead Way Investments Ltd* v *Lewis-Weare* [1985] 1 WLR 164 Lord Brandon set out a number of propositions of general application as to the qualifications which had to be fulfilled by way of residence in order to create the circumstances under which a person was occupying a dwelling house as a home. These were:

1. A person could have two dwelling houses, each of which he occupied as his home, so that, if either was let to him, his tenancy would be protected by the Rent Act 1977.
2. Where a person was a tenant of two different parts of the same house under different lettings by the same landlord, and carried out some of his living activities in one part of the house and the rest of them in the other part, neither tenancy would normally be protected. If, however, the true view of the facts was that there was, in substance, a single combined or composite letting of the two parts of the house as a whole, then the tenancies of both parts together would, or at least might, be protected.
3. Where a person owned one dwelling house which he occupied as his home for most of his time, and was at the same time the tenant of another dwelling house which he occupied only rarely for limited purposes, it was a question of fact and degree whether he occupied the latter dwelling house as his second home.

On applying these principles the House of Lords held that the tenant was not occupying the flat as his residence within s2(3) Rent Act 1977.

In addition, if the statutory tenant dies, his statutory tenancy may be taken over and continued by a member of his family residing with him for six months before his death, and this may happen twice; but where the tenant dies after 15 January 1989 succession depends on residence for two years before the tenant dies, and only one transmission is allowed (s39 Housing Act 1988).

Secondly, the landlord is only entitled to possession during either a protected contractual tenancy (a regulated tenancy) or a statutory tenancy if he can establish one of the grounds for possession set out in s98 and Schedule 15 of the Rent Act 1977, as amended by the Housing Act 1980. In any case the landlord is forbidden to obtain possession of premises let as a dwelling other than by proceedings in court (s3 Protection from Eviction Act 1977). The grounds for possession include the breach of a covenant by the tenant (Schedule 15, Case 1); the provision of suitable alternative accommodation: *Siddiqui* v *Rashid* [1980] 1 WLR 1018 and *Hill* v *Rochard* [1983] 2 All ER 21; nuisance or annoyance to neighbouring occupiers committed by the tenant (Schedule 15, Case 2). The court has a wide discretion to adjourn or suspend possession under the cases in Part I of Schedule 15 (the discretionary cases) and in those cases must also find that it is reasonable to order possession (s98).

Case 11 in Schedule 15 to the Rent Act 1977 has been amended by s1 Rent (Amendment) Act 1985 and now begins:

> 'Where a person (in this case referred to as "the owner occupier") who let the dwelling house on a regulated tenancy had, at any time before the letting, occupied it as his residence ...'.

This change was necessary because of the earlier decision of the Court of Appeal, in *Pocock* v *Steel* [1985] 1 WLR 229, that an owner-occupier could only make use of the original Case 11 if his occupation had immediately preceded the grant of the tenancy.

Subtenants are also protected. The normal rule at common law that all subtenancies determine when the head tenancy determines is suspended by s137. Provided that the subtenancy is lawful (that is, not in breach of a covenant against subletting) and protected as against the immediate landlord, then the subtenancy continues, with the landlord stepping into the tenant's shoes. See *Regalian Securities Ltd* v *Ramsden* [1981] 2 All ER 65.

The control over rent increases applies wherever a tenancy is protected, as either a regulated or a statutory tenancy. Either the landlord or the tenant may apply to the rent officer to have the rent registered. Once the rent is registered it is illegal for the landlord to demand more, and the tenant may sue to recover excess rent. A new (and increased) rent may only be registered every three years under the Rent Act 1977, although this has been reduced to two years for tenancies commencing after November 1980, by the Housing Act 1980. In addition, any increase is payable only by staggered increments. Registered rents are usually below the open market rent, as rent officers are not allowed to take scarcity value into account in determining the rent.

From the above, it is apparent that once a tenancy becomes protected under the

Rent Act 1977, the tenant is in a most favourable position. The gap in protection is found not in the mechanisms of the Act, but rather in the variety of means by which a tenancy may be excluded from the Act. Some of these means are provided by the Act itself, and others have been developed by landlords anxious to avoid having protected tenants. The extent of some of these non-statutory methods must now be measured in the light of the decision of the House of Lords in *Street* v *Mountford* [1985] 2 WLR 877.

Under the Act, the following are excluded:

1. Holiday lettings (s9): in *Buchmann* v *May* [1978] 2 All ER 993 the Court of Appeal held that if both parties agree that it is a holiday letting, and it is not an obvious sham, then the letting will be outside the Act.
2. Lettings to students (s8): this applies where the landlord is a university or similar body.
3. Lettings where the user is partly business and partly residential (s24): any business user takes the tenancy outside the Rent Act 1977.
4. Lettings where there is no separate dwelling house (s1): although one room can amount to a dwelling house, shared accommodation is not within the Act if the tenant shares 'essential living rooms' (ie does not have exclusive possession). See *Cole* v *Harris* [1945] KB 474. Essential living rooms include sitting rooms and kitchens, but not bathrooms.
5. Lettings where the landlord resides in another dwelling house in the same building (s12): this does not include a block of flats. However, provided that the tenancy would otherwise be protected (in other words, it would comply with the three requirements set out above), the tenancy has partial protection as a restricted contract.
6. Lettings where the rent includes any payment in respect of attendance or substantial payment in respect of board (s7): tenancies where the landlord provides breakfast are therefore not protected tenancies, although they can be restricted contracts.
7. All local authority tenants are outside the Rent Act 1977, but have been given similar protection by the Housing Act 1980 as secure tenants.
8. In the same way most housing association tenants are excluded by the 1977 Act, but are protected as assured tenants by the 1980 Act.

Tenants under restricted contracts are given partial protection, ss103–105 RA 1977. There is full rent control, but little in the way of security of tenure. Where the tenancy is a periodical tenancy, the tenant may apply for the operation of the notice to quit to be deferred for six months, and may apply again for a further deferment. He must however always apply before the notice to quit has expired. Tenants under terms certain cannot apply and have no security of tenure, neither do landlords have to show that they fall within any of the cases in Schedule 15; they may seek possession as of right under the common law. A 'restricted contract' is defined in s19(1) RA 1977 as:

> '... a contract ... whereby one person grants to another person, in consideration of a rent which includes payment for the use of furniture or for services, the right to occupy a dwelling as a residence.'

The largest gap in the legislation, however, is that it applies only to tenancies, not to licences. Over the years property owners have made wide use of this loophole and used ingenious devices for creating a licence which is a tenancy in all but name. In *Somma* v *Hazelhurst* [1978] 1 WLR 1014 a man and a woman who were not married were each granted a separate licence to occupy the same room in common with a person stipulated by the landlord. The landlord stipulated on the man's licence that the other occupant should be the woman, and vice versa. Both the occupants remained responsible only for their respective halves of the 'rent'. The Court of Appeal held that where both parties agree that there is to be a licence and not a tenancy, then they should be bound by that agreement, provided that the terms of the agreement are consistent with a licence. Here, neither of the two occupants had exclusive possession and they were not jointly liable for the whole 'rent'.

Therefore they were not joint tenants, but licensees, and outside the Rent Act 1977. This decision was expressly disapproved by the House of Lords in *Street* v *Mountford* (above). The fact that the distinction is now between tenant or lodger must curtail many of the former methods referred to above. It will not matter what name the parties give to the arrangement. See the earlier discussion at section 10.5 as to the joint decision of the House of Lords in *AG Securities* v *Vaughan* and *Antoniades* v *Villiers* [1988] 3 WLR 1205.

Residential tenancies created after 15 January 1989 may now come within the provisions of the Housing Act 1988. The 1988 Act was designed to deregulate new lettings but the Rent Act 1977 will continue to apply to tenancies existing on 15 January 1989.

1. The Housing Act 1988 only applies to new tenancies which may become either assured tenancies or assured shorthold tenancies. No assured tenancies under the Housing Act 1980 can be created after 15 January 1989.
2. Assured tenancies:
   a) These consist of a tenancy of a dwellinghouse let as a separate dwelling to an individual and occupied as the only or principal home. Rent must exceed two-thirds of the rateable value. Exceptions include business premises, student lettings, holiday lettings and certain resident landlords.
   b) Section 7 and Schedule 2 Housing Act 1988 sets out the grounds on which the landlord may seek possession. These grounds are split into eight mandatory grounds (Grounds 1–8) and eight discretionary grounds (Grounds 9–16). In the case of the discretionary grounds the court must be satisfied that it is reasonable to make an order. The grounds include:

      Ground 1 – possession now required where notice given before the tenancy commenced that possession may be so required. Compare Case 9 under Rent Act 1977;

Ground 6 –	wishes to redevelop the site;
Ground 9 –	where suitable alternative accommodation is available;
Ground 11 –	persistent delay in paying rent;
Ground 12 –	some obligation under tenancy 'broken or not performed';
Ground 16 –	a service tenancy and the employment has now ended.

c) There is no application of the fair rent rules, and the landlord can increase rent by giving a minimum of one month's notice. The notice can be referred to the Rent Assessment Committee to fix an open market rent for the premises. There is no control on the original rent charged, and the effect will be to allow market rents to be charged.

3. Assured shorthold tenancies:
   a) Section 20 provides for the creation of assured shorthold tenancies which are short, fixed-term lettings with the landlord guaranteed prossession at the end of the term. The term is for a minimum of at least six months with no maximum. A notice must be served on the tenant before it commences that it is an assured shorthold tenancy.
   b) The former protected shorthold tenancies are ended, but existing ones continue until they end by effluxion of time (s34).
   c) There is some rent control on the assured shorthold tenancy because the tenant may refer the rent to the Rent Assessment Committee at any time on the ground of excessive rent, and the committee can fix a lower rent by comparison with similar houses let on assured tenancies (s22(3)). A person cannot contract out of these shorthold provisions (s22(4)(b)).

Where residential tenancies are outside the protection afforded by the Rent Act 1977 or the Housing Act 1980, then they may be afforded some protection by the Landlord and Tenant Act 1954, or the Leasehold Reform Acts 1967–79.

Part I Landlord and Tenant Act 1954 protects tenants under long leases where the rent is less than two-thirds of the rateable value: who would, therefore, be outside the protection of the Rent Act 1977. If a lease had originally been for more than 21 years at this low rent and the premises are occupied as a separate dwelling at the time of the purported end of the lease, then such a long lease will continue on the same terms until one party issues a notice to terminate it (s3 Landlord and Tenant Act 1954). The effect of the 1954 Act is that the parties can agree a new tenancy or the landlord may seek possession but only on the very limited grounds set out in s12 LTA 1954.

The Leasehold Reform Acts 1967–79 (as amended by the Housing Act 1980) have further provisions which protect 'residential' tenants against eviction. If the tenant under a long lease, being a term of more than 21 years, of a home at a low rent has occupied the premises as his only or main residence for the last three years or three of the last ten years, then he may apply to the landlord either to purchase the freehold (ie enfranchise his lease) or to secure a 50-year extension of his lease. If the requisite conditions are satisfied, the landlord is bound to make a conveyance of the freehold at a price to be fixed in accordance with the relevant legislation. If the parties cannot agree the price it will be determined by the Lands Tribunal. If the tenant chooses lease extension rather than enfranchisement, once the extended term has commenced he must abide by this decision and cannot subsequently apply for enfranchisement. The benefit of a tenant's notice of his desire to purchase the freehold or obtain a 50-year extension of his lease under the Act can be assigned with the house. However, there is no right to enfranchise certain properties of particular historic interest or natural beauty. In *Tandon* v *Trustees of Spurgeon's Homes* [1982] AC 755 the House of Lords defined 'house' as a building designed or adapted for living in, ie for occupation as a residence, and then only exceptional circumstances would justify holding that the building could not be called a house.

Important changes to the Leasehold Reform Act 1967 have been effected by the Leasehold Reform Housing and Urban Development Act 1993. While the main innovation of the latter Act concerns flats, the changes to the 1967 Act are likely to be far-reaching. Four changes are particularly noteworthy. First, the right to enfranchise has been extended. Under the 1967 Act the right was restricted to houses having a rateable value limit of up to £1,500 in London and £750 elsewhere (this effectively excluded the owners of most higher-value houses from the provisions of the 1967 Act). The rateable value limits have now been abolished (s63 Leasehold Reform Act 1993). Accordingly, the tenants of higher-value houses who fulfil the remaining qualifying conditions (long lease at a low rent etc) now have the right to enfranchise under the 1993 Act. For many people that will be an attractive possibility. Secondly, an alternative low rent test has been introduced (s65 Leasehold Reform Act 1993). The new test, based as it is on the ground rent in the first year of the lease, should enable some leaseholders excluded by the existing test (which is based on the rent at the time of enfranchisement) to acquire the freehold. Thirdly, the price to be paid for enfranchisement of houses under the extended provisions has been revised (s66 Leasehold Reform Act 1993). Fourthly, leaseholders who only qualify under the 1967 Act because of the 1993 Act only have the right to enfranchise – they cannot opt to extend the lease for a further period of 50 years. This is probably a reflection of the fact that enfranchisement has proved infinitely more attractive than lease extension.

In addition, all residential tenants are protected from harassment and unlawful eviction by s1 Protection from Eviction Act 1977. To be lawful, eviction must be by due process of law, following possession proceedings (s3). Where the tenancy is a periodic one, four weeks' written notice to quit must be given (s5).

Section 27 Housing Act 1988 widens damages available in tort if a landlord unlawfully deprives a residential occupier of occupation of the premises or does some act calculated to interfere with the peace or comfort of the occupier.

In addition the criminal offence of harassment is changed in that it is now of necessity to prove that the landlord knew, or should have known, that his conduct would be likely to cause the occupier to give up his occupation.

The complaints that might legitimately be made about the legislation protecting residential tenants is not that there is insufficient protection, but rather that there is too much, and that this overprotection, combined with the haphazard way in which the legislation has evolved, has created a maze of legal provisions which baffles most people and encourages landlords to seek devious routes around the legislation protection given to tenants. The Housing Act 1980 has extended this protection, but has not simplified the law to any significant degree.

10.14 Agricultural tenancies

The law in respect of agricultural tenancies has recently been significantly reformed with the coming into force on 1 September 1995 of the Agricultural Tenancies Act 1995. The Act applies to agricultural tenancies created on or after that date. However, agricultural tenancies created before 1 September 1995 are still regulated by the Agricultural Holdings Act 1986. Given that there are a large number of agricultural tenancies in existence which were created before 1 September 1995 and that such tenancies are likely to be around for many years to come, a summary of both the 'old law' (ie pre 1 September 1995) and the 'new law' (post 31 August 1995) is set out below.

Pre 1 September 1995 tenancies

Agricultural tenancies created before 1 September 1995 are governed mainly by the Agricultural Holdings Act 1986. Agriculture has a wide meaning, including horticulture, seed growing, market gardening and grazing livestock.

The Acts apply to most agricultural tenancies, except grazing or mowing agreements for less than a year and tenancies for more than one year but less than two. Where agricultural land is let with non-agricultural land, it is a question of fact whether the whole is an agricultural tenancy.

Protection is given by:

1. Converting all tenancies that fall within the Act into periodic yearly tenancies determinable by notice to quit.
2. Restricting the grounds on which a notice to quit may be served and in most cases giving the tenant the right to serve a counter-notice. This, in effect, gives the Agricultural Land Tribunal jurisdiction to adjudicate whether the notice should take effect or not.
3. Permitting rent increases only at three-yearly intervals, the increase to be agreed or submitted to an arbitrator.
4. Entitling a tenant who has received valid notice to quit to compensation for improvements and disturbance.

Finally, any 'successor tenancies' arising out of these tenancies, even though arising after 31 August 1995, are still regulated under the 1986 Act.

Post 31 August 1995 tenancies

The Agricultural Tenancies Act 1995 fulfils a commitment made by the Conservative Party in their 1992 General Election manifesto to liberalise agricultural tenancy laws. The pattern of agricultural land ownership and tenure has changed significantly during the course of this century. At the turn of the century about 90 per cent of agricultural land was rented, whereas by 1993 the percentage had declined to 35 per cent. The Government and much of the industry concluded that this decline had been hastened by the introduction of security of tenure. One of the aims of the Agricultural Tenancies Act 1995 is to tackle the decline in the number of agricultural tenancies being offered.

The Act replaces the former regime relating to agricultural tenancies with the concept of a farm business tenancy which must comply with a range of conditions, eg a tenancy cannot be a farm business tenancy if it began before 1 September 1995 or if it is a tenancy beginning on or after that date under the statutory succession provisions of the Agricultural Holdings Act 1986. The new 'farm business tenancy' introduces a greater measure of flexibility. In particular, landlords and tenants can now negotiate the tenancy's length, rent levels and, within certain limits, rent reviews and repair provisions, without statutory intervention.

In essence, the Agricultural Tenancies Act 1995 is a 'deregulating' one. It gives the opportunity for landlords and tenants to enter into agreements to suit their own particular needs. It should lead to many new agricultural tenancies being created. Evidence suggests that this began to happen immediately, and that a significant number of new tenancies were granted in the first six months after the Act came into force. However, this was undoubtedly due as much to the enhanced reliefs for inheritance tax purposes which were also made available to landowners granting such tenancies as to the terms of the Act itself. Subject to certain conditions being satisfied, the value of the landlord's interest in the land attracts 100 per cent relief for inheritance tax purposes where a new agricultural tenancy is granted on or after 1 September 1995. Before the passing of the new Act, relief was available at only 50 per cent.

10.15 Business tenancies

The main statutory provisions relating to business tenancies are contained in Part II of the Landlord and Tenant Act 1954. This applies to tenancies of premises which are

> 'occupied by the tenant and are so occupied for the purposes of a business carried on by him',

and 'business' includes a trade, profession or employment (s23).

Personal occupation is not required where the tenant occupies by means of his servants. Tenancy includes all tenancies except a tenancy at will. See *Manfield & Sons* v *Botchin* [1970] 2 QB 612.

Certain tenancies, however, are expressly excluded. They include agricultural tenancies, tenancies protected by the Rent Acts, tenancies of licensed premises and service tenancies.

Security of tenure is given by providing that the tenancy can only be terminated by a notice in the prescribed form (s25). Unless the landlord stipulates in his notice one of the statutory grounds of opposition to a new tenancy set out in s30, the tenant may serve a counter-notice requiring the grant of a new tenancy. The House of Lords has confirmed that the 'corresponding date principle' applies to notices and applications under the 1954 Act: see *Dodds* v *Walker* [1981] 2 All ER 609. If one of the statutory grounds is stated the tenant may still apply to the court for a new tenancy, when the landlord must establish the ground relied upon.

If the parties cannot agree upon the terms of the new tenancy, they may apply to the court to determine the terms. See *O'May* v *City of London Real Property Co Ltd* [1982] 1 All ER 660.

Where the grounds of objection are that the landlord intends to demolish or reconstruct the premises, or intends to occupy them himself, the tenant is entitled to compensation. A tenant quitting the premises may also be entitled to compensation for improvements he has made.

10.16 Worked example

Q L leased a dwelling house to T for three years from 1 January 1994 at a rent of £2,000 a year. T covenanted not to under-let or part with possession of the property without first obtaining L's consent in writing and 'to carry out all external and internal repairs'. L covenanted that if he should decide to sell the dwelling house during the three-year term of the lease 'the property will first be offered for sale to the tenant at £40,000'. The lease reserves a right for L to re-enter into possession for any breach of covenant by the tenant.

Early in 1995 T asked L for consent to grant an underlease to A. L refused consent without giving reasons. T then executed an underlease to A for the residue of the three-year term and A went into possession.

Last winter the roof of the house was badly damaged by frost. If the roof was repaired the house would now sell for substantially more than £40,000.

Advise L who wishes: (1) to sue A for failing to repair the roof, and (2) to sell the house by auction immediately, with vacant possession, despite demands from T and A respectively that it be sold to them for £40,000.

When dealing with landlord and tenant questions it is advisable to:

1. draw a diagram showing the relationship of the parties;

2. list the covenants and their makers; and
3. list the breaches

before starting the answer.

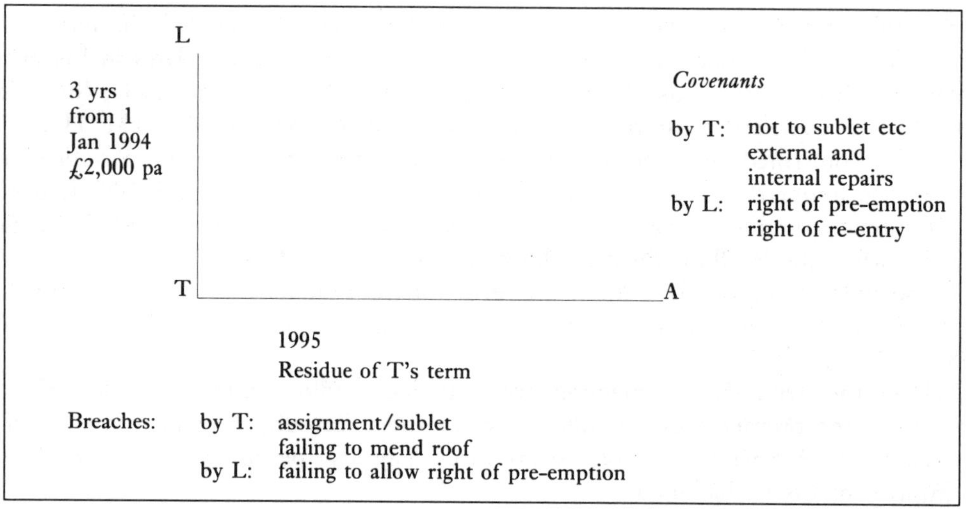

A The present position appears to be that T has assigned his lease to A. The purported sublease was for the whole of the residue of T's term, and therefore takes effect as an assignment, not as a subtenancy. The supposed subtenancy was executed, ie made by deed, and so the assignment will have been made by deed, so complying with s52(1) LPA 1925 and creating a legal assignment. L's original lease to T need not have been made by deed as the term was for three years and no fine was taken, so the exception in s54(2) LPA 1925 applies, and T's tenancy was legal.

The covenant not to underlet

The covenant in T's lease forbade subletting and parting with possession, not assignment. However, parting with possession covers both subletting and assignment, and as A has entered into possession as an assignee, T no longer has possession, as defined in s205(1)(xix) LPA 1925. But T's covenant was in the qualified form, and therefore s19 Landlord and Tenant Act 1927 implies the words 'such consent not to be unreasonably refused'. A refusal of consent without giving any reasons is prima facie unreasonable, and if L wishes to forfeit the lease for T's breach, he will bear the burden of showing that his refusal was not in fact unreasonable. On the other hand it could be argued that T never asked for L's consent to assign, only to sublet, and therefore T is in breach. An unlawful assignment is an irremediable breach (*Glass* v *Kencakes* (1966)), and provided that L has not waived the breach by accepting rent from A, he may be able to exercise his right, under the forfeiture clause, to forfeit the lease. L will first have to serve a s146 notice, specifying the breach complained of and requiring compensation in money, prior to taking possession proceedings.

The failure to repair the roof

As the lease was of a dwelling house, for less than seven years and commenced after 1961, s11 Landlord and Tenant Act 1985 applies. This implies into the lease covenants by L to keep the structure and exterior of the dwelling house in repair. Such covenants cannot be excluded or limited by any agreement to the contrary unless the County Court has sanctioned this as being reasonable. However, s11(2) expressly relieves the landlord from liability to rebuild or reinstate the premises as a result of damage due to fire, flood or other inevitable accident.

The issue is whether A can enforce the covenant. The benefit of all covenants contained in the lease between L and T passed to him by s78 LPA 1925. The roof was damaged by frost. It is arguable that this falls within the definition of 'other inevitable accident'. However, in order to escape liability L must also show that the house requires rebuilding or reinstatement and not just repairs. It is more likely that a court would hold that the house requires repairs, rather than reinstatement. That being so, L is bound by the implied covenant, and the roof is obviously part of the 'structure and exterior of the house', so making L responsible for the repairs, not T or A, so neither T nor A is in breach of their repairing covenant which applies only to internal repairs.

The right of pre-emption

What was originally granted to T was a right of pre-emption, that is, the right of first refusal once L decided to sell. A right of pre-emption is registrable as a C(iv) estate contract. Now that L has decided to sell, the right has become an option. The issue is whether either T or A can enforce it. L is the original grantor, and so the option remains enforceable against him whether or not it is registered as an estate contract under C(iv), or protected by notice on the register, as the case may be. However, an option is treated not as part of the lease, but as a separate agreement between the parties collateral to the lease. The agreement therefore between L and T was that T should have a right of pre-emption for three years commencing with the grant of the lease. Once L decided to sell the property the right of pre-emption became exercisable as an option. As between L and T, the original parties, the contract remains enforceable for three years. The question is whether A can enforce it. In *Griffith* v *Pelton* (1958) it was held that an option will not pass with an assignment of the lease to the assignee unless:

1. There was an express assignment of the option; or
2. The assignee was within the class of persons to whom the option or pre-emption was originally granted.

Therefore, whether or not A can enforce a right to purchase the freehold reversion will depend on the terms of the original grant by L and/or the terms of the assignment by T. In either case the option will be enforceable by an action for specific performance.

L's position is therefore not good. In order to forfeit the lease he will have to show that he did not unreasonably refuse consent. He is himself not in breach of his repairing covenants, but will be as soon as A informs him of the need for repair, and may already be liable if he has express knowledge of the need for repair. See *O'Brien* v *Robinson* (1973). In addition, the right of pre-emption, or option, being independent of the lease, may not come to an end if and when the lease is forfeited. See *Rafferty* v *Scholfield* (1897). L's best course of action is to discover how much the roof repairs will cost. If the cost of the repairs is equal to the difference between £40,000 and the present selling price of the house, he should sell to T or A, depending on whether or not the right of pre-emption was assigned.

11

Enforcement of Covenants between Freeholders

11.1 Introduction

This chapter deals with the enforcement of covenants affecting land where there is no privity of estate between the covenantee and covenantor. In other words, that is the enforcement of covenants between parties who do not stand in the relationship of landlord and tenant. It is important to grasp the distinction between the rules governing covenants between landlord and tenant (dealt with in Chapter 10) and those governing whether or not covenants affecting land can be enforced by and against persons between whom there is no privity of estate. There are two distinct sets of rules.

11.2 Definitions

A covenant is a promise contained in a deed. The deed may be (and usually is) a conveyance of a freehold estate in land, but the covenant may be contained in a separate deed. The type of promise contained in such deeds usually concerns the land, for example:

1. a promise not to build a factory;
2. a promise to maintain a fence;
3. a promise to keep land as open space.

But there is nothing to stop the parties to the deed making any type of promise, although promises not concerning the land are limited in their enforceability. The person who makes the promise is the 'covenantor'. The person to whom it is made is the 'covenantee'. Hence the person seeking to enforce the covenant (the plaintiff) will be the covenantee and the defendant will be the covenantor.

The land owned by the covenantee will have the benefit of the covenant, and so far as the covenant is concerned will be the 'dominant tenement'. The land owned by the covenantor will have the burden of the covenant and will be the 'servient tenement'. This can be illustrated by the following diagram where X originally owned the whole of Greenacre and sold part to Y, taking from Y a covenant not to use the land for business purposes.

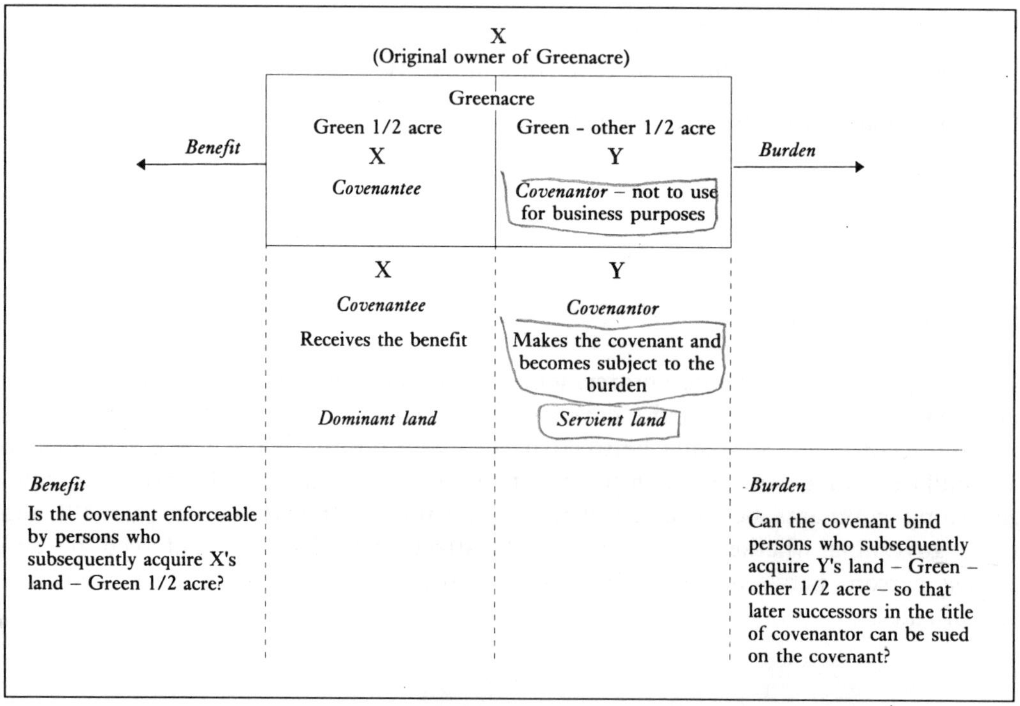

Before a covenant can be enforced by X against Y, two conditions must be fulfilled:

1. The covenantee (X) must have the benefit of the covenant.
2. The covenantor (Y) must be subject to the burden of the covenant.

The 'benefit' means the capacity to sue. The 'burden' means the liability to be sued.

The key to a proper understanding of this subject is to consider the benefit and burden separately. Both conditions must be satisfied. It is quite possible for the covenantee, X, to have the benefit, but for the covenantor, Y, not to be subject to the burden, or vice versa. Unless X has the benefit and Y has the burden, X cannot enforce a covenant against Y.

11.3 The creation of covenants

A owns two adjoining pieces of land, Blackacre and Whiteacre. There is a large house on Whiteacre, and Blackacre is open country. B wants to buy Blackacre and build a house there. A is happy to sell provided that he can ensure that B does not build a factory or use the land in some other way that will reduce the value of the land retained by A.

Therefore A makes it a condition of the sale to B that the conveyance of Blackacre to B contains a promise by B not to use Blackacre for any purpose except the building of one house. The covenant is made for the benefit of Whiteacre. As between A and B, the parties to the conveyance, this covenant remains enforceable under the normal rules of contract. The difficulties arise when either A or B sells the land as, though the covenant remains enforceable between them, B will no longer have any control over the land (if he has sold), so A's remedy will be limited to damages and he will be unable to ensure that the value of Whiteacre is not diminished by the building of a factory on Blackacre.

To deal with this situation rules have been developed which ensure that, in some circumstances, covenants are enforceable by and against successors in title of the original parties. If this is the case, the covenant is said to 'run with the land'. That is, the burden of the covenant can run with the land of the covenantor and the benefit of the covenant can run with the land of the covenantee.

There are two sets of rules governing the running of covenants: the common law rules and the equitable rules. The common law rules should be applied first, and then the equitable rules if the covenant is not enforceable at law. This may be demonstrated by way of a basic flow chart:

Running of covenants

	Benefit	*Burden*
Common law	Yes →	No ↓
Equity	(Yes)	Yes Provided that the covenant is negative/restrictive
		NB: Burden of a positive covenant does not run – neither at common law nor in equity

11.4 Enforcement of covenants at common law between original parties

Between original parties to the deed

The original covenantee can always enforce any express covenant against the original covenantor. But if the covenant was made for the benefit of land which the covenantee has parted with, then the covenantee may only recover nominal damages as he will not suffer any loss. The loss will be suffered by the present owner of the land. Hence if A sells Whiteacre to C, and B later builds four dwelling houses on Blackacre, A will be entitled to sue B for breach of covenant, but the loss will be suffered by C, so A will only be entitled to nominal damages.

Extension of original parties by s56 LPA 1925

At common law it was a strict rule that no one could sue on a deed made inter partes who was not a party to the deed. This rule has been relaxed by s56(1) LPA 1925, which provides that:

> 'A person may take … the benefit of any … covenant over or respecting land … although he may not be named as a party to the conveyance or other instrument.'

In order to qualify under s56 a person who was not a party to the original deed must show that the contract purported to be made with him (as covenantee), not just for his benefit. See *Beswick* v *Beswick* [1968] AC 58.

Hence, if in the conveyance of Whiteacre B covenanted with A and with the owners for the time being of Redacre and Greenacre (plots of land adjoining Blackacre), then the persons who are owners of Redacre and Greenacre at the time of the covenant can sue B on the covenant, even though they are not named as parties to the conveyance, because the covenant was expressed to be made with them for the benefit of their land.

Section 56 can only benefit persons who are in existence and identifiable when the covenant is made. Hence if the conveyance stated that the covenant was made with the owner for the time being of Redacre and his heirs and assigns, the only person who can benefit directly is the present owner. Future owners will be able to enforce the covenant only if they can show that the benefit of the covenant has run with Redacre (see sections 11.5 and 11.6).

11.5 Enforcement of covenants at common law by assignees

The benefit and burden of a covenant must be considered separately. *Note*: in order to be enforceable the covenantee must have the benefit and and covenantor must be subject to the burden; both conditions must be satisfied.

Benefit

The benefit of a covenant can be expressly assigned together with the land to which it relates. Hence, if B assigns Blackacre to C, he can also expressly assign the benefit of his covenant with A.

The benefit of a covenant runs with the land of the covenantee at common law, without express assignment, provided that the following four conditions are satisfied:

1. the covenant touches and concerns the land of the covenantee;
2. there is an intention that the benefit should run with land owned by the covenantee at the date of the covenant;
3. the covenantee must have the legal estate in the land which is to be benefited at the time of making the covenant; and
4. an assignee seeking to enforce the covenant must have the same legal estate in the land as the original covenantee.

The covenant must touch and concern the land

The rules here are the same as those governing pre-1996 leasehold covenants (see Chapter 10). The benefit of purely personal covenants will not run with the land.

> 'The covenant must either affect the land as regards its mode of occupation or it must be such as per se, and not merely from collateral circumstances, affects the value of the land.'

Per Tucker LJ in *Smith and Snipes Hall Farm* v *River Douglas Catchment Board* [1949] 2 KB 500.

The covenant must have been made for the benefit of land owned by the present covenantee

Hence, before C can enforce the covenant against A, he must show that the covenant was made for the benefit of Blackacre and that he (C) is the present owner of Blackacre. Once C assigns the land, he can no longer enforce the covenant. Only the original covenantee retains the right to enforce the covenant after he has assigned the land.

There is no requirement that the covenant has anything to do with any land owned by the covenantor. See *The Prior's Case* (1368) YB 42 Ed 3, Hil pl 14. Neither is it necessary to show that the assignee had notice of the existence of the covenant at the time of the assignment to him by the covenantee. Once the benefit is annexed to the land, it passes automatically. See *Rogers* v *Hosegood* [1900] 2 Ch 388.

The covenantee must have a legal estate in the land

Prior to 1875 the common law courts could not recognise the existence of equitable interests in land, so covenants could be enforced only by the owner of a legal estate.

Covenants made before 1926 can only be enforced at law where the assignee holds the same legal estate as the original covenantee. In *Smith and Snipes Hall Farm* v *River Douglas Catchment Board* (above) the Court of Appeal held that s78 LPA 1925 changed the law so that assignees did not need to have the same legal estate as the original covenantee so long as they derived title from the original covenantee. Hence both an assignee of the covenantee's freehold estate and the assignee's tenant could enforce a covenant – under s78 LPA 1925 the requirement is merely to be a 'successor in title'. In s78(2) this phrase is explained:

> 'to include the owners and occupiers for the time being of the land of the covenantee intended to be benefited'.

Note: the benefit of both positive and negative covenants can run at law.

The assignee seeking to enforce the covenant must have the same legal estate in the land as the original covenantee

Accordingly, if the original covenantee was an owner in fee simple, the benefit of the covenant could pass only to a third party who likewise owned the land in fee simple. There was limited authority for this requirement. The Court of Appeal decision in *Westhoughton UDC* v *Wigan Coal and Iron Co Ltd* [1919] 1 Ch 159 was frequently cited in support of this condition. However, in the opinion of Megarry and Wade the point was not clearly decided on that occasion (5th ed at p766 note 40).

Therefore, this final requirement constituted a rather doubtful feature of the common law rules on the passing of the benefit.

This rule, however, has been abrogated for covenants made after 1925 by s78 Law of Property Act 1925. As a result of this provision it is now sufficient to show that the person seeking to enforce the covenant is a 'successor in title' of the covenantee.

Burden

The burden of a covenant cannot run with freehold land at law, even by express assignment. Hence, at law a covenant can be enforced only so long as the original covenantor retains the land. The three methods covered below are potential exceptions to this rule. See *Austerberry* v *Oldham Corporation* (1885) 29 Ch D 750; *E & G C Ltd* v *Bate* (1935) 79 LJ News 203.

As the original covenantor remains liable on the covenant even though he has assigned the land, he may seek to protect himself by taking a covenant from his assignee that the assignee will observe the covenants. The covenantee may therefore be able to enforce the covenant by suing the original covenantor who will then sue the assignee. The disadvantage of this method is that once the chain of personal covenants becomes lengthy the chance that it will be broken by the disappearance or insolvency of one of the parties becomes greater.

A conveyancing device, as yet untested, is instead of conveying the land to grant a long lease at no rent containing the desired covenants. The lease is automatically enlarged by s153 LPA 1925 into a fee simple, but one made subject to all the obligations contained in the lease.

Under the so-called principle of benefit and burden as expressed in *Halsall* v *Brizell* [1957] Ch 169, where the burden (a covenant to contribute to the upkeep of a private road) was directly related to the benefit (the use by the covenantor of that road), the assignees of the covenantor could not take the benefit without taking the burden as well, even though the burden does not normally run at law. Upjohn J expressed the rule in these words:

> 'The defendants here cannot if they desire to use this house, as they do, take advantage of the trusts concerning the user of the roads contained in the deed and the other benefits created by it without undertaking the obligations thereunder. Upon that principle it seems to me that they are bound by this deed, if they desire to take its benefits.'

The use of the pure principle of benefit and burden was illustrated by Sir Robert Megarry VC in *Tito* v *Waddell (No 2)* [1977] Ch 106.

The extent of the principle was considered by the House of Lords in *Rhone* v *Stephens* (1994) The Times 18 March in which the issue was whether a positive covenant to maintain a roof was enforceable against a successor in title of the burdened land. Two clauses in the original conveyance were relevant to the litigation. Clause 2 imposed reciprocal benefits and burdens of support. Clause 3 imposed an obligation to repair the roof in question. The plaintiffs (who were seeking to enforce the positive covenant) argued that any party deriving any benefit from a conveyance had to accept any burden in the same conveyance. They submitted, in essence, that if a successor in title of the servient land took the benefit of clause 2 he had to accept the burden of clause 3. Lord Templeman rejected this contention in the following terms:

> 'The condition must be relevant to the exercise of the right. In *Halsall* v *Brizell* there were reciprocal benefits and burdens enjoyed by the users of the roads and sewers. In the present case clause 2 of the ... conveyance imposes reciprocal benefits and burdens of support but clause 3 which imposed an obligation to repair the roof is an independent provision. In *Halsall* v *Brizell* the defendant could, at least in theory, choose between enjoying the right and paying his proportion of the cost or alternatively giving up the right and saving his money. In the present case the owners of [the servient land] could not in theory or in practice be deprived of the benefit of the mutual rights of support if they failed to repair the roof.'

A covenant to pay money or to contribute to the upkeep of property may be construed as a rentcharge. In this case it may come within the definition of 'estate rentcharge' in s2 of the Rentcharges Act 1977, which was preserved by the 1977 Act.

> '"Estate rentcharge" is defined in s2(4) of the Rentcharges Act 1977 as
> "a rentcharge created for the purpose
> a) of making covenants to be performed by the owner of the land affected by the rentcharge enforceable by the rent owner against the owner for the time being of the land; or
> b) of meeting, or contributing towards, the cost of the performance by the rent owner of covenants for the provision of services, the carrying out of maintenance or repairs, the effecting of insurance or the making of any payment by him for the benefit of the land affected by the rentcharge or for the benefit of that and other land".'

The Wilberforce Committee published its report in 1965 the (*Report of the Committee on Positive Covenants Affecting Land*), recommending that the burden of positive covenants should run. The Law Commission has published three reports, in 1967, 1971 and 1984. The last report, numbered 127, entitled *Transfer of Land – The Law of Positive and Restrictive Covenants,* proposes fundamental changes in that both covenants and easements should be classified as land obligations, and the benefit and burden of a land obligation would run. The 1984 report of the Law Commission contains a draft Land Obligations Bill through which these proposals could be implemented.

Further comments on the decision in *Austerberry* v *Oldham Corporation* (1885) 29 Ch D 750 were made by the House of Lords in *Rhone* v *Stephens* (above). There the issue, as noted above, was whether a covenant to maintain a roof was enforceable against successors in title. In holding that the burden of this positive covenant did not run their Lordships affirmed the rule in *Austerberry* v *Oldham Corporation*, that the burden of a positive covenant did not run with freehold land at law. They further affirmed that the burden of restrictive but not positive covenants could run with freehold land in equity so as to bind successors in title of the servient land.

The case is noteworthy for the fact that the rule in *Austerberry* v *Oldham Corporation* was criticised in the Court of Appeal ((1993) The Times 21 January), and while recognising that it was bound by it the court suggested that the House of Lords 'might feel able to abolish or modify it'. The fact that the House of Lords has chosen not to do so means that once again we must wait to see what priority Parliament is prepared to allow for the important recommendations of the Law Commission in this regard.

The covenant may be construed as an easement. In *Crow* v *Wood* [1971] 1 QB 77 a right to have a fence kept in repair was held to be capable of being an easement. This could have a dramatic effect on positive obligations which involve the expenditure of money.

11.6 Example of the running of covenants at common law

A sells the fee simple of Blackacre to B, retaining Whiteacre. In the conveyance B (as covenantor) covenanted with A (covenantee) to:

1. maintain the dividing fence (V);
2. build only one dwelling house (W).

A (covenantor) covenanted with B (covenantee) to:

1. not build on Whiteacre (X);
2. build an extension to the dividing wall (Y).

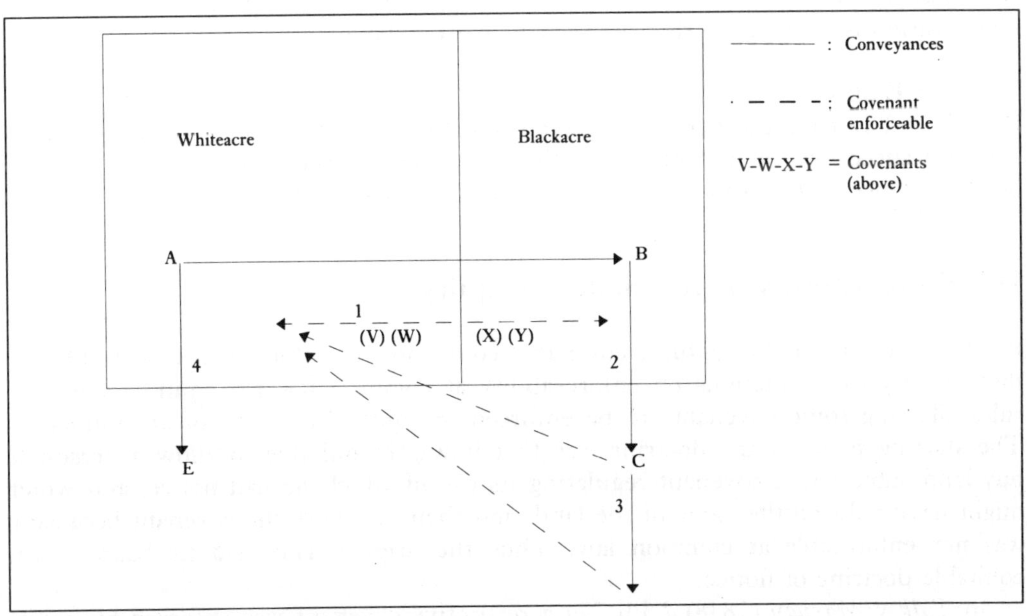

B subsequently conveys Blackacre to C.

C conveys it to D.
Later A conveys Whiteacre to E.

Enforceability of covenants in the above circumstances

Between A and B
All covenants are enforceable as A and B are original parties.

Between A and C
A is an original party, and so retains the benefit of covenants (V) and (W) and the burden of covenants (X) and (Y).

C is an assignee, so the burden of covenants (V) and (W) cannot pass to him. The benefit of covenants (X) and (Y) will pass to C provided that:

1. They touch and concern the land.
2. They were made for the benefit of Blackacre and C owns that land; and
3. C has a legal estate in Blackacre.

These conditions are fulfilled, and so C as covenantee has the benefit of covenants (X) and (Y). A as covenantor is subject to the burden, and so covenants (X) and (Y) are enforceable by C against A.

A has the benefit of covenants (V) and (W) but, as an assignee, C is not subject to the burden, and so C is not liable to A under covenants (V) and (W).

Between A and D
The position is identical to that between A and C (above).

Between E and D
Both E and D have the benefit of their respective covenants as covenantees, but as both are successors in title of the original covenantors, they are not subject to the burden. Hence neither can enforce a covenant against the other.

11.7 Enforceability of covenants in equity

Prior to the nineteenth century, covenants could not be enforced in equity. During that century the limitations on enforceability at common law led equity to develop rules allowing some covenants to be enforced in equity by means of an injunction. The starting point of the doctrine was that it was inequitable to allow a person to buy land subject to a covenant regulating its use of which he had notice, and which might have reduced the value of the land, and then to ignore the covenant because it was not enforceable at common law. Thus the original rule had its basis in the equitable doctrine of notice.

In *Tulk* v *Moxhay* (1848) 2 Ph 774 a restrictive covenant was enforced by equity against a successor in title who was not liable at common law, but who had purchased with notice of the covenant. The salient features of the case may be obtained from the following diagram:

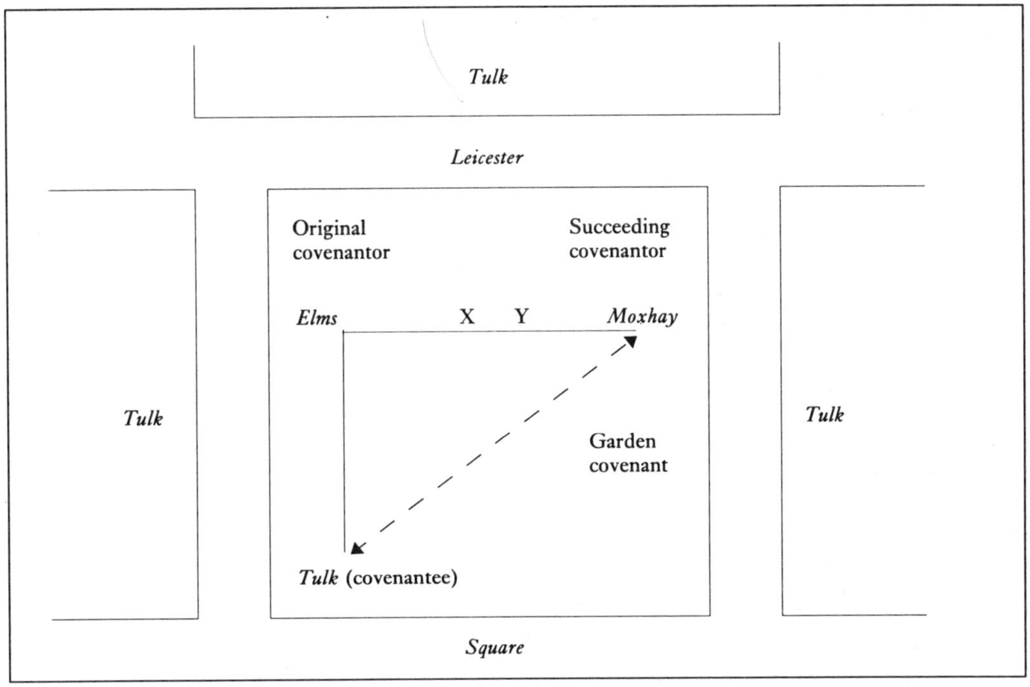

The covenant stated:

> '... at all times thereafter at his own costs to keep and maintain the said piece or parcel of ground and square garden in its present form and in sufficient and proper repair as a square garden and pleasure ground in an open state and uncovered with any buildings in a neat and ornamental order.'

At first equity enforced both positive and negative covenants, but by 1881 it was decided that only negative covenants were appropriate for equitable enforcement. The reason for this limitation was the courts' reluctance to make orders requiring constant supervision by the courts, as would be the case for an injunction enforcing a positive covenant.

The rule in *Tulk* v *Moxhay* has developed beyond the original emphasis on notice, so restrictive covenants are now capable of being proprietary interests in land, analogous to equitable easements. The benefit of a restrictive covenant can run in equity with the dominant tenement, and the burden with the servient tenement, provided that the requirements set out below are satisfied, and the requirements as to registration have been complied with where the covenant was created after 1925.

Registration of restrictive covenants

In order to be enforceable against a successor in title of the original covenantor, restrictive covenants created after 1925 must have been registered prior to the assignment.

Covenants made after 1925

Where the land is registered, the covenant should be registered as a minor interest, by the entry of a notice or a caution in the charges register of the land register. Where the land is unregistered, the covenant must be registered as a Class D(ii) land charge. Failure to register renders a restrictive covenant void against a purchaser for value of a legal estate in the land (s4(6) LCA 1972).

Covenants made before 1926

These are not registrable and the equitable doctrine of notice still applies. This is the best illustration of where the equitable rules of notice continue to apply today.

11.8 Enforceability in equity: original parties

The position in equity is the same as that at common law. The original covenantee can sue the original covenantor on the contract.

The original covenantee can sue successors in title of the original covenantor so long as the following conditions still apply:

1. He has retained land for the benefit of which the covenant was taken (ie the dominant tenement).
2. The burden has passed to the covenantor (see section 11.9).

The original covenantor remains liable even though he has parted with the land.

11.9 Enforceability in equity by successors in title

As at common law, a successor in title of an original covenantee will be able to enforce a covenant only if he has the benefit of the covenant and the covenantor is subject to the burden. Where both covenantee and covenantor are successors in title, the running of the benefit and the running of the burden must be considered separately.

The benefit of a covenant

A successor in title of the original covenantee will have the benefit of a covenant provided that four conditions are satisfied:

1. The covenant is negative in substance. The test is whether compliance with the

covenant will require the expenditure of money by the covenantor, or some other active step. It is the substance of the covenant which matters and not the form. See *Haywood* v *Brunswick Permanent Benefit BS* (1881) 8 QBD 403.

2. The covenant touches and concerns the land of the covenantee. The benefit of purely personal covenants cannot run with the land of the covenantee. The test for whether the covenant touches and concerns the land is the same as for leasehold covenants (see Chapter 10). See Farwell J in *Rogers* v *Hosegood* [1900] 2 Ch 388:

   > 'The covenant must either affect the land as regards mode of occupation, or it must be such as per se, and not merely from collateral circumstances, affects the value of the land.'

3. The covenantee has retained land capable of benefiting from the covenant and the covenant was made for the benefit of that land. In *Formby* v *Barker* [1903] 2 Ch 539 an assignee of the original covenantee was held to be unable to enforce a covenant because she had sold all the land benefited by the covenant.

   A landlord's reversion is a sufficient interest in land to allow him to enforce restrictive covenants contained in the head lease against subtenants (under the rule in *Tulk* v *Moxhay*, see above), where there is neither privity of estate nor of contract between the parties. See *Regent Oil Co Ltd* v *J A Gregory (Hatch End) Ltd* [1966] Ch 402.

   It is a question of fact whether a covenant is capable of benefiting land retained by the covenantee. Some degree of physical proximity between the dominant and servient tenements is required.
4. The benefit of the covenant has passed to the covenantee (see section 11.9).

Passing of the benefit

The benefit may pass by either of the methods below.

Express assignment

The benefit may pass by express assignment at the time the covenantee acquired the land. It must be shown that the covenant was intended to benefit the land acquired, but this can be done by extrinsic evidence if the conveyance is not clear. See *Newton Abbot Co-operative Society Ltd* v *Williamson & Treadgold Ltd* [1952] Ch 286.

The assignment need not be made by the original covenantee. It can be made by anyone in whom the benefit of the covenant is vested. See, again, *Newton Abbot Co-operative Society*.

Annexation

The benefit may also pass by annexation. The Court of Appeal decision in *Federated Homes Ltd* v *Mill Lodge Properties Ltd* [1980] 1 All ER 371 changed the law on annexation. It was held that where a restrictive covenant related to or touched and concerned the covenantee's land, s78(1) Law of Property Act 1925 annexed the benefit of the covenant to the covenantee's land. The covenant was enforceable at the suit of the covenantee and his successors in title, the person deriving title under him or them and the owner and occupier of the benefited land. The effect of s78(1) is that such a covenant ran with the covenantee's land and was annexed to it. The effect of this decision seems to be that the benefit of any covenant that touches and concerns the land of the covenantee is automatically annexed to the land of the covenantee when the covenant is made. Reference should be made to the critical article by G H Newsom entitled *Universal Annexation* in (1981) 97 LQR at page 32.

The previous rules on annexation, set out in *Rogers* v *Hosegood* (above), would therefore no longer appear to apply. Under the old rules it was necessary to show, by an indication in the document creating the covenant, or in the circumstances surrounding the creation, that the covenant was imposed for the benefit of the covenantee's land in order for the benefit to be annexed to the land.

There is no doubt that the decision in *Federated Homes* remains a sensitive issue. The decision was considered, at first instance, in *Roake* v *Chadha* [1983] 3 All ER 503 where it was held that s78 LPA 1925 could not be used to annexe the benefit of a covenant in the face of an express wording in the transfer which precluded any annexation whatsoever. The precise words of the covenant were:

> '... this covenant shall not enure for the benefit of any one owner or subsequent purchaser ... unless the benefit of this covenant shall be expressly assigned.'

Judge Paul Baker QC held that even though s78 is not expressly made subject to a contrary intention the covenant had to be construed as a whole. The precise words must, therefore, prevail that the benefit must be expressly assigned and annexation of the benefit could not be implied under s78. He concluded:

> 'The true position as I see it is that even where a covenant is deemed to be made with successors in title as s78 requires, one still has to construe the covenant as a whole to see whether the benefit of the covenant is annexed. Where one finds, as in the *Federated Homes* case, the covenant is not qualified in any way, annexation may be readily inferred, but where, as in the present case, it is expressly provided that "this covenant shall not enure for the benefit of any one owner or subsequent purchaser of any part of the Vendor's Sudbury Court Estate at Wembley unless the benefit of this covenant shall be expressly assigned", one cannot just ignore these words.'

The judge dealt with some of the comments on the *Federated Homes* decision and stated:

> 'I do not consider it to be my place either to criticise or to defend the decisions of the Court of Appeal. I conceive it my clear duty to accept the decision of the Court of Appeal as binding on me and apply it as best I can to the facts I find here.'

It was further held in *Federated Homes* that if a restrictive covenant is annexed to land then prima facie it is annexed to every part of the land without the need for express assignment in respect of a part of the land when the whole land has devolved through separate titles to the present covenantee.

No reference was made to *Re Ballard's Conveyance* [1937] Ch 473 or *Zetland* v *Driver* [1939] Ch 1, but to the extent that those decisions are based on the rule that a covenantee either must hold the whole of the land benefited by the covenant or show that the covenant was made for the 'whole or any part of the land', where he holds only a part of the land, they appear to have been overruled.

The problem of pre-1926 covenants was considered in *J Sainsbury plc* v *Enfield London Borough Council* [1989] 2 All ER 817.

W purchased a house in 1881 and this was inherited by his son in 1882. Neither father nor son lived in the house. In 1894 the son sold part of the land with the benefit of a restrictive covenant from the purchasers preventing the use of the land by the purchasers or their successors in title for building purposes other than for houses. In due course all the remaining land was sold. In 1985 the plaintiff contracted to buy the land conveyed in 1894 conditional on a declaration being obtained that the land was no longer subject to the restrictive covenants of the 1894 conveyance.

The declaration was granted by Morritt J because it could not be inferred from the 1894 conveyance that the benefit of the covenants was intended to be annexed to the land retained by the son in 1894. Also the words of s58(1) Conveyancing and Law of Property Act 1881 which provided that covenants relating to land of inheritance are deemed to be made with the covenantee, his heirs and assignees and to have effect 'as if heirs and assignees were expressed' could not effect annexation of the benefit of the covenant. The court also emphasised the difference in wording between s58(1) 1881 Act and s78(1) LPA 1925 with the result that the decision in *Federated Homes Ltd* v *Mill Lodge Properties* (above) could not be applied by analogy to pre-1926 restrictive covenants.

Building scheme

The benefit may also pass under a building scheme as defined in *Elliston* v *Reacher* [1908] 2 Ch 374 as modified by *Baxter* v *Four Oaks Properties Ltd* [1965] Ch 816 and *Re Dolphin's Conveyance* [1970] 1 Ch 654.

The conditions for enforceability are as follows.

1. The parties derived title from a common vendor.
2. There was a definite scheme of development.
3. The area affected was clearly defined.
4. There was an intention to impose a scheme of mutually enforceable restrictions on all purchasers of land in the development area and their successors in title.
5. Every purchaser bought his land knowing of the scheme of mutually enforceable restrictions.

In *Emile Elias & Co* v *Pine Groves* [1993] NPC 30 the conditions for a building scheme were not present. The area of the scheme was not defined, and there was no evidence that it was the intention of the parties to produce mutually enforceable covenants. Further, there was a lack of uniformity in the covenants imposed on lots of a similar nature (this was most unusual, given that the case concerned a high-class residential development).

Halsbury describes a building scheme as:

> '... a building scheme constitutes a local law for the area over which it extends and has the practical effect of rendering each purchaser and his successors in title subject to the restrictions and of conferring upon them the benefit of the scheme, as between themselves and all other purchasers and their respective successors in title.'

Subschemes may be created within the building scheme.

In *Brunner* v *Greenslade* [1970] 3 All ER 833 Megarry J held that where there is a head scheme of development relating to an original plot, any subpurchasers are presumed to be bound inter se by the covenants of the head scheme even though they have entered into no direct covenants with the subvendor or each other:

> 'They are bound inter se by an equity independent of contractual obligation.'

In the light of the decision in *Federated Homes* v *Mill Lodge* (above), the importance of building schemes as a means of annexing the benefit of a covenant to land is probably now decreased.

The burden of a covenant

A successor in title of the original covenantor will be subject to the burden of the covenant provided that the following four conditions are satisfied:

1. the covenant is negative in substance;
2. the covenant was made for the benefit of land retained by the covenantee;
3. the covenant must touch and concern the dominant land;
4. the burden of the covenant was intended to run with the land of the covenantor.

The covenant is negative in substance

Since the decision of the Court of Appeal in *Haywood* v *Brunswick Permanent Benefit Building Society* (1881) 8 QBD 403 it has been clearly established that only the burden of a negative covenant can be enforced in equity. What is crucial is not whether the covenant is worded positively or negatively but whether it is negative in substance (a covenant could be worded positively but still be negative in substance). A useful test in deciding whether a covenant is positive or negative is to ask the question whether it requires the covenantor or his successor 'to put his hand in his pocket'. If the answer is yes, the covenant is positive, not negative.

The covenant was made for the benefit of land retained by the covenantee

The covenant must be made for the protection of land retained by the covenantee: see *London County Council* v *Allen* [1914] 3 KB 642. There are several exceptions and qualifications to this requirement. For example, the interest of a mortgagee in mortgaged land is a sufficiently 'real' interest to enable it to enforce a restrictive covenant concerning the land. Further, there are a number of statutory exceptions to this requirement: see, for example, s609 Housing Act 1985.

The covenant must touch and concern the dominant land
In general the test for deciding whether a covenant touches and concerns the land is comparable to that applicable to pre-1996 covenants in a lease. In essence the covenant must benefit the land as land.

The burden of the covenant was intended to run with the covenantor's land
In the absence of an express statement to the contrary in the original conveyance or the assignment, by virtue of s79 LPA 1925 a covenant is deemed to have been made by the original covenantor and persons deriving title through or under him.

It is also necessary to show either that the covenant was registered before the assignment, if made post-1925, or that the assignee of the covenantor had notice of the covenant for pre-1926 covenants.

Because the burden runs in equity, the appropriate remedy is an injunction, awarded at the discretion of the court. The court may award damages in lieu of an injunction. An injunction will be the usual remedy because to award damages would be altering the basic contract between the parties. See *Wakeham* v *Wood* (1981) 43 P & CR 40.

11.10 Example of the running of covenants in equity

A owns the fee simple in two adjoining pieces of land, Blackacre and Whiteacre. He sells Blackacre to B, retaining Whiteacre. In the conveyance to B:

1. B covenants with A for the benefit of any adjoining or adjacent property retained by A:
   a) to maintain the dividing fence (a);
   b) to build only one dwelling house on Blackacre (b).
2. A covenants with B for the benefit of Blackacre:
   a) to refrain from building on Whiteacre (c);
   b) to build an extension to the dividing fence (d).

B subsequently conveys Blackacre to C, who in turn conveys to D. Later A conveys Whiteacre to E. E conveys part of Whiteacre to F. Covenants (b) and (c) are registered as D(ii) land charges by A and B.

See diagram below.

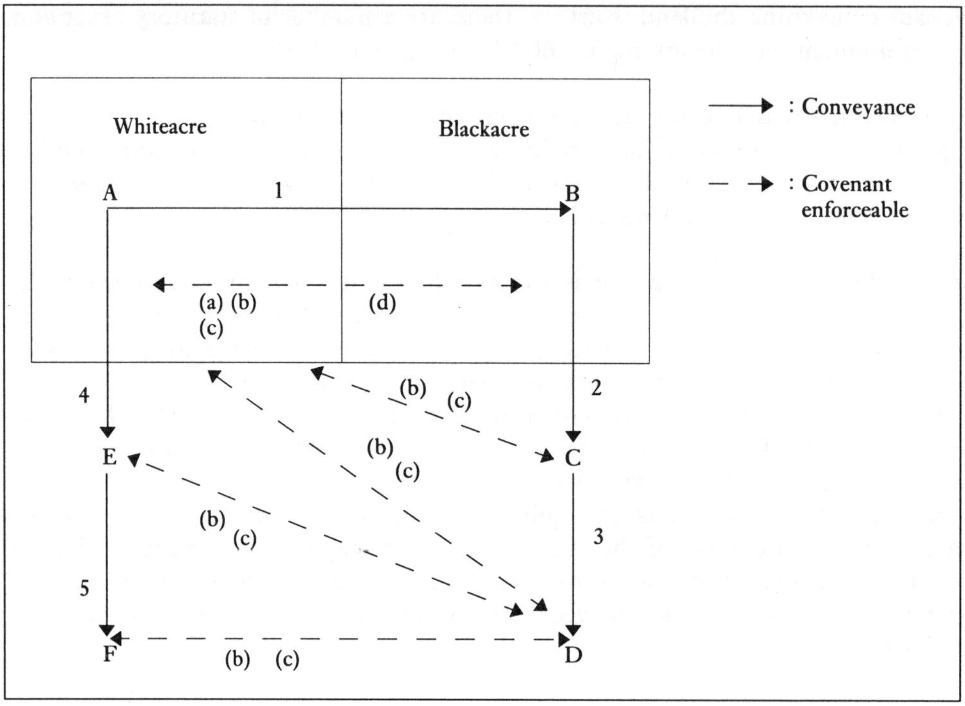

Enforceability of the covenants

Between A and B
All covenants are enforceable, as A and B are original parties.

Between A and C
A is an original party, so he retains the benefit of covenants (a) and (b) and the burden of covenants (c) and (d).

C is an assignee. He will be able to enforce covenants (c) and (d) if the benefit has passed to him, and covenants (a) and (b) will be enforceable against him if the burden has passed.

The benefit of covenants (c) and (d) will pass provided that:

1. The covenants are negative in substance.
2. The covenants touch and concern the land of the covenantee (C).
3. The covenantee (C) has retained land capable of benefiting and the covenant was made for the benefit of the land.
4. The benefit of the covenants has passed to C by express or implied annexation.

Covenant (d) is positive, so the benefit cannot run. Covenant (c) is negative, and satisfies conditions (2) and (3). The wording of the original conveyance, which states that the covenant is for the benefit of Blackacre and identifies Blackacre is sufficient for the benefit to be annexed to Blackacre by s78 LPA 1925. C therefore has the benefit of covenant (c).

The burden of covenants (a) and (b) will run provided that:

1. The covenants are negative in substance.
2. The covenants were made for the benefit of land retained by the covenantee (A).
3. The burden of the covenant was intended to run with Blackacre.

Covenant (a) is positive, so the burden cannot run. Covenant (b) fulfils all the requirements and was registered before the conveyance to C, so A can enforce it against C.

Between A and D
The position is identical to that between A and C.

Between E and D
Both E and D are successors in title of the original parties, so only restrictive covenants can be enforced between them.

In order to enforce covenant (b), E must show that:

1. The benefit has passed to him (see 'Between A and C' above).
2. D is subject to the burden (see 'Between A and C' above).
3. The covenant was registered prior to the assignment by B to C.

These conditions are satisfied.

In the same way, in order to enforce covenant (c) against E, D must show that:

1. The benefit has passed to him.
2. The burden has passcd to E.
3. The covenant was registered prior to the conveyance by A to E.

Again these conditions are satisfied.

Between F and D
Once the benefit and/or burden of a covenant becomes annexed to land, it is annexed to all or any part of that land. Hence both F and E can enforce covenant (b) against D, and D can enforce covenant (c) against F and E.

11.11 Discharge of restrictive covenants

In general a restrictive covenant remains enforceable indefinitely. There are various methods by which a restrictive covenant may be discharged:

The person entitled to the benefit expressly releases it, in other words waives his right to enforce it, by acquiescing to the breach of the covenant.

The person entitled to the benefit impliedly releases it by acting in such a way that it would be inequitable to enforce the covenant. See *Chatsworth Estates Co* v *Fewell* [1931] 1 Ch 224, where Farwell J explained the jurisdiction as:

> '... in many ways analogous to the doctrine of estoppel ... have the plaintiffs by their acts or omissions represented to the defendant that the covenants are no longer enforceable?'

It may be discharged or modified by the Lands Tribunal on application made under s84 LPA 1925 as amended by s28 LPA 1969. See *Re Hughes' Application* [1983] JPL 318.

The grounds for application are:

1. The person entitled to the benefit (being of full age and capacity) has expressly or impliedly consented.
2. The proposed discharge will not injuriously affect the person entitled to the benefit.
3. The restrictions are obsolete due to changes in the neighbourhood. This will not be so if the restriction is of real value, or the value of property is affected. See *Re Truman, Hanbury, Buxton & Co Ltd's Application* [1956] 1 QB 261; *Gilbert* v *Spoor* [1983] Ch 27.

The potential conflict between restrictive covenants and the obtaining of planning permission contrary to the covenants was further considered by the Court of Appeal in *Re Martin's Application* (1989) 57 P & CR 119.

There the restrictive covenant had been created under s37 Town and Country Planning Act 1962 (the predecessor of s52 Town and Country Planning Act 1971 which is now set out in s106 Town and Country Planning Act 1990). The covenant in question provided:

> '... that the said land ... shall not be used for any purpose other than as a private open space and that accordingly no building, structure or erection (other than fencing a summer house or garden shed if the owner shall so require) shall be placed thereon.'

In due course, and following an appeal to the Secretary of State for the Environment, an inspector granted outline planning permission for the erection of a two-storey detached house and garage on the protected land. Because of the existence of the covenant, the applicants applied to the Lands Tribunal to have the covenant discharged. The Tribunal dismissed the application, and this was confirmed by the Court of Appeal. The fact that planning permission had been obtained did not entitle the applicant to ignore the covenant. Fox LJ discussed the relationship between planning permission and covenants in these terms:

> '... the applicants' contention is wrong in so far as it suggests that the granting of planning permission by the Secretary of State necessarily involves the result that the Lands Tribunal must discharge the covenant. The granting of planning permission is ... merely a circumstance which the Lands Tribunal can and should take into account when exercising its jurisdiction under s84. To give the grant of planning permission a wider effect is, I think, destructive of the express statutory jurisdiction conferred by

> s84. It is for the tribunal to make up its own mind whether the requirements of s84 are satisfied ... All the facts of the case have to be examined by the Lands Tribunal.'

4. The restrictions are of no substantial advantage or value.
5. The restrictions are contrary to the public interest.

By s28 LPA 1969 the Lands Tribunal may discharge or modify a restrictive covenant by awarding compensation where appropriate, or may impose an alternative restrictive covenant.

A defendant in an action to enforce a restrictive covenant may apply for a stay of proceedings to allow an application to be made to the Lands Tribunal.

By s610 Housing Act 1985, the county court may modify a restrictive covenant to allow the conversion of a single dwelling house into two or more dwellings if planning permission has been obtained or if, owing to changes in the neighbourhood, the house cannot readily be let as a single dwelling.

Section 237 Town and Country Planning Act 1990 allows the local planning authority to develop in accordance with a planning permission even if this infringes a restrictive covenant. Compensation will then be payable.

When the fee simple of the burdened and the benefited land becomes vested in the same person the restrictive covenants are discharged due to this 'unity of seisin'. See *Texaco Antilles Ltd* v *Kernochan* [1973] AC 609; *Re Tiltwood, Sussex* [1978] Ch 269.

Section 84(2) LPA 1925 gives the court jurisdiction to declare whether land is affected by a restriction, the nature and extent of the restriction and by whom it is enforceable. In *Re Elm Avenue, New Milton, ex parte New Forest District Council* [1984] 2 All ER 632, the court examined the conflict between restrictive covenants and the statutory functions of a local authority which, in this instance, related to providing a car park. The court investigated the extent of its jurisdiction under s84(2) and Scott J stated:

> '... when an owner of land comes to the court for a declaration under s84(2) it does not seem to me that he can claim to be entitled to the declaration simply on the basis that if there had been an opponent who had been arguing for the benefit of the restrictions that opponent would have failed on a balance of probabilities' (at page 639).

The court accepted that the restrictive covenants could not prevent the use of the land by the council for a statutory purpose.

11.12 Worked example

In answering questions concerning covenants, the student should always keep two questions in mind:

1. Has the person seeking to enforce the covenant got the benefit of it?
2. Has the person against whom it is sought to enforce the covenant got the burden of it?

If the answer to both questions is 'yes' the covenant can be enforced. Both questions should *always* be considered in problems relating to restrictive covenants. In addition the dates of covenants should be considered to establish whether the rules of notice or registration apply.

Q Victor is the owner in fee simple of the 'Old Hall' which is situated in a 20-acre estate in pleasant rural countryside. Title to the Old Hall is registered.

In 1991, he sold five acres of the estate as a building plot to Patrick. In the conveyance, Patrick covenanted with Victor, his heirs and assigns that he would:

1. erect and maintain a boundary wall between his plot and the rest of the Old Hall estate;
2. use the land solely for private residential purposes;
3. pay £100 pa to Victor's daughter Mary.

In 1994, Patrick sold the five-acre plot (which by then had a house on it) to Quintin, 'subject to' the covenants entered into by him with Victor. In 1995, Victor sold the 'Old Hall' and the remaining 15 acres to Robert without reference to the covenants contained in the 1991 conveyance.

The boundary wall is now in need of repair. Further, Quintin is proposing to use the building on his land as a guest house and restaurant, and has never paid any money to Mary.

Advise Robert.

A The facts of the question can be represented diagrammatically as follows:

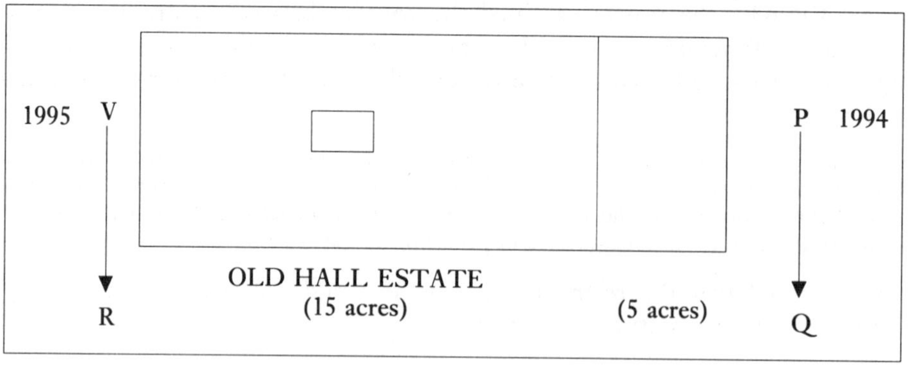

The Old Hall is the dominant land and the five-acre plot the servient land. Victor is the original covenantee and Patrick the original covenantor, and Robert and Quintin are their respective successors. In the ensuing paragraphs each covenant is dealt with separately.

1. *Erect and maintain a boundary wall – positive*
   Patrick's obligation to erect and maintain a boundary wall between his five-acre plot and the rest of the Old Hall estate ranks as a positive covenant. A positive

covenant is one which obliges the owner to do something on his land (a work covenant) or to contribute money towards work to be done or services to be rendered for the benefit of his land (a money covenant, eg a covenant to contribute towards the construction or maintenance of a private road). Here Patrick's covenant is a work covenant.

At common law the benefit but not the *burden* of a freehold covenant can run with the land, while in equity the benefit and burden of a restrictive (negative) covenant can also run with the land: *Austerberry* v *Oldham Corporation* (1885) and *Rhone* v *Stephens* (1994). It follows from this pre-emptive statement of the current law, that the burden of a *positive covenant* cannot run *directly* with freehold land either at law or in equity.

The covenant is enforceable between Victor and Patrick on the basis of privity of contract. However, since Patrick sold the servient land to Quintin in 1994 the burden of the covenant cannot be enforced *directly* against Quintin by either Victor or Robert.

However, the burden of the covenant may be enforced *indirectly* against Quintin. Because the original covenantor (Patrick) remains liable to the original covenantee (Victor) in respect of this covenant even if he subsequently sells the five-acre plot because of the privity of contract between them, it is advisable for an original covenantor to protect himself by taking a covenant of indemnity from the person to whom he sells the land (ie Patrick should have taken one from Quintin). If Patrick had taken a covenant of indemnity from Quintin it would mean that if he was then sued for any breach of the covenant by Victor he could sue Quintin on the indemnity covenant in order to recover any damages which he might have been required to pay Victor, or Victor's successor in title Robert (all the actions may be heard together by bringing in indemnifiers as third parties).

This indirect device for enforcing positive covenants is not foolproof. The person seeking to enforce the covenant must be able to locate the original covenantor. Further, the longer the chain the more liable it is to be broken by the insolvency or disappearance of one of the parties to it.

Here Robert cannot take action directly against Quintin for the non-repair of the boundary wall. He might be able to sue Patrick on the basis of privity of contract (the benefit of a covenant can run at law) if he could find him, and Patrick could then in turn sue Quintin on an indemnity covenant, if he took one from Quintin when he sold the five-acre plot to him.

The fact that the burden of a positive covenant cannot run *directly* with freehold land is one of the major weaknesses in English land law. It gives rise to difficulties in two contexts. First, as here, it causes difficulty in respect of covenants between neighbouring landowners as to such matters as fencing and boundary walls. Secondly, it also causes problems in relation to freehold flat blocks and other multi-unit developments (the fact that there is no *direct* enforcement of the burden of a positive covenant in relation to freehold land is one of the main reasons why most flat blocks in England and Wales are held on a leasehold basis) – for proposals for reform see Law Commission 1984 Report on Positive and Restrictive Covenants (Law Com No 127).

2. *Use the land solely for private residential purposes – negative*
A restrictive covenant is one which restrains a landowner in some respect from the uninhibited use of his property, eg a covenant which prevents the covenantor from using his land for the purpose of conducting trade or business. Here covenant (2) (to use the land solely for private residential purposes) is a restrictive one. The fact that the covenant is expressed in a positive form of wording is not significant – it is negative in substance.

a) Has Quintin got the burden?
As Quintin is not the original covenantor, he will only have the burden if certain conditions are satisfied. For the burden of a covenant to run in equity three conditions must be satisfied. First, the covenant must be a negative one: *Haywood* v *Brunswick Permanent Benefit Building Society* (1881). Here it is. Secondly, the covenant must have been made for the protection of land retained by the covenantee (Victor) *London County Council* v *Allen* (1914). Again this requirement would seem to be satisfied. Thirdly, the burden of the covenant must have been intended to run with the covenantor's (Patrick's) land. By virtue of s79 LPA 1925, covenants relating to the covenantor's land which are made after 1925 are deemed to have been made by the covenantor on behalf of himself, his successors in title and the persons deriving title under him or them unless a contrary intention appears. Here the covenant was entered into post-1925 and there is no contrary intention. Accordingly, the third requirement is satisfied.

There is one final matter to consider in relation to the burden of the covenant – registration. Since the land in question is registered, to be binding on Quintin the restrictive covenant must have been entered as a minor interest. For the purpose of the question it is assumed that the registration requirement has been satisfied. Accordingly, it seems that the burden of the covenant has passed to Quintin.

b) Has Robert got the benefit?
It is now necessary for Robert to show that the benefit of the covenant has passed to him. At common law the benefit of a covenant can run with freehold land if certain conditions are satisfied. However, since the burden of a covenant cannot run with freehold land directly at common law there is no real point in establishing whether the benefit of the covenant has passed to Robert at common law. Rather, it is crucial to consider whether the benefit has passed to him in equity.

For the benefit of a restrictive covenant to pass in equity to a successor in title of the covenantee (Robert) the covenant must 'touch and concern' or 'benefit' some land of the covenantee and the benefit must be transmitted in one or more of the ways prescribed by equity (annexation, assignment or scheme of development). Here, the covenant touches and concerns the remaining 15 acres of Old Hall estate. The key issue is whether the benefit has passed to Robert in one or more of the ways recognised by equity. On the facts, a scheme of development is not relevant.

Accordingly, it is necessary to consider annexation. Express annexation confers the benefit of the covenant upon the land and not individuals. Whether the benefit is so annexed to the land depends upon the wording of the covenants in the 1991 conveyance. In particular, it must be possible to identify the land to be benefited from such wording. In *Rogers* v *Hosegood* (1900) the covenant was deemed to be annexed since it referred to the dominant land. However, in *Renals* v *Cowlishaw* (1879) the covenant was not annexed because it only referred to 'the vendors, their heirs, executors, administrators and assigns' (ie no reference was made to any land). Here Patrick covenanted 'with Victor, his heirs and assigns'. This would not be enough for express annexation because there is no real identification of the benefited land.

However, statutory annexation is likely to be of help to Robert. In *Federated Homes Ltd* v *Mill Lodge Properties Ltd* (1980) the Court of Appeal held that where a restrictive covenant touches and concerns the covenantee's land, s78(1) LPA 1925 annexes the benefit of the covenant to the covenantee's land and the covenant is enforceable at the suit of the covenantee and his successors in title. On the strength of *Federated Homes* it would seem that Robert could show that the benefit of the covenant has passed to him. However, it is important to note that while the decision in *Federated Homes* was good news for conveyancers (s78 could come to the rescue if the express annexation formula used by them turned out to be deficient), the reasoning used by the Court of Appeal on that occasion is not beyond criticism.

Another consequence of *Federated Homes* has been to reduce the scope and need for assignment. An express assignment confers the benefit of a covenant on *persons*. Assignment involves passing the benefit of the covenant to each new owner by each conveyance of the benefited land. Here assignment is not available because in 1995 when Victor sold the Old Hall and remaining 15 acres to Robert he did so 'without reference to the covenants contained in the 1991 conveyance'.

Accordingly, provided that Robert can show statutory annexation (which seems likely), he will be able to enforce the restrictive covenant against Quintin. The remedy he would seek to stop Quintin using the building on his land as a guest house and restaurant would be an injunction.

3. *Pay £100 per annum to Mary – personal covenant*
   This covenant is enforceable between Victor and Patrick on the basis of privity of contract. However, it cannot be enforced against Quintin because it does not touch and concern the land. It is personal to the original parties.

12

Easements and Profits

12.1 Introduction: examples of easements

An easement is a right in the land of another which enables the landowner to restrict in some way the use of adjoining land by another party. Easements and profits are two kinds of rights which can be acquired over land belonging to another. Examples of easements are rights of light or of way; the extent of easements depends on how they are acquired.

The following feature among the most common rights which may or may not be easements:

Rights Capable of being Easements	*Rights not Capable of being Easements*
1. A right to receive light through a defined aperture in a building.	1. A right to a view: *Aldred's Case* (1610) (cf covenant in *Gilbert* v *Spoor* (1982))
2. A right to the passage of air through a defined channel: *Wong* v *Beaumont Property Trust* (1965).	2. A right of privacy: *Bernstein* v *Skyviews & General Ltd* (1977).
3. A right to have a building supported, eg by the wall of another building: *Dalton* v *Angus & Co* (1881).	3. A right to the general flow of air over land: *Chastey* v *Ackland* (1895).
4. A right to project a building over another person's land.	4. A right to have the wall of a separate building protected from the weather by an adjoining building: *Phipps* v *Pears* (1965).
5. A right to require the servient owner to fence his land: *Crow* v *Wood* (1971).	5. A right for the branches of a tree to overhang another person's land.
6. A right to store coal in another person's shed: *Wright* v *Macadam* (1949).	
7. A right to park a motor vehicle in a defined area: *Newman* v *Jones* (1982). Caveat – the use must not leave the servient owner without any reasonable use of his land: *London and Blenheim Estates Ltd* v *Ladbrooke Retail Parks Ltd* [1992] 1 WLR 1278.	
8. A right to the passage of piped water across another person's land: *Rance* v *Elvin* (1985).	
9. A right to fix a sign board on a neighbouring house: *Moody* v *Steggles* (1879).	
10. A right to store casks and trade produce on the servient land: *Att-Gen of Southern Nigeria* v *John Holt & Co (Liverpool) Ltd* (1915).	

It will be seen that easements of necessity are strictly limited to the circumstances of the necessity prevailing at the time of the grant. On the other hand the extent of an easement acquired by prescription depends on the extent of the user, and if the character or nature of the user remains constant there is no objection to an increase in its intensity. See *British Railways Board* v *Glass* [1965] Ch 538. Examples of profits are rights to take game or to cut turf. Easements can only belong to another landowner for the benefit of his land (compare restrictive covenants), but profits can exist 'in gross', that is, they can be held by people who are not landowners for their own benefit.

12.2 Essentials of an easement

In *Re Ellenborough Park* [1956] Ch 131 the Court of Appeal approved the classification made by Cheshire. There are four essentials:

1. There must be a dominant and a servient tenement.
2. The easement must accommodate the dominant tenement.
3. The dominant and servient owners must be different persons.
4. The right must be capable of forming the subject matter of a grant.

There must be a dominant and a servient tenement

This means that a right over land given to someone who does not own land capable of being benefited cannot be an easement. This is expressed in the statement that 'an easement cannot exist in gross'.

The easement must accommodate the dominant tenement

A right cannot be an easement unless it confers a benefit on the dominant tenement itself rather than its owner personally (compare 'touch and concern the land' in relation to covenants). In addition there must be some natural connection between the two tenements, although they need not be immediately adjacent. See *Hill* v *Tupper* (1863) 2 H & C 121.

The dominant and servient tenements must not be both owned and occupied by the same person

This derives from a basic principle that a man cannot have an easement over his own land. Rights habitually exercised by a man over part of his own land which would be easements if that part were separately owned and occupied are called 'quasi-easements'. An easement is a right 'in alieno solo' – in the land of another.

The right must be capable of forming the subject matter of a grant

This means that a right can only be an easement if it is of a kind that can be granted as an easement. The following tests are applied to determine whether the right is capable of being an easement:

1. The right must be of a kind already recognised as capable of being an easement. While this does not prevent new easements from being recognised as in *Re Ellenborough Park* (above), a right which does not resemble established easements will not in general be an easement, see *Phipps* v *Pears* [1965] 1 QB 76, and neither will a right which requires expenditure on the part of the servient owner: *Regis Property Co Ltd* v *Redman* [1956] 2 QB 612. But see *Crow* v *Wood* [1971] 1 QB 77 where a right to have a fence or wall kept in repair was held to be capable of being an easement. (Compare this with positive covenants: see section 11.5.) In spite of the expenditure of money required by such an easement Lord Denning said:

   > 'It seems to me that it is now sufficiently established, or at any rate, if not established hitherto, we should now declare, that a right to have your neighbour keep up the fences is a right in the nature of an easement which is capable of being granted by law so as to run with the land and to be binding on successors.'

   A right which amounts to a claim for joint possession of the servient tenement cannot be an easement. See *Copeland* v *Greenhalf* [1952] Ch 488; *Grigsby* v *Melville* [1974] 1 WLR 80.

   The statement of Lord St Leonards in *Dyce* v *Lady James Hay* (1852) 1 Macq 305 should be noted:

   > 'The category of servitudes and easements must alter and expand with the changes that take place in the circumstances of mankind.'

   This indicates that easements may have to be recognised to keep pace with modern technology.
2. The right must be capable of reasonably exact definition. Thus there can be no easement of a vague kind such as a right to privacy (*Browne* v *Flower* [1911] 1 Ch 219), or a right to an unspoilt view (*Aldred's Case* (1610) 9 Co Rep 57b).

   But a right to a view may be protected by a restrictive covenant as in *Gilbert* v *Spoor* [1983] Ch 27, or to a general flow of air (*Harris* v *De Pinna* (1886) 33 Ch D 238).
3. There must be a capable grantor.
4. There must be a capable grantee.

These two rules mean that there can only be an easement if at the time it arose the servient tenement was owned by someone capable of granting an easement (for example, a tenant cannot bind the reversion and so cannot grant an easement) and the dominant tenement was owned by a legal person capable of receiving a grant.

12.3 Legal and equitable easements

An easement can only be a legal interest in land if it is held for an interest equivalent to a fee simple absolute in possession or a term of years absolute (s1(2)(a) LPA 1925) and if it is created by statute, deed or prescription. A document not under seal cannot create a legal easement (s55 LPA 1925).

Any other easement is equitable

Where the servient tenement is unregistered land, an equitable easement created after 1925 is void against a purchaser of a legal estate for money or money's worth unless it is registered as a Class D(iii) land charge. See *Shiloh Spinners* v *Harding* [1973] AC 691.

Where the servient tenement is registered, equitable interests are minor interests protected by entry of a notice or a caution on the register. They may be capable of being overriding interests under s70(1)(a) LRA 1925. In *Celsteel Ltd* v *Alton House Holdings Ltd* [1985] 1 WLR 204 an equitable easement was held to come within s70(1)(a) because it was 'a right enjoyed with the land' for the purpose of Rule 258 of the Land Registration Rules 1925. It affected the registered title and so was an overriding interest which did not need to be protected by notice on the register as a minor interest.

12.4 Acquisition of easements

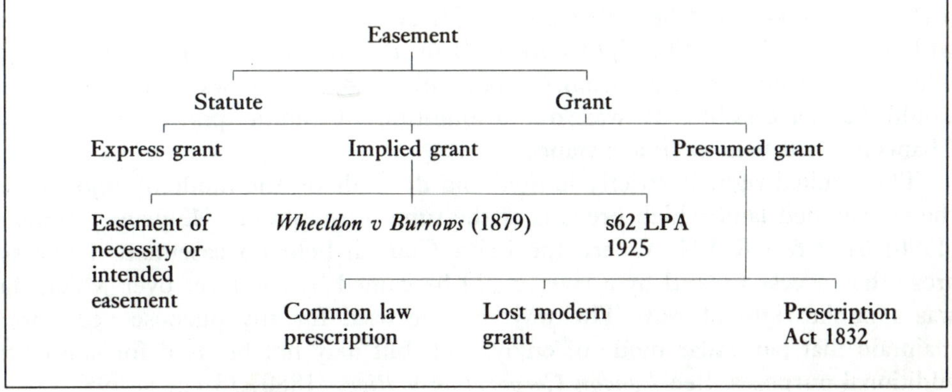

Methods of Acquisition of Easements

There are four ways in which an easement can be acquired:

Statute

Easements may be created by local Acts or may be given to public utilities, eg the early railway or canal companies.

Apart from statute, Cheshire expresses the rule at page 523 that the 'basic principle is that every easement must originate in a grant'.

Express grant or reservation

A grant is the giving of an easement by the servient owner to the dominant owner. A reservation is the reservation of rights by a landowner selling part of his land over the part sold. Before 1926 it was not possible to make a simple reservation; it had to be done by grant of the land to the purchaser and a regrant of the easement by the purchaser to the vendor. The effect of a grant or reservation is a matter of construction of the document, in the light of the general principles that a grant is construed against the grantor and a man may not derogate from his grant.

Implied grant or reservation

In favour of the grantor

As a grant is construed against the grantor, easements will only be impliedly reserved in favour of the grantor in two limited cases:

1. Easements of necessity. An easement of necessity is one without which the property retained cannot be used at all, and not one merely necessary to the reasonable enjoyment of the property. See *Union Lighterage Co* v *London Graving Dock Co* [1902] Ch 557 at 573.

   In *Nickerson* v *Barraclough* [1981] Ch 426 the Court of Appeal reversed in part Megarry V-C and held that a way of necessity could only exist in association with a grant of land. The right depended on the intention of the parties and the implication from the circumstances that unless some way was implied the land would be inaccessible. It was not a question of public policy, as the Vice-Chancellor had held at first instance.

   The implied right is strictly limited and depends on the mode of enjoyment of the surrounded land which prevails at the time of the grant: *Manjang* v *Drammeh* (1990) 61 P & CR 194. Where the Privy Council held no easement if necessity arose then access to land by a river could be gained by the river over which there was a public right of way. The way may be used for any purpose necessary to maintain that particular mode of enjoyment, but may not be used for subsequent additional purposes. See *London Corporation* v *Riggs* (1880) 13 Ch D 798.
2. Intended easements. These are easements necessary to carry out the clear common intention of the parties; for example, the grant of one of a pair of semi-detached houses, the other being retained, implies the mutual grant and reservation of easements of support.

This was considered by the Court of Appeal in *Stafford* v *Lee* (1992) The Times 16 November, where it was held that a common intention must be shown between the parties that the land was to be used in some definite and particular manner and that the easement was necessary to give effect to that intention. The common intention could be proved on a balance of probabilities by, for example, reference to any plan available amongst the title deeds.

Nourse LJ quoted Lord Parker of Waddington in *Pwllbach Colliery Co Ltd* v *Woodman* [1915] AC 634:

> 'The law will readily imply the grant or reservation of such easements as may be necessary to give effect to the common intention of the parties to a grant of real property, with reference to the manner or purposes in and for which the land ... is to be used. But it is essential for this purpose that the parties should intend that the ... land ... should be used in some definite and particular manner.'

Nourse LJ concluded:

> 'In those circumstances, on the balance of probabilities, the parties could only have intended that the land should be used for residential purposes. No other intention could reasonably be imputed to them. It followed that the easement claimed by the plaintiffs was necessary to give effect to the intention so established.'

In favour of the grantee

Because a grant is construed in favour of the grantee it is much easier for a grantee to acquire easements by implied grant. The types of easement which may be impliedly granted are:

1. Easements of necessity (see above).
2. Intended easements. These are more readily implied in the case of a grantee than of a grantor. See *Wong* v *Beaumont Property Trust* [1965] 1 QB 173; *Pwllbach Colliery Co* v *Woodman* (above).
3. Easements within the rule in *Wheeldon* v *Burrows* (1879) 12 Ch D 31. This case laid down that upon the grant of part of a tenement there would pass to the grantee as easements all quasi-easements over the land retained which:

    a) were continuous and apparent; or
    b) were necessary to the reasonable enjoyment of the land granted; and
    c) had been, and were at the time of the grant, used by the grantor for the benefit of the part granted.

Continuous and apparent. There must be some feature which gives a permanence to the right. A continuous easement is one which is enjoyed passively, eg a right to light, rather than one requiring some activity for enjoyment, eg a right of way. An apparent easement is one which can be discovered by a careful inspection by a reasonably expert observer. Despite the apparent exclusion of rights of way as not being 'continuous', the courts have always held that they come within the rule in *Wheeldon* v *Burrows* (above).

Necessary to the reasonable enjoyment of the land granted. In *Wheeler and Another* v *J J Saunders Ltd and Others* [1995] 2 All ER 697, the Court of Appeal provided useful guidance on this requirement. While recognising that there had been some doubt as to whether the requirement that the easement should be continuous and apparent was an alternative to the requirement that the easement be necessary for the reasonable enjoyment of the property granted, the court, on reviewing *Wheeldon* v *Burrows*, concluded that the court on that occasion had treated the first requirement as synonymous with the second. The test of what was necessary for the reasonable enjoyment of land was not the same as the test for a way of necessity (one without which the property could not be used at all). Peter Gibson LJ noted that in Cheshire and Burn's *Modern Law of Real Property* 'necessary' in the context of the doctrine of *Wheeldon* v *Burrows* indicated that the way 'conduces to the reasonable enjoyment of the property' (at p707). Further, Staughton LJ emphasised that the acquisition of easements under *Wheeldon* v *Burrows* was wider than acquisition of easements through the doctrine of necessity. Here, on the facts, access over the alleged servient land was not necessary for the reasonable enjoyment of the alleged dominant land. See Chapter 18, section 18.3, for further details.

The rule applies to a contract or a written or oral lease as well as to conveyances by deed.

Borman v *Griffith* [1930] 1 Ch 493: where a driveway was a feature which was there permanently and clearly suggested that it was in use as a means of access from a road across the servient property.

The doctrine of *Wheeldon* v *Burrows* is not limited to situations where a common owner sells off part of his land to the person claiming the easement and retains the other part (the traditional factual scenario when the doctrine is invoked). It can also apply where the common owner sells the quasi dominant land to one person and the quasi servient land to another, provided the sales to the different persons are contemporaneous: see *Swansborough* v *Coventry* (1832) 2 M & S 362.

4. *Section 62 Law of Property Act 1925.* By this section, unless a contrary intention is expressed, every conveyance of land passes with it (inter alia) all liberties, privileges, easements, rights and advantages whatsoever, appertaining or reputed to appertain to the land, or any part thereof or, at the time of conveyance, enjoyed with the land or any part thereof. This section does not apply to contracts, only conveyances, and will not apply to an agreement for a lease. See *Borman* v *Griffith* (above). The section has the effect of creating new easements (and profits) out of all kinds of quasi-easements and profits, not just those covered by the rule in *Wheeldon* v *Burrows,* provided the rights are those capable of being an easement or profit. An example of its operation may occur if a landlord renews a lease, having previously allowed the tenant to enjoy certain additional privileges. Unless these privileges are expressly excluded, the grant of the new lease converts them into easements enjoyed as of right.

Wright v *Macadam* [1949] 2 KB 744: where a right to use a coal shed was a right capable of being granted at law. As the right was being enjoyed with the property at the date of the 'conveyance' (in fact the renewal of a lease) and no contrary intention was expressed in that document, the right to store coal in the shed passed as an easement under s62 LPA 1925. See also *Goldberg* v *Edwards* [1950] Ch 247.

It was held in *Long* v *Gowlett* [1923] 2 Ch 177 that the section did not operate where the quasi-dominant and quasi-servient tenement were in the same ownership and occupation prior to the conveyance. The House of Lords has now given its approval to *Long* v *Gowlett* in holding that s62 only applies where there has been some diversity of ownership or occupation of the quasi-dominant and quasi-servient tenements prior to the conveyance: see *Sovmots Investments Ltd* v *Secretary of State for the Environment* [1977] 2 WLR 951 HL.

This has a serious limiting effect on the application of s62, and where land in common ownership and occupation is divided, a claimant will have to use *Wheeldon* v *Burrows* (above) to support any claim for implied easements.

An easement of light may be implied under either s62 LPA 1925 or the common law rules for implied easements. See *Lyme Valley Squash Club Ltd* v *Newcastle under Lyme Borough Council* [1985] 2 All ER 405.

5. Presumed grant or prescription (see section 12.5).

12.5 Prescription

The basis of holding that an easement is acquired by prescription is that if long user as of right is proved, the court will presume that the user began lawfully, ie as a result of a grant. There are three methods of prescription (prescription at common law, by lost modern grant and under the Prescription Act 1832), but they all rely on proof of continuous user 'as of right':

User as of right

From the earliest times English law has followed the Roman tests of user as of right, which are that it must be:

1. Nec vi: no force must be used in order to enjoy the claimed right, nor must user take place under protest from the servient owner.
2. Nec clam: if the user is secret the servient owner has no chance to protest, and the user is not as of right. See *Liverpool Corporation* v *H Coghill & Son Ltd* [1918] 1 Ch 307. However, the servient owner cannot say that the user was secret if he would have discovered it by reasonable inspection.
3. Nec precario: user enjoyed by permission cannot be as of right, even if there is no written contract or periodical payment. See *Gardner* v *Hodgson's Kingston Brewery Co Ltd* [1903] AC 229. The advantage of such a payment for the

servient owner is that it shows that the permission was renewed regularly; user after permission has lapsed may become user as of right if 'there is a change in circumstances from which revocation may fairly be implied', per Goff J in *Healey* v *Hawkins* [1968] 1 WLR 1967. This effect of permission was further considered by the Court of Appeal in *Jones* v *Price* (1992) The Independent 16 January. It was held that oral permission during the prescriptive period would negative user as of right and this would continue to be so while the common understanding of the parties remained that the user was permissive.

User in fee simple

The user must be by or on behalf of a fee simple owner against a fee simple owner. However, provided that user began against a fee simple owner, it does not make it ineffective for the purposes of prescription if the land is later leased or becomes settled. A tenant cannot acquire an easement by prescription against his landlord. See *Kilgour* v *Gaddes* [1904] 1 KB 457. It has also been held that a tenant cannot acquire an easement by prescription at common law or by lost modern grant against another tenant holding from the same landlord. See *Simmons* v *Dobson* [1991] 1 WLR 720.

The user must be continuous

This does not mean ceaseless user, but there must not be excessive intervals between each user, nor must there be long periods of non-user between periods of user. Continuity of user is not broken by an agreed variation in the user, see *Davis* v *Whitby* [1974] Ch 186 but a claim to use a right of way every 12 years to remove cut timber was held to be not continuous in *Hollins* v *Verney* (1884) 13 QBD 304.

Prescription at common law

At common law a grant would be presumed if continuous user as of right could be shown to have continued from 'time immemorial', which is 1189 (the first year of the reign of Richard I). As it soon became impossible to prove user back to that date, the courts adopted the rule that user since 1189 would be presumed if user for 20 years or more could be shown. This presumption could, however, be rebutted by showing that the right must have arisen since 1189, for example a right of light claimed for a building built after 1189.

Prescription by lost modern grant

Because it became very easy to prove, as 1189 became remote history, that the right must have arisen since that date, and therefore very difficult to prove common law prescription, the courts invented the fiction of 'lost modern grant'. If continuous user as of right is proved to have been enjoyed during living memory, or even for 20 years, but the right must have arisen since 1189, the court will presume that the right was granted by a document which is now lost. This presumption can be rebutted by proving:

1. That during the entire period when the grant could have been made there was nobody who could lawfully have made it. See *Oakley* v *Boston* [1976] QB 270 (where the servient owner had power to grant easements only if certain permission had been obtained and there was no evidence that this had been given either expressly or impliedly).
2. That in fact no grant was made.

For an application of the various methods of prescription, see *Tehidy Minerals Ltd* v *Norman* [1971] 2 QB 528, where it was decided that if rights of common had been enjoyed for 20 years a lost modern grant must be presumed unless such a grant was actually impossible. For a claim to succeed under lost modern grant the 20 years need not be continuous nor be the last 20 years immediately preceding the action. This provides some advantage compared with claims under the Prescription Act 1832 (below).

As to the need to supply a date when it is alleged the lost modern grant was made, see *Tremayne* v *English Clays Lovering Pochin Co Ltd* [1972] 1 WLR 657. This could be important because the activity might have become illegal at the alleged date of the grant. It has, for example, been illegal to pollute rivers since the Rivers Pollution Prevention Act 1876, and thus any claim for a presumptive right to pollute a river must have been established before 1876.

Note the comment of Buckley LJ in *Tehidy Minerals Ltd* v *Norman* (above):

> 'The co-existence of three separate methods of prescribing is, in our view, anomalous and undesirable, for it results in much unnecessary complication and confusion. We hope that it may be possible for the legislature to effect a long-overdue simplification in this branch of thc law.'

On the other hand, the *Tehidy* case itself does illustrate that the lost modern grant may be a necessary final resort for some claimants. See also the recommendations of the Law Reform Committee Report on the acquisition of easements and profits by prescription in its fourteenth report (1966).

Lost modern grant was considered by the Court of Appeal in *Bridle* v *Ruby* [1988] 3 All ER 64.

Having erected some houses, the estate developers transferred the freehold of two adjoining properties to the predecessors in title of the plaintiff and the defendants. As originally drafted, the transfer of the plaintiff's house reserved to its owner a right of way over the defendants' driveway, but this reservation was deleted on execution of the transfer. However, the plaintiff and his predecessors in title used the defendants' driveway for 22 years in the mistaken belief that a right of way had been granted to them. Following a dispute, the plaintiff sought to establish his right of way.

The Court of Appeal held that he was entitled to succeed as his mistaken belief about the legal origin of the alleged right of way did not prevent the user being as of right.

The question of tolerating a user of a track without objection from the owner of the land for sufficient years to support a claim for lost modern grant was considered by the Court of Appeal in *Mills* v *Silver* [1991] 2 WLR 324. Occasional use of a hill track by a neighbouring farmer without the permission of the landowner, but with his knowledge and acquiescence, was user as of right, creating the basis of a claim for an easement by presumption by lost modern grant. The case was lost on the basis that substantial improvement to the track was much more than repair to the track, and any prescriptive right did not authorise such work to the detriment of the landowner.

Prescription Act 1832

This Act was intended to simplify the acquisition of an easement by prescription, avoiding the difficulties of the common law and lost modern grant. Unfortunately it was drafted in very obscure terms. Rights to light and easements other than light are treated differently.

Easements other than light – s2 Prescription Act 1832

In order to establish a claim under the Prescription Act 1832 the claimant must show:

User as of right

This has the same meaning as for common law prescription except that there are rules relating to the effect of permission. These are:

1. Any consents, whether written or oral, given from time to time during the user defeat a claim under either of the statutory periods. See *Gardner* v *Hodgson's Kingston Brewery Co Ltd* [1903] AC 229.
2. A written consent given at the beginning of the user and extending throughout defeats a claim under either of the statutory periods.
3. An oral consent given at the beginning of the user and extending throughout defeats a claim under the shorter period but not the longer period.

User without interruption – s4 Prescription Act 1832

Interruption means some hostile obstruction and not merely non-user, although non-user may defeat a claim by showing insufficient enjoyment. The interruption is only effective in preventing an easement from being acquired if the claimant has acquiesced in the obstruction for a year after he has known of both the obstruction and the person responsible for it (s4). See *Davies* v *Du Paver* [1953] 1 QB 184, where Birkett LJ explained:

> 'Submission to or acquiescence in is a state of mind evidenced by the conduct of the parties ... it is a question of fact for the judge to decide on all the facts of the case ...'

This was echoed by Morris LJ:

> '... the date when submission or acquiescence begins must be determined as a question of fact having regard to all the circumstances.'

This question of interruption in the context of a claim to right of light was considered by the Court of Appeal in *Dance* v *Triplow* (1991) The Times 4 December. The emphasis is on the effective communication of any interruption to the defendant. The Court of Appeal set out the two elements necessary to prove interruption: first, the unwillingness to tolerate the interruption and, secondly, that some word or act made that clear to the defendant. If there is no such communication then this amounts to submission to the loss of the right. Balcombe LJ summarised the principle:

> 'The reason why the state of mind had to be evidenced by conduct was not merely to establish the existence of the state of mind but so as to establish that the state of mind was effectively communicated to the party concerned.'

User for one of the statutory periods

There are two alternative periods on which the claim may be based:

1. The shorter period: this is 20 years for easements. This operates negatively, in that proof of user for the shorter period simply assists a claim at common law by preventing the defence that enjoyment must have begun after 1189.
2. The longer period: this is 40 years for easements. This operates positively, in that proof of user for the longer period makes the right absolute and indefeasible.

Both periods are measured backwards from the action in which the right is questioned, so that an easement can only be acquired under the Prescription Act by the bringing of legal proceedings. See *Reilly* v *Orange* [1955] 2 QB 112 in which Jenkins LJ expressed the comment:

> 'What the Prescription Act 1832 requires as appears from the combined effect of s2 and s4 is the full period of 20 years.'

Deductions

The Act has complicated provisions for the deduction of certain periods when computing whether user for the requisite period before action has been shown. The effect of these provisions is shown in the following table.

	Term of years	*Life tenancy*	*Infancy*	*Lunacy*
Shorter period	Not deductible but period cannot start to run against tenant	Deductible	Deductible	Deductible
Longer period	Deductible provided that reversioner resists claim within three years of determination of term	As for term of years	Not deductible	Not deductible

Easements of light – s3 Prescription Act 1832

The amount of light was considered by the House of Lords in *Colls* v *Home & Colonial Stores Ltd* [1904] AC 179 to be:

> 'such an amount as was required according to the ordinary notions of mankind for the beneficial use of premises'.

In the case of business premises the right to light is sufficient light for the use of the premises for its ordinary business uses. In *Carr-Saunder* v *Dick McNeil Associates Ltd* [1986] 1 WLR 922 the configuration of rooms behind the windows with an acknowledged right of light was changed. The test was propounded by Millett J:

> 'The extent of the dominant owner's rights is neither increased nor diminished by the actual use to which the dominant owner has chosen to put his premises or any of the rooms in them; for he is entitled to such access of light as will leave the premises adequately lit for all ordinary purposes for which they may reasonably be expected to be used. The Court must, therefore, take account not only of the present use, but also of other potential uses to which the dominant owner may reasonably be expected to put the premises in the future.'

Thus development which restricted the dominant owner from subdividing the interior use of his premises as he wished was held to be an actionable nuisance:

> '... because the second floor can no longer (as it formerly could) conveniently be subdivided in such a way that the subdivided areas each receive an adequate amount of light.'

After many years this has now been further considered by the Court of Appeal in connection with the amount of light required for a greenhouse: see *Allen* v *Greenwood* [1979] 2 WLR 187 where, in a modern restatement of the rule, the court decided that the amount of light which may be acquired as an easement under s3 Prescription Act 1832 is the amount required for the use of a building for any ordinary purpose for which that building has been constructed or adapted. In this case, acquisition under s3 of an easement of light to a greenhouse must be sufficient for the cultivation of the plants. Goff LJ left the question of rights to light to activate solar heating panels for a future case, which will provide the opportunity to test in full the statement of Lord St Leonards in *Dyce* v *Lady James Hay* (1852) 1 Macq 305 that:

> '... the category of servitudes and easements must alter and expand with the changes that take place in the circumstances of mankind.'

Section 3 Prescription Act 1832 provides that the actual enjoyment of the access of light to a dwelling house, workshop or other building for 20 years without interruption shall make the right indefeasible unless enjoyed by written consent or agreement. This has created the following differences from the provisions relating to other easements (see above).

1. User need not be of right, provided that it is not enjoyed by written permission.
2. An easement of light can be acquired by a tenant against his landlord.
3. There is only one period – 20 years.
4. There are no deductions.
5. There is no presumption of a grant, and so it may be acquired against an owner who is not a capable grantee.
6. Interruptions: 'interruption' has the same meaning as for other easements: see s4 Prescription Act 1832. Any interruption should be a physical obstruction of the light by means of a screen or similar erection. But, under the Rights of Light Act 1959, the interruption can be purely nominal, by registering a notice as a local land charge. The notice (known as a 'light obstruction notice') must identify the servient and dominant tenements and the size and position of the notional obstruction. This notice remains effective for one year unless previously cancelled.

12.6 Extent of the easement

When the easement has been established, future questions may arise as to its content and extent. This would usually be a result of changes in the neighbourhood or of modernisation of methods of carriage over the years.

A straightforward increase in numbers may arise due to the success of a business. In *Woodhouse & Co Ltd* v *Kirkland (Derby) Ltd* [1970] 1 WLR 1185, Plowman J had to consider such an increase in custom and said this was '... a mere increase in user and not a user of a different kind or for a different purpose'.

The rule was effectively established in *British Railways Board* v *Glass* [1965] Ch 538. It was held that a general right of way is not limited to the user contemplated when the grant was made. An increase in the number of caravans using a site did not create an excessive user of a right of crossing in order to obtain access to the site which had been acquired by prescription. Harman LJ expressed the principle:

> 'A right to use a way for this purpose or that has never been ... limited to a right to use the way so many times a day or for such and such a number of vehicles so long as the dominant tenement does not change its identity.'

This question of the extent of the easement continues to create problems when the user is intensified or changed. If a user is a right of way, the intensification or change of user can have dramatic effect on the quality of life of the servient owner. In the case of express grant of a right of way 'at all times and for all purposes', this can accommodate changes in user and the consequent intensification of use, as seen in *White* v *Grand Hotel, Eastbourne* [1913] 1 Ch 113.

Notwithstanding that a right of way is granted in wide terms, it may be restricted by the physical characteristics of the path over which it subsists. In *White* v *Richards* [1993] RTR 318 a right of way in respect of motor vehicles existed over a dirt track which was 2.7 metres wide and some 250 metres long, with the servient owners' house just under three metres away from the track. The Court of Appeal held that the physical characteristics of the track were such as to require the words 'motor vehicles' in the grant to be restricted to those of limited dimensions and width (thus stopping the dominant owner taking 15 juggernaut lorries a day over the track). An express grant of a right of way does not carry with it an implied grant to a right to park, even for loading and unloading vehicles using the right of way. See *London and Suburban Land and Building Co* v *Carey* (1991) 62 P & CR 480.

Extent of easement of necessity

The above rule must be compared with that which applies in the case of an easement of necessity. There the extent of the implied right is strictly limited and depends on the 'mode of enjoyment' of the surrounding, servient, land at the time of the grant. The right may be used to maintain that 'mode of enjoyment' but for no other purpose.

Alteration to the dominant tenement

The fact that some land or another part of the building is added to the original dominant tenement will not necessarily destroy a right of way which was previously only appurtenant to the original dominant tenement. See *Graham* v *Philcox* [1984] 3 WLR 150, where it was held that the combining of a ground-floor and a first-floor flat into one dwelling where the right of way was only appurtenant to the first-floor flat did not affect the existence of the right.

Any such alteration must not, of course, make the user excessive.

Alteration to the servient tenement

In *Celsteel Ltd* v *Alton House Holdings Ltd* [1985] 1 WLR 204 an injunction was granted to restrain the building of a car-wash on the servient tenement which would restrict the width of access from nine metres to 4.14 metres. This would be a substantial interference with a right of way over the servient tenement.

Scott J identified two criteria: first, the interference would be actionable if it were substantial; and secondly, it would not be substantial if it did not interfere with the reasonable use of the right of way. The claim in this case satisfied the criteria, and an injunction was the appropriate remedy to restrain the construction of the car-wash, which would substantially interfere with the right of way.

12.7 Remedies for infringement of easements

Abatement

The owner of an easement may abate any obstruction to its exercise by removing it, provided that no more force is used than is reasonably necessary; there is no danger of injury to third parties; and there is no reasonable possibility of a breach of the peace occurring as a result. The law does not favour abatement.

Action

Possible remedies are an injunction, damages or a declaration. If damages are sought it is necessary to establish some substantial interference with the enjoyment of the easement. As to injunctions, a trivial or temporary infringement will not justify such a remedy.

Right of access – access order

By virtue of the Access to Neighbouring Land Act 1992 (see section 12.9) a landowner can apply to court for an 'access order' to give access to adjoining land. This could be obtained to enable a landowner to do work to preserve land in accordance with, for example, an easement, but is only available if the work cannot be carried out without entering the adjoining servient land.

12.8 Extinguishment of easements

There is no statutory procedure to discharge or modify easements as there is for restrictive covenants. There are four methods of extinguishing easements:

1. By statute – Commons Registration Act 1965.
2. By express release.
3. By implied release.
4. By unity of ownership and possession.

These are dealt with in turn.

By statute – Commons Registration Act 1965

For the effect of the Commons Registration Act 1965 in considering whether land is within a 'manor' under s22(1) 1965 Act: see *Corpus Christi College* v *Gloucestershire County Council* [1982] 3 WLR 849; *Hampshire County Council* v *Milburn* [1990] 2 WLR 1240.

The House of Lords overruled *Box Hill Common, Re; Box Hill Parish Council* v *Lacy* [1979] 2 WLR 177 in deciding that 'waste land of a manor' for the purposes of s22(1) includes both waste land at present belonging to a manor as well as waste land which formerly belonged to a manor.

If only part of the registration is challenged this is sufficient to challenge the validity of the whole registration. See *Re West Anstey Common* [1985] 2 WLR 677.

By express release

By implied release

1. There must be an actual intention to abandon the right. Non-user is not by itself enough, although non-user for a long period raises a presumption of intention to abandon: see *Moore* v *Rawson* (1824) 3 B & C 332 where a wall containing windows was replaced by a blank wall; this was held to be an abandonment of any right of light to the windows after 17 years.

   In *Benn* v *Hardinge* (1992) The Times 13 October the Court of Appeal re-emphasised this requirement. There non-user of a right of way for 175 years was not by itself enough to indicate an intention in the proprietor of the right to abandon it. The non-use of the dominant owner and his predecessors was explained by the Court on the basis that they had an alternative means of access to the fields in question (in other words, there was no need for them to use the disputed right of way). Finally, the court emphasised that a right of way was a piece of property of latent value whose abandonment was not to be readily inferred.
2. Alteration of the dominant tenement making the easement impossible or unnecessary may show an intent to abandon.

By unity of ownership and possession

Unity of both ownership and possession of the dominant and servient tenements extinguishes the easements. If there is only unity of possession the easement is merely suspended. If there is unity of ownership the easement continues until there is unity of possession.

12.9 Access to Neighbouring Land Act 1992

The Act came into force on 31 January 1993. It deals with the situation of a person who needs to gain access to neighbouring land in order to carry out works on his own land, for example to enter a neighbour's land in order to erect a new fence.

Until the Act, in all but an exceptional case, if A's neighbour refused A access then A could do nothing. In many cases this resulted in the deterioration of property, for example if A needed to repair his guttering but could only do so by placing a ladder on his neighbour's land. The Act gives effect to recommendations made by the Law Commission in its report *Right of Access to Neighbouring Land* (Law Com No 151).

The Act allows a landowner to apply to court for an access order to give access to neighbouring land (the servient land) for the purpose of carrying out any works which are reasonably necessary for the preservation of any land (the dominant land), except where making an access order would be unreasonable to the person to whose land access is required (s1). To get an order the applicant has to show that the work is either impossible or substantially more difficult to carry out without access to the servient land (substantially greater expense of the work without access to servient land is not a good reason for an order).

The effect of an access order is to require the respondent (servient owner) to permit the applicant to enjoy the access specified in the order. The right of access extends to anyone reasonably assisting the applicant (s3). The county court has initial jurisdiction in access proceedings, with power for proceedings to be transferred to the High Court (s7).

An access order could be obtained to enable a landowner to do work to preserve land in accordance with an easement. The Act has in effect created a statutory licence. However, it should be seen as a remedy of last resort. Clearly it is always going to be better to secure a neighbour's agreement to the access needed.

An access order is binding on the respondent's successors in title, subject to registration. In the case of registered land, an access order is not an overriding interest and must therefore be protected by a notice or caution (s5). In the case of unregistered land, an access order has to be registered in the register of writs and orders affecting land (s6(1)(d) Land Charges Act 1972).

12.10 Profits à prendre

A profit à prendre is a right to take something from the land of another. A profit may be either a several profit, that is, enjoyed by one person only, or a profit in common, enjoyed by one person in common with others.

Unlike an easement, a profit is not necessarily annexed to a dominant tenement, but may be in one of the following forms:

1. A profit appurtenant: this is a profit annexed to a dominant tenement by the act of the parties, and runs with it. Such a profit complies with the same rules as apply to easements and must generally satisfy the same four essentials as apply to easements under *Re Ellenborough Park* [1956] Ch 131 above.
2. A profit appendant: this is a profit annexed to land by the operation of law; probably the only one is a common of pasture, and no such common could be created after Quia Emptores 1290.
3. A profit pur cause de vicinage: this only exists when there are two adjoining commons which are not fenced off from each other, and the cattle put on one common have always been allowed to stray onto the other and vice versa.
4. A profit in gross: this type of profit is exercised independently of the ownership of the land, hence there is no dominant tenement.

12.11 Acquisition of profits à prendre

Profits à prendre can be acquired in four ways:

1. By statute: this is illustrated by the effect of the Inclosure Acts or certain Local Acts of Parliament.
2. By express grant: The grant must be by deed to create a legal profit.
3. By implied grant: s62 LPA 1925 applies to profits but the rule in *Wheeldon* v *Burrows* (1879) Ch D 31 does not.
4. By prescription:
   a) At common law.
   b) Lost modern grant.
   c) Section 1 Prescription Act 1832. The periods are 30 and 60 years. By s16 Commons Registration Act 1965, any period during which the servient tenement was requisitioned or grazing prevented for reasons of animal health must be deducted from a claim based on either period. The 1832 Act only applies to profits appurtenant.

12.12 Remedies for infringement of profits

These are the same as for easements, except that in the case of a profit the owner can sue a third party by proving possession without having to prove title.

12.13 Extinguishment of profits

Profits may be extinguished by the same method as easements.

12.14 Worked example

Q Alf is the tenant of an isolated cottage, owned by Bert, adjoining Greenfield, which is also owned by Bert. Since 1974 Alf has used a path across Greenfield to get to the pub, and Bert has never commented on this. In 1986 Alf started to make pottery in his cottage, and Bert has allowed him by oral permission to set up a stall on the edge of Greenfield adjoining the main road to sell his wares to passing motorists.

Three months ago, Bert sold Greenfield to Chris who has told Alf to remove the stall and to stop walking across Greenfield. Advise Alf.

Would the situation be different if in 1990 Bert had bought the freehold of Alf's cottage and then sold it to Alf?

In this type of question the student is asked to determine whether someone has a right to do something over someone else's land, in other words, is there an easement or profit. Where it is an easement, which is more usual in examination questions, two questions must be asked:

1. Does the right claimed fulfil the four essentials of an easement?
2. If so, has the person claiming the easement acquired it?

If the answer to either is no, there is no easement, but there may be a licence, and the student should not forget to discuss that possibility.

A It is best to treat the two items separately.

Using the path

There are a dominant and a servient tenement and the use of this path would seem to benefit the dominant tenement. This is a right of way, long recognised as an easement, and the freehold owner was in possession of the servient tenement.

As Alf is a tenant he could not acquire an easement on his own behalf, but he could do so for his landlord. Thus all the essentials of an easement are present.

As Alf and Bert are strangers, Alf could only acquire the easement by express grant, or by prescription. There is no express grant in this case. In order to establish a prescription claim, the user must have been as of right. In this case there was no force used, the user was not secret and no permission was given, and so the user was as of right. In order to establish a claim under s2 Prescription Act 1832, Alf must show user for either at least 20 years or at least 40 years after any relevant deductions measured from the date at which legal proceedings are brought. There are no periods of deduction in this case, and so if Alf brought proceedings immediately he could show more than 20 years' user. It is important that he acts within the next nine months to start an action claiming a declaration that there is a right of way and an injunction restraining Chris from preventing its use, because if there is an interruption by the owner of the servient tenement which is acquiesced in by the person claiming an easement for more than 12 months after he has known of the obstruction and the person responsible for it, then the claim will be defeated. If the interruption ceases, time starts to run afresh.

If Alf had bought the freehold of the cottage from Bert then there would be the relationship of grantor and grantee, and so easements could be acquired by implied grant. Use of the path is not an easement of necessity nor would it seem to be necessarily intended. As a tenant cannot acquire an easement against his landlord, Alf's user of the path during the time Bert owned both Greenfield and the cottage would be a quasi-easement. Under the rule in *Wheeldon* v *Burrows* (1879) quasi-easements over land retained by the grantor pass to the grantee provided that they are continuous and apparent and either necessary to the reasonable enjoyment of the land granted (see *Wheeler and Another* v *J J Saunders Ltd and Others* (1995)) or used by the grantor for the benefit of the part granted. While rights of way are not 'continuous' within the strict meaning of the rule, they have always been held to come within it, and so Alf would have acquired the right of way over Greenfield under the rule in *Wheeldon* v *Burrows* (1879). This would be a legal easement which would be binding on Chris.

The stall

There are a dominant and a servient tenement and a capable grantor and grantee. While there does not appear to be a decided case concerning the right to erect a stall on another's land, except in the special case of markets, the right to store goods on another's land, provided that it does not amount to possession of the land, is a recognised easement (see *Copeland* v *Greenhalf* (1952), *Attorney-General of Southern Nigeria* v *John Holt & Co (Liverpool) Ltd* (1915) and *Grigsby* v *Melville* (1973)), which is similar to the right claimed here. It is doubtful, however, whether this particular right benefits the cottage, the dominant tenement, or merely the occupant Alf.

This case is somewhat similar to *Hill* v *Tupper* (1863) in that the right claimed is for the benefit of the occupant's business. If the premises had been let as a pottery the result would be different.

If this right is not an easement, then all Alf has is a licence. If there was no consideration, then the licence was terminable at will by Bert, and so a fortiori Chris can terminate it. Even if it was a contractual licence it is unlikely that a court will hold Chris, a stranger to the contract, to be bound by it: see *Ashburn Anstalt* v *Arnold* (1989), where the Court of Appeal held obiter that a contractual licence could not bind a third party.

Assuming that the right is capable of being an easement, then Alf could only have acquired it by express grant, which there was not, or prescription. However he does not have sufficient length of user to found a claim in prescription and, even if he did, a claim under the 20-year period would be defeated because Bert gave permission.

If Alf had bought the freehold from Bert, then again he would only have acquired a right to set up the stall if it is capable of being an easement. If it is not capable, then all he has is a licence. If it is capable of being an easement, then he could have acquired it by implied grant. It would not appear to come under the rule in *Wheeldon* v *Burrows* (1879) as the easement is not continuous, but it would probably pass under s62 LPA 1925 as being analogous with *Wright* v *Macadam* (1949).

13

Licences

13.1 Introduction

In English law there is no general right to enter on land in the possession of another. A person doing so without the permission of the occupier is a trespasser. Hence the familiar (although incorrect) warning sign: 'Trespassers will be prosecuted'. The sign should read 'Trespassers will be sued' as trespass is a tort, not a crime.

A licence is a permission given by the occupier of land which allows the licensee to do some act which would otherwise be a trespass, for example to lodge in his house, to enter his cinema to see a film, or to camp on his land.

The law relating to licences has, in the last 100 years and especially in the last 20 years, changed and expanded. It was previously well established that a licence was merely a contractual arrangement between two persons subject to the normal rules of privity. It did not confer any interest in the land on the licensee. There are two major consequences of this view of licences:

1. A licensee whose licence was revoked could not obtain specific performance of the licence, but was left to his contractual remedy of damages.
2. A licence bound only the original parties, not successors in title of either.

Now the position is different with regard both to revocability and to third parties. The courts have used licences as a means of doing justice where the party had no recognised legal or equitable interest in the land, but it would be inequitable to deprive him of that land. In doing so they have expanded the effect of licences so that they now have some of the characteristics of proprietary interests in the land.

The law in this area is still developing and is not yet settled, particularly with regard to third parties. Cheshire at page 605 concludes:

> 'The law on this point is still in the process of development but it seems that a new right in alieno solo has emerged.'

The land law aspects of licences must also be considered in two distinct areas: first, as a lease-substitute. This aspect was considered in Chapter 10, and attention is drawn in particular to section 10.5. This aspect of the licence has itself undergone considerable expansion over the years as methods have been explored to overcome the security of tenure provisions of the Rent Act 1977 and, to a lesser extent, of the Landlord and Tenant Act 1954.

This expansion must now be reconsidered in the light of the decision of the House of Lords in *Street* v *Mountford* [1985] 2 WLR 877. It is as well to remember the conclusion expressed by Lord Templeman:

> 'Henceforth, the courts which deal with these problems will, save in exceptional circumstances, only be concerned to inquire whether as a result of an agreement relating to residential accommodation the occupier is a lodger or a tenant.'

Secondly, separate from the first point, the licence has developed into a distinct interest which merits the above conclusion by Cheshire that it is becoming 'a new right in alieno solo'. It is this second aspect of the licence which will be considered in this chapter.

Reference must also be made to the decision of the House of Lords in *AG Securities* v *Vaughan* and *Antoniades* v *Villiers* [1988] 3 WLR 1205. With the coming into force on 15 January 1989 of the Housing Act 1988, which allows landlords to create tenancies at full market rent, there will be less need for a landlord to try to avoid the Rent Acts by using a licence instead of a lease. As a consequence the lease/licence debate may no longer dominate as it has done in the past

Whether or not a licence is revocable or binds a third party will depend upon which type of licence has been created. There are four categories:

1. bare licences;
2. licences coupled with an interest;
3. contractual licences;
4 licences protected in equity or by estoppel.

In all discussions on licences it is as well to keep these four distinct categories in mind. They will be treated in this sequence in the subsequent sections.

13.2 Bare licences

These are licences granted otherwise than for valuable consideration – a mere permission and no more. Campers allowed to camp in a field free of charge would be bare licensees.

Revocability

A bare licence is revocable by the licensor at any time provided that he gives the licensee reasonable notice. Once the notice has expired, the licensee becomes a trespasser. In *Terunnanse* v *Terunnanse* [1968] AC 1086 it was held that a bare licence is automatically determined by the death of the licensor or the assignment of the land by the licensor.

Third parties

Bare licences are not binding on third parties, so if the licensor assigns the land the licensee cannot enforce the licence against the new owner and becomes a trespasser.

13.3 Licences coupled with an interest

The grant of a right to take something from the land of another, such as wood or game, creates an interest in land known as a profit à prendre (see section 12.10). In order to exercise the right, the grantee must also be given a licence to enter on the grantor's land. Such licences, because they are incidental to the enjoyment of an interest in land, are irrevocable and will bind third parties. The assignee of a profit à prendre will also acquire the licence.

The existence of the distinct rights should always be identified:

1. the licence to go on to the land;
2. the right to exploit the resources on the land, eg cutting timber.

13.4 Contractual licences

These are licences granted for valuable consideration. The licence may form the whole subject matter of the contract, as with a platform ticket or the hire of a room for the night. Or the licence may be part of a larger contract, such as the licence granted to a builder so that he may enter onto land to carry out building works.

Revocability

General principles

At common law, licences were held to be inherently revocable, even where granted for consideration, because they did not confer any interest in the land. A licensor could revoke a licence in breach of the terms of the contract. The licensee would thereby become a trespasser and his only remedy would be an action for damages for breach of contract.

In *Wood* v *Leadbitter* (1845) 13 M & W 838 the plaintiff, who had bought a ticket to a race meeting, was forcibly ejected from the ground. He sued for assault. It was held that the defendant licensor was empowered to revoke the licence at any time, and once he did so the plaintiff became a trespasser who could be lawfully ejected with reasonable force. His only remedy was damages for breach of contract, which were nominal.

After the Judicature Acts 1873 and 1875, which fused the administration of law and equity, the position was different. In *Hurst* v *Picture Theatres Ltd* [1915] 1 KB 1 the plaintiff had bought a cinema ticket and was forcibly ejected before the film was over. The Court of Appeal held that while the licensor had a power at law to revoke a licence in breach of contract, he could not do so in equity if (as was the case here) the contract was specifically enforceable. The plaintiff was therefore not a trespasser and was entitled to damages for assault.

The position where the contract is not specifically enforceable was considered in *Thompson* v *Park* [1944] KB 408 by the Court of Appeal, which affirmed the common law doctrine that a licensor had a power at law to revoke a licence even though he had no right to do so. If the contract was not specifically enforceable, the licensee became a trespasser, and an injunction restraining his trespass was available to the licensor.

In *Winter Garden Theatre (London) Ltd* v *Millennium Productions Ltd* [1948] AC 173 the House of Lords stated obiter that this doctrine no longer applied. Lord Greene explained the nature of the contractual licence as:

> '... it creates a contractual right to do certain things which otherwise would be a trespass ... the first thing to do is to construe the contract according to ordinary principles.'

An alternative explanation of the decision was given by Megarry J in *London Borough of Hounslow* v *Twickenham Garden Developments Ltd* [1971] Ch 233. This was that the conduct of the licensee justified the grant of an interlocutory injunction restraining that conduct even though he had acted under a disputed claim to a licence. This case is significant for the analysis of the contractual licence made by Megarry J (see below).

The issue arose again before the Court of Appeal in *Verrall* v *Great Yarmouth Borough Council* [1981] QB 202. The council had entered into a contract with the National Front giving them a licence to use one of the council's halls for their annual conference. Before the conference, the Conservative council was replaced by a Labour one which purported to revoke the licence, admittedly in breach of contract. The National Front sought specific performance of the contract. The council relied on *Thompson* v *Park* (above). The Court of Appeal rejected the council's case and an order for specific performance of the contract was made. Lord Denning MR stated:

> 'Since the *Winter Garden* case, it is clear that once a man has entered under his contract of licence, he cannot be turned out. An injunction can be obtained against the licensor to prevent his being turned out. On principle it is the same if it happens before he enters. If

> he has a contractual right to enter, and the licensor refuses to let him come in, then he can come to the court and in a proper case get an order for specific performance to allow him to come in.
>
> When arrangements are made for a licence of this kind of such importance and magnitude affecting many people, the licensors cannot be allowed to repudiate it and simply pay damages. It must be open to the court to grant specific performance in such cases.
>
> So I hold that the observations in *Thompson* v *Park* are no longer law. I agree with what Megarry J said about them in *London Borough of Hounslow* v *Twickenham Garden Developments Ltd*.' (See above.)

In the course of his judgment in the *Hounslow* case Megarry J made an analysis of the contractual licence, identifiying four major points relating to such licences as:

1. A licence to enter land is a contractual licence if it is conferred by contract: it is immaterial whether the right to enter the land is the primary purpose of the contract or is merely secondary.
2. A contractual licence is not an entity distinct from the contract which brings it into being, but merely one of the provisions of that contract.
3. The willingness of the court to grant equitable remedies in order to enforce or support a contractual licence depends on whether or not the licence is specifically enforceable.
4. But even if a contractual licence is not specifically enforceable, the court will not grant equitable remedies in order to procure or aid a breach of the licence.

In the latest (fifth) edition of Megarry and Wade at pages 802–3 the conclusion is expressed that:

> 'Equity may thus protect the licensee effectively at least before and during the period of the licence ... the judicial consensus is now to the effect that a licensor has no right to eject a licensee in breach of contract even where equity will not assist the licensee, and that if he does so forcibly the licensee can sue for assault.'

Commercial contractual licences

The basic principles to be applied to commercial contractual licences are:

1. Whether or not a licence is revocable depends on the terms of the contract, express or implied. In *Winter Garden Theatre (London) Ltd* v *Millennium Productions Ltd* (above) the respondents were granted a licence for value to use the appellants' theatre. The agreement made no express provision for the revocation of the licence by the licensors. The House of Lords held that whether or not a contractual licence was revocable depended upon the terms of the agreement. In this case, a term must be implied that the licence was not intended to be perpetual, but that it could be revoked by the licensor, on reasonable notice to the licensee.
2. A term that a licence is irrevocable can also be implied. See *Verrall* v *Great Yarmouth Borough Council* (above).

3. Whether or not the courts will grant equitable remedies to enforce a contractual licence depends upon whether the contract as a whole is specifically enforceable. See *LB of Hounslow* v *Twickenham Garden Developments Ltd* (above).
4. Even if specific performance is not available, the courts will not grant equitable remedies to a licensor to aid a breach of a contractual licence. See, again, *LB of Hounslow* v *Twickenham Garden Developments Ltd.*
5. In order to give business efficacy to a licence it may be necessary to imply a term that the premises are of sound construction and reasonably suitable for the purpose required by the licensees. See *Wettern Electric Ltd* v *Welsh Development Agency* [1983] 2 All ER 629, where Judge John Newey QC stated:

> '... the licence bore resemblance to a lease and many of the conditions in the latter resembled covenants in a lease. The defendant offered a licence in order to prevent protection of the plaintiffs under the Landlord and Tenant Act 1954. If the defendant had granted a lease to the plaintiffs it is clear ... that a term as to suitability could not be implied. Since, however, the plaintiffs were granted a licence, there is no reason why the prohibition of such a term in leases should be applied.
>
> It was possible for a term as to fitness for purpose to be implied in a licence ... the term was required to make the contract workable.'

Domestic contractual licences

Where persons occupy land under an informal family arrangement which has broken down, the courts have to decide on their legal relationship even though originally there was no intention on the part of the persons involved that their arrangement was to have legal consequences. In most cases, the court cannot spell out a legal relationship from the actual intentions of the parties, as the situation which has arisen was not foreseen and no provision was made for it. Hence:

> '... the court imputes to the parties a common intention which in fact they never formed and it does so by forming its own opinion as to what would have been the common intention of reasonable men as to the effect of the unforeseen event if it had been present to their minds.' (per Lord Diplock in *Pettitt* v *Pettitt* [1970] AC 777)

The original arrangement can usually be interpreted as giving rise to a variety of legal consequences, and the court must impose the legal relationship most appropriate in the present circumstances. A contractual licence will be imposed if that is the most fitting relationship (that is, if there has been or should be consideration and if the licence should be revocable), and the court will decide upon the terms of the contract according to what reason and justice require.

In *Tanner* v *Tanner* [1975] 1 WLR 1346, the Court of Appeal considered the case of an unmarried couple with children, where the father had bought the house for the mother and children to live in and the mother had given up a Rent Act protected flat to move into the house. The mother was found to have no proprietary interest in the house, but she did have a contractual licence allowing her to live there, which the father could not revoke until the children were no longer of school age. See also *Hardwick* v *Johnson* [1978] 1 WLR 683; *Chandler* v *Kerley* [1978] 1 WLR 693.

It should be noted that there are no hard and fast legal rules in this area of the law. The courts tend to work backwards. Once it is decided what an acceptable outcome would be, the courts fit the acts of the parties into a legal framework which produces the desired result. Money paid by one party to another can be construed as supporting a contractual licence or an estoppel (see section 13.5) or a resulting trust, whichever result would be the most appropriate in the circumstances. Megarry and Wade conclude at page 803:

> '... the contractual licence was employed as a flexible device for achieving an equitable result.'

Something of a check on the progress of the licence occurred in *Bristol & West Building Society* v *Henning* [1985] 1 WLR 778, where the Court of Appeal refused to recognise the existence of any protected equitable interest. If there is no express agreement or express trust the right to a beneficial interest under a constructive trust can only be established by proving an express or imputed intention that a party other than the legal owner should have a beneficial interest in the property. This intention must make it inequitable for the legal owner to claim the sole beneficial interest. In the course of his judgment Browne-Wilkinson LJ stated:

> 'In the absence of express agreement or express trust a right to a beneficial interest under a constructive trust could only be established by proving an express or imputed intention that a party other than the legal owner should have a beneficial interest in the property, which intention rendered it inequitable on the legal owner to claim the sole beneficial interest: *Gissing* v *Gissing* [1971] AC 886. In the same way in the absence of an express agreement such an intention or assumption must be proved in order to find the lesser property right of an irrevocable licence inferring a property interest.'

This final point is considered further in *Re Sharpe (A Bankrupt)* [1980] 1 WLR 219: see section 13.5. See also *Grant* v *Edwards* [1986] 3 WLR 114.

In *Stokes* v *Anderson* (1991) The Independent 10 January the Court of Appeal had to consider the beneficial interests of an unmarried couple in a house in which they had lived together. The decision was based on the common intention of the parties as indicated in *Gissing* v *Gissing* [1971] AC 886. In the course of his judgment, Nourse LJ made the following point:

> 'It was possible that the House of Lords would one day decide to solve the problems presented by these cases by assimilating the principles of *Gissing* v *Gissing* and proprietary estoppel as suggested in *Grant* v *Edwards* [1986] Ch 638 but this court must continue to regard cases such as the present as being governed by *Gissing* v *Gissing* principles, at any rate until their application would not produce a just result.'

Successors in title

The basic principle is that contractual licences are not binding on successors in title, even with notice. The contract binds only the parties to it, and does not confer any proprietary interest in land capable of running with the land. See *King* v *David Allen*

& Sons Billposting Ltd [1916] 2 AC 54; *Clore* v *Theatrical Properties Ltd* [1936] 3 All ER 483.

The decision in *Errington* v *Errington and Woods* [1952] 1 KB 290 is often cited as authority for the proposition that a contractual licence will bind third parties with notice, but the fact is that this case could also have given rise to an estoppel (see section 13.5 below) and Lord Denning's judgment can be interpreted on that basis. The decision has in any case been frequently criticised (though never overruled). In *Binions* v *Evans* [1972] Ch 359 Stephenson LJ left open

> 'the vexed question whether a contractual licence has been elevated to a status equivalent to an estate or interest in land'.

This criticism, albeit an obiter dictum on the facts, has been renewed by Fox LJ in *Ashburn Anstalt* v *Arnold* [1988] 2 All ER 147 where it was said that a contractual licence is not an interest in land binding on a purchaser, even one with notice. The fact that *Ashburn Anstalt* v *Arnold* has been overruled by the House of Lords in *Prudential Assurance Co Ltd* v *London Residuary Body* [1992] 3 WLR 279 in no way affects the essence of this comment by Fox LJ. This serves to remind of those earlier decisions where it had been held that a contractual licence is only a personal obligation. See *King* v *David Allen* and *Clore* v *Theatrical Properties*, above. Fox LJ concluded on these earlier cases:

> 'Down to this point we do not think that there is any serious doubt as to the law. A mere contractual licence to occupy land is not binding on a purchaser of the land even though he has notice of the licence.'

He then went on to consider *Errington* v *Errington* and said that although the decision may have been correct it went too far in saying that a contractual licence is binding on third parties except purchasers for value without notice. He gave three alternative justifications for the decision: as an estate contract, an estoppel or a constructive trust. As indicated below, the constructive trust may come to play an increasingly important part in this area of land law, but as Fox LJ states:

> 'The court will not impose a constructive trust unless it is satisfied that the conscience of the estate owner is affected. The mere fact that that land is expressed to be conveyed "subject to" a contract does not necessarily imply that the grantee is to be under an obligation, not otherwise existing, to give effect to the provisions of the contract.'

He went on to say:

> 'In matters relating to the title to land, certainty is of prime importance. We do not think it desirable that constructive trusts of land should be imposed in reliance on inferences from slender materials.'

In spite of this final caveat it may well be that the constructive trust will develop into the common solution to these problems at the expense of further development of the licence by estoppel as a new right in alieno solo.

In *DHN Food Distributors Ltd* v *London Borough of Tower Hamlets* [1976] 3 All

ER 462 Lord Denning MR stated that a contractual licence under which one company (the legal owner) gave another company the right to occupy premises indefinitely, gives rise to a constructive trust, under which the legal owner is not entitled to turn out the licensee.

Third party rights were not in issue in this case, but the decision would imply that a successor in title with notice would take subject to equitable rights arising under a constructive trust, even where the original licence was purely contractual.

13.5 Licences protected by estoppel or in equity

The equitable doctrines of estoppel and the constructive trust have been increasingly used by the courts to protect the position of licensees where it would be contrary to justice to allow strict legal principles to be applied. The courts are very flexible in their approach, and once the licensee has established that equity should intervene on his behalf the court will then consider how best to protect him. In effect the licence is made irrevocable or binding on third parties, but this result may be achieved by giving the licensee a recognised legal or equitable interest in the land. So a licensee may be held to be entitled to a full fee simple or a tenancy or an irrevocable licence under a constructive trust. But see the decision of the Court of Appeal in *Bristol & West Building Society* v *Henning* [1985] 1 WLR 778, above, which may be an indication of a change of attitude by the court in such cases.

The equitable doctrines which empower the courts to interfere in this manner with established property rights are proprietary estoppel, constructive trusts, and mutual benefit and burden. These are all described below.

Proprietary estoppel

This is a type of estoppel which operates to prevent the revocation of a right affecting land which one party has been led by the other to believe to be permanent. When A, the owner of land, allows B to expend money on that land or otherwise act to his detriment under an expectation created or encouraged by A that he will be allowed to remain on the land or acquire an interest in the land, then A will not be allowed to defeat that expectation and deny B's right to remain on or to acquire an interest in the land. The principle was first expressed in this form in a dissenting judgment in *Ramsden* v *Dyson* (1866) LR 1 HL 129. In such problems a first requirement is to identify the necessary estoppel factor, which may be some active encouragement to proceed and/or the expenditure of money.

Proprietary estoppel differs from promissory estoppel (as propounded in *Central London Property Trust* v *High Trees House Ltd* [1947] KB 130) in that it acts as both a sword and a shield. In other words it can found a cause of action as well as a defence. As a sword, proprietary estoppel allows the promisee to enforce a promise to convey a legal estate, or convey an interest in land, or grant an irrevocable licence, where the promise would be unenforceable under normal land law principles.

As a shield, proprietary estoppel protects the promisee from the exercise of the promisor's full legal rights, by raising an equity which the court must protect by the grant of an appropriate estate, interest or status in the land. See Cumming-Bruce LJ in *Pascoe* v *Turner* [1979] 1 WLR 431:

> 'One distinction between this class of case and the doctrine which has become known as promissory estoppel is that where estoppel by encouragement or acquiescence is found on the facts, those facts give rise to a cause of action. They can be relied upon as a sword not merely as a shield.'

The cases outlined below show the variety of ways in which the doctrine has been applied.

In *Dillwyn* v *Llewellyn* (1862) 4 De GF & J 517 a father gave possession of land to his son and attempted to convey the fee simple to him in writing. The son entered on the land and, with his father's assent, spent £14,000 on building a house for himself there. The father left the son only a life interest in the land by his will. After his father's death, the son claimed to be entitled to the full fee simple. The House of Lords held that the father's representations, together with the son's expenditure, gave the son the right to call for the imperfect transaction to be perfected, and the full fee simple should be vested in him. In this case the estoppel factor was the spending of the money by the son on building the house, together with the acquiescence of his father in his doing so.

In *Bannister* v *Bannister* [1948] 2 All ER 133 it was held that an irrevocable licence for life arose through proprietary estoppel, and that as the interest of the licensee fell within the definition set out in s20(1)(iv) SLA 1925, of 'a tenant for years determinable on life, not holding merely under a lease at a rent', she became a tenant for life under the SLA and was entitled to have the legal title vested in her.

This decision has been criticised, as the licensee acquired a far greater interest in the land than could have been intended, and it has not generally been followed, the minority judgment of Lord Denning in *Binions* v *Evans* [1972] Ch 359 being preferred. On the other hand the majority of the Court of Appeal in *Binions* v *Evans* *did* adopt this decision in spite of the consequences this could have under the SLA 1925.

The debate on the effect of the decision in *Binions* v *Evans* was considered by Vinelott J in *Ungurian* v *Lesnoff* [1989] 3 WLR 840. The Settled Land Act 1925 again provided the solution where an intention to reside in a house for life was construed from very complex facts leading to the purchase of a house in London. As tenant for life the defendant could call for the execution of a vesting deed and the appointment of trustees. Once the settlement was completed she could use the power of sale within the SLA. Vinelott J considered the solutions within *Binions* v *Evans* itself in these terms:

> 'Although ... every judgment of Lord Denning is entitled to the greatest respect, I do not

> find the reasons he gives for the conclusion that the defendant in *Binions* v *Evans* ... was not a tenant for life persuasive. A person with a right to reside in an estate during his or her life, or for a period determinable on some earlier event, has a life or a determinable interest as the case may be. The estate is necessarily limited in trust ... by way of succession. That is so whether the trust is express or arises by operation of law. Of course, the power of sale given to a tenant for life by the SLA 1925 may override and defeat the intentions of the settlor or of the parties to a transaction which gives rise to a constructive trust or settlement.'

The judge concluded that if the property were sold under the SLA powers the defendant tenant for life could

> 're-invest the proceeds in the purchase of another house or ... enjoy the income from them'.

The following cases illustrate the modern application of the doctrine. In many of the cases it will be seen that the estoppel factor is raised by the expenditure of money on the land of another person.

In *Hopgood* v *Brown* [1955] 1 WLR 213, A and B owned adjoining plots of land. It was agreed between them that A could build a garage up to a certain boundary line. The garage in fact stood partly on B's land. B's successor in title claimed possession of that part of the land occupied by A's garage. The Court of Appeal refused possession. B was estopped by his conduct and A's expenditure from asserting his strict legal rights. A's bare licence was converted into either an irrevocable licence or an easement binding on B's successor in title because the latter had constructive notice of the encroachment from the title deeds.

The situation in *Inwards* v *Baker* [1965] 2 QB 29 began in 1931, at A's suggestion, B built a bungalow on A's land under the impression that he would be allowed to live there as long as he wished. Again note this estoppel factor. A died in 1951. The trustees of his will were aware of B's occupation and allowed B to stay there until 1963 when they sought possession. Possession was refused by the Court of Appeal on the grounds that B had acquired, as against A, an irrevocable licence arising by proprietary estoppel. The licence gave B the right to remain in occupation for his lifetime. The trustees (A's successors in title) were bound by B's licence because they had acquiesced in B's continued occupation after they had notice of it. Lord Denning MR said:

> '... if the owner of land requests another, or indeed allows another, to expend money on the land under an expectation created or encouraged by the (owner of the land) that he will be able to remain there, that raises an equity in the licensee such as to entitle him to stay.'

In *Crabb* v *Arun District Council* [1976] Ch 179 the plaintiff owned two plots of land, only one of which (plot A) had an exit to the highway. In reliance upon the defendants' assurance that he would be allowed a right of way across their land onto the highway from plot B, the plaintiff sold plot A without reserving a right of way across it from plot B to the exit. There was no formal grant of an easement by the defendants. Shortly afterwards, the defendants fenced off the exit points from plot B, which they had themselves installed. The plaintiff sought an injunction. The Court of Appeal held that the defendants were estopped from going back on their assurance and that the interest that the plaintiff should be granted was a right of way across the defendants' land free of charge. Lord Denning MR took the opportunity to restate the fundamental principle:

> '... the first principle upon which all courts of equity proceed, that is, to prevent a person from insisting on his strict legal rights ... when it would be inequitable for him to do so having regard to the dealings which have taken place between the parties'.

Pascoe v *Turner* [1979] 1 WLR 431 dealt with the situation where, upon leaving his mistress (the defendant) for another woman, the plaintiff told her that the house they had shared (of which he held the fee simple) was hers, as was everything in it. He later repeated this assurance. In reliance upon this, the mistress spent money on furnishings and decoration, with the acquiescence of the plaintiff. Later the plaintiff sought possession, having purported to terminate the defendant's licence. The Court of Appeal held that the plaintiff's promise, together with the defendant's expenditure and the plaintiff's acquiescence in that expenditure, allowed the defendant to set up a proprietary estoppel. The defendant's equitable rights arising under that estoppel could only be satisfied by the grant to her of the fee simple of the house. Cumming-Bruce LJ concluded:

> '... the equity to which the facts in this case give rise can only be satisfied by compelling the plaintiff to give effect to his promise and her expectations. He has so acted that he must now perfect the gift. The plaintiff is ordered to execute a conveyance forthwith at his expense, transferring the estate to the defendant.'

In *Greasley* v *Cooke* [1980] 1 WLR 1306 Lord Denning MR further explored the detriment which must be suffered by the promisee to found proprietary estoppel. In 1938 the defendant, aged 16, came to live as a maidservant in a house occupied by a widower, his three sons, Kenneth, Hedley and Howard, and his mentally retarded daughter. After 1946 Kenneth and the defendant lived together as man and wife. From 1948 onwards the defendant received no wages, but continued to look after the house and nursed the daughter until she died in 1975. She had been given vague assurances by Kenneth and Hedley that she had taken to mean that she could live in the house as long as she wished, but after Kenneth's death in 1975, Hedley and Howard's daughters, in whom the house vested, sought possession. The Court of Appeal held:

1. The statements by Kenneth and Hedley were sufficient to amount to assurances for the purposes of proprietary estoppel.
2. That being so there is a rebuttable presumption that the defendant acted on the faith of those assurances, and it is for the plaintiff to provide evidence that she did not.
3. There must be some detriment, but the expenditure of money is not a necessary element of such detriment. It is sufficient that the party to whom the assurance is

given acts on the faith of it in circumstances in which it would be unjust and inequitable for the party making the assurance to go back on it.

In *Williams* v *Staite* [1978] 2 WLR 825 the defendant had been held in previous proceedings to be entitled to an irrevocable licence for life, arising through proprietary estoppel and binding on the plaintiff's predecessor in title. The plaintiff purchased with notice of the licence. The issue was whether the defendant's behaviour (swearing at the plaintiff, blocking one entrance and committing other acts calculated to reduce the plaintiff's enjoyment of his property) entitled the plaintiff to revoke the licence. The Court of Appeal held:

1. The defendant's behaviour was not sufficiently improper to lead the court to deprive him of the equitable relief he sought, but there could be circumstances in which the court would refuse to restrain the revocation of an equitable licence. Thus certain conduct could make an irrevocable licence revocable, but that conduct did not arise in this case.
2. Where a party is seeking to establish a right to an equitable licence (rather than claiming protection for an existing licence) then the court must take that party's conduct into account in determining whether a sufficient answer to his equity has been made out by the other party. In other words the courts may refuse to recognise and enforce rights claimed under proprietary estoppel if there has been serious misconduct by the claimant.

In *Matharu* v *Matharu* (1994) The Times 13 May the doctrine was used to give a widow a licence to occupy a house for life. In that case the plaintiff owned a house in which his son and daughter-in-law (the defendant) were living. The house was in the plaintiff's sole name. The son carried out extensive improvements to the house at his own expense with the plaintiff's approval. In 1991 the son died. Up until 1990 the defendant had assumed that the house was owned by her husband. Further, she claimed that she was encouraged in that belief by the plaintiff. During 1991 the defendant, at her own expense, installed a modern kitchen in the house. Subsequently the plaintiff claimed possession. The Court of Appeal held that the defendant was able to establish proprietary estoppel. However, on the facts the defendant had no beneficial interest in the property (there had been no common intention between the plaintiff, defendant and her husband that the property was to be shared beneficially). The defendant's equity could be satisfied by giving her a licence to remain in the house for life (or such shorter period as she might decide) provided that she was responsible for the outgoings on the house and kept the premises in good decorative repair. Accordingly, the plaintiff was unable to gain possession of the house.

See also *Re Sharpe* (*A Bankrupt*) [1980] 1 WLR 219 explained in outline later in this section.

Evidence of estoppel may be based on future prospective rights

In *Re Basham (Deceased)* [1986] 1 WLR 1498 it was held that the principle of proprietary estoppel was not limited to acts done in reliance on a belief relating to an existing right, but did extend to an act done in reliance on a belief that future rights would be granted. Also proprietary estoppel could be raised in relation to grants of rights over residuary estate. On the facts the plaintiff had established that she had acted to her detriment in reliance on her belief, encouraged by the deceased, that she would ultimately benefit by receiving the deceased's property when he died. She was absolutely and beneficially entitled to the whole of the deceased's estate.

If the occupiers of a property carry out repairs and improvements which enhance the value of the property, they can only claim an interest in that property if they can prove they had acted in the belief that they would acquire an interest in the property and that belief had been encouraged by the landlord. In *Brinnand* v *Ewens* (1987) The Times 4 June no such belief could be proved. In his judgment Nourse LJ set out four ingredients which were necessary to establish proprietary estoppel:

1. The claimant must show that he had prejudiced himself or acted to his detriment.
2. Acting in that way must have taken place in the belief either that he had sufficient interest in the property or that he would obtain such an interest.
3. The belief must have been encouraged by the owner of the land or others acting on his behalf – this may be considered as the estoppel factor.
4. There must be no bar to the equity.

The courts continue to explore the limits of proprietary estoppel. In *J T Developments* v *Quinn* (1991) 62 P & CR 33 the Court of Appeal held that a proprietary estoppel could arise out of negotiations even where there was no binding agreement for a lease. In addition it appears that such estoppel is binding on third parties either as an overriding interest under s70(l)(g) LRA 1925 or by virtue of the rules of notice in unregistered land. This remains an area which would benefit from some very clear guidance from the courts.

Constructive trusts

The courts have also protected a licence by means of imposing a constructive trust on purchasers with notice of the licence. This was first developed by Lord Denning MR in his dissenting judgment in *Binions* v *Evans* [1972] Ch 359.

The defendant had been given a right to live in a cottage rent-free for the rest of her life on terms that only she was entitled to give notice. She was responsible for some repairs. The cottage was sold to the plaintiffs expressly subject to her right to live there, and the plaintiffs paid a lower price because of this. When the plaintiffs sought possession it was refused, the majority of the Court of Appeal following *Bannister* v *Bannister* [1948] 2 All ER 133 and holding that the true construction of the arrangement was that the defendant became a tenant for life under the Settled

Land Act 1925 by virtue of s20(1)(iv), and that her interest had not been overreached on sale.

Lord Denning's minority reasoning was as follows:

1. The initial grant had been of no more than a contractual licence, revocable by the defendant.
2. The sale to the plaintiffs with express notice of and subject to the licence and at a lower price as a result meant that an equity arose, which took the form of a constructive trust imposed on the plaintiffs at the time of purchase to hold the cottage on trust for the defendant to occupy it for the rest of her life. Consequently the plaintiffs were not entitled to possession.

Constructive trusts have been used by the courts where the person seeking to revoke the licence is a successor in title of the licensor (as in *Binions* v *Evans*). The reason for this is that proprietary estoppel, strictly speaking, cannot be maintained against a third party who did not make the representations. But a constructive trust can be imposed upon a successor in title where it would be inequitable to allow him to disregard any rights the licensee might have.

Constructive trusts are exempted by s53(2) LPA 1925 from the requirement that the creation or disposition of equitable interests be evidenced in writing. A constructive trust was used to bind a successor in title of the licensor in *Re Sharpe (A Bankrupt)* [1980] 1 WLR 219 where the original agreement had been oral. There the successor in title was the licensor's trustee in bankruptcy, who was bound by the bankrupt's equitable obligations, but not by merely contractual obligations. The possible hardening of attitudes by the court may be detected in the decision of the Court of Appeal in *Bristol & West Building Society* v *Henning* [1985] 1 WLR 778, considered above at section 13.4.

This attitude of the Court of Appeal in *Henning* must be compared with that in *Grant* v *Edwards* [1986] 3 WLR 114 where the Court of Appeal held that where an unmarried couple live in a house which is in one name only then the other party is entitled to a beneficial interest in the property if a constructive trust can be established by showing that it would be inequitable for the legal owner to claim sole beneficial ownership. It is possible to establish such a constructive trust by showing a common intention that both parties should have a beneficial interest (proved directly or by inference from their actions) together with the fact that the claimant had acted to his or her detriment on the basis of this common intention, believing that by so acting a beneficial interest would be obtained. On the facts there was the necessary common intention, and the plaintiff had acted to her detriment by making formal contributions to the household expenses, thus releasing money to make necessary mortgage repayments.

The problem in the future may well be to establish whether a constructive trust arises at all following the decision of the House of Lords in *Lloyds Bank plc* v *Rosset* [1990] 2 WLR 867. Lord Bridge expressed a restrictive principle in some circumstances where a constructive is alleged and considered the problem where the courts are asked to rely on conduct of parties to infer a common intention to share property beneficially and to give rise to a constructive trust. He concluded:

> 'Direct contributions to ... [the] ... purchase price by ... [a] ... partner ... not the legal owner whether initially or by payment of mortgage instalments would readily justify ... the creation of a constructive trust ... [it is] ... extremely doubtful whether anything less would do.'

The courts are still exploring the limits of proprietary estoppel but take care not to extend the principle too far. This caution was seen in *Layton* v *Martin* (1985) The Times 11 December.

So far there has been no decision dealing with the issue of whether a successor in title without notice is bound. As the licence by estoppel becomes established as a new right in alieno solo, a question to be considered is whether it should continue to rely upon the doctrine of notice for protection against third parties. A possible solution, which would avoid the complications of the Settled Land Act 1925 and still give protection to the licensee against subsequent purchasers of the land, would be for the licence to become registrable under the Land Charges Act 1972. The advantage of such a procedure can be seen in cases with facts like those of *Inwards* v *Baker* [1965] 2 QB 29. A similar solution was adopted under what is now the Matrimonial Homes Act 1983 to protect the right of a deserted spouse to occupy the matrimonial home.

There is little doubt that this reliance upon the equitable doctrine of notice undermines the objects of the 1925 property legislation, which was designed to simplify conveyancing by collecting together as many third party rights as possible within the land charges register.

The lease-substitute aspect of the licence could also be seen to be undermining the legislation relating to security of tenure by creating 'sham' licences. This aspect received severe criticism from the House of Lords in *Street* v *Mountford* [1985] 2 WLR 877; that decision restores the role of the Rent Act in affording security of tenure to tenants. There are counter-views to this idea of making licences by estoppel registrable as land charges, and Cheshire at page 604 is strongly critical of the idea:

> '... licences have been held not be registrable under the Land Charges Act (1972). Indeed it would be a disaster for the licensee if they were ... if they were registrable and not registered they would be void against a purchaser who actually knew of the licence.'

No doubt a similar argument could be advanced in respect of the deserted spouse, but registration does bring certainty into an area where there is a singular lack of certainty at present.

In the case of land with registered title there appears little doubt that the licence by estoppel would be a 'right' protected by 'actual occupation' to create an overriding interest under s70(1)(g) LRA 1925 (see Chapter 7).

Mutual benefit and burden

Equity will also enforce a licence against successors in title with notice where the original licence also conferred a benefit on the licensor which the successor in title is enjoying. See *E R Ives Investments Ltd* v *High* [1967] 2 QB 379.

In these circumstances, the successor in title is not entitled to take the benefit acquired through the licence without submitting to the burden imposed by the licence. The rule was described by Lord Denning in *E R Ives*:

> 'When adjoining owners of land make an agreement to secure continuing rights and benefits for each of them in or over the land of the other, neither of them can take the benefit of the agreement and throw over the burden of it.'

The application of a similar benefit and burden rule in relation to positive covenants was seen in *Halsall* v *Brizell* [1957] Ch 169 – see Chapter 11.

Re Sharpe (A Bankrupt) [1980] 1 WLR 219. In January 1975 the debtor purchased a property for £17,000 with the help of £12,000 lent to him by his aunt as part of an arrangement whereby the aunt was to live with the debtor and his wife in the property and they were to look after her. On 27 April 1978 a receiving order was made against the debtor. On 30 April his trustee in bankruptcy contracted to sell the property with vacant possession to a purchaser for £17,000. Prior to the contract the trustee twice wrote to the aunt asking whether the £12,000 was a gift or a loan, and if it was a loan whether any consideration or security had been given for it, but she did not reply to the letters, probably because of her old age and bad health. After the date of the contract, however, she made a claim to the property, claiming either a beneficial interest under a resulting trust by virtue of the loan or alternatively a right under an irrevocable licence to occupy the property until repayment of the loan. The trustee in bankruptcy claimed possession of the property against the debtor and his aunt. The questions arose (1) whether the aunt had any interest in the property and (2) if so whether it was binding on the trustee in bankruptcy.

Browne-Wilkinson J held that the aunt did have an interest in the property binding on the trustee in bankruptcy. The making of a loan did not create a resulting trust in favour of the lender. Where parties proceeded on a common assumption that one of them was to have a right to occupy the property, and that one expended money or otherwise acted to her detriment in reliance on that assumption, the court would imply an irrevocable licence or constructive trust. This conferred on the aunt an interest in the property binding on the trustee in bankruptcy. Her conduct in failing to reply to the trustee's letters was not such as to preclude her from enforcing her interest.

He concluded with these words:

> 'Finally, I must reiterate that I am in no way deciding what are the rights of the purchaser from the trustee as against Mrs Johnson. It may be that as a purchaser without express notice in an action for specific performance of the contract his rights will prevail over Mrs

> Johnson's. As to that, I have heard no argument and express no view. I do, however, express my sympathy for him in the predicament in which he finds himself.
>
> I therefore dismiss the trustee's application for possession against Mrs Johnson.'

The judge expressed his views on the present state of the law as being:

> '... very confused and difficult to fit in with established equitable principles. I ... hope that ... the whole question can receive full consideration in the Court of Appeal so that, in order to do justice to the many ... people ... who never come into court at all but who wish to know with certainty what their proprietary rights are, the extent to which these irrevocable licences bind third parties may be defined with certainty.'

14

Mortgages

14.1 Introduction

A mortgage was defined by Lindley MR in *Santley* v *Wilde* [1899] 2 Ch 474 as:

> '... a conveyance of land or an assignment of chattels as security for the payment of a debt or the discharge of some other obligation for which it is given'.

The person who borrows the money and provides the security is called the mortgagor and the person who lends the money the mortgagee. Always remember that a mortgage is a security for money lent.

If the mortgagor has a legal interest in property and he gives the mortgagee a legal interest by way of security, then the mortgage is legal. If the mortgagor has merely an equitable interest, for example the beneficial interest of the tenant for life under the SLA 1925, then the mortgage must be equitable. A mortgagor with a legal interest can, however, create an equitable mortgage of that legal interest. The type of mortgage depends on what the mortgagee gets, not necessarily on what the mortgagor has.

In considering the law relating to mortgages the statutory rules set out in ss85–120 Law of Property Act 1925 should be considered as well as the extensive case law on the subject.

14.2 Creation of a mortgage

By s85 LPA 1925 a mortgage made after 1925 can be made in one of two ways:

1. By demise for a term of years absolute.
2. By charge of deed expressed to be by way of legal mortgage: s87 LPA 1925.

By demise for a term of years absolute

The mortgage is made in the form of a lease of the mortgagor's property with a proviso (known as the proviso for cesser on redemption) that the lease should be determined when the mortgage is redeemed, that is, when all the capital and interest are paid off. If the mortgage is of a freehold the term of the lease is usually 3,000 years, if of a leasehold then the mortgage is a sublease for about ten days less than the mortgagor's unexpired term.

Subsequent mortgages are created by granting a lease (or sublease in the case of mortgages of leaseholds) for at least one day longer than the previous mortgage.

A mortgage which purports to be by way of conveyance of the fee simple operates as a mortgage by demise for a term of 3,000 years (s85(2) LPA 1925).

By charge by deed expressed to be by way of legal mortgage: s87 LPA 1925

This method of creating a mortgage was first introduced by the LPA 1925, and is usually called a 'legal charge'. It is a simpler document than the mortgage by demise, but it imposes exactly the same rights on both mortgagor and mortgagee. Its main advantage is that freeholds and leaseholds can be mortgaged together in one document, which is not possible when the mortgage is by demise. The legal charge is a legal interest within s1(2)(c) LPA 1925 and will not be in breach of a covenant against subleasing which would be true of a mortgage by demise of leasehold property.

14.3 Legal and equitable mortgages

Legal mortgages

A legal mortgage can only be created by deed in one of the two ways discussed above, by demise or by way of legal charge, and can only be created in respect of a legal estate.

Equitable mortgages

An equitable mortgage which may be of either the legal estate or an equitable interest can be created in one of the following ways:

A mortgage of an equitable interest is always equitable. Such a mortgage can be made by conveyance of the whole equitable interest with a proviso for reconveyance on redemption. The mortgage need not be by deed, but it must be in writing signed by the mortgagor or his agent (s53 LPA 1925). As to the question of priority, see section 14.16.

A mortgage of a legal estate not made by deed must be equitable. It acts as a contract to create a legal mortgage when made in writing and signed by or on behalf of both parties to the mortgage. See s2 Law of Property (Miscellaneous Provisions) Act 1989. Equity treats it as an actual mortgage, provided that the money has actually been advanced.

Formerly the deposit of title deeds was treated as an act of part performance, but the repeal of s40(2) LPA 1925 by s2 Law of Property (Miscellaneous Provisions) Act 1989 has seen the end of this form of equitable mortgage. This was confirmed in *United Bank of Kuwait plc* v *Sahib and Others* (1994) The Times 7 July. There may, in the future, be scope for using equitable estoppel to justify the holding of the title deeds by the alleged mortgagee. In practice the deposit of title deeds is usually accompanied by a written agreement in order to make the parties' intentions clear.

The three methods of creating an equitable mortgage of the legal estate are:

1. Depositing with the lender the title deeds to the legal estate as security for the loan: the deposit of the title deeds must be intended to be by way of security for the loan and not for any other purpose, and this deposit of title deeds must now be accompanied by some agreement made in writing setting out the terms of the mortgage and be signed by or on behalf both parties to the mortgage.
2. By express agreement made in writing: this must satisfy s2 Law of Property (Miscellaneous Provisions) Act 1989.
3. By equitable charge: this is creating a charge on the land – which is *not* a charge by deed expressed to be by way of legal mortgage (which would then be within s87 Law of Property Act 1925) – without any agreement to make a legal mortgage and without a deposit of title deeds. This form of equitable charge has been the subject of considerable recent judicial comment.

In Cedar Holdings Ltd v *Green* [1979] 3 WLR 31 it was alleged that an ineffectual legal mortgage might be a charge in equity on one of the two joint tenants' beneficial interest. This was denied by the Court of Appeal, which held that a beneficial interest in the proceeds of sale of land held on the statutory trust for sale was not an interest in land due to the operation of the doctrine of conversion. See also *Property Discount Corporation Ltd* v *Lyon Group Ltd* [1981] 1 All ER 379.

As indicated in Chapter 8, section 8.18, the decision of the Court of Appeal in *Cedar Holdings Ltd* v *Green* [1981] Ch 129 was criticised by Lord Wilberforce in *Williams & Glyn's Bank* v *Boland* [1981] AC 487, and was said to have been wrongly decided. This criticism was considered and followed by the Court of Appeal. In *First National Securities Ltd* v *Hegarty* [1984] 3 All ER 641 it was held that a legal charge of a house held in joint ownership, that had only been created by the husband using a forgery of his wife's signature, failed as a legal charge, but did create a valid equitable charge on the husband's beneficial interest in the house. This should be compared with the decision of the Court of Appeal in *Thames Guaranty Ltd* v *Campbell* [1984] 2 All ER 585, where the existence of any equitable charge was denied in favour of the innocent wife, who was entitled to have the land certificate returned to her. Slade LJ commented:

> 'Even if Mr Campbell had had a beneficial interest in the property, he would not have been entitled to part with the land certificate without the consent of Mrs Campbell as joint owner of the legal estate ... Mrs Campbell [was] entitled to request the return of the land certificate to the joint custody of herself and Mr Campbell.'

See also the decision of the Court of Appeal in *Springette* v *Defoe* (1992) The Independent 24 March.

14.4 The right to redeem and the equity of redemption

The right to redeem is the mortgagor's right to pay off all the capital and interest owing under the mortgage and take his land free from the mortgagee's rights. There are two distinct rights to redeem.

1. The legal right to redeem is the contractual right at law to redeem on the precise day fixed by the mortgage, neither before nor after. At common law, if the mortgage was not redeemed on the precise day fixed then the mortgagee took the land. Hence the intervention of equity to protect the mortgagor.
2. The equitable right to redeem is the right conferred by equity to redeem at any time after the legal date of redemption has passed on reasonable terms. Because of this right, it is possible for the legal date of redemption to be fixed for a day shortly after the mortgage is created (normally six months), although both parties intend that the mortgage should not in fact be redeemed for many years. An

early legal date of redemption is normally specified in the mortgage deed because certain of the mortgagee's remedies do not arise until that date has passed.

The equitable right to redeem is not the same as the equity of redemption. The 'equity of redemption' is the total of the mortgagor's rights in the property given by equity, which arise as soon as the mortgage is made. The equity of redemption is an interest in land which can be dealt with just like any other interest in land. The two may be demonstrated in this way:

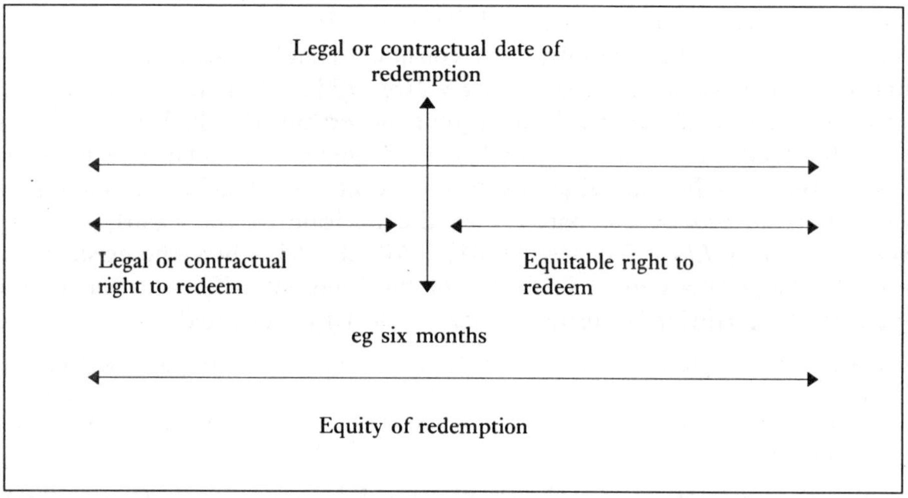

The language of the mortgage sometimes creates difficulties because of the date inserted in the mortgage deed when the money must be repaid. A literal interpretation of the mortgage would indicate that if the borrower failed to repay the mortgage on this date, he would forfeit the land. This is contrary to the concept that the land is no more than a security for the loan, and even though this contractual date for repayment has passed the borrower will be allowed to repay the loan and have the title to the land restored in his name free from the mortgage. It is this right that is known as the 'equitable right to redeem'. The sum of the contractual and equitable rights of the mortgagor are known as his 'equity of redemption'. See Lord Parker in *Kreglinger* v *New Patagonia Meat and Cold Storage Co Ltd* [1914] AC 25:

> 'The equity to redeem, which arises on failure to exercise the contractual right of redemption, must be carefully distinguished from the equitable estate which, from the first, remains in the mortgagor, and is sometimes referred to as an equity of redemption.'

14.5 The rights of the mortgagor

The right of redemption

Since a mortgage is only a security, any provision which prevents or unduly restricts the right of redemption is void as repugnant to the true nature of the transaction; the maxim is 'once a mortgage always a mortgage'. Equity will protect the mortgagor's rights of redemption from any attempt by the mortgagee to prevent the mortgagor from redeeming the mortgage. This takes the form of the following two rules:

The test of a mortgage is in substance not form
If the transaction is in substance a mortgage, it will be as treated as such by equity, which will allow the mortgagor to redeem even if in form the document purports to be something else, for example an absolute conveyance or an option to purchase.

There must be no clogs on the equity
The basis of this topic is in the words of Lord Eldon in *Seton* v *Slade* (1802) 7 Ves 265:

> 'Any stipulation which may deprive the mortgagor of his equitable right to redeem or prevent him getting back his property on payment of the loan in substantially the same state as when the mortgage is made is void in equity. There must be no clog or fetter on the exercise by the borrower of the right to redeem, ie "once a mortgage always a mortgage".'

The phrase 'once a mortgage always a mortgage' means that once a transaction is seen to be a mortgage no provision in the contract will be allowed to stand if it is inconsistent with the right of the mortgagor to recover his security on discharging his debt.

This rule as to clogs on the equity of redemption may be dealt with under three headings:

1. The mortgage must not be irredeemable – 'once a mortgage always a mortgage'.
2. The mortgagor must be able to redeem free from conditions in the mortgage (the equity of redemption must not be clogged).
3. Rights of the mortgagor under the Consumer Credit Act 1974.

The mortgage must not be irredeemable – 'once a mortgage always a mortgage'. Equity will not allow any term in a mortgage which expressly makes a mortgage irredeemable or redeemable only by a limited class of persons or for a limited period. Similarly, it will not allow a term which has the effect of preventing or limiting redemption. A term in a mortgage which gives the mortgagee an option to purchase the mortgaged property is void even if is not oppressive. See *Samuel* v *Jarrah Timber and Wood Paving Corporation Ltd* [1904] AC 323; *Lewis* v *Frank Love Ltd* [1961] 1 WLR 261. However, once the mortgage has been made, equity will not interfere if the mortgagor then gives the mortgagee such an option. The time between the two events must be at least one day. See *Reeve* v *Lisle* [1902] AC 461.

The right of pre-emption is valid whenever it is given because it is the mortgagor who then decides whether he is going to sell or not.

A term which postpones the date of redemption may be valid provided that it is reasonable and not oppressive, and that it does not in fact make the right to redeem worthless. See *Fairclough* v *Swan Brewery Ltd* [1912] AC 565, and *Knightsbridge Estates Trusts Ltd* v *Byrne* [1939] Ch 441 in which Sir Wilfred Greene MR stated:

> 'Equity is concerned to see two things, one that the essential requirements of a mortgage transaction are observed and the other that oppressive and unconscionable terms are not enforced ... The resulting agreement was a commercial agreement between two important corporations experienced in such matters and has none of the features of an oppressive bargain where the borrower is at the mercy of an unscrupulous lender.'

If the mortgage is part of a business contract, and one of the effects of a term postponing redemption is to make the contract unlawful as being in restraint of trade, the postponement is inoperative. See *Esso Petroleum Co Ltd* v *Harper's Garage (Stourport) Ltd* [1968] AC 269.

In *Alec Lobb (Garages)* v *Total Oil Great Britain* [1985] 1 All ER 303 the Court of Appeal had to consider a lease and leaseback arrangement of a garage and petrol filling station which was to receive all its supplies from one source only for 21 years. This was held not to be void as an unreasonable restraint of trade where the lease was for 51 years and its full market value was paid. The essence of this transaction was that the company had raised finance on the premises by lease and underlease rather than a mortgage with the object that the garage would then continue trading. Dillon LJ was of the opinion that the restraints on trading in the leaseback were reasonable. Dunn LJ agreed that there was ample consideration for the grant of the lease, and also the underlease was necessary if the plaintiffs were to continue trading from the site. He concluded:

> 'Public policy did not require that such arrangements should be unenforceable. On the contrary public policy should encourage a transaction which enabled trading by the plaintiffs to continue, and preserved an outlet for Total's product.'

The mortgagor must be able to redeem free from conditions in the mortgage (the equity of redemption must not be clogged). A collateral advantage which is not oppressive and not in restraint of trade will be enforced during the currency of the mortgage – see *Biggs* v *Hoddinott* [1898] 2 Ch 307; *Esso* v *Harper* (above); *Multiservice Bookbinding Ltd* v *Marden* [1978] 2 WLR 535 – but not after the redemption of the mortgage: see *Noakes & Co Ltd* v *Rice* [1902] AC 24; *Bradley* v *Carritt* [1903] AC 253.

In the case of commercial mortgages entered into by parties bargaining on equal terms, the courts may be prepared to enforce a collateral advantage even after redemption by treating it as if it was a separate agreement, part of the consideration for entering the mortgage. In *Kreglinger* v *New Patagonia Meat and Cold Storage Co*

Ltd [1914] AC 25 Lord Parker summarised the rules relating to collateral advantages in these words:

> 'There is now no rule in equity which precludes a mortgagee from stipulating for any collateral advantage, provided such collateral advantage is not either:
> 1. unfair and unconscionable, or
> 2. in the nature of a penalty clogging the equity of redemption, or
> 3. inconsistent with or repugnant to the contractual and equitable right to redeem.'

See also *Cityland and Property (Holdings) Ltd* v *Dabrah* [1968] Ch 166 where a term in the mortgage was unenforceable as being oppressive and unreasonable because the whole balance of the premium and loan became immediately repayable on default.

There appears to be no objection to index-linked mortgages, even though the fluctuations in the respective values of the currency create a substantial rise in repayments. See *Multiservice Bookbinding Ltd* v *Marden* (above), where Browne-Wilkinson J held that there was nothing contrary to public policy in the index-linking arrangement. The parties were of equal bargaining power, and the terms were not unfair, oppressive or morally reprehensible. Index-linked arrangements by a building society were also held to be valid in *Nationwide Building Society* v *Registry of Friendly Societies* [1983] 3 All ER 296.

Rights of the mortgagor under the Consumer Credit Act 1974. The Consumer Credit Act 1974 establishes a code to regulate the supply of credit not exceeding £15,000 made to an individual or to partnerships. A personal credit agreement by which a creditor provides credit not exceeding £15,000 is a 'regulated consumer agreement'. The mortgage must come within the rules relating to regulated consumer agreements, and loans by a building society or local authority for house purchase are exempt, but not loans made by a bank for house purchase.

1. *Protection of the mortgagor: ss137–140*
   The court is given power to re-open a credit agreement if it is extortionate. This power extends to all credit bargains by an individual 'whenever made'. This provision (s137) covers regulated, exempt and credit bargains exceeding £15,000 unless the mortgagor is a corporate body.

   Section 138 of the Act explains 'extortionate' to mean situations where the payments are 'grossly exorbitant' or if they 'otherwise grossly contravene the ordinary principles of fair dealing': see *A Ketley* v *Scott* [1981] ICR 241.

   The wide discretion given to the court 'to do justice between the parties' is set out in s139. The court may re-open the agreement and, to relieve a debtor or surety from payment of any sum in excess of what is fairly due and reasonable, may direct accounts to be taken, or set aside the whole or part of the obligation, or alter the terms of the credit agreement.

2. *Postponement of the right to redeem and the 1974 Act*
   Under s94 a debtor under a regulated agreement has the right, on giving notice to the creditor, to redeem prematurely at any time. Any provision in the

agreement which limits his rights in this respect is void. A provision to postpone the contractual right to redeem in a regulated agreement would be void. Compare this with the decision in *Knightsbridge Estates Trusts Ltd* v *Byrne* [1939] Ch 441.

14.6 Redemption

Who can redeem?

The right to redeem may be exercised by any person who is interested in the equity of redemption, including assignees, subsequent mortgagees, and a lessee under a lease granted by the mortgagor but not binding on the mortgagee.

Method of redemption: s115 LPA 1925

After 1925 a mortgage is discharged by a receipt, endorsed on or annexed to the mortgage deed, which names the person paying the money and is signed by the mortgagee. The mortgagor who is exercising his right to redeem must pay the principal, all arrears of interest (for however long due) and all costs properly incurred by the mortgagee in exercising his powers under the mortgage.

If the payee is not the person entitled to the immediate equity of redemption the receipt operates as a transfer of the mortgage to him. On redemption the mortgagee will return any title deeds he is holding to the mortgagor, unless he is aware of a subsequent incumbrancer to whom he should transfer the deeds. A mortgagee who hands the deeds to the mortgagor will not thereby incur liability to a later incumbrancer if he has no notice of him; mere registration of a land charge is not sufficient, actual notice is required (s96(2) LPA 1925). This is another occasion where the equitable rules of notice still apply. As a result all subsequent mortgagees who do not obtain the title deeds should both register their mortgage, as appropriate, and give notice of their interest to all prior mortgagees.

Effect of redemption

Where the mortgage is redeemed by the mortgagor and there are no subsequent incumbrances, the effect is that the property is left free from incumbrances.

If the mortgage is redeemed by a subsequent mortgagee the effect is that the prior mortgage, with all its rights, is transferred to the subsequent mortgagee. If a prior mortgage is redeemed by the mortgagor he cannot take a transfer of this mortgage which might prejudice subsequent mortgagees; it must be discharged.

If there are several incumbrancers and one of them seeks to redeem a prior mortgage by an action, then the maxim 'redeem up, foreclose down' applies. For example, if A mortgages his property to M, N, O, P and Q in succession, and P wishes to redeem N's mortgage, this could affect the value of O's, Q's and A's interests in the land. M is not affected because his mortgage has priority. The court will order that P redeems both N's and O's mortgages, and also that both Q and A should have the opportunity of either paying off the prior incumbrances or asking for a sale; if they do neither their interests will be foreclosed. This principle only applies to redemptions sought in a court action. All parties interested in the mortgagor's equity of redemption, that is the mortgagor and all subsequent incumbrancers, must be made parties to the foreclosure action. In this way they will then have an opportunity to redeem or demand a transfer of the mortgages prior to their mortgages.

Extinguishment of the equity of redemption

The equity of redemption may be extinguished by:

1. Foreclosure } see below, section 14.7, the rights of the mortgagee.
2. Sale }
3. Limitation Act 1980 (see Chapter 15): this applies where the mortgagee has been in possession of the mortgaged land for 12 years without receiving any principal or interest money and without giving any written acknowledgement of the mortgagor's title.
4. The mortgagor surrendering the equity of redemption to the mortgagee, provided that there is no provision in the mortgage deed that this should be done. This would be void under the 'once a mortgage always a mortgage' rule.

The right to sue

As against third parties the mortgagor in possession has always been able to bring an action in his own name. The mortgagor can now bring an action in his own name against a tenant by s98 LPA, provided that the mortgagee has not given effective notice of his intention to enter into possession or enter into receipt of the rents and profits. Section 98 authorises the mortgagor to sue for possession, for the rent and profits and to protect the property eg against a trespasser.

14.7 The rights of the mortgagee to enforce his security: remedies of the mortgagee

The mortgagee whose mortgagor defaults on payments under the mortgage is given several remedies. Some of these are primarily a method of recovering his capital, others are for enforcing payment of interest.

As a mortgage is merely a security for money lent, these remedies are given to the mortgagee solely to enable him to recover his money. The five major remedies may be seen as:

Common law	*Statutory or express in deed*	*Equity*
Possession	Sale	Foreclosure
Sue on the personal covenant	Appointing a receiver	

14.8 The remedies of the legal mortgagee

Sue on the personal covenant to repay

By taking this action the mortgagee is taking a normal action for debt, and is not seeking to enforce the security. The action will be barred after 12 years if the mortgage is by deed, six years in other cases (Limitation Act 1980). This remedy is available in addition to the others, so that if insufficient money to cover the mortgage debt is obtained when the security is realised the mortgagee could sue the mortgagor on the personal covenant for the remainder.

Foreclose

This is a very severe remedy which is a form of confiscation of the mortgagor's whole interest. Foreclosure is the process whereby a court declares that the mortgagor's equitable right to redeem is extinguished, leaving the mortgagee as the legal and equitable owner of the property. There are two conditions to the exercise of this remedy:

1. The legal date of redemption must have passed. This is because foreclosure is the extinguishing of the equitable right to redeem, which does not arise until the legal right to redeem has gone.
2. There must be a court order. The mortgagee must bring an action in the Chancery Division of the High Court, and all parties interested in the equity of redemption must be made parties, that is, all subsequent mortgagees to the mortgagee seeking to foreclose and the mortgagor. The writ requires the mortgagor to pay or be foreclosed, and if he does not pay a foreclosure order nisi is made requiring him to pay by a fixed date. If he does not do so the order is made absolute.

Foreclosure has the disadvantage for the mortgagee that even after the foreclosure order has been made absolute the foreclosure can be opened by the court, in other words, the equity of redemption can be revived, provided that it is equitable to do so. In general the court is reluctant to order foreclosure, especially if the value of the property is greater than the amount owing on the mortgage, and may instead order a sale at the request of any person interested (s91 LPA 1925). When the mortgaged property is or includes a dwelling house and the mortgage money is repayable by instalments (the common building society type of mortgage) the court has wide powers in the foreclosure action to adjourn the proceedings or suspend its order (Administration of Justice Act 1973 s8(3)).

Sell

The mortgagee had no power of sale at common law and in equity, but this was remedied by statute, and the current provisions are contained in ss101–107 LPA 1925. The power of sale is the remedy most commonly used, as it enables a mortgagee to recover his capital speedily, and is usually combined with an action to obtain vacant possession to allow the best price to be obtained.

A distinction has to be made between when the power of sale arises, and when it becomes exercisable.

The power of sale (s101)

This arises when:

1. The mortgage has been made by deed.
2. The legal date of redemption has passed, see *Payne* v *Cardiff RDC* [1932] 1 KB 241 (in the case of repayment by instalments, the legal date for redemption arises when one instalment is overdue).
3. There is no contrary intention expressed in the mortgage deed.

If the mortgage money is not due this statutory power of sale is not available but, apparently, the court may be able to order a sale instead of foreclosure under s91 LPA 1925 – see *Twentieth Century Banking Corporation Ltd* v *Wilkinson* [1977] Ch 99.

Exercise of the power of sale (s103)

Once the power of sale has arisen it becomes exercisable when one or more of the following conditions is fulfilled:

1. Notice requiring repayment of the mortgage money has been served on the mortgagor and default has been made in payment of part or all of it for three months thereafter.
2. Some interest under the mortgage is two months or more in arrears.
3. There has been a breach of some provision contained in the LPA 1925 or the mortgage deed (other than the covenant for payment of the mortgage money or interest) which should have been observed or performed by the mortgagor or by someone who concurred in making the mortgage.

Until the power of sale has arisen the mortgagee has no power of sale, and any purported sale to a purchaser conveys only the mortgagee's mortgage, ie a transfer of the mortgage.

Once the power of sale has arisen the mortgagee can transfer good title even though the power has not in fact become exercisable, the mortgagor having a remedy in damages against the mortgagee if the power has been irregularly or improperly exercised (s104 LPA 1925). Thus a purchaser from a mortgagee must only satisfy himself that the power of sale has arisen, but he must act in good faith, and if he is aware that the power has not in fact become exercisable he will not get a good title.

A second or subsequent mortgagee can sell subject to any prior incumbrances or, if the prior mortgagee(s) concur(s), free from incumbrances.

Although the mortgagee only has a term of years, or its equivalent, he will convey the fee simple or other the whole interest of the mortgagor.

Mode of sale

The statutory power of sale is exercisable without a court order. The mortgagee is not a trustee of the power of sale, and may adopt any method of sale, but he must act in good faith and take reasonable care. In exercising the power of sale the non-building society mortgagee must obtain the true market value of the property. See Salmon LJ in *Cuckmere Brick Co Ltd* v *Mutual Finance Ltd* [1971] Ch 949:

> '... a mortgagee in exercising his power of sale does owe a duty to take reasonable precautions to obtain the true market value of the mortgaged property at the date on which he decides to sell.'

This duty is owed to both the mortgagor and any guarantor of the mortgagor's debt. See *Standard Chartered Bank* v *Walker* [1982] 3 All ER 938.

A similar obligation to achieve 'the best price that can reasonably be obtained' is imposed on building societies by s13(7) and Schedule 4 para 1(1)(a) of the Building Societies Act 1986. See *Tomlin* v *Luce* (1889) 43 Ch D 191; *Cuckmere Brick Co* v *Mutual Finance Ltd* (above).

The duty of a mortgagee to third parties upon exercising the power of sale was considered by the Court of Appeal in *Parker-Tweedale* v *Dunbar Bank plc (No 1)* [1990] 3 WLR 767. The duty to the mortgagor to take reasonable care to obtain the true market value of the property at the time of sale was confirmed. This duty of care does not extend to the beneficiary under a trust of which the mortgagor was a trustee. In this case, as a result of three separation agreements, the wife became the sole legal owner and mortgagor of the property, but the plaintiff, the husband, was entitled to the net surplus proceeds from the sale of the property. Nourse LJ discussed the principle settled in *Cuckmere Brick Co Ltd* v *Mutual Finance Ltd* (above) that the mortgagee owes the mortgagor 'a duty to take reasonable care to obtain a proper price for the mortgaged property' at the sale. He then went on to say:

> 'But there is no support, either in the authorities or in principle, for the proposition that where the mortgagor was a trustee, even a bare trustee, of the mortgaged property, a like duty is owed to a beneficiary under the trust of whose interest the mortgagee had notice.'

He explained that the duty owed by the mortgagee to the mortgagor arose out of the particular relationship between them, and then concluded:

> 'Once it was recognised that the duty owed by the mortgagee to the mortgagor arose out of the particular relationship between them, it was readily apparent that there was no warrant for extending its scope so as to include a beneficiary under a trust of which the mortgagor was the trustee.'

The obligation on the mortgagee was to take reasonable care to obtain a proper price being the true market value. It is the mortgagee's decision when to sell once the power of sale has become exercisable. See *Countrywide Banking Corporation* v *Robinson* [1991] 1 NZLR 75.

A sale by the mortgagee to himself, either directly or through a third party, may be set aside

In *Williams* v *Wellingborough Borough Council* [1975] 1 WLR 1327 a council house was sold to the tenant with the purchase money left on the mortgage. Following default, the purported sale by the council to itself was held to be void.

The problem of the mortgagee exercising his power of sale was considered by the Privy Council in *Tse Kwong Lam* v *Wong Chit Sen* [1983] 3 All ER 54, and it was held that there was no inflexible rule that a mortgagee exercising his power of sale under a mortgage could not sell to a company in which he had an interest. However, the mortgagee and the company had to show that the sale was made in good faith and that the mortgagee had taken reasonable precautions to obtain the best price reasonably obtainable at the time. This would be shown by taking expert advice as to the method of sale, the steps which ought reasonably to be taken to make the sale a success, and the amount of the reserve. Sale by auction did not necessarily prove the validity of the transaction, since the price obtainable at an auction which produced only one bid might be less than the true market value. On the facts, the mortgagee did not succeed in showing that all reasonable steps had been taken to achieve the best price reasonably obtainable.

Lord Templeman stated:

> 'In the result their Lordships consider that in the present case the company was not debarred from purchasing the mortgaged property but, in view of the close relationship between the company and the mortgagee and in view in particular of the conflict of duty and interest to which the mortgagee was subject, the sale to the company can only be supported if the mortgagee proves that he took reasonable precautions to obtain the best price reasonably obtainable at the time of sale.'

Proceeds of sale

The mortgagee is trustee of the proceeds of sale. The proceeds must be used in the following order:

1. discharge of any prior incumbrance, if the property was sold free from them;
2. discharge of the expenses of sale;

3. discharge of money due to the mortgagee under the mortgage;
4. pay the balance to the next subsequent mortgagee or, if none, to the mortgagor. The subsequent mortgagee will hold the balance on trust to discharge the money due to him and to pay the balance to the next person entitled.

Court order for sale

In addition to the power given to the mortgagee, the court is given a wide power to order a sale at the instance of any person interested by s91 LPA 1925: see *Twentieth Century Banking Corporation Ltd* v *Wilkinson* [1977] Ch 99. Here the legal date for redemption was not until 1988, and so the statutory power of sale under s101 had not arisen. Templeman J held that the mortgagor was so seriously in arrears that he was in breach of a fundamental condition which barred the legal right of redemption. This allowed the mortgagee to foreclose, and a sale was ordered under s91 instead of foreclosure. The judge considered the basis of this right in these words:

> 'The defendants would in law be entitled to their property back if they complied with all their covenants ... In default of such compliance, the defendants have no legal right to recovery of their property, but equity accords them a right, namely an equitable right to redeem. That equitable right to redeem can, in a proper case, be terminated by an order for foreclosure. If the lenders are entitled to foreclose, the court in its discretion may order a sale instead.'

A court can order a sale of mortgaged property even against the wishes of the mortgagee. In *Palk* v *Mortgage Services Funding* [1993] 2 All ER 481 the plaintiffs decided to sell their home when the husband's company failed. The defendant mortgagee refused to agree to a sale negotiated by the plaintiffs because the sale price would not have been enough to pay off the mortgage debt. Furthermore, the mortgagees had secured a suspended possession order and were hoping to let the property in order to generate income pending an upturn in the housing market when they would sell it. Of central significance to the case was the fact that the sum due under the mortgage was increasing by about £43,000 per year whereas the anticipated income from letting was between £13,000 and £14,000 per year. The Court of Appeal stated that it had an unfettered discretion under s91(2) LPA 1925 to order a sale of mortgaged property even against the wishes of the mortgagee. In the exceptional circumstances of this case, they concluded that it was just and equitable to order a sale (even though a significant amount of the debt would remain outstanding and unsecured).

Take possession

The previous two remedies, foreclosure and sale, enable a mortgagee to recover his capital, while both this one and the next, appointing a receiver, leave the capital intact and enforce payments of interest.

The mortgagee has a right to possession as soon as the mortgage is executed:

s95(4) LPA 1925. In *Four Maids Ltd* v *Dudley Marshall (Properties) Ltd* [1957] Ch 317 Harman J described the right in these words:

> 'The right of the mortgagee to possession in the absence of some contract has nothing to do with default on the part of the mortgagor. The mortgagee may go into possession before the ink is dry on the mortgage unless there is something in the contract, express or implied, whereby he has contracted himself out of that right. He has the right because he has a legal term of years in the property.'

The right arises even if the mortgagor is not in any default. This is because, if the mortgage is by demise, the mortgagee is a tenant and therefore entitled to possession as against the mortgagor, and a mortgagee whose mortgage is by legal charge has by statute the same rights as a mortgagee by demise.

There is nothing inconsistent about granting a mortgagee a possession order, suspended subject to conditions as to payment being met by the mortgagors, and a concurrent money judgment for the entire mortgage debt, suspended for as long as the possession order remains suspended. See *Cheltenham & Gloucester Building Society* v *Grattidge* (1993) The Times 9 April where the building society started possession proceedings and claimed payment of the balance of the amount due because at the time there was widespread incidence of negative equity and it was concerned that the equity in the mortgaged property might not be enough to pay off the entire mortgage debt. The Court of Appeal held it could not make an immediately enforceable order for the payment of the entire mortgage debt. However there was no reason why it should not make a suspended order under s71(2) County Courts Act 1984 – suspended for as long as the possession order remained suspended.

The attitude of the court to an action for possession in the wrong circumstances is illustrated by *Quennel* v *Maltby* [1979] 1 WLR 318, in which the Court of Appeal held that so long as interest was paid and there was nothing outstanding, equity had the power to restrain any unjust use of the right to possession. In this case possession was being sought to defeat the protection afforded to a tenant by the Rent Act 1977, and the mortgagee was held not to be acting in good faith.

Relief of mortgagor

Even though the mortgagee has a right of possession he must obtain a court order before he can take possession. Before 1936 the action was brought in the King's Bench Division and the order was given automatically, but in that year possession actions were transferred to the Chancery Division, which thereafter refused an order if it was inequitable to grant it, and allowed an adjournment or stay of execution to give the mortgagor a chance to redeem the mortgage.

When the mortgaged property includes a dwelling house the court is given a discretion by s36 Administration of Justice Act 1970 (as amended) to adjourn the proceedings or to grant a stay of execution where it appears likely to the court that the mortgagor is likely within a reasonable time to pay any sums due to remedy any default. See *Western Bank* v *Schindler* [1977] Ch 1, where the Court of Appeal held that this section applied whether or not the mortgagor was in arrears or default. For the continuing application of this rule where the mortgage does not contain a default clause, see *Habib Bank Ltd* v *Tailor* [1982] 1 WLR 1218.

When the mortgage is an instalment mortgage it is further provided by s8 AJA 1973 that the mortgagor may be required to pay off arrears only, not to pay the whole of the mortgage monies. This statutory discretion has been extended in favour of a mortgagor under an endowment mortgage: *Centrax Trustees Ltd* v *Ross* [1979] 2 All ER 952. In *Bank of Scotland* v *Grimes* [1985] 2 All ER 254 the Court of Appeal confirmed that s8 AJA 1973 was intended to cover both instalment mortgages and endowment mortgages. Griffiths LJ said:

> '... the words to defer payment were inserted in s8 to cover endowment mortgages where there was no obligation to repay the capital until the end of the duration of the loan.'

The question of what constitutes a 'reasonable period' for bringing payments up to date for the purposes of s36 AJA 1970 (as amended) fell to be considered in *Cheltenham & Gloucester Building Society* v *Norgan* [1996] 1 All ER 449. There N was sole owner of a period farmhouse which was subject to a mortgage. N's repayments faltered and the building society issued a summons to repossess the farmhouse. The county court judge estimated that N's arrears were £20,000 and that a period of two to four years was the maximum that would normally be allowed for clearing arrears (even though here the mortgage had 13 years still to run). He concluded that it would be impossible for N to meet that target and therefore the building society was entitled to have possession. N appealed and her appeal was allowed. A key consideration was what constituted a 'reasonable period' for bringing payments up to date for the purposes of s36 1970 AJA. The court unanimously agreed that 'the logic and spirit of the legislation' required that the court should take the full term of the mortgage as its starting point and pose at the outset the following question: 'Would it be possible for the borrower to maintain payment off of the arrears by instalments over that period?' The court identified a number of considerations which were likely to be relevant in establishing a reasonable period, including the following:

1. how much could the borrower reasonably afford to pay both now and in the future?;
2. if the borrower had a short term problem in meeting his mortgage commitments, how long was the difficulty likely to last?;
3. why had the arrears accumulated?;
4. how much remained of the original term?; and
5. were there any reasons affecting the security which should influence the length of the period for payment?

Accordingly, the case was remitted back to the county court to work out a new repayment scheme over the remaining 13 years of the loan.

This is unquestionably a landmark ruling. It formalises the process of capitalisation where the arrears are added to the original loan. Clearly some homeowners who fall into arrears with their mortgages will now have a better chance of keeping their homes. It is likely that large numbers of homeowners fighting repossession will now take their lenders to court in order to secure a comparable deal to that obtained by Mrs Norgan. However, it will clearly not help all homeowners facing repossession. Many people in that position are unable (because of redundancy, separation, etc) to meet their mortgage repayments, let alone try to pay off large arrears. See Chapter 18, section 18.4, for further details.

The Court of Appeal has refused to lay down strict rules for district and circuit judges as to the procedural aspects of possession proceedings. If a mortgagee argues that the truth of what the court is told by a mortgagor should not be accepted without formal evidence, then it is necessary for the mortgagor to file affidavit evidence. However, in the absence of such a submission it is for the judge to decide whether or not to act on the basis of informal evidence or material. See *Cheltenham & Gloucester Building Society* v *Grant* (1994) The Times 9 May, where the judge acted on the basis of information given to him informally by those representing the defendant mortgagor, and the Court of Appeal ruled that the way in which the district judge had exercised his discretion could not be interfered with.

Finally, the court can suspend a possession order under s36 Administration of Justice Act 1970 (as amended) when the proposed means of dealing with the arrears is a sale by the borrowers of the mortgaged property in order to discharge the entire debt, rather than (as is usually the case) a scheme whereby the mortgagor proposes only to repay the arrears while at the same time keeping the property. See *Target Home Loans* v *Clothier and Clothier* [1994] 1 All ER 439, where the Court of Appeal postponed a possession order for three months to enable the defendant mortgagors to sell their home with a view to discharging the entire mortgage debt (the property in question was already on the market and an early sale was anticipated).

Duties of a mortgagee in possession

A mortgagee who takes possession may use the income arising from the land in lieu of the interest payments due to him under the mortgage, and he may use any surplus to pay off the capital or may hand it over to the person next entitled. If he is a second or subsequent mortgagee he must make any payments due to prior mortgagees. A mortgagee in possession may not derive any personal advantages and must account strictly to the mortgagor. This means that he is liable for any loss caused by his own negligence. A brewery which let a free house as a tied house only selling its own beer was held liable for the difference in rent between a free house and a tied house in *White* v *City of London Brewery Co* (1889) 42 Ch D 237.

If the mortgagee occupies the premises himself he must pay a fair rent, and he must do reasonable repairs. In effect possession is only a satisfactory remedy where the mortgagee can collect fixed rents.

Possession and the question of undue influence

The question of fiduciary duty owed by a creditor who seeks possession and the possible effect of undue influence has become an increasing problem since safeguards were introduced to overcome the problems for mortgagees created by the decision in *Williams & Glyn's Bank* v *Boland* [1981] AC 487. In *National Westminster Bank plc* v *Morgan* [1985] 2 WLR 588 the House of Lords held that before a transaction could be set aside on the grounds of undue influence it had to be shown that it constituted a disadvantage to the person influenced and seeking to avoid it. Any question of presumption of undue influence will only become relevant if the transaction is shown to constitute such a disadvantage. On the facts of this case the proposals were designed to rescue the home from an earlier mortgagee's action for possession. Lord Scarman warned that:

> '... there was no precisely defined law setting limits to the equitable jurisdiction of a court to relieve against undue influence. A court in the exercise of such jurisdiction was a court of conscience ... and whether a transaction was or was not unconscionable ... depended on the particular facts of the case.'

The question of undue influence was also considered by the Court of Appeal in *Kingsnorth Trust Ltd* v *Bell* [1986] 1 WLR 119. The Court of Appeal held that where, under the influence of her husband, a wife executed a mortgage of the matrimonial home without knowing his true purpose in wanting the advance, then her rights in the property retained their priority to the mortgagee's rights. Dillon LJ concluded:

> 'The moral was that where a creditor (or intending lender) desired the protection of a guarantee or charge on property from a third party other than the debtor and the circumstances were such that the debtor would be expected to have influence over that third party, the creditor ought for his own protection to insist that the third party has independent advice.'

In recent years one of the most dynamic areas of mortgages has concerned the following situation – property jointly owned by husband and wife; wife provides security for her husband's business debts following undue influence etc by the husband; husband defaults on repayments; lender seeks to recover possession of the property and the wife alleges that her consent to the security was obtained by undue influence or misrepresentation on the part of her husband which is binding on the lender through actual or constructive notice. The leading case in this regard is that of the House of Lords in *Barclays Bank* v *O'Brien and Another* [1993] 3 WLR 786. There a matrimonial home was in the joint names of a husband and wife. The husband, but not the wife, had an interest in a company. In order to raise capital for this company the husband negotiated a loan from the bank, with the bank taking a legal charge over the matrimonial home as security. He misrepresented the transaction to his wife by telling her that she would be signing the mortgage for a fixed amount of £60,000 that would only last for three weeks and which would enable him to increase his shareholding in the relevant company (in fact they had guaranteed all the company's debts to the bank). The husband signed the relevant documents in the absence of his wife, and when the wife went to sign the legal charge the effect of the deal was not explained to her, nor was she advised to obtain independent legal advice despite the fact that the bank had asked its staff at the relevant branch to explain the deal to her and advise her to take such advice before signing. The company got into financial difficulties, the bank called in the guarantee, and when the husband failed to pay the sum owing the bank sought to realise its security by seeking a possession order in respect of the matrimonial home.

The House of Lords held that the wife was able to have the legal charge against the matrimonial home set aside because the bank was fixed with constructive notice of the husband's misrepresentation. This notice arose as follows: the bank was put on enquiry when the wife offered to stand surety for her husband's debts by a combination of two factors. Firstly, the transaction on its face was not to the wife's financial advantage. Secondly, there was a substantial risk in such transactions that in getting a wife to act as surety the husband had committed a legal or equitable wrong that entitled the wife to set the transaction aside. To avoid such constructive notice it was necessary for the bank to have taken steps (in the absence of the husband) to bring home to the wife the risk that she was running as surety and advise her to take independent advice. This the bank had not done. Finally, their Lordships said that their ruling would also apply to unmarried couples, heterosexual or homosexual, in a relationship where there was a risk of one of them exploiting the other's emotional involvement and trust.

This decision of the House of Lords is undoubtedly a landmark ruling, since as a result of it wives (and others in an analogous position) who agree that their family homes can be used as security for their husbands' debts now have greater protection against the loss of their properties. However, it is important to emphasise the context of the decision – that of a wife signing a mortgage as surety for the debts of her husband. This reality was emphasised by the House of Lords in *CIBC Mortgages plc* v *Pitt and Another* [1993] 3 WLR 802. There a matrimonial home was in the joint names of husband and wife. The only encumbrance on it was a mortgage in favour of a building society. The husband told the wife that he wanted to borrow money on the security of their home in order to use the money so raised for buying shares on the stock market. The wife was unhappy with this idea but eventually agreed to it as a result of pressure from her husband. Both husband and wife signed the mortgage application form, which stated that the purpose of the loan was to pay off the existing mortgage and use the balance to buy a holiday home, and both signed the mortgage offer and legal charge. The wife did not read the documents before signing, nor was she advised to seek legal advice about the transaction. After the existing mortgage was discharged, the rest of the loan was paid into a joint account and the husband used the money to speculate on the stock market. Following the stock market crash of October 1987 the husband was unable to keep up the mortgage payments, and the plaintiffs applied for a possession order in respect of the matrimonial home. The wife contested the application on the basis that she had been induced to sign the relevant documents by undue influence on the part of her husband.

In dismissing the wife's appeal the House of Lords held that the rules laid down in *Barclays Bank plc* v *O'Brien and Another* (above) only applied to cases in which the wife was effectively a surety in that the money was given to her husband or her husband's company. Here Mrs Pitt was, with her husband, a joint borrower of the money. Although she had established undue influence by her husband, the plaintiffs would not be affected by it unless they had notice of it. Here they had no such notice because the loan had been advanced to the husband and wife jointly and there was nothing to suggest to the plaintiffs that it was anything other than a normal advance to a married couple for their joint benefit. The plaintiffs had no duty to advise the wife separately. The mere fact that there was a risk of undue influence because one of the borrowers was the wife of the other was not, in itself, enough to put the plaintiffs on inquiry.

In view of the clear factual differences between this case and *Barclays Bank* v *O'Brien,* the decision in the former is in no way inconsistent with that in the latter case.

Post O'Brien *developments*

Since *Barclays Bank plc* v *O'Brien and Another*, several important issues left unresolved by the House of Lords on that occasion have been considered by the Court of Appeal. Two issues in particular have been addressed: those of independent legal advice and whether a charge which has been induced by misrepresentation should be set aside in full or should be upheld as valid to the extent to which the chargor thought the charge was valid.

Independent legal advice

A creditor in *O'Brien*-type cases has to take reasonable steps to bring home to the wife the risks she is running in signing the document, and has to advise her to take independent legal advice in order to rebut a presumption of undue influence by the husband. The requirement of independent legal advice has fallen to be considered on at least three occasions: *Massey* v *Midland Bank plc* [1995] 1 All ER 929; *Banco Exterior Internacional* v *Mann and Others* [1995] 1 All ER 936; and *Bank of Baroda* v *Rayarel and Others* (1995) The Times 19 January. Each of these cases is considered in turn.

In *Massey* v *Midland Bank plc*, M owned a house and was persuaded by misrepresentations by her lover, P, to charge her house to the plaintiff bank as security for an overdraft granted to a business venture in which P was involved. The bank advised M directly to seek independent advice and P arranged for his own solicitor to advise her. The solicitor advised M in the presence of P and she signed the charge. The solicitors confirmed to the bank that they had given M independent advice and thereafter the bank granted the loan. Subsequently, the company went into liquidation and the bank sought possession of the house. The deputy judge held that the bank was unaffected by P's dishonesty and granted them an order of possession. M appealed but her appeal was dismissed. The bank was put on inquiry by the circumstances in which M had agreed to provide the security. However, its actions (requiring M to be advised and requiring confirmation of such advice) prevented it from being fixed with constructive notice of P's misrepresentations. The bank was entitled to conclude that M had received independent advice from the firm of solicitors and to assume that the solicitor dealing with the matter had acted honestly and given proper advice. The case gives important guidance on the issue of independent advice. It decided that it was enough if the advice to the woman was independent of the lender, even though it was not independent of the man who made the misrepresentations. Further, at variance with *Barclays Bank plc* v *O'Brien and Another* (above) the court found for the bank even though the solicitor explained the nature of the bank's charge to the woman in the presence of her lover. On the *O'Brien* view of the matter the explanation should have been given in the man's absence. See Chapter 18, section 18.4, for further details.

In *Banco Exterior Internacional* v *Mann and Others* [1995] 1 All ER 936, the husband (first defendant) wanted to charge the matrimonial home as security for a loan to be granted by the plaintiff bank to his company. The bank sent the relevant documents to the company, marked for the husband's attention, to enable the wife (second defendant) to sign a declaration that her rights would be postponed to the bank's charge over the matrimonial home. In a covering letter, the bank required the wife's declaration to be signed by her in the presence of a solicitor who would certify that he had explained its effect to her. However, nothing was said about the need for a solicitor to be acting only for the wife. In fact, the documents were sent to a solicitor who for some time had acted for both the husband and his company. The solicitor explained the declaration to the wife, who stated that she had no real choice but to sign. The solicitor then certified that he had explained the nature and effect of the declaration to her. Subsequently the company went into liquidation and the bank sought a possession order. The Court of Appeal held that a presumption of undue influence by the husband over the wife in respect of the transaction had arisen, but that the bank had taken reasonable steps to ensure that the undue influence of the husband had been counteracted. It had required the wife to sign the declaration in the presence of a solicitor, who was required to certify that before it was executed its nature and effect had been explained to her. As to the independent legal advice aspect, the bank had received the solicitor's warranty that he had explained to the wife the nature and effect of the declaration. It was for the solicitor to consider whether he was able to do this without any conflict of interest. The bank could rely on the fact that the solicitor undertook the task as demonstrating that he was sufficiently independent for that purpose. Accordingly, the validity of the charge was upheld. In line with *Massey* v *Midland Bank plc* (above) the court decided that the person advising a wife or unmarried partner in an *O'Brien*-type case had only to be independent of the creditor and did not also have to be independent of the principal debtor (the husband). However, in *Mann* the court went further than *Massey* because in *Mann* the bank never even spoke to the wife whereas in *Massey*, as previously noted, the bank advised the woman directly to seek independent advice.

In *Bank of Baroda* v *Rayarel and Others* (1995) The Times 19 January the Court of Appeal stated that a bank dealing through a solicitor with a wife acting as surety for a loan to her husband's company could usually assume that the solicitor had properly advised the wife (ie that he had done his job properly). Accordingly, the bank was not required to take any additional steps to avoid being fixed with constructive notice of the husband's undue influence etc so as to enable the wife to escape liability for the debt.

This decision is in line with *Massey* v *Midland Bank plc* (above). In these cases the Court of Appeal seems to be saying that the bank/lender in an *O'Brien* situation can discharge its responsibilities as to independent advice by delegating to a third party solicitor.

The charge

The Court of Appeal has also had to consider whether a charge which has been induced by misrepresentation should be set aside in full or should be upheld as valid to the extent to which the chargor thought the charge was valid. In *TSB Bank plc* v *Camfield* [1995] 1 All ER 951 a husband and wife entered into a transaction in order to secure loan facilities for the husband's company from the plaintiff bank. The security for the loan was the matrimonial home, over which the bank took a legal charge. The wife was induced to stand as surety by an innocent misrepresentation by her husband that their maximum liability for the loan was limited to £15,000 when in fact it was unlimited. The husband's business failed and the bank brought proceedings against the husband and wife. The county court judge gave judgment for the bank against the wife for £15,000 and made an order for possession of the home, subject to the wife making payment in full within six months. The wife appealed, claiming that she was entitled to have the charge set aside in toto. The Court of Appeal allowed the appeal; the case came within the principles laid down in *Barclays Bank* v *O'Brien* (above). As to the bank's view that the court could set aside the charge on terms that the wife had acknowledged that it was a valid security for £15,000, the court agreed with the view expressed by Ferris J in the unreported first instance case of *Allied Irish Bank* v *Byrne* (1 February 1994) that the wife's right to set aside the transaction (because she could rely on misrepresentation by her husband to resist liability to the lender pursuant to a charge) was 'an all or nothing process'. Accordingly, the bank was not entitled to an order that the charge be partially enforceable against the wife.

These cases of undue influence are a direct consequence of the requirement for a greater awareness by the mortgagee of the existence of persons in actual occupation of premises offered as security for a mortgage and the rights of such persons. This mainly arises in registered land, due to the decision in *Williams & Glyn's Bank* v

Boland [1981] AC 487, but it should not be disregarded where the title to the land is not registered because of the possible effect of constructive or imputed notice in the mortgagee. See *Kingsnorth Finance Co Ltd v Tizard* [1986] 1 WLR 783.

Appoint a receiver

This achieves much the same result as taking possession without the responsibilities. It is a statutory power given by s101 LPA 1925, which arises and becomes exercisable under the same circumstances as the power of sale (see above). There is no requirement for a court order. The receiver is deemed to be the agent of the mortgagor (s109(2)). In registered land the mortgagee must be registered as proprietor before pursuing this remedy.

In *Lever Finance Ltd* v *Needleman's Trustee and Kreutzer* [1956] Ch 375 a transferee of a mortgage of registered land sought to exercise his statutory power to appoint a receiver. It was held that he could not do so until he had obtained his own registration as proprietor of the charge. Until then the receiver was merely an ordinary agent of the mortgagee.

Income received by the receiver
This must be applied in the following order:

1. payment of rates, taxes and other outgoings;
2. payments which rank in priority to the mortgage;
3. his own commission and insurance premiums, and the cost of repairs if so desired in writing by the mortgagee;
4. interest due under the mortgage;
5. if the mortgagee so directs in writing, repayment of the principal sum, otherwise the surplus to be paid to the person next entitled.

14.9 The remedies of the equitable mortgagee

Sue the mortgagor for the debt
As with a legal mortgage (see section 14.8), the mortgagee can take a normal action to recover the debt.

Foreclose

This is the equitable mortgagee's main remedy. The court ordering the foreclosure will direct the mortgagor to convey the legal estate to the mortgagee. The court may order a judicial sale instead of foreclosure: s91 LPA 1925.

Sell

The statutory power of sale only applies when the mortgage is made by deed. A power of sale may be given expressly in mortgages not made by deed, but this has been held to give the mortgagee the power to sell only his equitable interest. This may be extended to a power to sell the legal estate by inserting a power of attorney or declaration of trust in the mortgage deed. Under the latter the mortgagor declares that he holds the legal estate on trust for the mortgagee and authorises the mortgagee to appoint himself or a third party as trustee instead of the mortgagor, to enable a conveyance of the legal estate to a third party to be effected.

Take possession

An equitable mortgagee has no right to take possession, but the court may award him possession.

Appoint a receiver

If the mortgage is by deed the equitable mortgagee has the statutory power to do this, otherwise he has the right to have a receiver appointed by the court (s37 Supreme Court Act 1981). A receiver appointed by the court is not strictly an agent and is personally liable for his actions as a receiver. He will be required by the court to provide a security.

14.10 Other rights of the mortgagee

The right to fixtures (quicquid plantatur solo, solo cedit)

The mortgagee is entitled to all fixtures on the land at any time during the mortgage unless the mortgage provides otherwise: see *Meux* v *Jacobs* (1875) LR 7 HL 481; *Hulme* v *Brigham* [1943] KB 152; *Gough* v *Wood & Co* [1894] 1 QB 713.

The right to title deeds

The first mortgagee is entitled to possession of the title deeds. The mortgagor is entitled to inspect the deeds and make copies of them on reasonable notice. In the case of registered land the mortgage must be registered as a registered charge. The land certificate will be held by the Land Registry and the mortgagee will receive a charge certificate.

The right to insure against fire at the mortgagor's expense

This allows a mortgagee to protect the value of his security. In practice it is usually specified in the mortgage deed that the mortgagor will himself insure the mortgaged property. The statutory power in s101 LPA 1925 is not adequate because the amount insured must not exceed that on the mortgage deed or, if no amount is specified, two-thirds of the amount required to reinstate the property if totally destroyed.

Note the right under the Fires Prevention (Metropolis) Act 1774 of any person interested in the insured property (including the mortgagor) to require that the insurance money be applied to make good the damage.

14.11 The right to tack further advances

The right to tack is the right of a mortgagee under certain circumstances to add a subsequent loan to an existing loan on the same property mortgaged by the same mortgagor and so to gain priority for this subsequent loan over any intermediate loans by other mortgagees.

Before 1926 subsequent equitable mortgagees without notice of a prior equitable mortgage could buy out the legal mortgage and thus squeeze out any intermediate equitable mortgage. This method of buying priority was known as 'the plank in the shipwreck' – 'tabula in naufragio'. This form of tacking by a subsequent mortgagee was abolished by s94 LPA 1925. After 1925 the only form of tacking that may take place is by the prior mortgagee.

Tacking is best understood if demonstrated by a linear diagram in the following form:

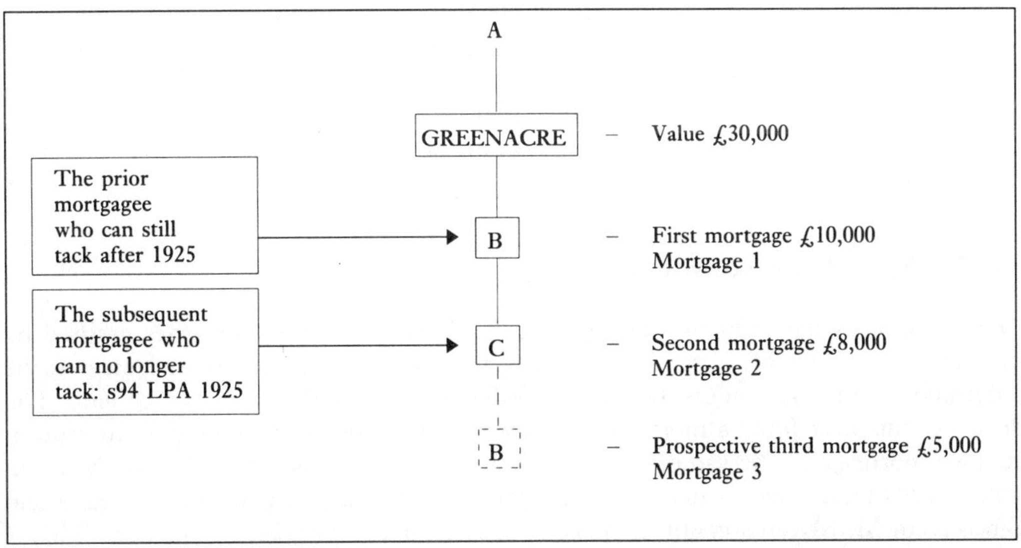

If A now wishes to borrow a further £5,000 on the security of Greenacre and B is prepared to lend the £5,000, he will wish to know whether he can 'tack' mortgage 3 to mortgage 1 in order to obtain priority for his combined loan of £15,000 before C.

Section 94 provides that the two loans may be tacked if one of three conditions is satisfied:

1. B has arranged with C to enable mortgage 1 and mortgage 3 to be added together.
2. There is an obligation in mortgage 1 to make further advances.
3. B has no notice of mortgage 2 created with C.

Thus the effect of s94 LPA 1925 is that the prior mortgagee (and only the prior mortgagee) has a right to make further advances which will rank in priority to subsequent mortgages created before the further advances provided that the following apply:

1. An arrangement to this effect has been made with subsequent mortgagees.
2. The prior mortgagee has no notice of the subsequent mortgage at the time of the further advance. A prior mortgagee may tack where he has no notice of intervening mortgages when he makes his further advance. Registration is notice for this purpose except where the prior mortgage was made expressly to secure a current account or other further advances, where only express notice will prevent tacking. A second mortgagee should give express notice of his mortgage to the first mortgagee as well as registering it. This exception to the rule that registration is equal to actual notice was designed to meet commercial needs. In the case of a bank a security to cover a customer's overdraft would not be as effective if further drawings were made dependent upon a search in the land charges register. It should be noted that this exception covers all mortgages where the contract contemplates further advances on the same security.
3. The prior mortgage imposes an obligation on the mortgagee to make the further advances, for example where an overdraft to a specified limit is secured by a mortgage.

14.12 The right to consolidate

Consolidation is the right of a person who holds two or more mortgages granted by the same mortgagor on different properties to refuse in certain circumstances to be redeemed as to one, unless he is also redeemed as to the other or others. The doctrine thus may force a mortgagor who wishes to redeem one mortgage to redeem another mortgage at the same time. The mortgagee can consolidate the securities, in other words treat them as one. If A mortgages by separate instruments Pinkacre and Blueacre to M, M can sometimes make A redeem both mortgages or neither. This is fair; M might have lent more money on Pinkacre than it was worth, relying on

Blueacre where the security was ample. He should not be left with the bad security after the good has been redeemed. 'He who seeks equity must do equity.' Again this may be seen in diagrammatic form:

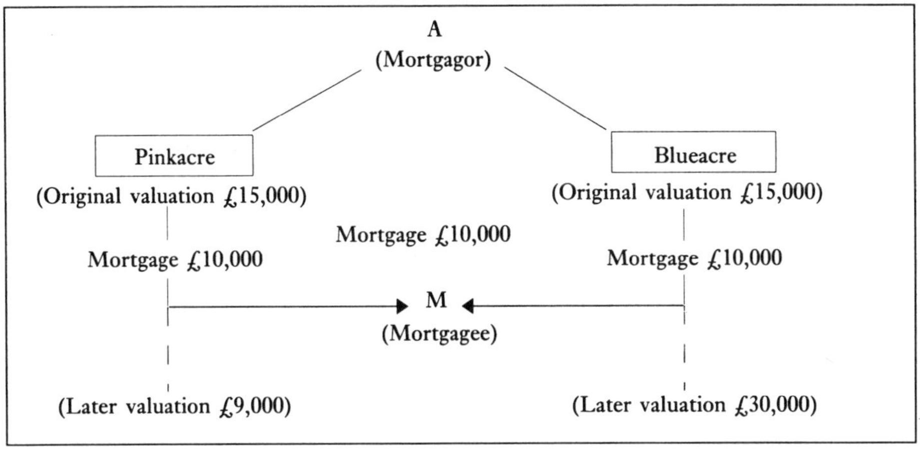

A enters into two separate mortgages of Pinkacre and Blueacre borrowing £10,000 on the security of each property. For some reason, perhaps a new road or a new industrial estate created nearby, the value of Pinkacre falls but the value of Blueacre reflects the current increase in land values. The total security is adequate at £39,000, but M is under-secured on Pinkacre. If A seeks to redeem Blueacre and leave M holding only Pinkacre, then M would be under-secured (£10,000 loan on property valued at £9,000). The doctrine of consolidation helps M by stating that if A seeks to redeem Blueacre he will only be allowed to do so on condition that he also redeems Pinkacre. M can insist on the simultaneous redemption of both mortgages. Waldock in *The Law of Mortgages* says:

> 'The principle upon which the court acts is that after the mortgagor is in default on his contract his right to redeem exists only in equity and, in seeking the assistance of equity, he must himself do equity.'

Before consolidation can take place, the following four conditions must be satisfied:

1. The right to consolidate must be reserved by at least one of the mortgage deeds, since s93 LPA 1925 forbids consolidation unless the right to consolidate is expressly reserved.
2. Both mortgages must have been created by the same mortgagor. If they have not been so created, there can never be consolidation, but according to *Sharpe* v *Rickards* [1909] 1 Ch 109 it is not necessary for them to have been created in favour of the same mortgagee.

3. The legal date of redemption must have passed on all the mortgages which it is desired to consolidate, as otherwise the mortgagor has a legal right to redeem which cannot be made subject to an equitable doctrine.
4. At one and the same time all the mortgages must have been vested in one person, and all the equities in another. If redemption is sought at that time, the mortgagee can consolidate. Even if this state of affairs has ceased when redemption is sought and the equities are then owned by different persons, a mortgagee who holds both mortgages can consolidate. The principle is that once a right to consolidate has arisen, a person who takes either of the equities takes subject to the right.

Note: There cannot be consolidation against a transferee of one of the equities by reason of anything which occurs after he acquires the property.

Examples

1.

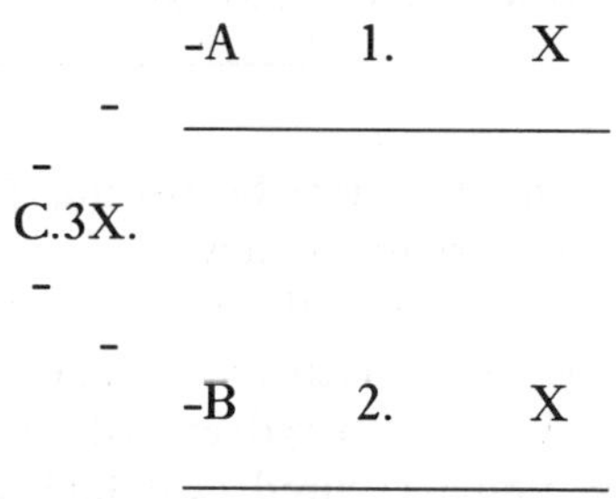

Steps

1. A mortgages one estate to X.
2. B mortgages another estate to X.
3. C purchases both equities of redemption.

Here there can be no consolidation since condition (2) above is not fulfilled. Both mortgages were not created by the same mortgagor.

2.

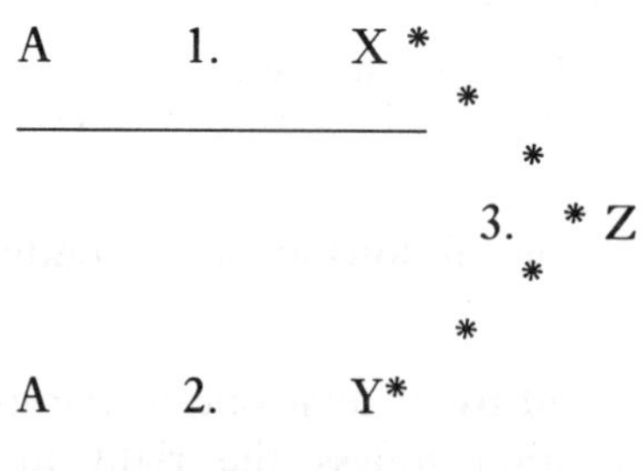

Steps

1. A mortgages one estate to X.
2. A mortgages another to Y.
3. Z purchases both mortgages.

Here Z can consolidate, provided that the right was reserved and the legal date for redemption has passed.

3.

A 1. X	*Steps*
	1. A mortgages one estate to X.
-A 2. X	2. A mortgages another to X.
- 3.	
B-	3. A sells second estate to B.

Here X acquired a right to consolidate after step 2. He can compel B, who purchased subject to that right, to take a transfer of the mortgage on the first estate if he wishes to redeem the mortgage on the second estate. This would leave the parties as:

1.

A ——————— B
(Mortgagor) (Mortgagee)

4.

A 1. X*	*Steps*
	1. A mortgages one estate to X.
3.* *Z	2. A mortgages another to Y.
A 2. Y*	3. Z purchases both mortgages.
B- 4.	4. A sells second estate to B.

Here Z acquired the right to consolidate after step 3 (see example (2) above). He can compel A, who wishes to redeem the mortgage on the first estate, to purchase the mortgage on the second estate also. The effect of this would be:

2.

B ——————— A
(Mortgagor) (Mortgagee)

Conclusion

Megarry and Wade point out at page 959 that this right of consolidation 'causes less trouble than might be supposed'. On the other hand it can create problems for an innocent purchaser of a mortgage who may be presented with the requirement to redeem an unsuspected second mortgage, as in the case of B in example (3) above. Megarry and Wade conclude:

> 'There may well be doubts as to the wisdom of equity in allowing a mortgagee who has made two distinct bargains, one good and one bad, to use the success of one to rescue him from the failure of the other. But the doctrine has existed almost as long as the equity of redemption itself and is too well settled to be questioned.'

14.13 The rights common to both parties

To grant a lease

1. A lease granted by the mortgagor before the mortgage is created is binding on the mortgagee provided that it is a legal lease or, if it is an equitable lease, it is registered as a land charge Class C(iv) if the land is unregistered, or the tenant is in actual occupation if the land is registered.
2. At common law, any lease granted by either party during the existence of the mortgage was not binding on the other without his consent.

By s99 LPA 1925 either party, provided that he is in possession or has appointed a receiver, can grant a lease binding on the other party, as long as:

1. No contrary intention is expressed in the mortgage deed.
2. If the lease is an agricultural or occupational lease, the term does not exceed 50 years, or 999 years for building leases.
3. The lease:
   a) reserves the best rent obtainable without a fine;
   b) takes effect in possession not more than 12 months after execution;
   c) contains a covenant by the tenant to pay the rent and a condition for re-entry on the rent being more than 30 days in arrear.
4. A counterpart executed by the lessee is delivered to the other party to the mortgage within one month.

The use of the statutory power of leasing by the mortgagor is often expressly excluded by the mortgage: *Rhodes* v *Dalby* [1971] 1 WLR 1325. If a mortgagor grants a lease when the statutory power is excluded it is void against the mortgagee although valid against the mortgagor: *Dudley and District Benefit Building Society* v *Emerson* [1949] Ch 707. If the mortgagee refuses to acknowledge such a lease and seeks to exercise one of his remedies against the mortgagor, the lessee may protect his interest by redeeming the mortgage.

Quennel v *Maltby* [1979] 1 WLR 318 suggests that the mortgagee will only be able to exercise the remedies if they are used in good faith for the purpose of enforcing the security and not for any other ulterior motive, such as avoiding the effects of the Rent Act 1977.

To accept the surrender of a lease

By s100 LPA 1925 either party, if in possession or having appointed a receiver, can accept the surrender of a lease provided that within one month of the surrender he grants a new lease within his statutory powers for a term at least as long as that unexpired of the surrendered lease and at a rent at least equivalent to it. If these conditions are not complied with the surrender is void and the old lease continues.

14.14 Priority of mortgages in unregistered land

The rules of priority which apply depend on whether the mortgage is of a legal estate or an equitable interest, and whether the land is registered or unregistered. The pre-1926 principles will only be mentioned in so far as they still apply, the main rules relating to priority now being those laid down by the 1925 legislation. In this section we are considering mortgages of the legal estate only. For mortgages of the equitable interest see section 14.16.

The basic problem relating to priorities may be represented in the diagram below:

Priority of mortgages of the legal estate after 1925

A	– Mortgagor
Greenacre	– Value £50,000
B	– First mortgagee (£10,000) obtains title deeds
C	– Second mortgagee (£10,000). Register as land charge immediately
D	– Third mortgagee (£10,000). Register as land charge immediately
E	– Fourth mortgagee (£10,000). Register as land charge immediately

The mortgage with B is not registrable because the title deeds were deposited as security. The mortgages with C, D and E are not so protected and must be registered as land charges in order to obtain protection. Provided that this is carried out immediately the mortgage is entered into, no priority problems should arise after 1925. It is only if C or D fails to register that the question of priority becomes significant.

Priority of mortgages when the land is unregistered depends on whether the mortgage is registrable or not (see Chapter 6) as a land charge Class C(i) or Class C(iii). There are four possible situations:

1. Both mortgages are unregisterable.
2. First mortgage is unregisterable, second is registerable.
3. First mortgage is registerable, second is unregisterable.
4. Both mortgages are registerable.

These will be dealt with in turn.

Both mortgages unregistrable

While this is unlikely, it is possible for the first mortgagee to have only some of the title deeds, the remainder being deposited with the second mortgagee, or the mortgagor may have recovered the title deeds from the first mortgagee in order to hand them to a second mortgagee. See *Northern Counties Fire Insurance Co* v *Whipp* (1884) 26 Ch D 482.

Priority of such mortgages is not dealt with by the 1925 legislation, so the pre-1926 rules apply, and these rules are different for legal and equitable mortgages. There are four possibilities:

Both mortgages legal

They will rank in order of creation, unless the first mortgagee has by his misconduct disentitled himself to priority. The types of misconduct which have been held to have this effect are:

1. Fraud: this would be if the first mortgagee was party to a scheme with the mortgagor to allow the second mortgagee to believe that the property was unencumbered.
2. Estoppe: if the first mortgagee by word or conduct allows the mortgagor to deal with the property as if there were no mortgage, he will lose his priority to a subsequent mortgagee.
3. Gross negligence: if the first mortgagee has negligently failed to obtain the title deeds (*Walker* v *Linom* [1907] 2 Ch 104), or failed to retain them (*Northern Counties Fire Insurance Co* v *Whipp* (above)) he may lose his priority.

First mortgage legal, second equitable

The first will have priority unless the mortgagee is guilty of fraud, estoppel or gross negligence (see above).

First mortgage equitable, second legal

The primary rule is that the first mortgagee has priority unless the second is a bona fide purchaser for value without notice. In practice, however, the courts seem to have held that in the absence of actual notice the second has priority (*Hewitt* v *Loosemore* (1851) 9 Hare 449) unless he has been guilty of 'gross negligence' (*Oliver* v *Hinton* [1899] 2 Ch 264).

Both mortgages equitable

The priority is in order of creation unless the first mortgagee is guilty of fraud, estoppel or gross negligence (see above).

First mortgage unregistrable, second registrable

The first mortgage will have priority unless forfeited by the fraud, estoppel or gross negligence of the mortgagee (see above).

First mortgage registrable, second unregistrable

This situation is governed by s4(5) LCA 1972 which provides that a registrable charge (Class C(i) or Class C(iii)) which is not registered is void

> 'against a purchaser of the land charged ... or of any interest in such land, unless the land charge is registered in the appropriate register before the completion of the purchase'

and by s198 LPA 1925 which provides that such registration constitutes actual notice for all purposes connected with the land. Therefore, if the first is registered before the second is created, the first has priority; if it is not registered when the second is created, the second has priority.

Both mortgages registrable

If the first mortgage is registered before the second is created then the first has priority by the above principles – see the diagram above.

Similarly, if the second mortgage is registered before the first is registered then the second has priority. If, however, the second mortgage is created before the first is registered, but is registered after the first, there is a conflict between the statutory provisions. By s4(5) LCA 1972 the first is void against the second, and so the second has priority regardless of when it was registered. However, s97 LPA 1925 provides that mortgages rank according to their date of registration, and so the first has priority. There has been no reported judicial consideration of this conflict. This has been described as the 'circulus inextricabilis' and has, to date, only been an exercise for the academic writer rather than for the practitioner. The problem may be illustrated in this way:

January	–	A takes a first legal mortgage and obtains the title deeds as security.
June	–	B takes a second legal (puisne) mortgage.
July	–	C takes a third legal (puisne) mortgage.
August	–	B registers a land charge Class C(i).
September	–	C registers a land charge Class C(i).

There is no doubt that the title deeds protect A's priority, but who has priority between B and C?

If s97 LPA 1925 is applied, then B has priority over C because that was the order of registration.

If s4(5) LCA 1972 is applied, then C has priority over B because B's mortgage is void against C at the time of the creation of C's mortgage in July. Most of the textbook writers believe that this second solution will prevail and this section will provide the answer. Cheshire states at p721 that after 1925 the question of priorities

> 'depends upon a combination of s97 of the Law of Property Act 1925 and s4(5) of the Land Charges Act 1972, but it would appear that the latter is the dominating enactment'.

Megarry and Wade at p1,000 appear to agree in these words:

> 'How this conflict could be resolved is uncertain, but it might well be that s4(5) [LCA 1972] would be held to prevail, despite the argument (not a strong one) that s97 would then be meaningless.'

The priority of mortgages of unregistered land may be summed up by the following table. 'R' stands for registrable, 'NR' for non-registrable:

First	*Order of creation*	Second
1. NR		NR
Priority depends on whether mortgages are legal or equitable.		
a) Legal		Legal
Order 1		2 unless first guilty of fraud etc
b) Legal		Equitable
Order 1		2 unless first guilty of fraud etc
c) Equitable		Legal
Order 1		2 unless second BFP
d) Equitable		Equitable
1		2 unless first guilty of fraud etc
2. NR		R
1		2 s13 LPA 1925
3. R		NR
a) If first not registered before second created		
Order 1		2 s198 LPA 1925
b) If first registered before second created		
Order 2		1 s4 LCA 1972
4. R		R
a) If first registered before second created		
Order 1		2 s198 LPA 1925
b) If second created and registered before first registered		
Order 2		1 s4 LCA 1972
c) If both created before first registered, second registered after first, conflict		
Order 1		2 s97 LPA 1925
2		1 s4 LCA 1972

14.15 Priority of mortgages in registered land

Creation of legal mortgage

The provisions of the Land Registration Act 1925 relating to mortgages are, according to most writers, unnecessarily obscure and complicated. There are two methods of creating a legal mortgage of registered land:

1. By a deed creating a registered charge (s25 LRA 1925): when such a deed is registered the mortgagor must surrender his land certificate to the Registry, which retains it during the currency of the mortgage and issues a charge certificate to the mortgagee.
2. By creating a legal mortgage in the same way as for unregistered land and protecting it by a notice or by an ordinary caution: s106(3) LRA 1925 as amended by Administration of Justice Act 1977 s26(1).

A mortgagee can only exercise his statutory powers if he is a registered chargee. See *Lever Finance Ltd* v *Needleman's Trustee and Kreutzer* [1956] Ch 375.

Creation of equitable mortgage

The creation of an equitable mortgage of registered land is more complex. The following methods exist:

1. By protection by a notice or by ordinary caution as for legal mortgages, whether the mortgage is by deed or otherwise: s106 LRA 1925, as amended by AJA 1977 s26(1) (see above). Section 26(1) AJA 1977 abolishes the special mortgage caution formerly protecting mortgages by deed not registered as registered charges. The mortgage now only takes effect in equity and can be protected by an ordinary notice or caution, and until then it may be overridden as a minor interest.
2. A simple deposit of the land certificate creates a lien on the registered land (s66 LRA 1925), which should be protected by a notice of deposit, which will operate as a caution. See *Barclays Bank Ltd* v *Taylor* [1974] Ch 137, discussed in detail below. Such notices of deposit are frequently used by banks.
3. Possibly, by registration as a registered charge if it is made by deed.

Priority

The rules relating to priority of mortgages are also complex, and depend on the nature of the mortgage.

Registered charges

By s29 LRA 1925 registered charges rank in the order in which they are entered on the register (cf s97 LPA 1925) and not in the order in which they are created. See *Williams & Glyn's Bank* v *Boland* [1981] AC 487.

Other mortgages

The position of mortgages not protected by registration or the former special mortgage caution was considered in *Barclays Bank Ltd* v *Taylor* (above). An equitable mortgage was created by the deposit with the bank of the land certificate, the bank registering a notice of deposit. The registered proprietors then contracted to sell the property to the Taylors, who entered a caution to protect their estate contract. At first instance Goulding J held that the bank's charge was not protected because it was a charge by deed, and s106(2) LRA 1925 appeared to say that this could be protected by a special caution and in no other way. However, the Court of Appeal held that the bank's mortgage was effective in equity, and thus took priority to that of the Taylors, who also had only an equitable interest. Such mortgages would appear to rank in priority in order of date of entry of the caution or notice of deposit. Section 26 Administration of Justice Act 1977 has amended s106 by abolishing the special mortgage caution and providing that mortgages of registered land may be made in the same ways as mortgages of unregistered land, but unless they are registered charges they will take effect only in equity and should be protected as a minor interest by entry of a notice or caution. The section makes no provision as to priority.

14.16 Priority of mortgages of an equitable interest

This is governed by the rule in *Dearle* v *Hall* (1828) 3 Russ 1 as amended by ss137 and 138 LPA 1925. For further details see the Equity and Trusts syllabus and the standard textbooks.

Dearle v *Hall* provides that priority depends upon the order in which the trustees received notice from the mortgagees. This rule originally applied to personalty, but s137(1) applies the rule to all dealings with equitable interests after 1925. It provides:

> 'The law applicable to dealings with equitable things in action which regulates the priority of competing interests therein, shall, as respects dealings with equitable interests in land, capital money, and securities representing capital money effected after the commencement of this Act, apply to and regulate the priority of competing interests therein.'

The object of the rule in *Dearle* v *Hall* was to enable a person to discover, by inquiries addressed to the trustees, whether the owner of an equitable interest had created any earlier incumbrances.

In the case of registered land the order of priority of equitable interests was formerly governed by s102(2) LRA 1925. This was repealed by s5 Land Registration Act 1986. The effect of this is to abolish the Minor Interests Index and provide that priority between dealings with equitable interests in registered land will also be determined by the rule in *Dearle* v *Hall*. The consequence of this is that in both registered and unregistered land the rule of priority for equitable mortgages will be the order in which notice is received by the trustees from the mortgagees.

14.17 Summary of the rules of priority in unregistered land

Before 1926

Legal or equitable interests in land
The order of creation is subject to the doctrine of the purchaser without notice, or to the rules relating to fraud, estoppel and gross negligence (see *Northern Counties of England Fire Insurance Co* v *Whipp* (1884) 26 Ch D 482); or excuses for non-production of title deeds. See *Hewitt* v *Loosemore* (1851) 9 Hare 449; *Oliver* v *Hinton* [1899] 2 Ch 264.

Equitable interests in personalty
The order in which notice was received by the owner of the legal estate. See *Dearle* v *Hall* (above).

After 1925

Legal estates in land

1. Where the title deeds are obtained, the order of creation of mortgages.
2. If the title deeds are not obtained, registration as a land charge (note the conflict between s97 LPA 1925 and s4(5) LCA 1972).

Conclusion: one must register before the completion of the next transaction.

Equitable interests in any property
Section 137(1) LPA 1925 applies the above rule in *Dearle* v *Hall*: priority depends upon the order in which notice of the mortgage is received by the appropriate trustees.

15

Adverse Possession

15.1 General principles

Definition: 'adverse possession' means possession inconsistent with the title of the true owner.

Acquisition of title by adverse possession is one aspect of the law of limitation of actions: the prevention of stale claims and the prevention of endless litigation by the extinction of the right of action after a certain period of time. Limitation of actions is purely statutory. Once an owner's right to take an action for possession against a squatter is barred by lapse of time his title to the land is extinguished, and the squatter acquires it by being in possession. The title he acquires, however, is only the title of the owner he dispossesses, so he may be evicted by a person having a better title.

15.2 Limitation periods

These are now laid down by the Limitation Act 1980. The main periods for land law purposes are:

1. Six years for simple contracts, arrears of rent, tort (s5).
2. Twelve years for actions on a deed (s15):

> 'No action shall be brought to recover land after the expiration of 12 years from the date on which the right of action accrued.'

3. Twelve years for actions for recovery of land or money charged on land (s16).

The limitation period in respect of land owned by the Crown or by a corporation sole is, however, 30 years (Schedule 1, Part II).

15.3 Running of time

In order to determine when the action has become barred it is necessary to discover when time began to run, including any factors which could postpone this date, what will start time running afresh and what can suspend the running of time.

When time begins to run

When the owner is entitled to possession
Time begins to run as soon as:

1. The owner has been dispossessed or has discontinued his possession.
2. Adverse possession has been taken by some other person. As stated above, adverse possession is possession inconsistent with the title of the true owner, and whether the possession of the other person was adverse is a matter of fact depending on the circumstances of each case.

In *Wallis's Cayton Bay Holiday Camp Ltd* v *Shell-Mex and BP Ltd* [1975] QB 94 Lord Denning described the nature of the claim:

> 'Possession by itself is not enough to give a title. It must be adverse possession. The true owner must have discontinued possession or have been dispossessed and another must have taken it adversely to him. There must be something in the nature of an ouster of the true owner by the wrongful possessor.'

The meaning of 'discontinued possession' or dispossession was further considered by Sir John Pennycuick in *Treloar* v *Nute* [1976] 1 WLR 1295:

> 'The person claiming by possession must show either (1) discontinuance by the paper owner followed by possession, or (2) dispossession ... (ouster) of the paper owner ... where the person claiming by possession establishes possession in the full sense of inclusive possession, that by itself connotes absence of possession on the part of the paper owner.'

There must be an intention to 'exclude the owner as well as other people'. This question of intention was explained by Slade J in *Powell* v *McFarlane* (1977) 38 P & CR 452:

> '... the courts ... will require clear and affirmative evidence that the trespasser, claiming that he has acquired possession, not only had the requisite intention to possess, but made such intention clear to the world. If his acts are open to more than one interpretation and he has not made it perfectly plain to the world at large by his actions or words that he has

> intended to exclude the owner as best he can, the courts will treat him as not having had the requisite animus possidendi and consequently as not having dispossessed the owner.'

From the cases it is clear that adverse possession must be a question of fact in which circumstances such as the nature of the land and the way in which the land is enjoyed must be taken into account.

The intention to possess was the subject of further consideration by the Court of Appeal in *Buckinghamshire County Council* v *Moran* [1989] 2 All ER 225. A plot of land had been conveyed to the plaintiffs in 1955. To the south the plot was bounded by a laurel hedge; to the west there was a privet hedge; to the east there was a fence in poor condition along the road frontage and to the north was Dolphin Place with nothing to separate the plot from it. From about 1967 the previous owners of Dolphin Place had maintained the plot and treated it as part of their garden; they had mowed the grass and trimmed the hedges. In 1971 Dolphin Place was conveyed to the defendant

> 'together with ... all such estate right title and interest as the vendors may have in or over [the plot]'.

The vendors made a statutory declaration to the effect that since 1967 they had cultivated the plot and from time to time parked a horse-box there and that no one had challenged their right to occupy it. They further declared that their permission had been sought to lay an electric cable across the plot. The plaintiffs sought possession of the plot and the defendant claimed that they had been dispossessed by him more than 12 years before they instituted the proceedings. The judge found that the plaintiffs had never discontinued their possession of the plot, and that finding was not now challenged. Nevertheless, he declared that the defendant was the freehold owner of the plot, and the plaintiffs appealed.

The appeal was dismissed: the defendant had shown both factual possession and the requisite intention to possess.

Slade LJ:

> 'Under the Limitation Act 1980, as under the previous law, the person claiming a possessory title had to show either discontinuance by the paper owner followed by possession or dispossession (or, as it was sometimes called "ouster") of the paper owner ...
>
> If the law was to attribute possession of land to a person who could establish no paper title to possession, he must be shown to have both factual possession and the requisite intention to possess (animus possidendi). A person claiming to have dispossessed another similarly had to fulfil both those requirements. However, a further requirement which the alleged dispossessor claiming the benefit of the [Limitation Act 1980 had to satisfy was] to show that his possession has been adverse within the meaning of ... paragraph 8 of Schedule 1 ...
>
> The crucial question was whether Mr Moran was in adverse possession of the plot on 28 October 1973 ...
>
> On the evidence it would appear clear that by 28 October 1973, Mr Moran had acquired complete and exclusive physical control of the plot. He had secured a complete enclosure of the plot and its annexation to Dolphin Place. Any intruder could have gained access to the plot only by way of Dolphin Place, unless he was prepared to climb the

locked gate fronting the highway or to scramble through one or other of the hedges bordering the plot.

Mr Moran had put a new lock and chain on the gate and had fastened it.

He and his mother had been dealing with the plot as any occupying owners might have been expected to deal with it. They had incorporated it into the garden of Dolphin Place.

The more difficult question was whether Mr Moran had the necessary animus possidendi ... the animus possidendi involved the intention, in one's own name and on one's own behalf, to exclude the world at large, including the owner with the paper title, so far as was reasonably practicable and so far as the process of the law would allow.

As a number of authorities indicated, enclosure by itself prima facie indicated the requisite animus possidendi: *Seddon* v *Smith* (1877) 36 LT 168, 169.

However, the placing of the new lock and chain and gate did amount to a final unequivocal demonstration of Mr Moran's intention to possess the land.'

The above decision of the Court of Appeal was applied by a differently constituted Court of Appeal in *Morrice* v *Evans* (1989) The Times 27 February. In 1974 Mr and Mrs Evans purchased a property from Mrs Dummett; adjoining the property was the plot in question. The plot was overgrown and neglected; it was owned by Mrs Dummett, but it was not included in the conveyance to the Evanses. The only access to the plot was via the Evanses' garden, and there was no marked boundary separating the two pieces of land. At all times the Evanses used the plot as part of their garden, but in 1975 Mrs Dummett's son-in-law and agent, Mr Morrice, told Mr Evans to stop using the greenhouse on the plot, and he had done so.

Mrs Dummett died in 1985 and by 1986 the plot was vested in her daughter, Mrs Morrice. On 18 September 1987 Mrs Morrice commenced proceedings seeking a declaration that she was the freehold owner of the plot and entitled to possession of it. The declaration was made and the Evanses appealed, relying on s15(1) of the Limitation Act 1980.

The appeal was dismissed.

Balcombe LJ:

'Paragraphs 1 and 8 of Schedule 1 to the [1980] Act (relating to the time that a right of action was to be treated as accruing) made it clear that for Mr and Mrs Evans to succeed in their claim to title to the plot by adverse possession, they had to establish that before 18 September 1975 – that is, 12 years before the date of the commencement of action:

1. that Mrs Dummett was dispossessed or discontinued her possession of the plot; and
2. that since that date Mr and Mrs Evans had been in adverse possession of it ...

The law on adverse possession had been recently clarified by the Court of Appeal's decision in *Buckinghamshire County Council* v *Moran* [1989] 2 All ER 225 where adverse possession of a plot treated as a garden was held to be established to as to entitle the possessor to a declaration that he was the freehold owner of it.

On whether the necessary animus possidendi existed in that case, Slade LJ had cited what he himself had stated in *Powell* v *McFarlane* (1977) 38 P & CR 452, 471–2, that "the animus possidendi involves the intention, in one's own name and on one's own behalf to exclude the world at large, including the owner with the paper title ... so far as was reasonably practicable and so far as the process of the law would allow".

Mr Evans' evidence had been that "if Mr Morrice told me not to do something, I accepted that I was not to do it". That evidence, together with the facts of the case,

> showed that the judge was clearly right to conclude that Mr Evans had not the necessary animus possidendi to establish the relevant adverse possession of the plot.'

It must be shown that the claimant has accepted the assertion of the right by the paper owner, and the mere assertion alone by the true paper owner of a claim to possession in land contained in a letter sent to the squatter is not sufficient to prevent the squatter obtaining title by adverse possession.

The question of intention is a continuing problem for the courts.

The erection of a fence for some 24 hours was not a sufficient act of possession. This did not constitute a sufficient degree of exclusive physical control. See *Marsden* v *Miller* (1992) The Times 23 January, in which Scott LJ stated:

> 'To obtain possession of land, both a mental element and a factual element were requisite. The factual element had to involve an appropriate degree of exclusive physical control. The mental element, the Animus 2 precedent, had to consist of an intention to take possession to the exclusion of all others.'

Successive squatters

A squatter can give as good a title as he has. If the first squatter is dispossessed, the second squatter acquires any time which has already run, but if the first squatter abandons possession before the second takes possession, time starts running afresh.

The fact that where a squatter dispossesses another squatter, and the first squatter abandons his claim, then the second squatter can add the time enjoyed by the first squatter to achieve the necessary 12 years' adverse possession was illustrated by *Mount Carmel Investments Ltd* v *Peter Thurlow Ltd* [1988] 3 All ER 129, where it was confirmed by the Court of Appeal. In this case the first squatter had abandoned his claim and the defendants as second squatters were entitled to rely on the combined period of 14 years' possession to give them a title under s15(1) Limitation Act 1980.

Future interests

The remainderman or reversioner must sue for possession either within 12 years of the commencement of the adverse possession, or within six years of his interest vesting in possession, whichever is the longer. The second period is not available when the land is entailed and the reversioner or remainderman's interest could have been barred by the tenant in tail.

Leaseholds

Time does not begin to run against the reversioner if the tenant is dispossessed until the lease expires, because until then he has no right to possession. A tenant cannot acquire title against his landlord during the currency of the lease because his possession is not adverse. See *Fairweather* v *St Marylebone Property Co Ltd* [1963] AC 510. Failure to pay the rent only bars the landlord's right to recover any unpaid instalment after six years. The landlord's title will, however, be barred if a third party is in adverse receipt of rent for 12 years. If the rent is 'not less than ten pounds a year' see Schedule 1 Part I paragraph 6 Limitation Act 1980.

Tenants at will and at sufferance

Tenant at will. Formerly time ran from one year after the grant of the tenancy unless rent was paid or a written acknowledgement of the landlord's title was given, which caused time to start running afresh. This rule was abolished by the Limitation Act 1980, and now time runs in favour of a tenant at will from the time his tenancy comes to an end.

Tenant at sufferance. Time runs from the commencement of the tenancy because in one sense his possession is already adverse. A tenant who remains in occupation at the expiry of his lease whether periodic or for a term of years without paying rent and without the landlord's consent is a tenant at sufferance, and time begins to run from the expiry of the lease.

Rentcharges

A rentcharge is defined in s38(1) Limitation Act 1980 as a

> '... periodical sum of money charged upon or payable out of land, except a rent service or interest on a mortgage of land'.

Time runs from the last payment of rent to the owner of the rentcharge.

Section 38(8) Limitation Act 1980 provides:

> 'References in this Act to the possession of land shall, in the case of ... rentcharges, be construed as references to the receipt of the ... rent, and references to the date of dispossession or discontinuance of possession of land shall, in the case of rentcharges, be construed as references to the date of the last receipt of rent.'

Mortgages

1. The mortgagor's right to redeem is barred after 12 years' possession by the mortgagee without receiving payment by or on behalf of the mortgagor. Receipt of rent and profits from the mortgaged land is not enough to stop time running. *Note*: this is an exception to the rule that the possession must be adverse.
2. The mortgagee's rights under the mortgage are barred after 12 years from the date when repayment became due without any payment by the mortgagor or written acknowledgement of the mortgagee's rights. Time will have to begin running again if the mortgagor makes any written acknowledgement or pays any interest or capital (s29(4) Limitation Act 1980).

Trusts

Adverse possession of trust property does not bar the trustee's title until all the beneficiaries are barred; for example, if land is held on trust for sale for X for life, then to Y for life and then to Z, 12 years' possession by S, a squatter, against X will bar only X; time will not start to run against Y until X's death, and similarly time will not run against Z until Y's death, and S will only bar the trustee's legal estate by 12 years' adverse possession after Y's death.

Section 18 Limitation Act 1980. A trustee can never acquire title by limitation against the beneficiaries. Time does not run in favour of a beneficiary against the trustees unless the beneficiary is solely and absolutely entitled. This would occur when a purchaser is let into possession before conveyance.

Postponement of the limitation period

The date from which time begins to run may be postponed by:

The owner being under a disability
If the owner was under a disability, for example was an infant or a patient under a Mental Health Act, when the adverse possession began he has an alternative period of six years from the end of his disability to take action, subject to a maximum period of 30 years from the beginning of adverse possession (s28(1) and (4) Limitation Act 1980). A supervening disability has no effect on the running of time; the disability must end at the time when the cause of action accrued.

Fraud, fraudulent concealment or mistake
Time does not begin to run until the claimant discovers the fact or could have discovered the fact with 'reasonable diligence' (s32(1) Limitation Act 1980).

Starting time running afresh

Time may be started running afresh by a payment or by a written and signed acknowledgement of the plaintiff's title (s29 Limitation Act 1980). Once the limitation period has elapsed the owner's title cannot be revived by any payment or acknowledgement.

Suspension of the period

Once time has started to run it will run continuously. Suspension of the running of time can only be done by statute; for example, during the Second World War, running of time was suspended against any person who was an enemy or detained in enemy territory by the Limitation (Enemies and War Prisoners) Act 1945.

15.4 Effect of lapse of time

Once the limitation period has been achieved:

1. The owner's title is extinguished in that he can no longer take legal proceedings to recover the property. Section 17 Limitation Act 1980 provides:

   '... at the expiration of the period prescribed by this Act for any person to bring an action to recover land ... the title of that person shall be extinguished.'

2. The squatter acquires the title that the person he dispossessed had, subject to all third party rights. A squatter, not being a purchaser for value, takes subject even to unregistered registrable rights, but there is no actual transfer of title to him and his protection is negative in that he is protected from interference by the person who has been dispossessed. The nature of the squatter's title was described by Lord Radcliffe in *Fairweather* v *St Marylebone Property Co Ltd* [1963] AC 510:

   'He is not at any stage of his possession a successor to the title of the man he has dispossessed. He comes in and remains in always by right of possession, which in due course becomes incapable of disturbance as time exhausts the one or more periods allowed by statute for successful intervention. His title, therefore, is never derived through but arises always in spite of the dispossessed owner.'

3. Leases: unless the landlord has reserved a right of forfeiture for breach of covenant and a covenant is broken he cannot eject a squatter until the lease has expired. If, however, the dispossessed tenant surrenders his lease, the lease merges with the reversion and the landlord can sue immediately for possession.

   Fairweather v *St Marylebone Property Co Ltd* (above) was distinguished in respect of land with registered title by Browne-Wilkinson J in *Spectrum Investment Co* v *Holmes* [1981] 1 WLR 221. In the case of registered land, if the squatter registered his rights under the LRA 1925, once the limitation period has run, those rights could not be defeated by a subsequent surrender of the lease between the original lessee and the landlord. In *Fairweather* the House of Lords held that a surrender of the lease enabled the landlord to eject the squatter forthwith. The House of Lords did not have to consider the effect of registration of the squatter's title.

   The result is the same if the tenant acquires the landlord's reversion. The tenant will continue to remain liable under the covenants in the lease if he was the original tenant, that is, if there is privity of contract, but not if there was only privity of estate. There is no privity of estate between a squatter and the landlord, and so only restrictive covenants are directly enforceable against him. He is, however, liable to distress if the rent is not paid. If he does pay rent he will become a periodic tenant.

   A squatter is not entitled to relief from forfeiture under s146 LPA 1925.

Registered land

Section 75 LRA 1925 provides that the Limitation Act 1980 shall apply to registered land in the same way as to unregistered land, with one important distinction: that when an interest would have been extinguished in the case of unregistered land then in the case of registered land it will not be extinguished. Instead it is deemed to be held in trust by the registered proprietor for the person who has acquired title against him.

Section 75(1) LRA 1925 provides:

> '(1) The Limitation Acts shall apply to registered land in the same manner and to the same extent as those Acts apply to land not registered, except that where, if land were not registered, the estate of the person registered as proprietor would be extinguished, such estate shall not be extinguished but shall be deemed to be held by the proprietor for the time being in trust for the person who, by virtue of the said Acts, has acquired title against any proprietor, but without prejudice to the estates and interests of any other person interested in the land whose estate or interest is not extinguished by those Acts.
> (2) Any person claiming to have acquired a title under the Limitation Acts to a registered estate in the land may apply to be registered as proprietor thereof.'

The effect of s75 is that no legal title can vest in the adverse possessor until he has been registered as proprietor. Until then the registered proprietor's estate is held on trust for the adverse possessor.

In addition, s70(1)(f) LRA 1925 provides that 'rights acquired or in course of being acquired under the Limitation Acts' are overriding interests (see Chapter 7).

15.5 Proof of squatter's title

The fact of long possession alone is not enough to produce a good title between vendor and purchaser. In order to provide a good title by limitation a vendor must prove the following:

1. the title of the former owner to the particular land;
2. the extinction of that title in favour of the vendor.

This is a particularly heavy burden of proof because the vendor will normally have no documents of title in order to support his claim to be able to sell. Problems may well arise relating to restrictive covenants that remain in force. See *Re Nisbet and Pott's Contract* [1906] 1 Ch 386.

If a person has been in occupation of land for 14 years following a contract to purchase which was never completed by a conveyance, then possession is not adverse because there was always an answer to any action, namely that the possession was by virtue of the contract. See *Hyde* v *Pearce* [1982] 1 WLR 560.

15.6 Worked example

Q Twenty years ago a small farm was settled on A for life with remainder to B in fee simple. A was not interested in farming, and for the last 14 years Y has been farming one of the fields. A has now got planning permission to build on the land and wishes to evict Y. Advise A. Would your answer be different if A had died five years ago and the legal fee simple for the farm had been vested in B by A's personal representatives 18 months after A's death?

A In the absence of fraud or of unusual circumstances, as in *Wallis's Cayton Bay Holiday Camp* v *Shell-Mex* (1975), farming the land is adverse possession against A. As Y has been doing so for more than 12 years, A's life interest is extinguished and he cannot evict Y. On A's death B will have six years to claim possession, and so the land can be recovered then. It is possible that if A surrendered his life interest to B, with intent to extinguish it under s105(1) SLA 1925, B would be able to start a possession action immediately.

If A had died five years ago but the legal fee simple for the farm had been vested in B by A's personal representatives 18 months after A's death, this would have meant that the farm became vested in possession three and half years ago. Time runs against the remainderman, B, either from 12 years from the commencement of adverse possession or within six years of his interest vesting in possession, whichever is the longer (s15(2) Limitation Act 1980).

If the first alternative is chosen, being 12 years from the commencement of adverse possession, time would have run out for B. But the second period means that time only begins to run from the date the interest vests in possession in B and so the adverse possession of Y does not, at this stage, extinguish B's title. B must bring an action for possession within the next two and half years.

16

Future Interests: The Rules against Perpetuities and Accumulations

16.1 Introduction

The law dealing with perpetuities and accumulations should be considered purely as an exercise in logic. It has very little to do with the rest of land law, but once grasped the principles are very straightforward. The most important distinction is between vested and contingent interests (see section 16.2). The rule against perpetuities applies only to contingent interests.

It should also be noted that the rules apply only to future interests, that is, interests taking effect otherwise than in possession. An interest in possession gives an immediate right to the enjoyment of the land. A future interest gives a right of enjoyment at some time in the future. This is explained in Megarry and Wade at p231:

> 'A future interest in land is an interest which confers a right to the enjoyment of the land at a future time ...'

Future interests are divided into two categories:

1. Interest in reversion: this is that part of the grantor's interest not disposed of by the grant, which will revert back to him or his successors when the estates which have been created come to an end.
2. Interest in remainder: this is that part of the grantor's interest that is disposed of by the grant, provided that it is postponed to an interest in possession created at the same time. The future interest must be held by someone other than the original grantor, or his successors, and the name is derived from the fact that possession will remain away from the original grantor.

   The grant by X, a fee simple owner, to A for life, remainder to B for life, remainder to C in tail creates:

   a) one interest in possession: A's life interest;
   b) two interests in remainder: B's life interest, C's fee tail;
   c) one interest in reversion: X's fee simple.

The rule against perpetuities applies only to interests in remainder. This is because interests in reversion are always vested.

16.2 Vested and contingent interests

Interests in remainder can be either vested or contingent. An interest is vested when the grantee of the interest is certain that he will be entitled to the interest at some time in the future, as soon as the interests prior to his own have determined. An interest is contingent if the grantee cannot say with certainty whether or not he will be so entitled. The time at which it must be decided whether a grant is vested or contingent is the date at which the grant takes effect:

1. if by will, the date of the testator's death;
2. if inter vivos, the date of the grant.

Note: the word 'vested' does not mean that the grantee is entitled in possession. A future interest can be vested. The test to be adopted is to ascertain whether the owner is absolutely entitled at the present time to assume possession whenever it may fall vacant.

Vested interests

A future interest is vested provided that three conditions are satisfied:

1. the identity of the grantee or grantees must be known; and
2. all conditions attached to the grant must have been complied with; and
3. the respective shares of the beneficiaries must be known.

Contingent interests

An interest is contingent if any of the three conditions is not satisfied. It will stay contingent until all the conditions are satisfied. Megarry and Wade explain this also at page 231:

> 'A contingent interest is one which will give no right at all unless or until some future event happens.'

It is vital to understand the distinction between vested and contingent interests, as the rule against perpetuities (see 'Importance of the distinction' below, and section 16.3 below) applies only to contingent interests.

Examples of vested and contingent interests

1. Gift by will 'to A for life, remainder to B'.
   At testator's death A and B are alive.
   B's interest in remainder is vested as all three conditions are satisfied.
2. Gift by will 'to A for life, remainder to B when he reaches 21'.
   At testator's death A is alive and B is 14.
   B's interest in remainder is contingent: condition 2 is not satisfied as B has not reached 21. The gift to B will vest when he reaches 21.
3. Gift by will 'to A for life, remainder to all the children of A'.
   At testator's death A is alive with two children.
   The children's interest in remainder is contingent. A may have more children. Thus condition 1 is not satisfied; the identify of all possible children of A is not known. Nor is condition 3 satisfied: the respective shares will depend on how many children A has. The gift will vest when A dies, as no more children can then be born to A.

Importance of the distinction

If someone holds a vested interest then he cannot lose it. If he holds a contingent interest, it is uncertain whether he will obtain the benefit from the property concerned. Thus at death a vested interest will always pass under the will or intestacy, but a contingent interest does not.

If an interest is contingent it is subject to the rule against perpetuities, but if it is vested it is not subject to the rule.

16.3 The rule against perpetuities

Unless and until an interest in land becomes vested, the interest cannot be sold. Before the Settled Land Act 1882, a landowner could ensure that land remained in the family by creating a long succession of future interests. These interests were not necessarily contingent, but often were, in order to provide for circumstances unknown to the settlor – whether, for instance, his grandson would have two or three sons.

In order to prevent land from being tied up in contingent (and hence inalienable) future interests for generations, the rule against perpetuities was developed. The common law rule was settled by the beginning of the nineteenth century, and its aim was to allow a landowner to tie up land in contingent future interests so as to benefit his children and grandchildren, but no further. To achieve this, gifts had to vest within the lifetime of persons alive at the date the gift took effect. A man's children were normally alive at his death, but his grandchildren need not be. As donors frequently made it a condition of receipt of the interest that the grandchildren should reach 21, 21 years was allowed in addition to the lifetime during which the gift had to vest.

The common law rule was very strictly interpreted by the courts, which applied pure logic rather than common sense. Hence many gifts failed because they might not vest within the period, even though it was highly likely that they would vest. The possibility of failure renders the gift void ab initio.

In response to these problems, the common law rules were supplemented by first the LPA 1925 and then the Perpetuities and Accumulations Act 1964, which applies to gifts taking effect after 15 July 1964 which would fail at common law.

In applying the rule against perpetuities the following steps should be followed:

1. Determine which interests are interests in remainder.
2. Determine whether any interests in remainder are vested or contingent (see section 16.2).
3. Apply the common law rules to the contingent future interests.
4. If the gift fails at common law and it took effect after 15 July 1964, apply the PAA 1964 rules.

16.4 The common law rule against perpetuities

The rule is as follows: the grant of a *contingent* interest is *void ab initio* at common law unless it is certain that the interest will *vest*, *if it vests at all*, within the perpetuity period. The perpetuity period consists of a *life or lives in being* when the grant takes effect, plus 21 years. The italicised words and phrases are explained below.

Contingent
This means the gift is not vested. That is, one or more of the three requirements for a vested interest have not been met:

1. The identity of the beneficiary or beneficiaries is not known.
2. A condition has not been fulfilled.
3. The respective shares of the beneficiaries are not known.

Void ab initio
The gift, if it fails at law, is void from the moment that it takes effect. The interest concerned will be held by trustees on trust for the residuary legatees.

Vest
A gift vests when all three conditions in 'Contingent' above become satisfied. It then ceases to be contingent.

If it vests at all
It is not necessary to show that the gift will actually vest. It must merely be shown that it is possible for it to vest within the period.

A life or lives in being
This means the lifetimes of persons alive at the date that the gift comes into effect.

Calculation of the perpetuity period

The period starts at the date the instrument takes effect, that is, the date of the testator's death if the gift is by will, or the date of the instrument if it is an inter vivos gift. The period stops after the lifetime(s) of the life/lives in being plus 21 years.

Lives in being at common law
A life in being is the lifetime of anyone alive when the gift takes effect. It is necessary to know the date of death of lives in being, and so it is obviously impractical to apply this wide definition. Lives in being are consequently limited to the following:

1. lives in being expressly nominated by the testator; or if there are no nominated lives,
2. lives in being relevant to whether or not the gift will vest (implied lives).

Nominated lives. It is common for a testator to nominate lives in being. There is no requirement that any of the nominated lives in being have any interest in the gift, hence a donor can ensure a relatively lengthy perpetuity period by nominating a number of lives in being.

It is necessary for the persons administering the gift to be able to ascertain when the nominated lives die, and so it is usual to select the descendants of a named monarch. The monarch should be fairly recent as otherwise it will not be possible to trace all his descendants. In *Re Moore* [1901] 1 Ch 936, the testatrix nominated as lives in being all the persons alive at the date of her death. The gift was held void. In *Re Villar* [1929] 1 Ch 243, a testatrix who died in 1926 nominated all the descendants of Queen Victoria (died 1901, having had 11 children) alive at the time of her death. There were then approximately 120 descendants, scattered all over Europe. It was held that the difficulty in ascertaining their dates of death was not sufficient to render the gift void. The valid clause read:

> '... ending at the expiration of 20 years from the day of the death of the last survivor of all the lineal descendants of her late Majesty Queen Victoria who shall be living at the time of my death'.

In *Re Leverhulme (No 2)* [1943] 2 All ER 274 a 'Queen Victoria' clause was held valid, but it was suggested that no further use be made of Queen Victoria's descendants. Today it is normal to use the descendants of George V, or George VI. The lives must be human lives and not trees: see *Re Kelly* [1932] IR 255.

Example of nominated lives in being.

> 'The lives in being are all those lineal descendants of George VI alive at my death.'

The testator died in September 1981. At that date there were ten lineal descendants of George VI alive, the youngest being a few weeks old. The perpetuity period runs from September 1981 until the death of the longest lived of those ten plus 21 years.

Implied lives. If there are no expressly nominated lives, the lives in being are the lives of persons who are concerned in the gift. In practice, it is only necessary to consider the lifetimes of persons who are relevant to whether the gift will vest.

Example of implied lives in being.

1. Gift by will 'to my grandson, John'.
   The lives in being will be John and his parents, if they are alive when the gift takes effect.
2. Gift by will 'to all my grandchildren to attain 21'.
   At the date of the testator's death, two of his children and two of his grandchildren are alive. The lives in being are the two children and the two grandchildren. The perpetuity period will run from the death of the testator until 21 years after the death of the last of the lives in being to die. Note that any grandchildren born after the testator's death will not be lives in being.

The two children are lives in being because they are relevant to when the gift will vest. The gift must vest, if it vests at all, 21 years after the death of the last of the children, as it is only after those events that it is certain that no more grandchildren can be born, and that all the grandchildren will be 21.

In *Re Drummond* [1988] 1 WLR 234 a 1924 settlement directed property to be held for the settlor for life, thereafter to his daughters for life and thereafter, as to each daughter's share, for such of the children or issue of that daughter as she should appoint, in default of appointment for her children equally at 21 or, if female, at their earlier marriage, and failing such children, for the settlor's daughters (if living) or their issue (taking their parents' share) equally at 21.

The Court of Appeal had to consider the destination of a share under this concluding limitation. The problem was to decide when to close the class of 'issue' in this final limitation. By a majority the Court of Appeal decided the appropriate time to close the class was on the death of the life tenant as the life in being. This reasoning was supported by the words introducing all the trusts subsequent to the daughter's life tenancy and was, in the words of Nourse LJ:

> '... the natural and convenient time for ascertaining the class of the issue of a deceased life tenant'.

The words referred to the date of the deaths of the objects of the gifts, and the gift to the 'issue' took effect as a gift to the issue then living.

As a result no interest might vest outside the perpetuity period and the share under the final limitation was, therefore, valid.

Application of the common law rule

The following steps should be gone through:

1. Is the gift vested or contingent; have all three conditions been complied with?
2. If contingent, when will it vest; in other words, when will all three conditions be complied with?
3. Is it absolutely certain that the gift must vest, if it vests at all, within the lifetimes of persons alive at the time the gift takes effect plus 21 years?

Examples

1. Gift by will 'to A for life, remainder to A's first son to reach 21'.
   At the date of the testator's death, A is alive, a bachelor with no children.
   Apply steps:

   a) A's gift is vested.
      The gift to A's son is contingent.
      His identity is unknown and he has not reached 21.
   b) The gift to A's son will vest when he reaches 21. (Note that A may never

have a son. This does not matter. The test is whether any son that A might have would reach 21 within the period.)

c) The life in being is A. Hence the perpetuity period is A's lifetime (which is extended to include the gestation period) plus 21 years. Any son born to A must be born within A's lifetime and must reach 21 within 21 years of A's death.

Therefore, the gift will vest, if it vests at all, within the perpetuity period.

2. Gift by will 'to A for life, then to the first of A's sons to be called to the Bar'.
On testator's death, A is alive with no children.
Apply steps:

a) A's interest is vested. His son's is not; his identity is not known and the condition (being called to the Bar) has not been fulfilled.
b) The gift must vest when A's son is called to the Bar.
c) The life in being is A. The perpetuity period is A's lifetime plus 21 years. The son must be born, at the latest, within nine months of A's death. But he may be called to the Bar more than 21 years after A's death.

Hence, the gift to A's son is void at common law.

Future parenthood at common law

At common law any possibility, however remote, that a gift may not vest within the period renders the gift void. The law is not concerned with the probability that the gift will vest, but the possibility that it might not.

Consequently, the possibility that one of the lives in being may have another child (who would not be a life in being, and who might qualify under the terms of the gift after the perpetuity period) must be taken into account. The fact that it is extremely unlikely, or physically impossible, for such a child to be born is ignored. In *Jee* v *Audley* (1787) 1 Cox Eq Cas 324 a gift was held void because the court presumed that it was possible that a 70-year-old woman might have another child.

Megarry and Wade comment at page 245:

> 'Even when it can be proved that the birth of further children is a physical impossibility, the rule at common law maintains the same stubborn disregard for the facts of life.'

Example

Gift by will 'to all the grandchildren of A to reach 21'.

At the testator's death, A is a 64-year-old woman with two daughters and no grandchildren. The lives in being are hence A and her two daughters. At common law the gift fails. This is because the following sequence of events might occur:

1958 Testator dies.

1960 A has a daughter, B. B is not a life in being.

1967 A and her elder daughters are all killed in a car crash. The perpetuity period now has 21 years left to run. B is seven years old.

1987 B has a child, A's grandchild. This grandchild will not be 21 until 2008. The perpetuity period ran out in 1988.

Legal impossibility is not ignored at common law. In *Re Gaite's Will Trusts, Banks* v *Gaite* [1949] 1 All ER 459 there was a gift by will to A for life and then to such of A's grandchildren living at the testator's death or born within five years thereof who should attain the age of 21 years. At the testator's death, A was a 67-year-old widow with children. The remainder to A's grandchildren was contingent.

It had to be assumed that A could have more children. These children would not be lives in being because they would not be alive at the testator's death; therefore those children could have children (A's grandchildren) who would reach 21 more than 21 years after the death of A and those of her children alive at the testator's death. Therefore, some of the beneficiaries under the will would fulfil the condition after the end of the perpetuity period.

However, the gift to the grandchildren was valid. This was because it was limited to grandchildren born within five years of the testator's death. Therefore to qualify, any grandchild of A would have to be born to A's hypothetical child before that child was five years old. This is a legal impossibility as the age of consent is 16.

The possibility that a trustee might not fulfil his duties under the trust is also ignored: see *Re Atkins' Will Trusts* [1974] 1 WLR 761.

The result of the decisions on future parenthood is that a contingent gift will fail at common law if the beneficiaries are the grandchildren of anyone alive at the testator's death.

Unborn spouses

The possibility that a life in being might marry a spouse who was not born at the date of the testator's death may cause a gift to fail at common law.

Example

Gift by will 'to my son A for life, remainder to his widow (if she survives him) for life, remainder to any of their children living at the death of the survivor'.

At the testator's death A is a bachelor. The life in being is thus A. A may marry a woman born after the death of the testator, and so his potential wife cannot be treated as a life in being. This makes the gift to A's children void, as A's widow might survive for more than 21 years after the death of A, so the gift to the children may not vest until after the perpetuity period.

Hence any gift to children to take effect on the death of the survivor of their parents will fail unless:

1. Both parents are alive at the testator's death.
2. The children to benefit are limited to the children of persons alive at the testator's death, which is done by naming both parents: 'the children of A and B'.

16.5 Modifications to the common law rule before 1964

There are three ways in which the harshness of the common law rule is modified in order to save gifts otherwise void:

1. Class closing under the rule in *Andrews* v *Partington.*
2. Age reduction under s163 LPA 1925.
3. Alternative contingencies.

These will be dealt with in turn.

Class closing under the rule in Andrews *v* Partington

The rules as to class closing apply only to class gifts. A class gift is a gift of property to all persons who come within some description, the property being divisible in shares varying according to the number of persons in the class. Thus gifts of property to 'all my children who attain 25', 'all the nephews and nieces of my late husband', or 'A, B, C, D, and E if living' are all class gifts.

The perpetuity rule applies to class gifts in two ways:

1. The gift cannot vest until the size of the respective shares is known. Hence if, at the date the gift comes into effect, it is possible that any class member could become entitled to a share after the end of the perpetuity period, the whole gift fails, and no member of the class can take any share.

   Example
   Gift by will 'to A for life, and remainder to all A's grandchildren'.
   If A is alive at the testator's death, the gift to the grandchildren will be void because A might have more children whose children might be born (and thus qualify for membership of the class of grandchildren) after the end of the perpetuity period.

2. If any member of the class might take a vested interest outside the perpetuity period, the whole gift fails, even though all the other members qualify inside the period.

   Example
   Gift by will 'to A for life, then to all the children of A to attain 25'.
   If A is alive at the testator's death, the gift to A's children is void, because a child might be born to A who might not reach 25 until after the end of the perpetuity period.

The rule in *Andrews* v *Partington* (1791) 3 Bro CC 401 is a rule of convenience, allowing members of a class to become entitled to their share as soon as they become qualified. It states that a numerically uncertain class closes as soon as the first member becomes entitled to claim his share. The class is thereupon limited to potential members who are already born. Potential members born later are not entitled to any share. As each member becomes entitled, he is given his share. If a potential member dies before qualifying, the shares of the remaining members of the class are adjusted.

The rule can save class gifts otherwise void for perpetuity only if one member of the class has qualified when the gift takes effect.

Examples

1. Gift by will 'to A for life, remainder to all the grandchildren of A'.
   If A is alive at the testator's death, the gift will be saved by the rule in *Andrews* v *Partington* if any grandchildren have been born by the testator's death. The class will then be limited to those grandchildren already born who are all lives in being and whose shares must vest within the perpetuity period.
2. Gift by will 'to A for life, remainder to all the children of A to attain 25'.
   If A is alive at the testator's death, the gift to the children will be valid only if one of the children is already 25. The class is then limited to those of A's children already born. If there are four, aged 26, 24, 22 and 21, they will be entitled to a quarter share each. If one of the younger ones dies before the age of 25, the shares are adjusted to a third each.

Note: the gift in the above example could also be saved by age reduction. See below.

Age reduction under s163 LPA 1925

Gifts conditional on the beneficiary reaching an age greater than 21 are often void at common law.

Example

Gift by will 'to all the children of A to reach 25'.
This gift could be valid only if:

1. A was dead at the time the gift took effect, so no more children could be born.
2. A was alive, but one of A's children was already 25 so the class could be limited to lives in being.

If A is alive, and no child has reached 25, the gift will fail at common law.

Section 163 LPA 1925 allows the age of 21 to be substituted for the excessive age provided that:

1. The gift came into effect after 1925 and before 15 July 1964.
2. The gift would otherwise be void.
3. The excess is in the age of a beneficiary or class of beneficiaries.

In the example above, the age of 21 can be substituted for 25 if the gift would otherwise fail.

Alternative contingencies

Where the vesting of a gift is dependent upon the occurrence of either one or the other of two events, the strict common law rules are relaxed. If the gift is 'to A if X happens or if Y happens', and event X must occur within the perpetuity period, but event Y may occur outside the period, then by the strict common law rules, the gift is void. But in these circumstances the 'wait and see' principle of the PAA 1964 (see section 16.8 below) is applied at common law. It is not necessary to decide whether the gift is valid when it comes into effect. Instead the trustees can wait and see which of the two alternative events happens. If the validating event happens, the gift is valid; if it does not, the gift is void.

In *Re Curryer's Will Trusts* [1938] Ch 952 there was a gift by will to the testator's grandchildren to take effect on the death of the last surviving child of the testator or on the death of the last surviving widow or widower of the testator's children, whichever happened later. The gift to the grandchildren would be valid if it took effect on the death of the last surviving child of the testator. The alternative contingency is void because of the possibility of an unborn spouse (see section 16.4). It was held that the trustees could wait and see if all the widows and widowers did in fact die before the last surviving child.

In order for the 'wait and see' exception to apply, the alternative contingencies must be expressly stated in the instrument or will. In *Proctor* v *Bishop of Bath and Wells* (1794) 2 Hy Bl 358 property was left by will to the first son of A to become a clergyman or, if A had no sons, to B. Both A and B were alive at the date of the testator's death. B claimed the property on the death of A. It was held that the gift over to B in fact depended on two alternative contingencies. Either A had no sons, or none of his sons became a clergyman. As the alternatives were not expressed, the wait and see exception did not apply, and the gift over to B was void, as it was dependent upon a prior void gift (see section 16.6).

16.6 Gifts which follow void gifts

Gifts which follow void gifts are divided into three categories:

1. Vested gifts: a vested gift following a void gift is valid.

   Example
   Gift for life 'to first son of A to marry, remainder to B in fee simple'.
   If A is alive when the gift comes into effect, the gift to A's son is void, for perpetuity. B's gift is vested, and can take effect in possession at once. B is thus entitled to the fee simple.

2. Contingent but independent gifts: a contingent gift that follows a void gift is valid provided that it is independent of the prior void gift.

Example
Gift for life 'to first son of A to marry, remainder in fee simple to B when he attains 21'.
If A is alive at the date of the gift, the gift to A's son is void. If B is under 21, the gift to B is contingent. But the gift to B is contingent upon B reaching 21, not upon A's son marrying. B will be entitled on A's death. Hence the gift to B is valid, and he will be entitled to the fee simple as soon as he reaches 21.

3. Contingent and dependent gifts: a contingent gift that follows a void gift, and is dependent upon it, is itself void ab initio.

Example
Gift for life 'to the first son of A to marry, but if no son of A marries, to B in fee simple when he attains 21'.
If A is alive, the gift to A's son is void. If B is an infant, the gift to B is contingent. But B's gift is also dependent upon A's gift. B is entitled only if both he reaches 21 and A does not marry. B's gift is thus void.

The gift over in *Proctor* v *Bishop of Bath and Wells* (above) was contingent and dependent and hence void.

16.7 Determinable and conditional interests

Determinable interests

Neither a determinable fee simple nor a possibility of reverter is subject to the rule against perpetuities at common law. But see section 16.8.

Conditional interests

Conditions precedent
These are subject to the perpetuity rule at common law. Hence a gift to 'A provided that he survives B' is subject to the rule and will be void if B could die outside the perpetuity period.

Conditions subsequent
The grant of a conditional interest involves both the grant of a conditional fee simple and the creation of a right of re-entry (see Chapter 6). The conditional fee simple is not affected by the rule, but the right of re-entry is void if it could take effect outside the perpetuity period. The conditional fee simple is converted into an absolute interest if the right of re-entry is void.

Example
Gift of 'fee simple in possession to testator's grandchildren provided that no grandchild marries outside the Jewish faith'.
The provision might not take effect until after the perpetuity period and is void; the grandchildren are absolutely entitled.

16.8 Perpetuities and Accumulations Act 1964

The PAA 1964 applies to gifts coming into effect after 15 July 1964 that are void at common law. The common law rules are applied first; the Act modifies the common law rules.

Section 1: the perpetuity period

A period of 80 years or less may be substituted for the normal perpetuity period in the instrument creating the gift.

Section 2: future parenthood

Where a gift would be void at common law because of the possibility of future parenthood, it may be valid under the PAA 1964. Section 2(1)(a) provides that for the purposes of the rule it shall be presumed that women are capable of having children only between the ages of 12 and 55, and that men's capacity is limited to the age of 14 or over.

Any presumption arising in the case of a living person under s2(1)(a) may be rebutted, and it would be possible to give evidence of actual capacity (s2(1)(b)). These presumptions only arise in any legal proceedings.

Section 3: wait and see

Under the common law the general rule was that it must be clear when the instrument took effect that the interest could not vest outside the perpetuity period. There was no 'wait and see' facility. Where a gift would be void apart from the provisions of s3, s4 (age reduction, class closing) and s5 (the unborn spouse), then s3 allows the trustees to wait and see if the gift does in fact vest within the perpetuity period. Under s3 the interest is to be treated as valid until it is clear that it cannot vest within the period.

Examples

1. Gift 'to A (a man), for life, remainder to those of A's grandchildren to reach 21'. If A is alive at the date of the gift, the gift to the grandchildren is void at

common law. Under the Act, it is possible to wait and see whether the gift will in fact vest. This will be known when A dies. If he had no more children after the testator's death, the gift will vest, as the grandchildren's parents are lives in being (see below). If A did have more children, then any potential grandchildren as yet unborn at A's death can be excluded from the class: s4(4) (see below).

2. Gift 'to the first son of A to be called to the Bar'.
   If A is alive when the gift is made, it is void at common law. Under the Act, the trustees can wait and see whether any son of A does become a barrister within the perpetuity period.

Sections 3(4) and 3(5): lives in being

When the 'wait and see' provisions of this Act (see above) are to be applied, then the perpetuity period must be calculated with reference to statutory classes of lives in being, unless the donor has nominated a fixed period of 80 years or less. By s3(5) these classes are:

1. the person by whom the disposition was made – the donor;
2. a person to whom or in whose favour the disposition was made, that is to say:
   a) in the case of a disposition to a class of persons, any member or potential member of that class – the donee;
   b) in the case of an individual disposition to a person taking only on certain conditions being satisfied, any person as to whom some of the conditions are satisfied and the remainder may in time be satisfied – the donee;
   c) in the case of a special power of appointment exercisable in favour of members of a class, any member or potential member of the class – the donee;
   d) the first two provisions (above) equally apply to special powers of appointment – the donee;
   e) a person on whom any power, option or right is conferred – the donee;
3. a person having a child or grandchild who qualifies as a statutory life under (2) above or would if subsequently born so qualify – the donee's parents and grandparents;
4. any person on the failure or determination of whose prior interest the disposition is limited to take effect – the owner of a prior interest.

If any of these categories is too numerous for determination it may be disregarded.

The lives in being under the Act do not differ, in practical terms, from lives in being implied at law, although the Act is wider.

Section 3(5) does not apply unless the 'wait and see' provisions are applied. Where the gift was made before 1964, or is valid at common law, a royal lives clause can be used.

Section 4(1): age reduction

Where a gift would be void because it is limited to persons attaining an age of more than 21, then the age may be reduced to that which will allow the gift to be valid, so long as the reduced age is not less than 21. This provision differs from s163 LPA 1925 in that the reduction need not be to 21 years.

Example
Gift 'to all the grandchildren of A to attain 30.' A is alive, with no children.
The 'wait and see' provisions are applied until A's death. There are three grandchildren aged two, four and six. Section 4(1) can then be applied, reducing the qualifying age to 23, the age which will allow the gift to vest within the perpetuity period, that is, 21 years from A's death.

Section 163 LPA 1925 is repealed for gifts made after 15 July 1964.

Sections 4(3) and 4(4): class reduction

Class reduction under the Act operates in a fashion similar to, but more straightforward than the rule in *Andrews* v *Partington* (1791) 3 Bro CC 401 (see section 16.5).

Under s4(3), persons can be excluded from the class of potential beneficiaries where their inclusion would prevent the age reduction provisions from operating to save the gift.

Example
In the example above relating to s4(1), age reduction to 23 will not save the gift if any of A's children are still capable of having children. Section 4(3) can be used to exclude any potential unborn grandchildren from the class of beneficiaries.

Section 4(4) allows the exclusion of members from the class of beneficiaries where their inclusion would cause the gift to fail for remoteness, and age reduction is not appropriate.

Example
Gift 'to all the children of A who marry'.
If, at the end of the perpetuity period, any of A's children are not married, they can be excluded from the class, leaving only the married children as beneficiaries.

Section 5: unborn spouses

Section 5 prevents the possibility of an unborn spouse from causing a gift to fail. The 'wait and see' provisions are applied first, and if it becomes apparent that an unborn spouse will survive the perpetuity period, the gift can then be treated as though it were to take effect immediately before the end of the period.

Example
Gift 'to A for life, remainder to his widow (if she survives him), remainder to any of their children living at the death of the survivor.'
A is a bachelor, who marries a woman who was born after the death of the testator, and she survives A. The trustees should wait until the end of the perpetuity period, and if A's widow is still alive, the gift to the children can be saved by treating the gift to the children as taking effect immediately before the end of 21 years after the death of A, rather than upon the death of A's widow.

Section 6: gifts following void gifts

Where the Act applies, no gift is itself void only because it is dependent upon a prior gift which is void for remoteness. Each distinct gift must stand or fall by itself, and the perpetuity period must be applied to each in isolation.

This removes the complications of the common law rules (see section 16.6). Section 6 operates as soon as the gift is made, and the 'wait and see' provisions do not have to be applied.

Example
Gift for life 'to the first son of A to marry, but if no son of A marries, to B in fee simple when he reaches 21.'
A is alive and B is under 21. Section 6 allows the gift to B to be valid ab initio. There is no need to wait and see if any son of A does marry within the perpetuity period.

Section 9: options relating to land

The Act makes one important change in the common law rules on options, which make all options, except an option to renew a lease, subject to a 21-year perpetuity period. Under the Act, options are divided into two classes:

1. Options for a lessee, contained in a lease, to purchase the freehold or a superior tenancy: these options are not subject to the perpetuity rule, provided that the option ceases to be exercisable not later than one year after the end of the lease and is exercisable only by the lessee or by his successors in title.
2. All other options: these are subject to a perpetuity period of 21 years and no longer. The 'wait and see' principle applies, hence the owner of an option must use it within 21 years of its grant, after which time the option is void.

In all cases, the perpetuity rules apply only to options being enforced against successors in title. Prior to 1964 the perpetuity rule did not apply to the original parties to an option. Section 10 PAA 1964 changes the common law rule in respect of instruments taking effect after 15 July 1964, and as a result the perpetuity rule now applies to options to purchase between both the original parties and successors in title.

Section 12: determinable and conditional interests

The Act changes the common law rules for grants made after 15 July 1964 by making determinable interests subject to the perpetuity rule, so that the common law distinction between determinable and conditional interests no longer exists.

16.9 Powers

Powers, because they are concerned with the disposition of property, come within the perpetuity rule. The application of the rule depends on the type of power.

General powers

1. They must be exercisable within the perpetuity period.
2. They need not be exercised within the perpetuity period.
3. When they are exercised, the interest must vest within the perpetuity period reckoned from the date of their exercise (ie a second perpetuity period).

General testamentary powers

1. They must be exercisable within the perpetuity period.
2. They must be exercised within the perpetuity period.
3. When they are exercised, the interest must vest within the perpetuity period reckoned from the date of their exercise (ie a second perpetuity period).

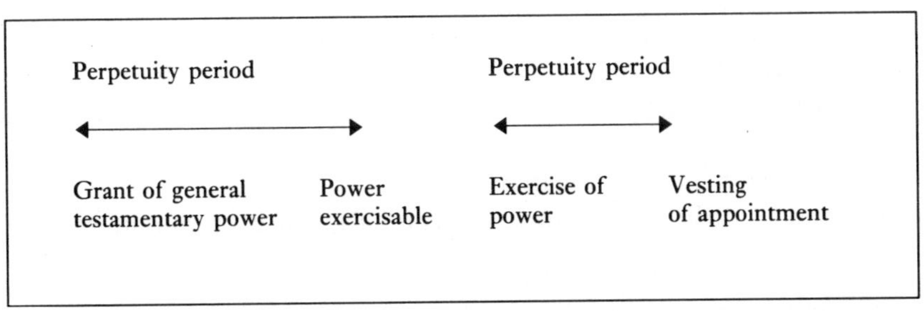

Special powers

1. They must be exercisable within the perpetuity period.
2. They must be exercised within the perpetuity period.
3. The interest appointed must vest within the original perpetuity period.

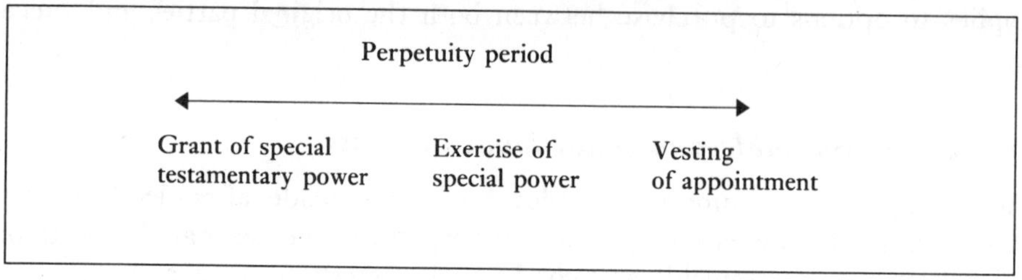

If a power cannot be exercised beyond the perpetuity period it is valid, even though an invalid appointment may be made under it.

For powers granted after 15 July 1964 the 'wait and see' provisions of the PAA 1964 apply. The Act also does not recognise any type of hybrid power except a general testamentary power, treating every power as special unless:

1. It is expressed by the instrument creating it to be exercisable by one person only.
2. The donee of the power, being of full age and capacity, can exercise it to transfer the whole appointable interest to himself unconditionally.

16.10 Exceptions to the perpetuity rule

1. Certain contracts, eg options to purchase (s9 PAA 1964): see section 16.9.
2. Limitations after entails: the 1964 Act has no effect.
3. A gift to charity followed by a gift over to another charity: the gift over will not be void merely because the event may take place after the end of the perpetuity period.
4. Restrictive covenants.
5. Forfeiture clauses in leases by which the tenant agrees that if at any time the terms of the lease are broken the landlord may re-enter and bring the lease to an end.
6. Mortgages: it does not apply to the postponement of a mortgagor's right to redeem. See *Knightsbridge Estates Trusts Ltd* v *Byrne* [1939] Ch 441.
7. Resulting trusts: these were not subject to common law but are now subject to PAA 1964.
8. Right of survivorship in joint tenancy.
9. All powers and remedies for enforcing rentcharges are exempted by s11(1) PAA 1964.

Megarry and Wade state at page 295:

> 'The general effect of the exemptions is to enable rights which are merely ancillary to other valid interests to be exercised outside the perpetuity period.'

16.11 The rule against accumulations

An accumulation is a direction to add income from a fund to the capital rather than distributing it. Originally accumulations were subject only to the rule against perpetuities, but at the end of the eighteenth century a celebrated case, *Thellusson* v *Woodford* (1799) 11 Ves 112, caused a change in the law. The case showed that a long period of accumulation, which was valid under the rule against perpetuities, could theoretically result in a fund containing a significant part of the national wealth. Parliament hastily intervened by passing the Accumulations Act 1800, often said in the past to be one of the worst-drafted Acts on the statute book.

The present law is contained in the Law of Property Act 1925 ss164–166, as amended, for instruments taking effect after 15 July 1964, by the Perpetuities and Accumulations Act 1964 s13(1).

The statutory periods

Income can only be accumulated for one of the following periods:

1. the life of the settlor or settlors; 2. 21 years from the death of the settlor; 3. the minority or respective minorities of any persons living or en ventre sa mère at the death of the settlor; 4. the minority or respective minorities only of any person or persons who, under the limitations of the settlement would, if of full age, be entitled to the income directed to be accumulated;	LPA 1925 s164
Plus	
5. 21 years from the date of the settlement; 6. the duration of the minority or respective minorities of any person or persons in being at the date of the settlement.	PAA 1964

Purchase of land

Where the accumulation is directed for the purpose of purchasing land, only period (4) may be selected: s160(1) LPA 1925. The choice of period is a matter of construction of the instrument directing accumulation.

Excessive accumulation

If the accumulation period may possibly exceed the perpetuity period, the direction to accumulate is totally void. The Perpetuities and Accumulations Act 1964 has not affected this rule.

If the accumulation period cannot exceed the perpetuity period but exceeds the relevant accumulation period, the direction to accumulate is good for the relevant accumulation period and only the excess is void.

If a direction to accumulate is wholly or partially void, the income for the void period passes to the person or persons who would have been entitled if no direction to accumulate had been made. There is no acceleration of subsequent interests.

The rule in *Saunders* v *Vautier* (1841) 4 Beav 115 enables a beneficiary of full age who has an absolute, vested and indefeasible interest in property to terminate any accumulation and require that the property be vested in him.

Exceptions to the rule against accumulations

Section 164(1) LPA 1925 gives three exceptions to the rule:

1. accumulation for the payment of the debts of any grantor, settlor, testator or other person;
2. accumulation to raise portions for children;
3. accumulation of the produce from timber or wood.

16.12 Revision summary

One of the problems with this area of land law is the collecting of the material into some cohesive whole for revision purposes. The following table is suggested as a method of revision, based on the normal style of question which invites the candidate to consider the law before and after the Perpetuities and Accumulations Act 1964 became effective.

Topic	*Before 16 July 1964 common law or LPA 1925*	*After 15 July 1964 Perpetuities and Accumulations Act 1964*
1 Perpetuity period	Lives in being – no restriction as to number selected	s1 – add a fixed period not exceeding 80 years
2 Possibility of vesting	Applied rigidly – any remote chance then void – 'fertile octogenarians': *Jee* v *Audley* (1787)	s2 – male under 14 and female under 12 or over 55 presumed incapable of having children
3 'Wait and see' rule	No general 'wait and see' rule – significant date was the moment of vesting	s3 – an interest is to be treated as valid until it is clear that it cannot vest within the period
4 Age contingencies	Fail if contingent on beneficiary attaining an age greater than 21: s163 LPA 1925 substituted 21 as the relevant age	s4(1) (repealed s163 LPA 1925) – substitutes the age nearest to that specified which will save it from being void for remoteness (no longer reduced to 21)
5 Class gifts	Composition of class and share of each member of the class must be known within perpetuity period – gift is wholly valid or wholly void. But – closing of classes – if uncertainty as to numbers, class will close as soon as first member becomes entitled: *Andrews* v *Partington* (1791)	ss4(3) and 4(4) – member whose interest can vest only outside the period and is not saved by reducing the age is excluded from the gift – and gift in favour of the rest of the class is valid
6 Subsequent interests	A limitation which follows a void limitation and is dependent on it is void, even though it must vest during the perpetuity period	s6 – no longer fails because 'ulterior to and dependent upon' a void gift – now each gift stands or falls by itself and perpetuity rules applied to each in isolation
7 Accumulations	Rule applies to directions to accumulate income – the income could be accumulated for some period as property could be made inalienable, ie for the perpetuity period: *Thellusson* v *Woodford* (1799), then see Accumulations Act 1800, then ss164–166 LPA 1925	ss164–166 LPA 1925 and s13 of 1964 Act. Now a total of six possible accumulation periods, comprising life, or 21 years, or minority: see Megarry and Wade: 'In determining the appropriate period, the starting point is to ascertain which of the periods the testator or settlor seemingly had in mind.'

16.13 Worked examples

Q Jack died in 1960 leaving the following bequests in his will:

1. I leave Blackacre to the first son of my old friend Graham to become a barrister or, if no such son becomes a barrister, or, if he has no son, to my nephew Robert.
2. I leave Whiteacre to my daughter Vivianne for life, and then to such of her children as attain the age of 21 and to such of her grandchildren who shall attain the age of 21 born to any of her children who shall die before reaching 21. At Jack's death Vivianne was aged 60, with two children and no grandchildren.

   a) Advise on the validity of these dispositions.
   b) Would your answer be different if Jack had died in 1970?

A 1. a) If Graham is dead the gift to the son is valid because all Graham's sons must be lives in being and if any of them are to become barristers they must do so in their own lifetimes. The gift over to Robert, who is a life in being, must therefore also be valid.

If Graham is alive he could have another son, born after Jack's death, who is not a life in being, and that son could be the first to become a barrister more than 21 years after the death of all the lives in being. That gift is therefore void at common law. The gift to Robert is expressed to depend on two alternative contingencies:

i) That Graham will have sons but none of them will become barristers.
ii) That Graham will have no sons.

The first of these contingencies is too remote, but the second is valid as it will be known whether that occurs at the death of Graham, a life in being. When the gift depends on express alternative contingencies the common law allows one to 'wait and see'. If it is the valid contingency which occurs, the gift to Robert is valid; if the other occurs, then Robert's gift is void: *Re Curryer's Will Trusts* (1938).

b) If Graham is dead the gift is valid at common law so the 1964 Act does not apply.

If Graham is alive, the 'wait and see' provisions of s3 should be applied. The statutory lives in being will be Graham and his wife, Graham's parents and his wife's parents and any sons of Graham alive at Jack's death. The gift over to Robert is in itself valid and is not void merely because it is dependent on s6.

2. a) This is a class gift. The gift to the children would be valid, but the gift to the grandchildren invalidates the whole gift because Vivianne could have

another child, who could die leaving a child who could attain 21 more than 21 years after the death of all the lives in being. The common law takes no account of the fact that Vivianne, being aged 60, is most unlikely to have another child. The gift might be saved, however, by the rule in *Andrews* v *Partington* (1791), if at least one child has attained 21. In that case the class will close, with the children alive at Jack's death as potential beneficiaries.

b) The fertility presumptions of s2 PAA 1964 apply, and so Vivianne can be presumed to be incapable of having another child. This means that all the children she can possibly have are lives in being, and any children they might have must attain the age of 21 within 21 years from the death of the lives in being, so the gift is valid.

17

Statutory Restrictions on the Use of Land

17.1 Introduction

This very complex subject is dealt with in outline only. For more details see Megarry and Wade Chapter 19 (5th edn). It is most unlikely to be the subject of a direct question (apart from the statutory rules relating to the protection of tenants), but a broad appreciation of the restrictions will help in the understanding of modern land law.

17.2 Planning control

This is well covered by Cheshire, Chapter 29, at page 943. The system of planning control is governed by the Town and Country Planning Act 1990. Any person who wishes to 'develop' his land must first obtain planning permission from the local planning authority. 'Development' covers almost every type of building operation and material change of use, except alteration to a building which does not affect its external appearance or change to another use within the same category, for example from a theatre to a cinema. Once planning permission is granted, the benefit attaches to the land and for anyone who has an interest in the land. 'Development' is defined in s55(1) Town and Country Planning Act 1990 as:

> '... the carrying out of building, engineering, mining or other operations in, on, over or under land or the making of any material change in the use of any buildings or other land'.

Section 55(2) contains a list of activities which do not amount to development under this definition. Any development that does not come within the exceptions set out in s55(2) must be the subject of an application for planning permission submitted to the local planning authority. In deciding whether to grant planning permission the local planning authority must take into consideration the provisions of the development plan and 'any other material considerations'.

The local planning authority may grant or refuse permission or grant permission subject to such conditions 'as they think fit'. Any conditions must:

> 'fairly and reasonably relate to the permitted development. The planning authority are not at liberty to use their powers for an ulterior object, however desirable that object may seem to them to be in the public interest.' (per Lord Denning MR in *Pyx Granite Co Ltd* v *Minister of Housing and Local Government* [1958] 1 QB 554)

If the applicant is not satisfied he can appeal to the Secretary of State within six months. This appeal may be made the subject of a public inquiry or be dealt with by correspondence only. The decision of the Secretary of State, or his inspector, can be challenged in the courts within three months on a point of law.

The use of land for caravan sites is more closely controlled, and there are special controls for historical buildings, conservation areas, national parks, advertisements and trees.

If there is a breach of planning control the local planning authority may serve an enforcement notice, specifying the steps to be taken to remedy the breach and giving a time in which this is to be done. Failure to comply is a criminal offence, and the local planning authority may itself enter the land and take steps to enforce the notice.

In certain cases the owner of the land which loses value because permission has been refused, or where the grant of permission reduces the value of the land or makes it virtually unsaleable ('planning blight'), may get compensation or may be able to make the local authority acquire the land by way of a purchase notice.

In furtherance of development plans for an area a local authority has powers to purchase property in the area compulsorily, the owner getting the open market value of the land in compensation. As compulsory purchase is an interference with private ownership, the acquiring authority must always have statutory authority to acquire land for the particular purpose. Once the compensation has been agreed the legal estate is vested in the acquiring authority by normal conveyancing procedures.

17.3 Protection of tenants

This has been dealt with in Chapter 10. The major statutes are:

Residential tenants:	Rent Act 1977, Housing Acts 1980–1988.
Business tenants:	Landlord and Tenant Act 1954.
Agricultural tenants:	Agricultural Holdings Act 1986 and Agricultural Tenancies Act 1995.

17.4 Public health and housing provisions

There are a large number of provisions intended to prevent the serious deterioration of houses and to deal with those that have become uninhabitable. The obligations of landlords of certain types of tenanted property to repair under the Landlord and Tenant Act 1985 have already been discussed (see Chapter 10). Sections 8–10 provide for the declaration by the local authority of clearance areas when the majority of the buildings in the area have become unfit for human habitation or otherwise dangerous. The authority then has power to clear and redevelop the area. When an individual house becomes unsafe through lack of repair, the local authority can serve the owner with a dangerous structure notice, requiring the necessary repairs to be done. If individual rooms are not fit for human habitation, in particular basement rooms, the local authority can serve a closure order, which forbids the use of those rooms unless and until certain works are done to make them habitable.

17.5 Taxation

The pattern of land-holding has been greatly affected by the enormous increase in taxation that has taken place in the present century, in particular the introduction of estate duty which made the strict settlement of successive interests very expensive in terms of tax burdens. If the land produces an income this is taxed as income tax.

Most settlements of land made today are designed to reduce the burden of taxation, and trusts are most usually varied (under the Variation of Trusts Act 1958) for that purpose.

17.6 Betterment

There have been a number of schemes to recoup from landowners some of the enhanced values of the land due to public decisions represented by the granting of planning permission. The latest of these schemes was contained in the Community Land Act 1975 which was repealed by the Local Government Planning and Land Act 1980.

17.7 Conclusion

The link between land law and conveyancing must always be kept in mind. Megarry and Wade reminds the reader of this at page 1143:

> 'Formerly a conveyancer was concerned to see that his client obtained a good title to the land ... A good title to the land must still be obtained, but the conveyancer must also investigate whether his client will be able to use the land for the purposes he has in mind, or whether those purposes are liable to be frustrated by planning control and by the rights of protected tenants.'

For this reason a study and understanding of land law is essential. It is hoped that these pages have made this ability to understand land law a little easier than it might otherwise be.

18

Recent Cases

18.1 Co-ownership

Re Dennis (A Bankrupt) [1995] 3 All ER 171 Court of Appeal (Sir Thomas Bingham MR and Kennedy and Millett LJJ)

Severance of an equitable joint tenancy by bankruptcy

Facts

D and his wife owned two properties as beneficial joint tenants. In September 1982, D committed an act of bankruptcy (he failed to comply with a bankruptcy notice) and so a bankruptcy petition was presented against him. D's wife died in February 1983 leaving her estate to her two children in her will. In May 1983 a receiving order was made against D and in November 1983 he was adjudicated bankrupt.

The question arose whether the vesting of D's property in the trustee, which severed the joint tenancies, occurred at the date of the act of bankruptcy by retrospective effect of the adjudication, or at the date of adjudication of bankruptcy. If the former, the joint tenancies were severed before the wife's death and her share as a tenant-in-common would devolve under her will. If the latter, the joint tenancies were not severed before the wife's death and the wife's share would pass on her death to D as survivor, with the result that on adjudication the whole interest in the properties vested in the trustee and was available to D's creditors.

The judge held that under s38(a) Bankruptcy Act 1914 title to the bankrupt's property only vested in the trustee when the adjudication order was made. The wife's personal representatives appealed.

Held

Appeal allowed. Where a joint tenant of property was adjudged bankrupt under the

Bankruptcy Act 1914, the title of the trustee in bankruptcy to that property related back to the first act of bankruptcy even though the debtor was not adjudged bankrupt until some later date. Consequently, the joint tenancies had been severed in September 1982 (date of bankruptcy) and not in November 1983 (date of adjudication). Since the relation back of the trustee's title to the act of bankruptcy was an automatic statutory consequence, he could not then lay claim to the property and at the same time deny that it had vested in him at that earlier date. Just as the trustee could elect to rely on the doctrine of relation back to base a claim to property formerly belonging to the debtor and to claim that a joint tenancy had been severed where it was the debtor who had died in the intervening period, the personal representatives of a deceased joint tenant could also rely on the doctrine to deprive the trustee of his claim to an interest which had accrued to the debtor under the principle of survivorship.

Here the joint tenancies had been severed on D's act of bankruptcy in September 1982 (ie before the wife's death) and therefore the wife's share devolved under her will. Accordingly, the court declared that a one-half share in the properties formed part of the wife's estate.

Commentary

The significance of this case is that it clearly establishes that the severance of an equitable joint tenancy due to an act of bankruptcy by one of the joint tenants will occur on the date of the act of bankruptcy and not the later date of adjudication of bankruptcy.

Re Palmer (Deceased) (A Debtor) [1994] 3 All ER 835 Court of Appeal (Balcombe, Evans and Roch LJJ)

Joint tenancy – principle of survivorship – joint tenant debtor dying before insolvency administration order made – whether order severed the joint tenancy held by the deceased immediately prior to death

Facts

In 1989, P, a solicitor, together with his wife bought a property as joint tenants. Following allegations of serious misconduct the Law Society commenced inquiries into the conduct of P's practice but before these inquiries were completed P died, on 22 November 1990.

At his death there were substantial claims against his estate by former clients of the deceased's firm and the Inland Revenue, which could only be met if P's share of the jointly owned property devolved as part of his estate rather than passing to his wife under the principle of survivorship. In consequence of the deceased's indebtedness his executor obtained, in 1991, an insolvency administration order under the Administration of Insolvent Estates of Deceased Persons Order 1986 (the order was made under s421 Insolvency Act (IA) 1986).

The respondent was appointed trustee of the estate and he sought a declaration under s283 Insolvency Act 1986 as modified by Schedule 1 of the 1986 Order that his title to P's estate operated retrospectively so as to take effect before P died. (If correct this would have severed the joint tenancy before P died, thus creating a tenancy-in-common with the result that the deceased's share would devolve to the estate and provide assets for the creditors.) Under s283 IA 1986, as modified, a deceased debtor's estate comprised 'all property belonging to [him] or his personal representative ... at the date of the insolvency administration order', while under para 12 of Schedule 1 to the 1986 Order the administration order was to be taken as being made 'on the date of death of the deceased debtor'. Vinelott J granted the declaration sought. He concluded that:

1. the insolvency administration order was to be treated as being made on the date of death (legislative fiction); and
2. according to judicial fiction the order was to be taken as being made on the first moment of that day.

By combining the legislative fiction and the judicial fiction he concluded that the order had been made before P died and thus the joint tenancy had been severed before death so that an undivided half-share devolved as part of P's estate. P's widow appealed.

Held

The rule that a judicial act was presumed to have been made on the first moment of the day when it was done and took precedence over other non-judicial acts on the same day (judicial fiction) could not be allowed to operate so as to render a statutory instrument ultra vires primary legislation.

Here the judge had wrongly combined the judicial fiction and the legislative fiction to reach the conclusion that the insolvency order had been made before P died. That construction rendered the 1986 Order ultra vires because the administration order would then go beyond what was sanctioned by s421 of the 1986 Act – namely making an order dealing with the insolvent estate of a deceased person.

The 1986 Act clearly referred to the estate of a 'deceased person'. Nothing in the 1986 Act altered the ordinary meaning of the 'estate of a deceased person', which in the case of the estate of a deceased joint tenant did not include his unsevered interest under a beneficial joint tenancy since that passed by the principle of survivorship to the surviving joint tenant and did not pass to his personal representative or form part of his estate. It was not possible to use the 1986 Order in combination with the judicial fiction to make an insolvency administration order applicable to the property of a person who had not yet died.

On the proper application of the 1986 Act and the 1986 Order the insolvency administration order took effect at the moment P died and not on the first moment of the day he died. This meant that when P died the joint tenancy had not been severed because the insolvency administration order only became effective then. Accordingly, P's interest in the joint tenancy had passed, by survivorship at the moment of his death, to his widow and was not affected by the insolvency administration order.

Commentary

The key issue in this case was when did the respondent acquire title to the deceased's property under the insolvency administration order? The court, in holding that it was at the moment of death rather than the first moment of the day of death (ie immediately prior to death), was in essence re-emphasising the primacy of the principle of survivorship. It was not prepared to see that principle side-stepped in favour of the very creative approach to the interpretation of the relevant legislation contended for by the respondent.

It is important to emphasise that P died before the order was made. If he had been declared bankrupt during his lifetime that would have severed the joint tenancy – from the date of the act of bankruptcy.

18.2 Leases and tenancies – including covenants relating to the leasehold

Hooper* v *Sherman [1994] NPC 153 Court of Appeal (Steyn, Rose and Morritt LJJ)

Whether an exchange of correspondence regarding an oral agreement concerning land could amount to a valid exchange of contracts to transfer land for the purposes of s2 Law of Property (Miscellaneous Provisions) Act 1989

Facts

H and S lived together for several years in a house which was in their joint names but in unequal shares, with S having the greater share. The property was subject to a mortgage in respect of which each was jointly liable. The relationship between the couple deteriorated and culminated in S applying for an ouster and non-molestation order. However, before the application was heard a compromise agreement was reached by the parties. Under the agreement (which was *not* expressed to be subject to contract) H would transfer all his interest in the house to S in return for her assuming sole responsibility for the mortgage. Further, H undertook not to assault S and to vacate the house. S's solicitor wrote a letter to H's solicitor confirming the fact of an agreement and detailing its terms. H's solicitor replied in a letter marked 'without prejudice'. This letter confirmed the fact of agreement and stated that H was prepared to transfer his share in the house to S provided the mortgagee agreed to release him from all his obligations under the mortgage. Difficulties arose when the mortgagee would not agree to release H until there had been a period of six months' satisfactory payments by S.

Faced with this delay, H said the arrangement was unsatisfactory and applied under s30 Law of Property Act 1925 for an order that the house be sold. A preliminary issue arose as to whether there was any contract in existence between the parties. The issue was whether the two letters satisfied the requirements of s2(1) Law of Property (Miscellaneous Provisions) Act 1989.

At first instance there was a preliminary ruling that H and S had made a legally valid contract to transfer H's share of the property and mortgage liability to S by an exchange of letters. H appealed, contending that the letter from his solicitors did not contain all the terms of the agreement and emphasising that it had been marked 'without prejudice'.

Held

Appeal dismissed (Morritt LJ dissenting). H's counsel made two important concessions. First that 'exchange of contracts' was not a term of art. Second, that in accordance with Law Commission Report No 164 (which formed the basis of the 1989 Act) it was still possible to make a contract by correspondence. The majority accepted that these concessions had been rightly made and concluded that the letters which the parties' solicitors wrote to each other (ie exchanged) after the oral agreement was entered into amounted to an 'exchange of contracts' within s2 of the 1989 Act. Since the letters both dealt with all the essentials, the parties, the subject matter and the consideration they amounted to an exchange of contracts and constituted a valid agreement under s2 of the 1989 Act even though one letter referred to undertakings which the other did not mention. Finally, marking the letter from H's solicitors 'without prejudice' did not prevent a contract from being formed because 'without prejudice' did not have the same effect as 'subject to contract'.

Commentary

Although the facts of the case do not concern leases, it is an important decision on the formalities for disposing of an interest in land and should be read in conjunction with the following case which does concern leases. See *Commission for the New Towns* v *Cooper (GB) Ltd* [1995] 2 All ER 929 below.

Commission for the New Towns v *Cooper (GB) Ltd* [1995] 2 All ER 929 Court of Appeal (Stuart-Smith, Farquharson and Evans LJJ)

Whether an exchange of correspondence about an oral agreement concerning land could amount to a valid exchange of contracts to transfer land for the purposes of s2 Law of Property (Miscellaneous Provisions) Act 1989

Facts

In 1986, EHL (C's predecessor in title) became a tenant of commercial premises on an underlease from MK (CNT's predecessor). An agreement was reached between the parties whereby MK was to do certain building work to be paid for by the underlessee. The parties made three other agreements by deed which gave EHL a variety of options. The first was a 'put option' which was a covenant by MK to take an assignment of the underlease from EHL under certain conditions. The second was a 'larger premises option' allowing EHL to opt to transfer to larger premises. The third was a 'side land option' allowing EHL to acquire land alongside the existing premises. Both the put option and the larger premises option were expressed to be personal to EHL.

In 1988, C (the defendant) acquired the unexpired residue of the term of the underlease by assignment. However, the business made losses and in 1990 C's American parent company analysed the cost of closing the business, including the penalty payable on the surrender of the underlease.

In 1991, C decided instead to try to obtain from MK the put option that had previously been enjoyed by C's predecessor (EHL) without MK realising it (C's intention was to use that option to enable it to reduce its liquidation costs by avoiding the penalty payment for termination of the underlease). The parties met on 11 January 1991 with no formal agenda. The negotiations centred upon a dispute concerning the building work. C did not mention the put option at all but indicated that as part of a comprehensive settlement it expected to obtain the rights previously enjoyed by EHL and specifically mentioned the side land option (they did this merely to raise a reference to the separate deeds which existed – they had no interest in the side land option). A provisional agreement was reached at the meeting under which C agreed to pay £45,000 in full resolution of the dispute over the building work and MK agreed to treat C 'in all respects as having the same rights and benefits under the original documentation' as its predecessors had had and to grant C a new side land option.

At the end of the negotiations C, on the same day, sent a faxed letter confirming the provisional agreement. In particular the letter included the following sentence: 'You confirmed at our meeting that you will treat Coop Ind (UK) Ltd in all respects as having the same rights and benefits under the original documentation as Edison Halso Limited'.

On 14 January, MK, by way of response, sent a copy of the recommendation to confirm the agreement which was to be put to MK's executive management committee for its approval. The executive committee approved the agreement.

On 16 January, C, by faxed letter, sought written confirmation from MK of the accuracy of the 11 January letter. Later that day MK gave C the written confirmation required. As soon as agreement had been reached, C immediately sought to exercise the put option so as to require MK to take an assignment of the underlease. MK denied that it had granted a put option and sought rectification of the agreement.

The judge held that:

1. C had acquired the put option and that the plaintiff was not entitled to

rectification because it had not been shown that C knew of the plaintiff's mistake; and

2. the correspondence between the parties did not satisfy the requirements of s2 Law of Property (Miscellaneous Provisions) Act 1989 (contracts for the sale or disposition of an interest in land should be in writing) so the plaintiff was not bound by the agreement (ie there was no enforceable agreement to grant the put option).

C appealed against the judge's decision on the second issue and the plaintiff cross-appealed against his decision on the first issue. The issue on C's appeal was whether an exchange of correspondence concerning an oral agreement concerning land could satisfy s2 of the 1989 Act.

Held

Cross-appeal allowed. Appeal dismissed. The contract did not include the put option. Where one party to a contract intended the other to be mistaken as to the terms of their agreement and made false and misleading statements to divert the other's attention from discovering the mistake he could not insist on performance of the contract to the letter, but might be bound by the agreement which the other party mistakenly thought was being made. The other party might be entitled to rectification of the contract even where it could not be shown that his mistake was induced by any misrepresentation.

As to the s2 issue, a contract to grant a put option in the form enjoyed by C's predecessor in title was a disposition of an interest in land within the meaning of s2 of the 1989 Act. Accordingly, it was required to be evidenced in writing, either in one document recording the agreement signed by both parties or by an exchange of contracts (C contended that the exchange of letters of 16 January was a sufficient exchange of contracts within the meaning of s2). Stuart-Smith LJ drew a distinction between the formal 'exchange of contracts' and simple letters of offer and acceptance. Here the letters relied upon did not record all the express terms of the agreement already reached. Rather, they were the final offer and acceptance which concluded the negotiations. The closing stages of correspondence by which an agreement was reached, ie the final offer or counter-offer and an unqualified acceptance of it, could not also constitute the 'exchange of contracts' which was required by s2 before a contract could be made. An additional exchange of documents setting out or incorporating all 'the terms which the parties have agreed' must take place or the parties must sign a simple document which sets them out. Although the correspondence would have amounted to a sufficient note or memorandum under s40 Law of Property Act 1925, it did not constitute an exchange of contracts and therefore could not satisfy the more stringent requirements of s2 of the 1989 Act.

Commentary

As a result of this case and that of *Hooper* v *Sherman* [1994] NPC 153 (below), there are now two conflicting Court of Appeal decisions on the question whether an exchange of correspondence regarding an oral agreement concerning land can satisfy the requirements of s2 Law of Property (Miscellaneous Provisions) Act 1989.

It is submitted that the reasoning in *Commission for the New Towns* v *Cooper* was firmly based on the premise that the aim of s2 was to narrow the circumstances in which an enforceable contract for the disposition of an interest in land could exist. There the court was trying to put 'clear blue water' between a formal 'exchange of contracts' and simple letters of offer and acceptance. Whether the court was right to do this is open to conjecture. It seems to be perfectly feasible for letters of offer and acceptance to incorporate all the terms of the agreement and be signed by both parties as required by s2. An obvious consequence of these conflicting decisions is uncertainty for conveyancing practitioners. A definitive statement on the point from the House of Lords would be welcome.

18.3 Easements and profits

Wheeler and Another v *J J Saunders Ltd and Others* [1995] 2 All ER 697 Court of Appeal (Staughton and Peter Gibson LJJ and Sir John May)

Aspects of the doctrine of *Wheeldon* v *Burrows*

Facts

W owned a farmhouse adjacent to farmland let to S Ltd. Originally the farmhouse and farmland were in common ownership. The common owner sold the house (quasi dominant land) to W and also disposed of the farm (quasi servient land). There were two ways of gaining access to the house. First, there was direct access from a road (the east entrance). Second, there was access across part of the farmland (the south entrance). However, the conveyance of the house to W did not contain an express grant of a right of way over the farmland in favour of the house. S Ltd took the view that W was not entitled to cross the farmland to reach the house and blocked the access strip with a wall of breeze blocks. W commenced proceedings against S Ltd on several matters including the latter's obstruction of the right of way to the house. At first instance, W obtained damages for the obstruction and a mandatory injunction requiring S Ltd to demolish the wall. S Ltd appealed. The appeal concerned several issues. The 'easement issue' was whether an implied easement had been granted to W under the rule in *Wheeldon* v *Burrows* (1879) 12 Ch D 31.

Held

Appeal allowed in part (S Ltd succeeded on the easement point but not on another ground of appeal). Under the doctrine of *Wheeldon* v *Burrows*, easements were implied in favour of a grantee which were continuous and apparent or necessary for the reasonable enjoyment of the property granted and which had been and were at the time of the grant used by the common owner for the benefit of the part granted. While recognising that there had been some doubt as to whether the requirement that the easement should be continuous and apparent was an alternative to the requirement that the easement be necessary for the reasonable enjoyment of the property granted, the court, on reviewing *Wheeldon* v *Burrows,* concluded that the court on that occasion had treated the first requirement as synonymous with the second. The test of what was necessary for the reasonable enjoyment of land was not the same as the test for a way of necessity (one without which the property could not be used at all). Peter Gibson LJ noted that in Cheshire and Burn's *Modern Law of Real Property* 'necessary' in the context of the doctrine of *Wheeldon* v *Burrows* indicated that the way 'conduces to the reasonable enjoyment of the property' (at p707). Here, on the facts, the south entrance (access across S Ltd's land) was not necessary for the reasonable enjoyment of the house since the east entrance would do just as well. The fact that the latter was four inches narrower than the south entrance was not critical. The court noted that the gate at the south entrance was usually shut and this led Staughton LJ to conclude that it was 'not the main entrance and was probably only used on rare occasions' (at p702). Here access over the farmland was not necessary for the reasonable enjoyment of the house – not least because there was another means of access. Accordingly, W did not have an implied easement of way. The mandatory injunction requiring S Ltd to remove the wall was discharged and the award of damages for the obstruction was reversed.

Commentary

The case is significant for at least two reasons.

First, it clarifies several aspects of the doctrine of *Wheeldon* v *Burrows* (1879). In particular, it provides useful guidance on the requirement that the easement be necessary for the reasonable enjoyment of the property granted. Further, Staughton LJ emphasised that the acquisition of easements under *Wheeldon* v *Burrows* is wider than acquisition of easements through the doctrine of necessity.

Second, the case demonstrates that the acquisition of easements under the doctrine of *Wheeldon* v *Burrows* is not limited to situations where a common owner sells off part of his land to the person claiming the easement and retains the other part (the traditional factual scenario when the doctrine is invoked). Here the common owner sold the quasi dominant land (the house) to the plaintiff and disposed of the quasi servient land (the farm) to the defendant. The doctrine of *Wheeldon* v *Burrows* can apply to a factual scenario like the instant case provided the sales to the different persons are contemporaneous (see *Swansborough* v *Coventry* (1832) 2 M & S 362). Here the claim to the right of way over the farmland under *Wheeldon* v *Burrows* failed because it was not necessary for the reasonable enjoyment of the house.

18.4 Mortgages

Cheltenham & Gloucester Building Society* v *Norgan [1996] 1 All ER 449
Court of Appeal (Evans and Waite LJJ and Sir John May)

Mortgage arrears – court's discretion under the Administration of Justice Acts 1970 and 1973 to grant relief – starting point for determining the reasonable period for repayment of the outstanding arrears is the outstanding term of the mortgage

Facts

Since 1974, N, her husband and family lived in a period farmhouse. N became sole owner of the farmhouse (said to be worth about £225,000) when she bought out her husband's half-share. In 1986, £90,000 was borrowed by way of mortgage from the Guardian Building Society using the farmhouse as security. Under the terms of the mortgage, if at any time any monthly instalment was in arrears and unpaid for one month after becoming due, the mortgagee would be entitled to take possession of the property. N fell into arrears with the interest payments on the mortgage after her husband's business ran into difficulties. By April 1990, when the Guardian Building Society was taken over by Cheltenham and Gloucester Building Society, N owed about £7,000. The Cheltenham and Gloucester was a member of the Council of Mortgage Lenders whose statement of current practice provided means of helping some borrowers in difficulty, including lengthening the term of a repayment loan, deferring interest payments for a period and capitalising interest. The building society obtained a county court order for possession but execution was suspended as N made strenuous efforts to pay off her arrears.

In September 1993, a district judge refused to block the possession order any longer. In June 1994, that decision was upheld by Judge O'Malley in Shaftesbury County Court. He estimated that N's arrears were £20,000 and decided that a period of two to four years was the maximum that would normally be allowed for clearing arrears (even though here the mortgage had 13 years still to run). He concluded that it would be impossible for N to meet that target and therefore the building society was entitled to have its possession order enforced.

Held

Appeal allowed. At common law the court had only a very limited jurisdiction to grant relief to a borrower in default under a mortgage. It could only adjourn the application for a short time to give the borrower the chance to pay up in full: *Birmingham Citizens' Permanent Building Society* v *Caunt* [1962] Ch 883. However, the rigour of the common law position had been mitigated by the Administration of Justice Acts 1970 and 1973. Under the Acts the court had a discretion to treat the sum due under the mortgage as being only the arrears of instalments or interest and to allow a reasonable period for the borrower to pay off the arrears if it appeared he was likely to be able to do so. The question was what exactly constituted a 'reasonable period' for bringing payments up to date? The court unanimously agreed that 'the logic and spirit of the legislation' required, especially in cases where the parties were proceeding with the type of arrangement provided for in the statement of current practice, that the court should take the full term of the mortgage as its starting point and pose at the outset the following question: 'Would it be possible for the borrower to maintain payment off of the arrears by instalments over that period?' The court identified a number of considerations which were likely to be relevant in establishing a reasonable period, including the following.

1. How much could the borrower reasonably afford to pay both now and in the future?
2. If the borrower had a short-term problem in meeting his mortgage commitments, how long was the difficulty likely to last?
3. Why had the arrears accumulated?
4. How much remained of the original term?
5. Were there any reasons affecting the security which should influence the length of the period for payment?

Accordingly, the case was remitted back to the county court to work out a new repayment scheme over the remaining 13 years of the loan. Finally, the building society was ordered to pay the costs of the case.

Commentary

What will be the effect of this landmark ruling? It formalises the process of capitalisation where the arrears are added to the original loan. Clearly some homeowners who fall into arrears with their mortgages will now have a better chance of keeping their homes. It is likely that large numbers of homeowners fighting repossession will now take their lenders to court in order to secure a comparable deal to that obtained by Mrs Norgan. However, it will clearly not help all homeowners facing repossession. Many people in that position are unable (because of redundancy, separation etc) to meet their mortgage repayments, let alone try to pay off large arrears. Further, the Council of Mortgage Lenders has expressed concern that it might persuade borrowers to take 'a mortgage payments holiday' knowing that if their case ever got to court they would be given a long period to pay off their arrears.

Massey v *Midland Bank plc* [1995] 1 All ER 929 Court of Appeal (Neill, Steyn and Peter Gibson LJJ)

Man and woman in long-standing relationship; woman persuaded by misrepresentations by the man to sign a charge over her home in favour of the bank as security for a loan being granted by the bank to the man. Whether the bank bound by constructive notice of the man's misrepresentations?

Facts

M owned a house and was persuaded by misrepresentations by her lover, P, to charge her house to the plaintiff bank as security for an overdraft granted to a business venture in which P was involved. The bank indicated to P that M had to be independently advised by a solicitor before it would proceed with the transaction. P arranged for his own solicitors to advise M and the bank sent the charge to them. M was advised by P's solicitor, who explained the nature of the bank's charge to her in the presence of P. M signed the charge and the solicitors confirmed to the bank that they had advised her and explained the charge to her. Thereafter, the bank lent the money to P. Subsequently the company went into liquidation and the bank sought possession of M's house. M resisted on the ground that she had been induced to sign the charge by P's misrepresentations (in particular, he fraudulently exaggerated the prospects of the new business) and undue influence, and that the bank was affected by P's wrongdoing. The deputy judge held that the bank was unaffected by P's dishonesty and granted them an order of possession. M appealed.

Held

Appeal dismissed. The bank was put on inquiry by the circumstances in which M had agreed to provide the security. However, its actions (taking reasonable steps to ensure that M's agreement to the charge had been properly obtained and receiving confirmation from the solicitors that they had explained the charge to her) prevented it from being fixed with constructive notice of P's misrepresentations. The bank was entitled to conclude that M had received independent advice from the firm of solicitors and to assume that the solicitor dealing with the matter had acted honestly and given proper advice. The bank was under no duty to enquire into what had happened at the interview between M and the solicitors.

Commentary

In recent years one of the most dynamic areas of mortgages has concerned the following situation – property jointly owned by husband and wife; wife provides security for her husband's business debts following undue influence etc by the husband; husband defaults on repayments; lender seeks to recover possession of the property and the wife alleges that her consent to the security was obtained by the husband's undue influence/misrepresentation which is binding on the lender through actual or constructive notice. The lead case in this regard is *Barclays Bank plc* v *O'Brien and Another* [1993] 3 WLR 786, where the House of Lords, in a landmark ruling, gave wives who agreed that their family home could be used as security for their husbands' debts greater protection against the loss of their property. In particular, their Lordships said that to avoid having constructive notice in such a situation it was necessary for the lender to take steps (in the absence of the husband) to bring home to the wife the risk she was running as surety and advise her to take independent advice.

It is submitted that the decision in *Massey* is significant for at least three reasons.

First, the court followed their Lordships' dicta in *O'Brien* in holding that the *O'Brien* ruling was not restricted to a husband and wife situation, but applied also to unmarried couples provided they were in a relationship where there was a risk of one of them exploiting the other's emotional involvement and trust. Here the couple were unmarried. Second, the case gives guidance on the issue of 'independent advice'. It decided that it was enough if the advice to the woman was independent of the lender even though it was not independent of the man who made the misrepresentations. The Court of Appeal seems to be saying that the bank/lender in this type of situation can discharge its responsibilities vis-à-vis independent advice by delegating to a third-party solicitor. This view of the matter was supported by a differently constituted Court of Appeal in *Bank of Baroda* v *Rayarel and Others* (1995) The Times 10 January. Third, at variance with *Barclays Bank plc* v *O'Brien and Another* the court found for the bank even though the solicitor explained the nature of the bank's charge to the woman in the presence of her lover. On the *O'Brien* view of the matter the explanation should have been given in the man's absence.

Index

Special Offer!

Would you find a revision guide, summarising the major legal developments during the previous academic year useful?

Law Update 1996 could be yours for only £2.50 reduced from the RRP of £6.95.

Simply fill in the following questionnaire and return it to:
Andrea Dowsett, Publisher, HLT Publications, 200 Greyhound Road, London W14 9RY

If you return your questionnaire before 31st January 1997, you will be entitled to a copy of our Law Update 1996 at the reduced price of £2.50.

Student Questionnaire

Which course are you studying?

Course: ______________________________

Institution: ______________________________

Address: ______________________________

Which HLT title have you bought? ______________________________

Did you buy it:

a) at the beginning of the academic year ☐

b) half way through the academic year ☐

c) before your exams ☐

Did you buy it because:

a) you have used HLT books before ☐

b) it was recommended by your lecturer ☐

c) it was recommended by a friend ☐

d) you chose it from the bookshop ☐

Is the coverage in the book:

a) too detailed ☐

b) not detailed enough ☐

c) just right ☐

Would you describe the book as good value for money compared to other textbooks in the area?

Yes ☐ No ☐

How many HLT titles have you bought in the past? ☐

Which ones?

____

Are there any subject areas you would like to see an HLT book on?

____

____

Any other comments?

____

____

____

Do you own or have easy access to a PC? If so what kind of PC (hardware/software) do you use?

____

Simply fill out your name and address below and send it with your questionnaire and a cheque made payable to 'HLT Publications' for £2.50. Address on previous page.

Name: ______________________________

Address: ______________________________

____

____

____

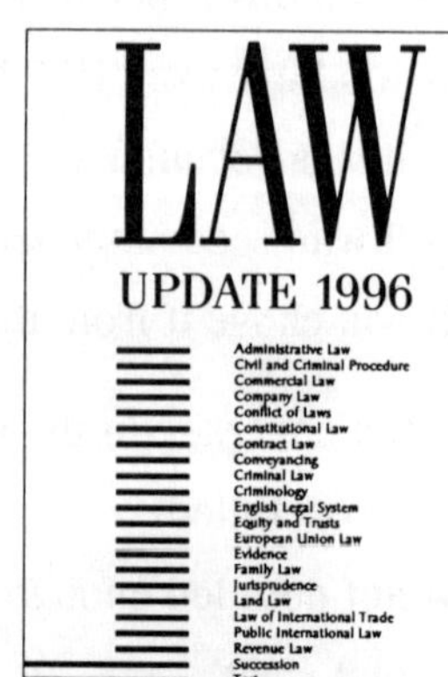

To complete your order, please fill in the form below:

Module	Books required	Quantity	Price	Cost
		Postage		
		TOTAL		

Prices include postage and packing in the UK.

For Europe, add 15% postage and packing (£20 maximum).

For the rest of the world, add 40% for airmail.

ORDERING

By telephone to **01892 724371**, with your credit card to hand.

By fax to **01892 724206** (giving your credit card details).

By post to:

HLT Publications, The Gatehouse, Ruck Lane, Horsmonden, TONBRIDGE, Kent TN12 8EA.

When ordering by post, please enclose full payment by cheque or banker's draft, or complete the credit card details below.

We aim to despatch your books within three working days of receiving your order.

Name:

Address:

Postcode: Telephone:

Total value of order, including postage: £

I enclose a cheque/banker's draft for the above sum, or

charge my ☐ Access/Mastercard ☐ Visa ☐ American Express

Card number

☐☐☐☐ ☐☐☐☐ ☐☐☐☐ ☐☐☐☐

Expiry date ☐☐☐☐

Signature: .... Date: ....